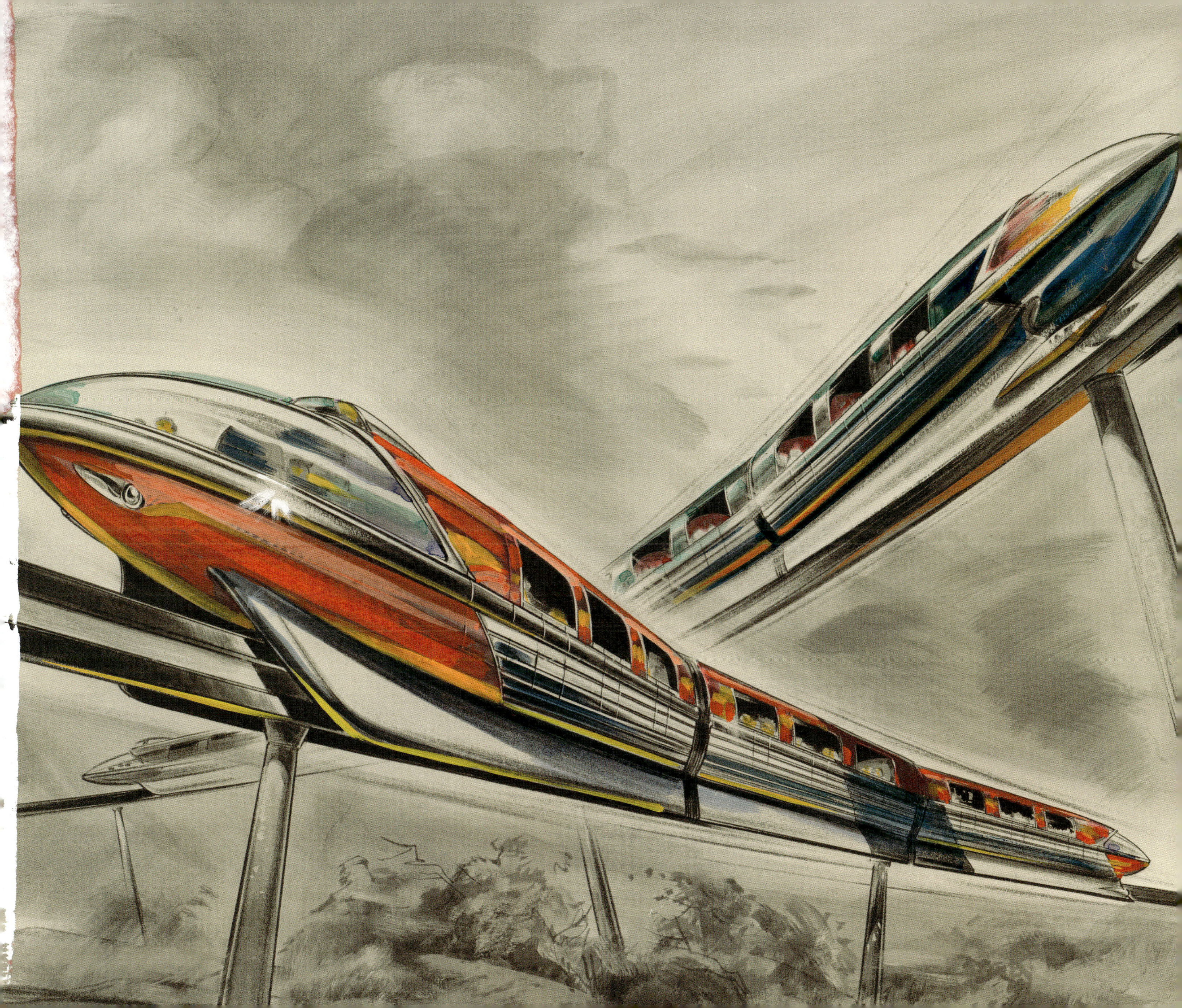

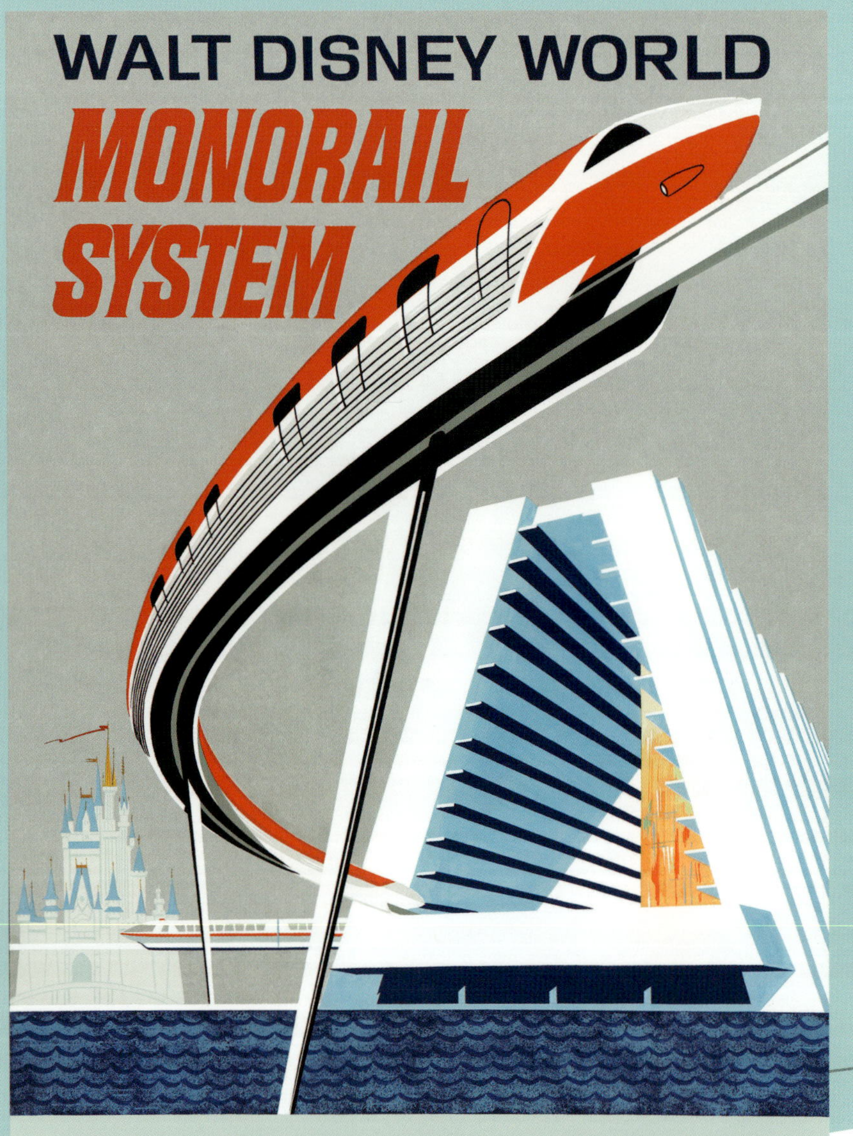
WALT DISNEY WORLD
MONORAIL
SYSTEM
BOARD AT HOTELS
and MAIN ENTRANCE

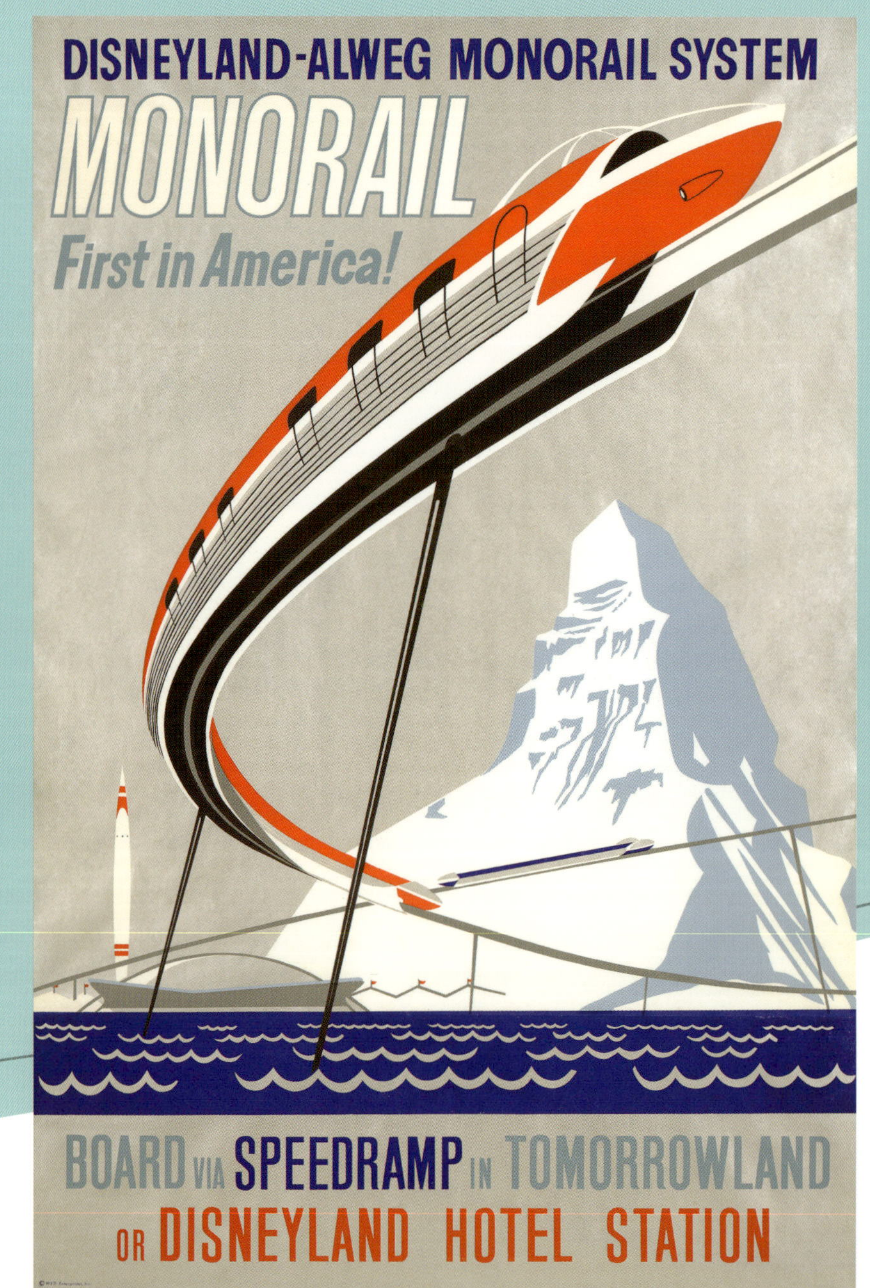
DISNEYLAND-ALWEG MONORAIL SYSTEM
MONORAIL
First in America!
BOARD VIA SPEEDRAMP IN TOMORROWLAND
OR DISNEYLAND HOTEL STATION

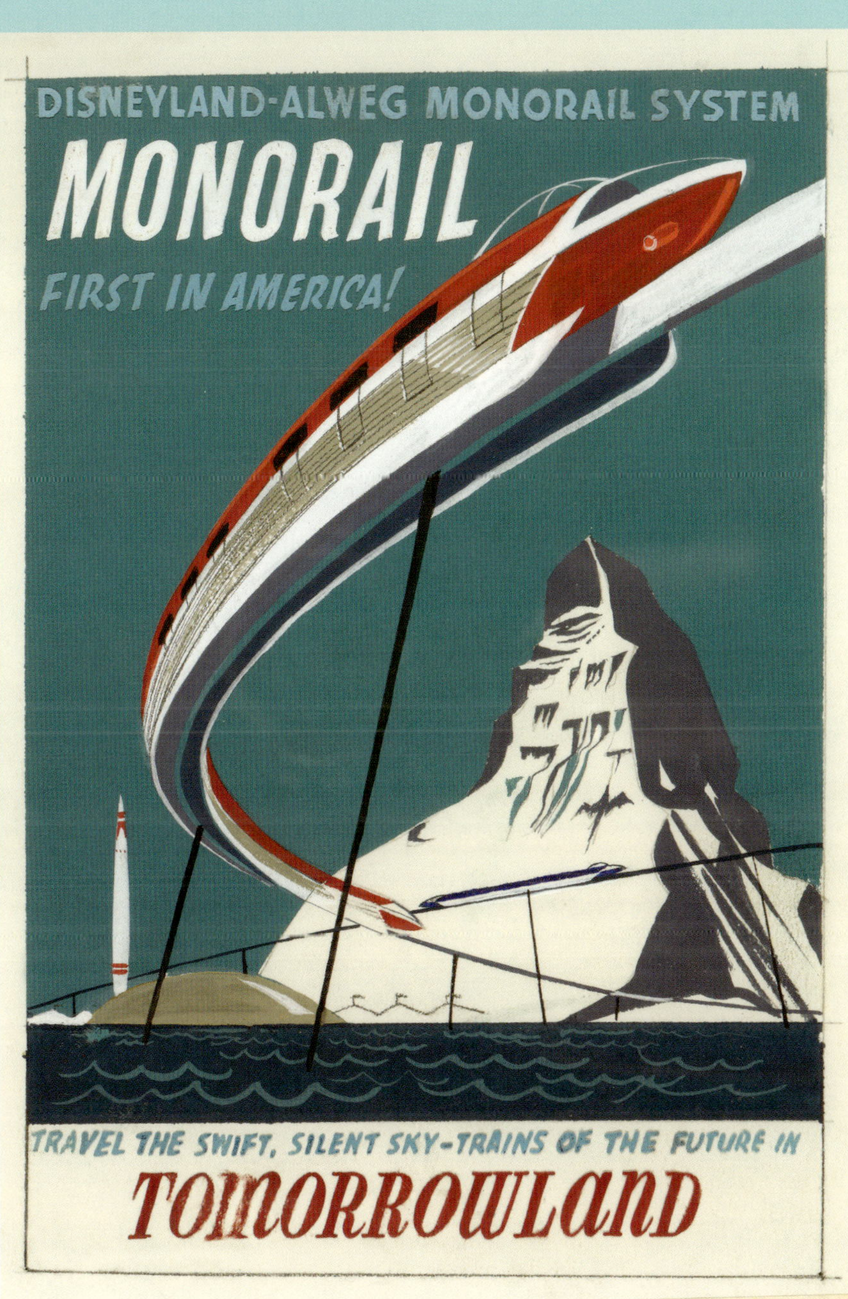

THE DISNEY MONORAIL

IMAGINEERING A HIGHWAY IN THE SKY

JEFF KURTTI

VANESSA HUNT

PAUL WOLSKI

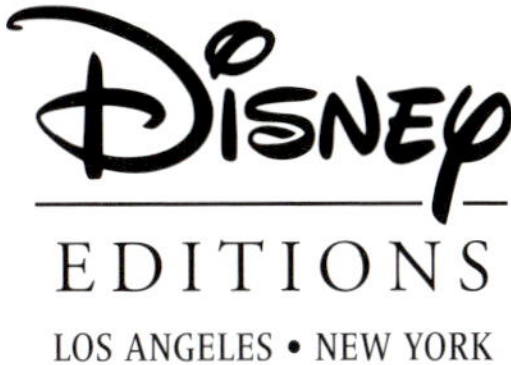

EDITIONS

LOS ANGELES • NEW YORK

For information address Disney Editions, 1200 Grand Central Avenue, Glendale, California 91201.

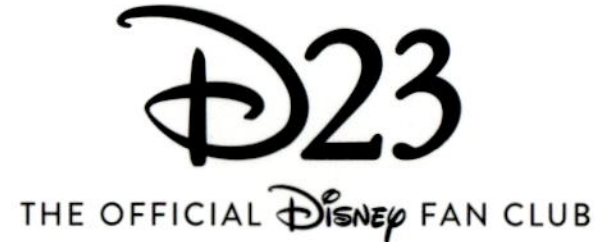

PAGE ONE: John Hench color styling in acrylic and watercolor over Bob Gurr drawing, 1959.
PAGE TWO, LEFT: Attraction poster, Walt Disney World Monorail System, Walt Disney World Resort. Adapted by Collin Campbell, 1971.
PAGE TWO, RIGHT: Attraction poster, Disneyland Monorail, Disneyland. Paul Hartley, 1961.
PAGE THREE: Comprehensive rough design for attraction poster, Disneyland Monorail, Disneyland. Paul Hartley, 1961.
OPPOSITE: Cover of *Vacationland* magazine, Fall 1959.
FOLLOWING SPREAD: Composite photograph/illustration preview of Harbor Boulevard view at parking entrance to Disneyland, 1958.

Editorial Director:
Wendy Lefkon

Senior Editor:
Jennifer Eastwood

Senior Designer:
Lindsay Broderick

Managing Editor:
Monica Vasquez

Production:
Kate Milford
Karen Romano
Marybeth Tregarthen

Book design:
Vanessa Hunt
Paul Wolski

ISBN: 978-1-4847-3767-5
FAC-039745-22020

Printed in South Korea

First Hardcover Edition,
September 2020

10 9 8 7 6 5 4 3

Visit www.disneybooks.com

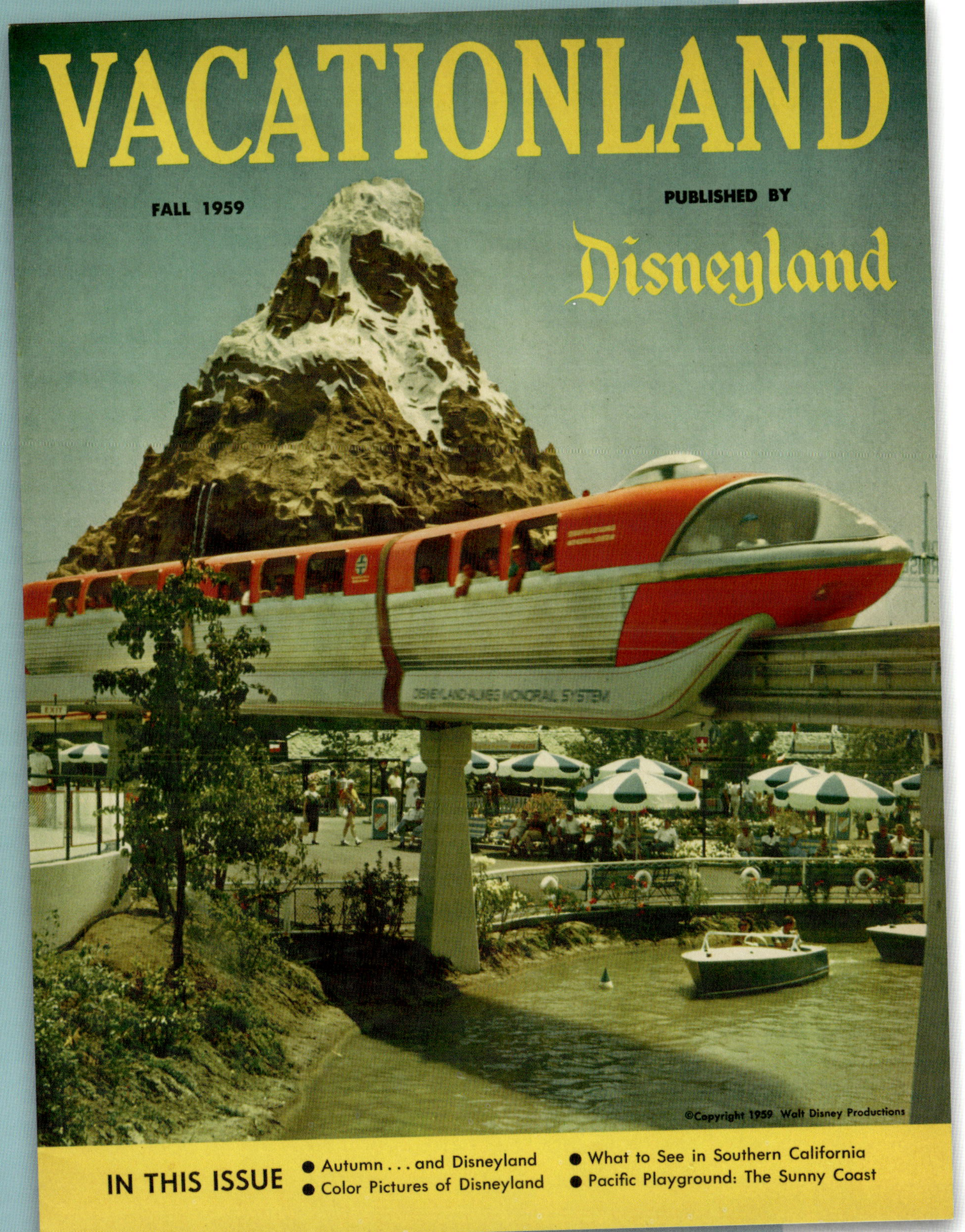
VACATIONLAND
FALL 1959
PUBLISHED BY
Disneyland
DISNEYLAND-ALWEG MONORAIL SYSTEM
©Copyright 1959 Walt Disney Productions
IN THIS ISSUE
Autumn . . . and Disneyland
Color Pictures of Disneyland
What to See in Southern California
Pacific Playground: The Sunny Coast

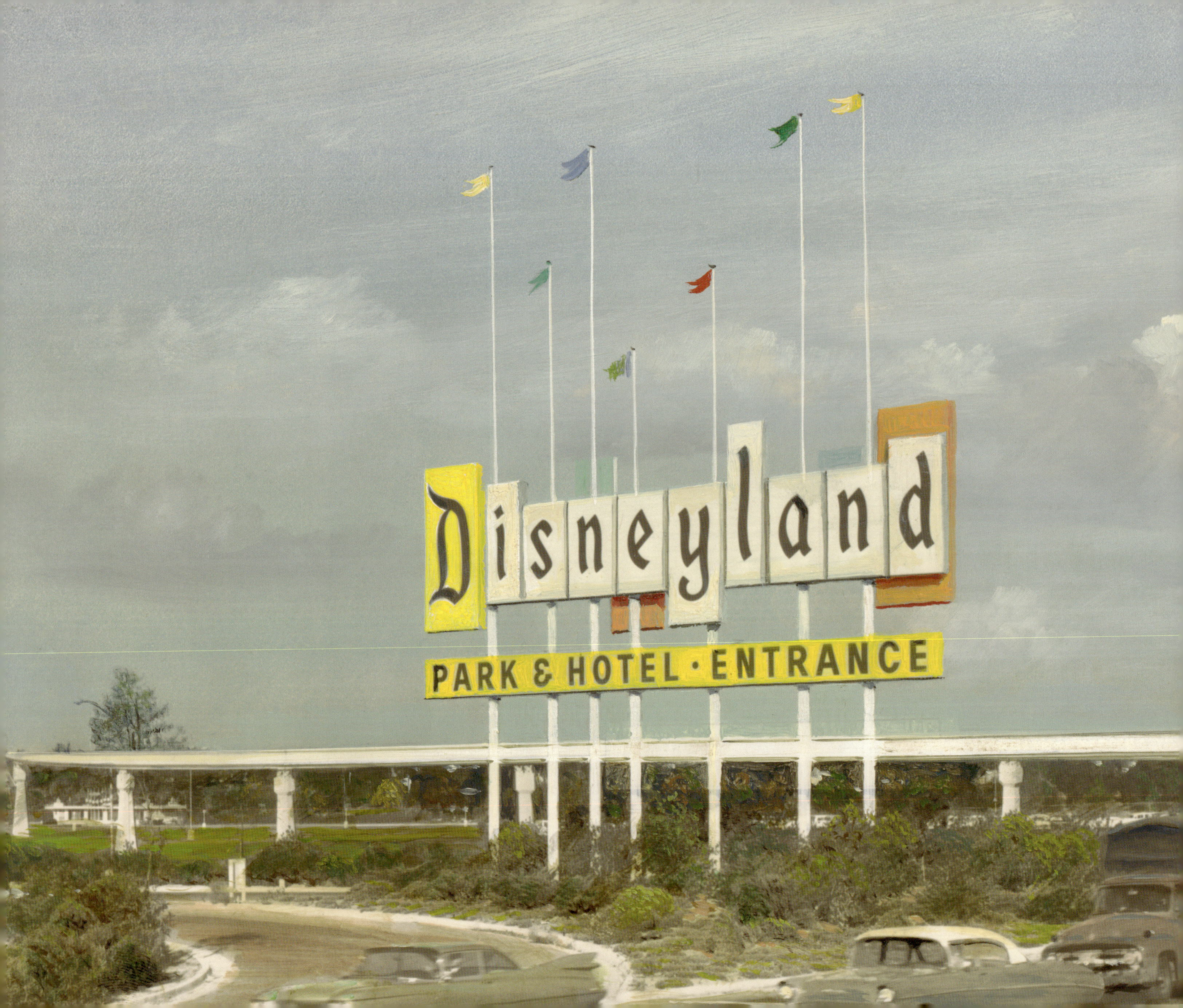
Disneyland
PARK & HOTEL · ENTRANCE

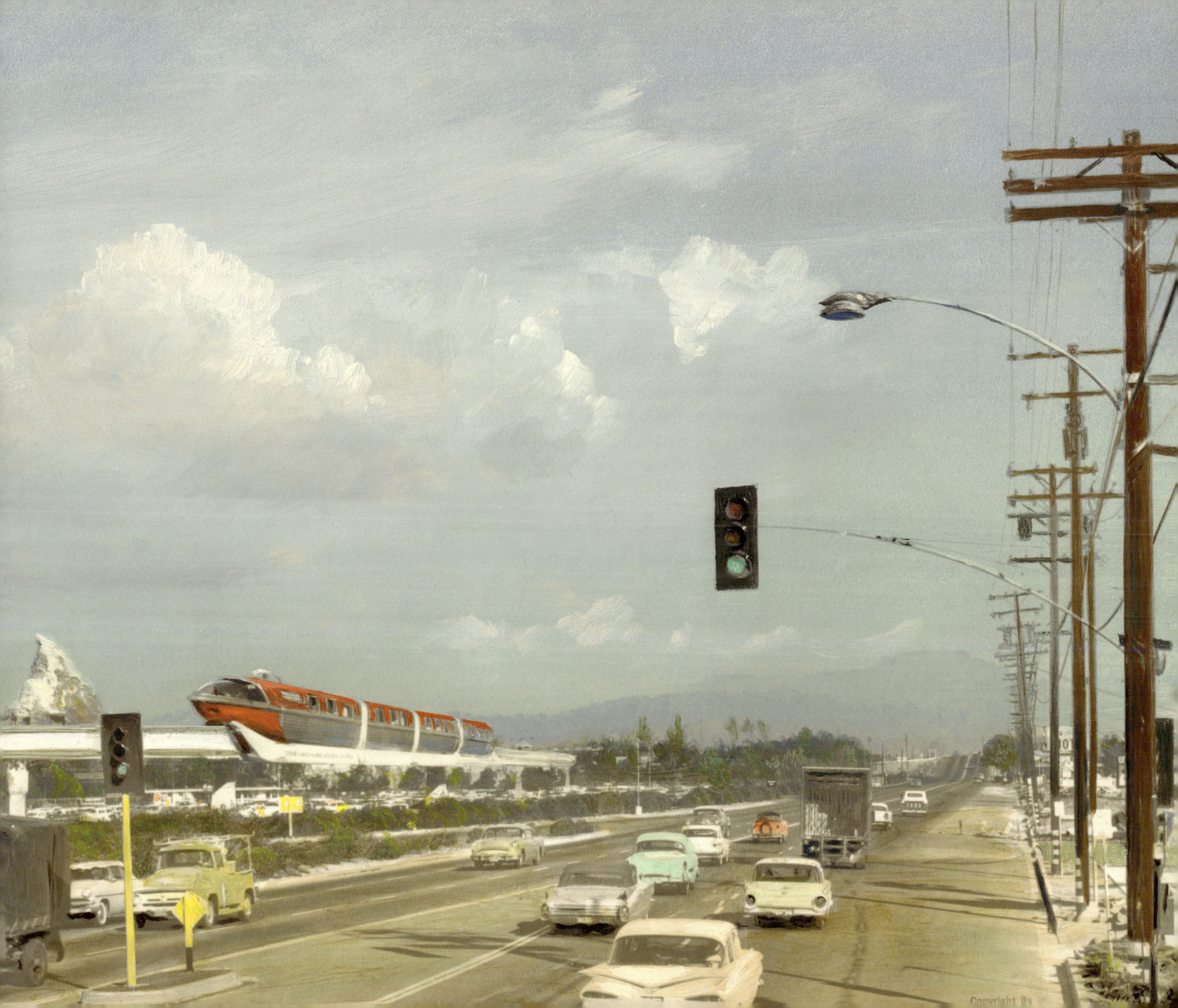
Copyright By

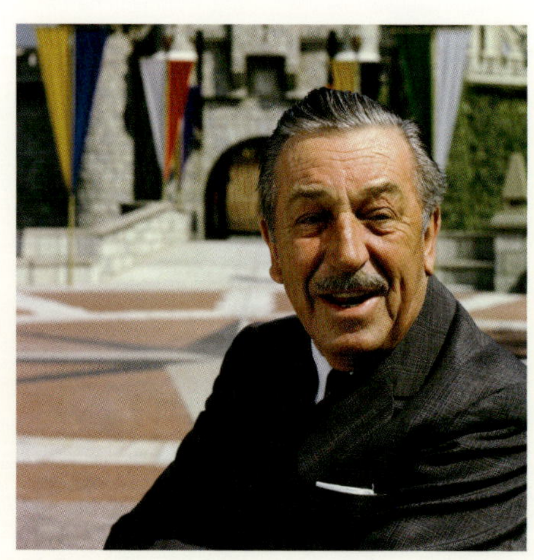

A vista into a world of wondrous ideas, signifying man's achievements . . . a step into the future, with predictions of constructive things to come. Tomorrow offers new frontiers in science, adventure, and ideals: the Atomic Age, the challenge of outer space, and the hope for a peaceful and unified world.

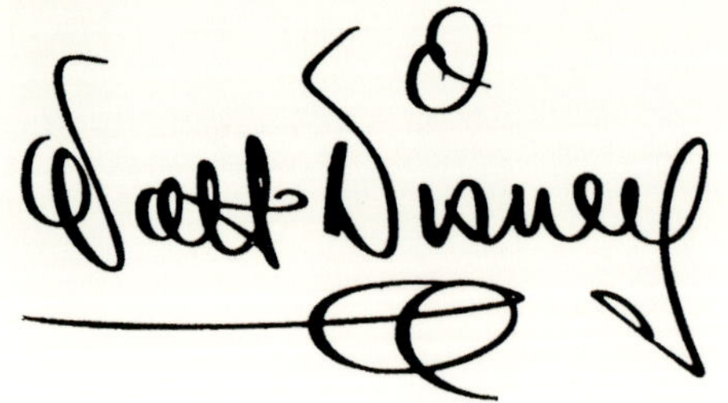

CONTENTS

A Childhood Memory and a Vision of the Future

By Tricia Nixon Cox and Julie Nixon Eisenhower

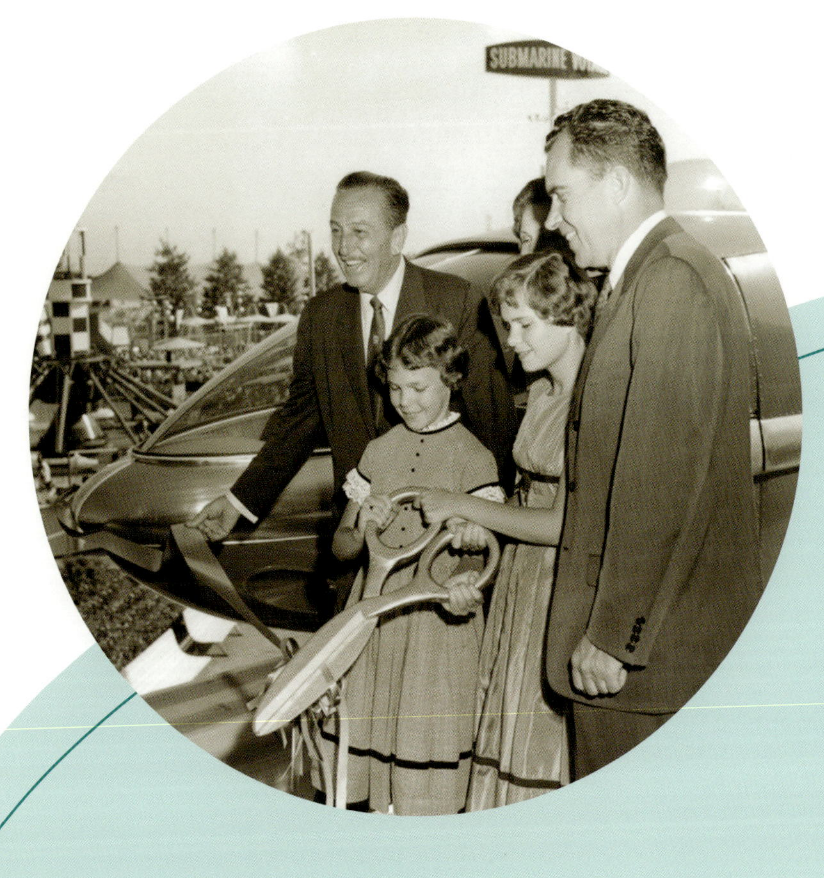

The first major expansion of Walt Disney's young theme park included the installation of a special elevated railway known as the Monorail.

And we had the opportunity to spend June 14, 1959, in the Anaheim park, when we cut the ribbon to open that Monorail with our parents, Richard and Pat Nixon (at that time, our father was the US vice president, under President Dwight D. Eisenhower), and Walt and his family. We then took the very first ride on it around the looped track with the legendary entertainer Art Linkletter as our driver.

We could not have imagined what a popular icon the Monorail would become. For six decades, it has provided countless families that special Disney experience—just as it did ours.

That was a jam-packed day: early in the morning, we posed with a huge pair of gold-painted wooden scissors during a press preview of the dedication ceremony. Then we tried out the new Matterhorn Bobsleds, rode Snow White's Adventures, and had lunch in Walt's private apartment, located on the second story of the Main Street Firehouse. It was the perfect day for two young girls—made all the better because we happened to be on summer break from our school . . . in Washington, DC!

And at 4 p.m. that very afternoon, we used the scissors to cut the ribbon live on television—and officially unveil Disneyland's Monorail. But the stubborn scissors

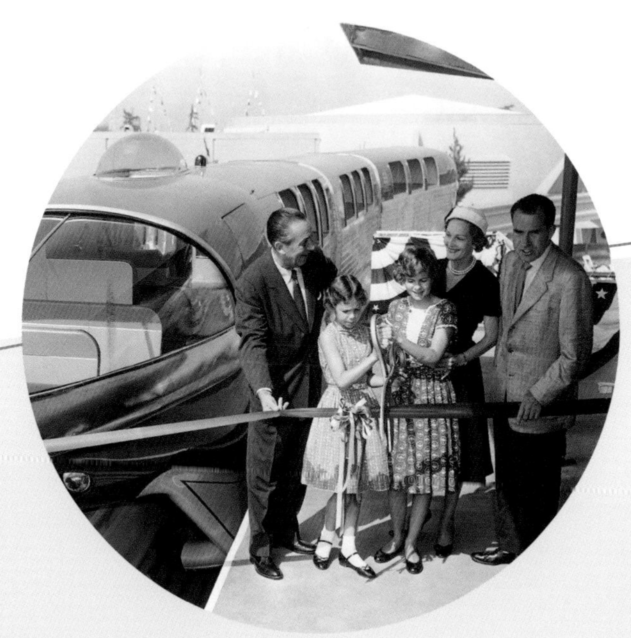

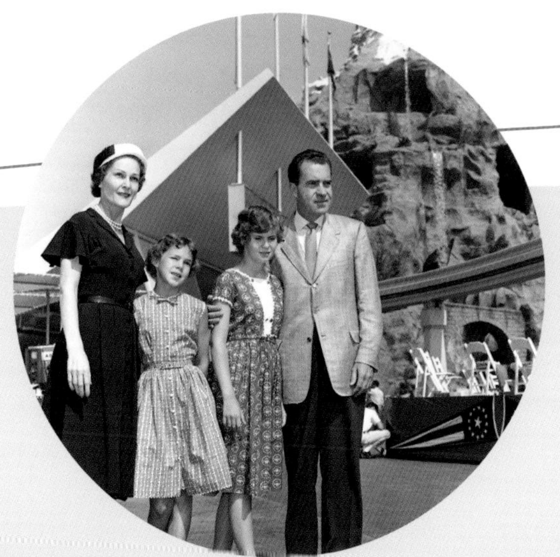

didn't exactly cooperate. Eventually, Walt had to come to the rescue and rip the ribbon in half because the scissors wouldn't work at all!

Walt also threw a parade down Main Street, U.S.A. to honor our parents with two thousand celebrities, plus special dignitaries and members of the press; Walt's family was also there, including Lilly, his brother Roy, and his daughter Diane, who would become a dear friend of ours for many years. No Disneyland parade is complete without a red, white, and blue reviewing stand and a musical company of seventy-six trombones!

It was the biggest event at the park since Disneyland's opening four years earlier.

Like millions of other American families, our family had visited Disneyland—and would later visit Walt Disney World in Florida—many times; in fact, we visited as often as we could. Our parents cherished Walt's years of friendship, not to mention his warmth, creativity, and contagious sense of humor. He was, on that warm June day, as charming as ever.

Walt's excitement for life continues to inspire millions across the globe. For example, his excitement about the Monorail was clearly evident to us just over sixty years ago, as he prided himself on having conceived not only of a new Disneyland attraction but also of a new vision for the future of American transportation. He saw the Monorail as a revolutionary method of mass transit that would stretch far beyond the physical limits of Disneyland—and serve as an easy-to-use system that people everywhere could hop on and off of, all around California, much like a bus or a subway.

While the scale of Walt's vision never quite came to be, the Monorail at Disneyland has expanded to an astounding 2.5 miles since its opening! It now carries eager children (and accompanying adults) from the outskirts of the park right into the heart of all the magical happenings.

So, in many ways, Walt's vision did, in fact, come true.

And Disneyland was—and remains, as it is now—the "Happiest Place on Earth," thanks to that vision.

Those two young girls who had the good fortune of being at Disneyland that June day a little over sixty years ago are today thankful to the extended Disney family for their many years of friendship and grateful for the trust and confidence that Walt, Lilly, and the Disney family had in our parents. And we truly treasure the many memorable visits to Disneyland and Walt Disney World we have taken since with our parents, and now with our own children and grandchildren.

OPPOSITE AND ABOVE: Three images of Vice President Richard Nixon and his family from the opening of the Disneyland-Alweg Monorail System on Sunday, June 14, 1959. The photo opposite is from the official dedication that afternoon, as broadcast on ABC-TV. The photos above were staged in the morning, to enable wire services and newspapers east of the Rockies to include them in their Monday morning editions.

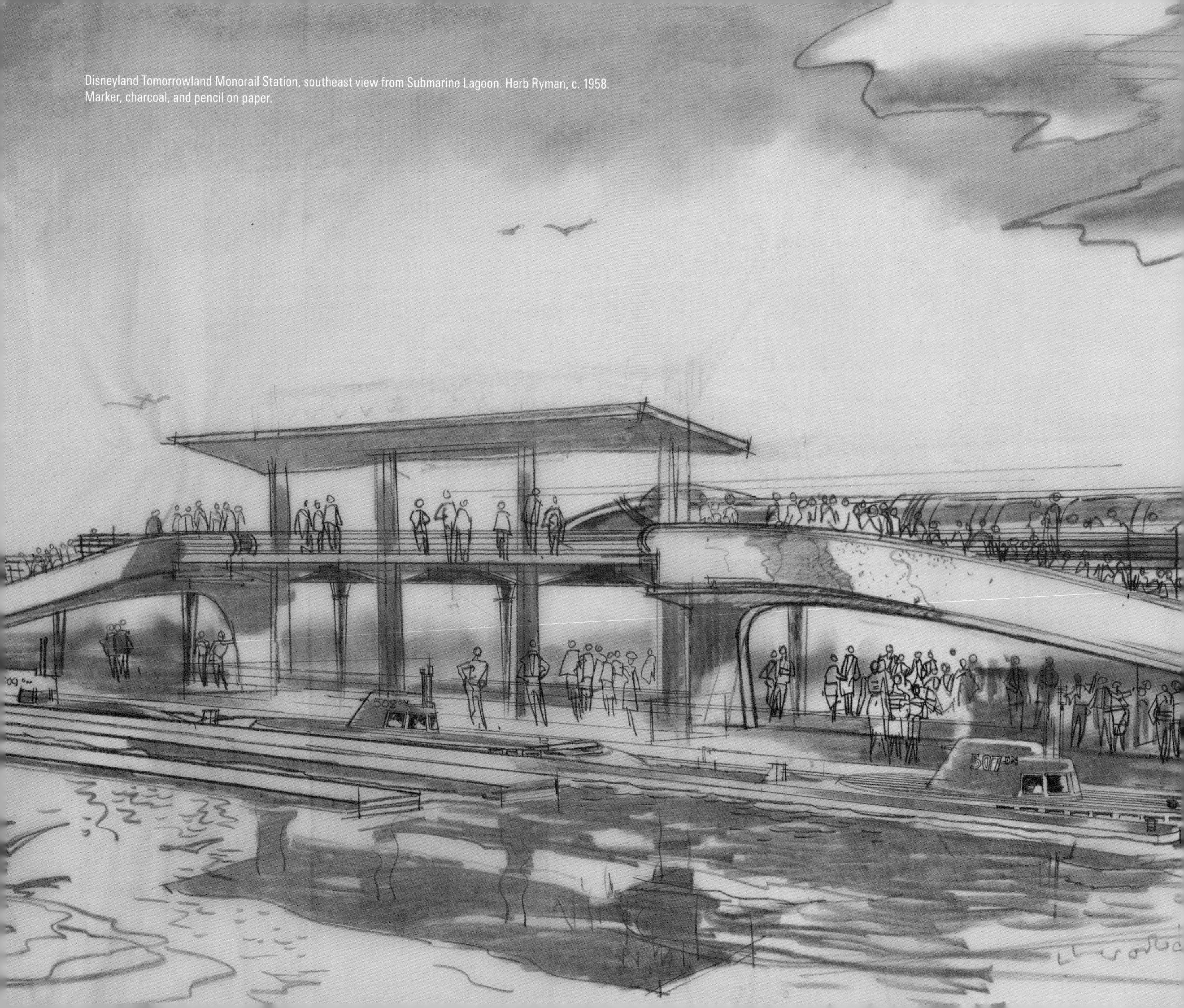

Disneyland Tomorrowland Monorail Station, southeast view from Submarine Lagoon. Herb Ryman, c. 1958.
Marker, charcoal, and pencil on paper.

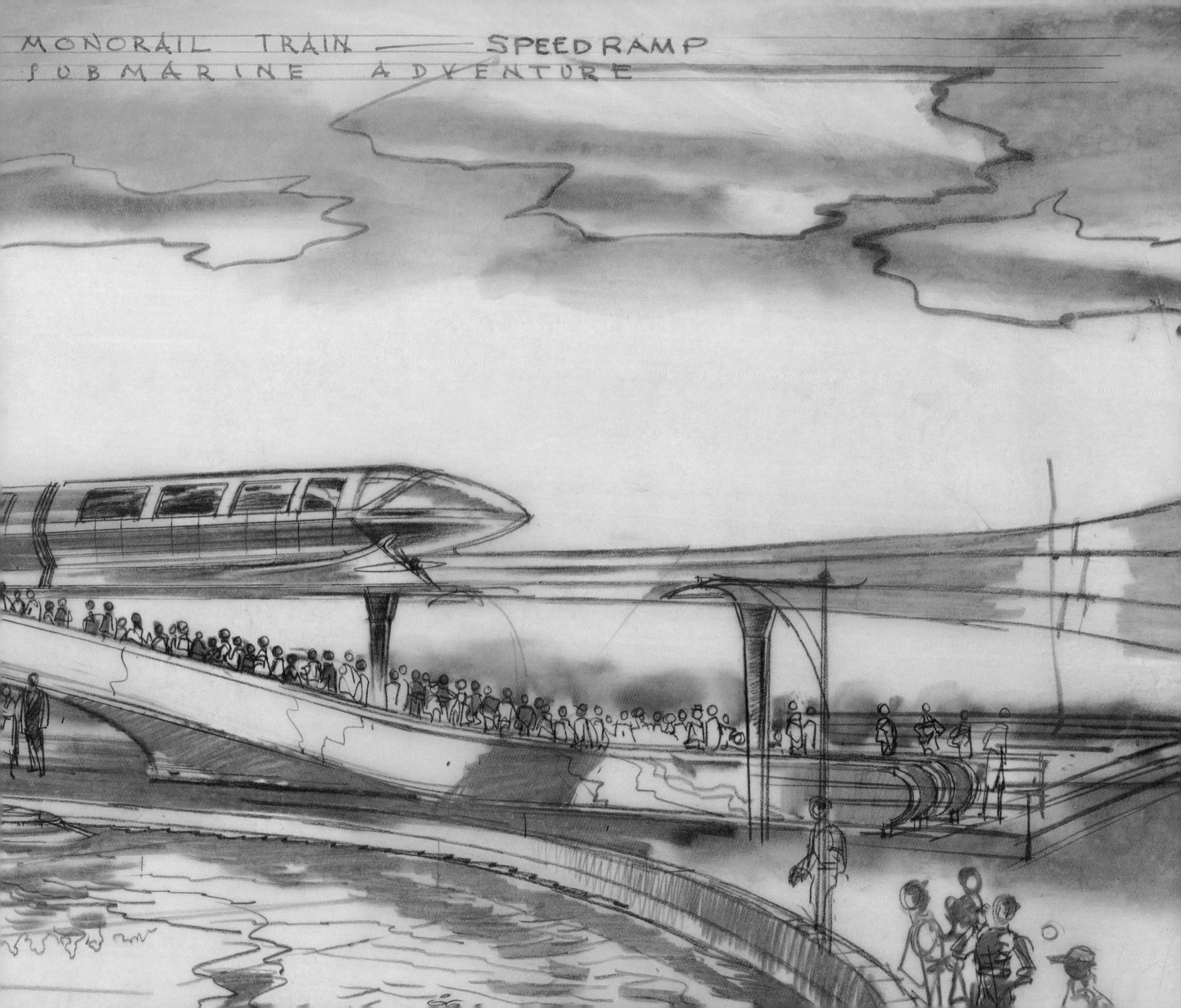
MONORAIL TRAIN — SPEEDRAMP
SUBMARINE ADVENTURE

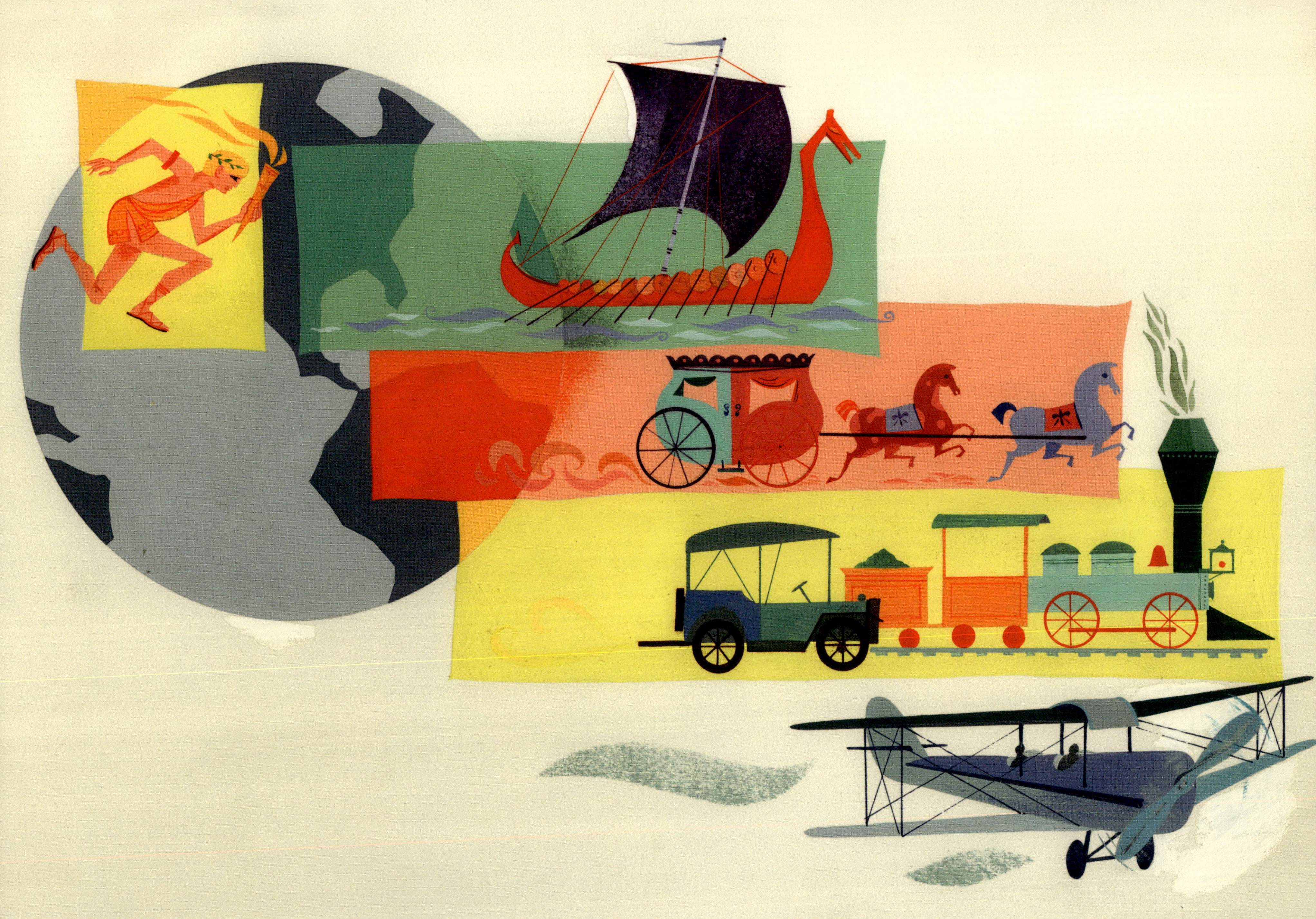

Illustration for article "Our Shrinking World," *Walt Disney's Magazine*, Volume IV, Number 5, August 1959. Paul Hartley. Gouache on illustration board.

CHAPTER 1

A Great Big Beautiful Tomorrowland

Walt Disney by award-winning Armenian-Canadian portraitist Yousuf Karsh, 1959.

Tomorrow can be a wonderful age. Our scientists today are opening the doors of the Atomic Age to achievements which will benefit our children and generations to come. . . . You will actually experience what many . . . predict for the world of tomorrow.

—Walt Disney

Walt Disney on the Move

"You see, our whole forty-some-odd years here has been in the world of making things move," Walt Disney said in a 1963 interview. Early in his career that had meant a specific type of animation—making still drawings and objects "move" in order to tell stories, create characters, and elicit emotions. Later, realistic figures of birds, animals, and people became a symbol of "animation innovation" within Disneyland, and at the 1964–1965 New York World's Fair.

Less frequently connected to the work and character of Walt Disney is another category of animation, a kind of movement that influenced him throughout his life: an interest in, an avocation of—indeed, a passion for—passenger transportation.

With this in mind, it's helpful to remember Walt in the context of his times.

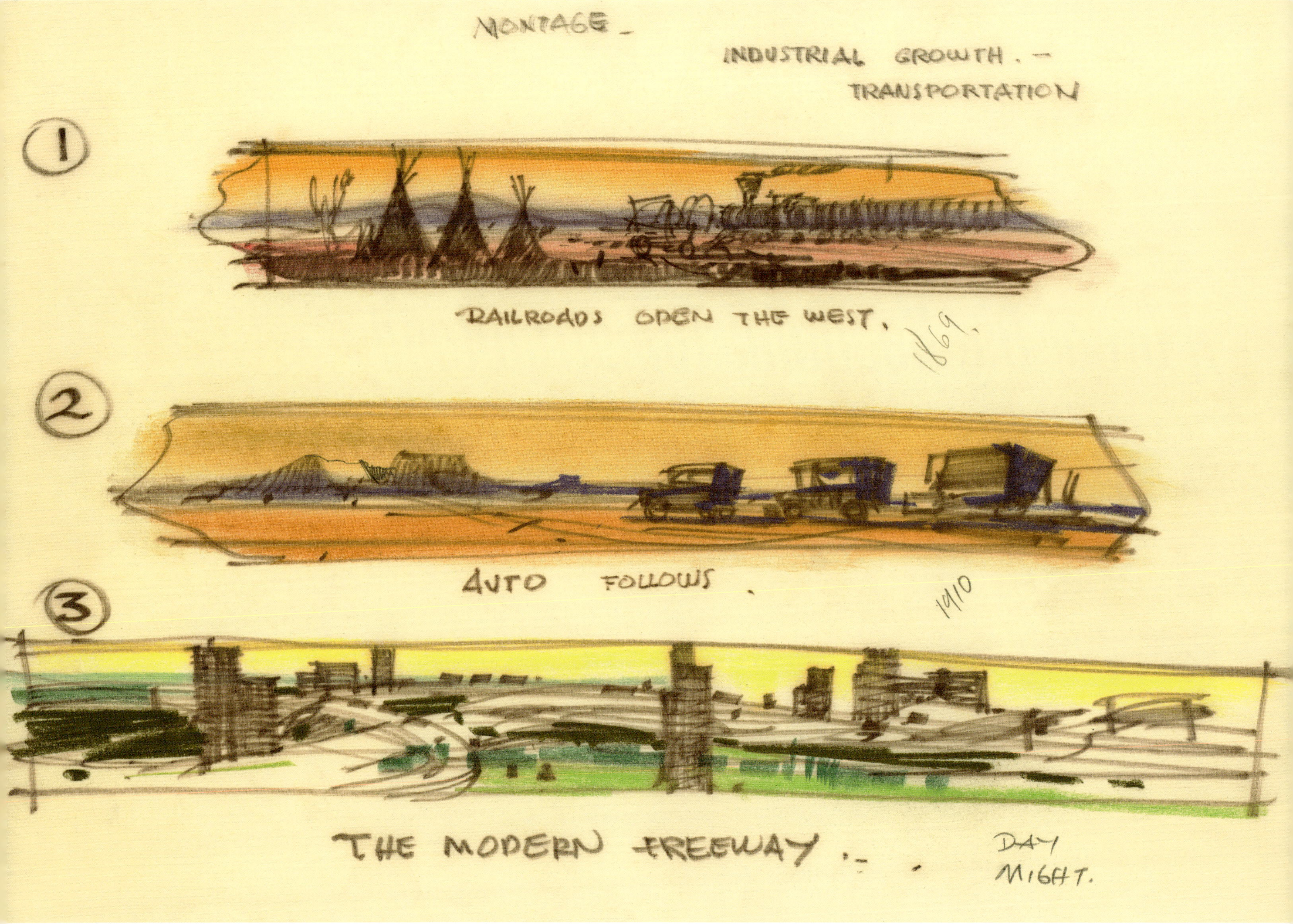

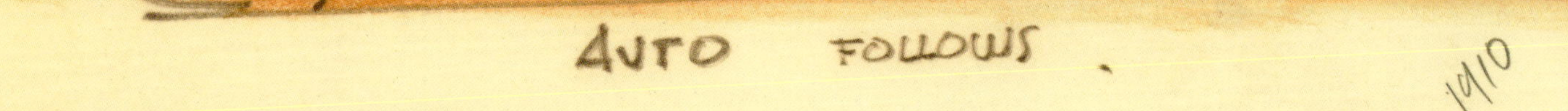
MONTAGE _
INDUSTRIAL GROWTH. –
TRANSPORTATION
1
RAILROADS OPEN THE WEST.
1869.
2
AUTO FOLLOWS.
1910
3

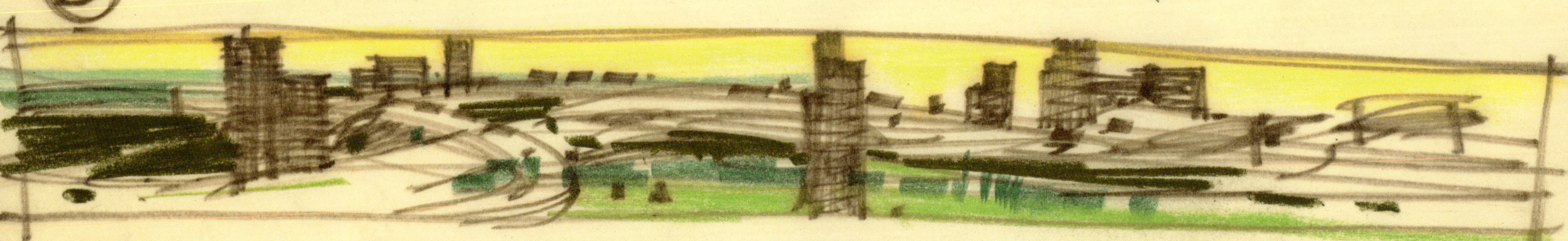
THE MODERN FREEWAY. –
DAY
NIGHT.

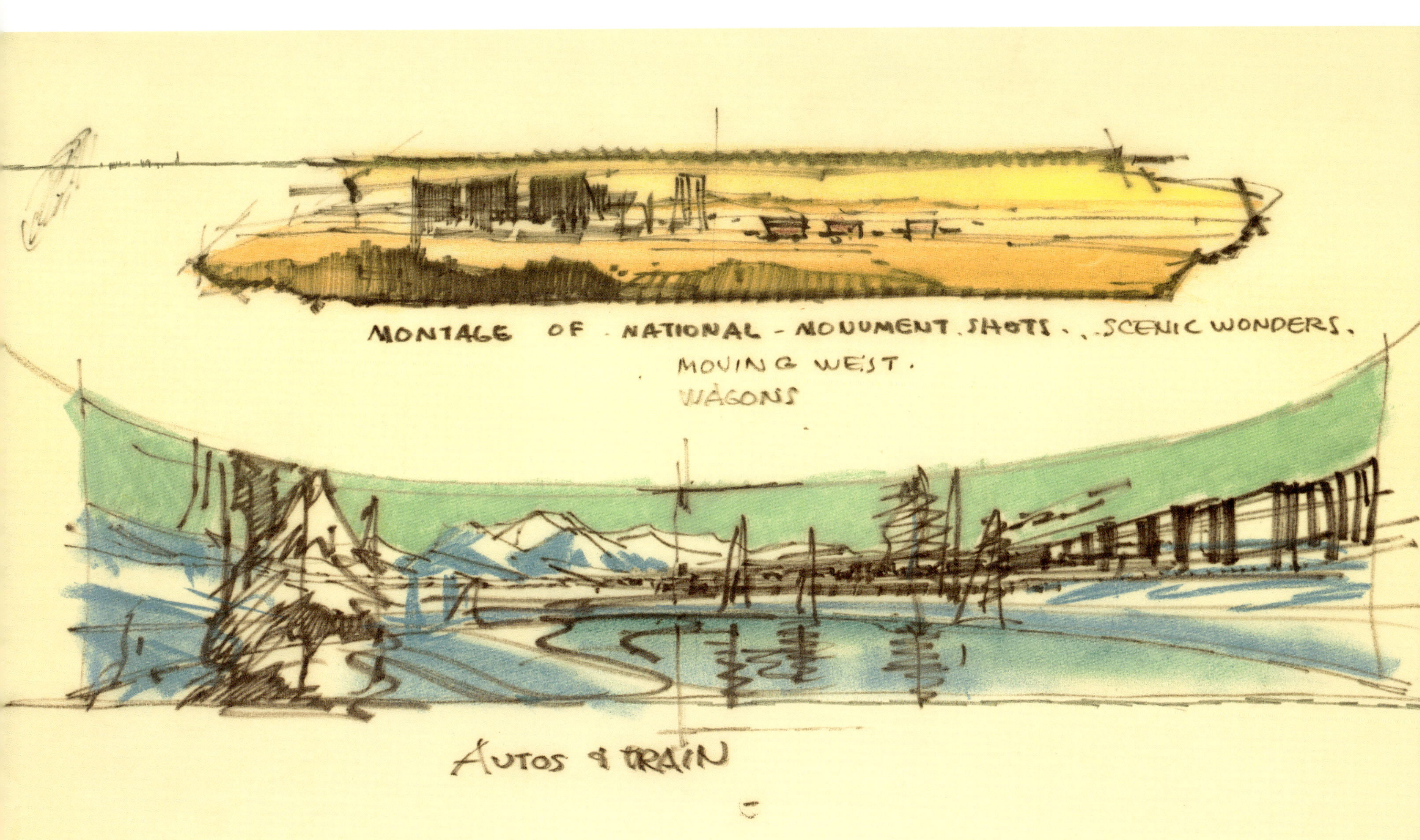

OPPOSITE AND ABOVE: Concept art by Herb Ryman, 1964, for *Magic of the Rails*, a Circle-Vision 360 film prepared for the Swiss Federal Railways and shown at an exposition in Lucerne, Switzerland, and later in Germany.

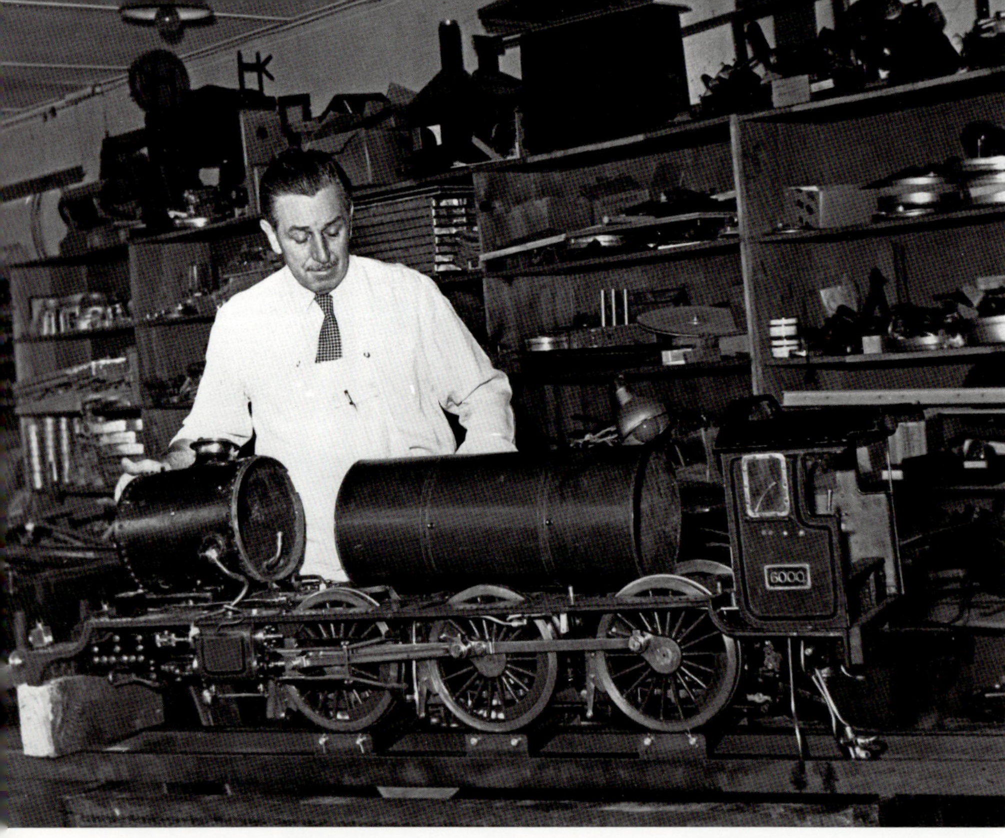

Walt in the Studio Machine Shop, at work on his 1:8-scale live steam locomotive, the *Lilly Belle*, 1949.

Certainly, like so many his age, Walt was subject to a certain "romance of the rails"; the whistle of the nearby train seemed to be a potent lure for young people of his era. There was little variety or adventure for a kid growing up in the American Midwest in the early years of the twentieth century. Limited and landlocked, many people never left the few square miles surrounding their birthplace. For Walt, though, the appeal of exploration was strong—fueled by the tales of immigrant and peripatetic relatives, and the adventures he read about in literary fiction.

The most prevalent, most powerful, most modern, and most elegant mode of transport in Walt's formative years was the railroad. The Wright brothers' historic flight in Kitty Hawk, North Carolina, took place when Walt was about two years old. The Ford Model T debuted when he was about seven. (Walt recalled that in 1908 his town of Marceline, Missouri, had only two automobiles.) All these inventions, breakthroughs, and events occurring at such an impressionable point in Walt's life certainly informed his point of view on a subject that he would continue to pursue and explore for the rest of his life: the notion and action of human advancement.

Progress and the Concept of Manifest Destiny

Walt grew up steeped in a culture that deeply believed in the uniquely American notion of "Manifest Destiny," a conviction that America had been chosen to carry out the task of expansionism to "drive out the wilderness" and bring "the light of civilization" to the North American continent.

This aggressive idea of expansion was realized in the swift movement of Euro-American people and the establishment of communities through the "New World" from the Eastern Seaboard to the West Coast over a brief century; even to this day, a prevailing cultural logic of this philosophy and the certainty of its ideas is an undercurrent of the American identity.

Connected to this philosophical idea was the physical means by which the population moved across the continent. Tied to this migration was the concept of concurrent technological innovation used to create advances in the shipment, speed, and efficiency. This had come to generally mean a modernization, advancement, and improvement in science, technology, design, and methodology that became a component of a perceived overall improvement in economics and society.

Within these ideas lay the beginnings of a larger notion that would be so ingrained in Walt Disney's personal identity, and a word that would become a theme to his life's work: *progress*.

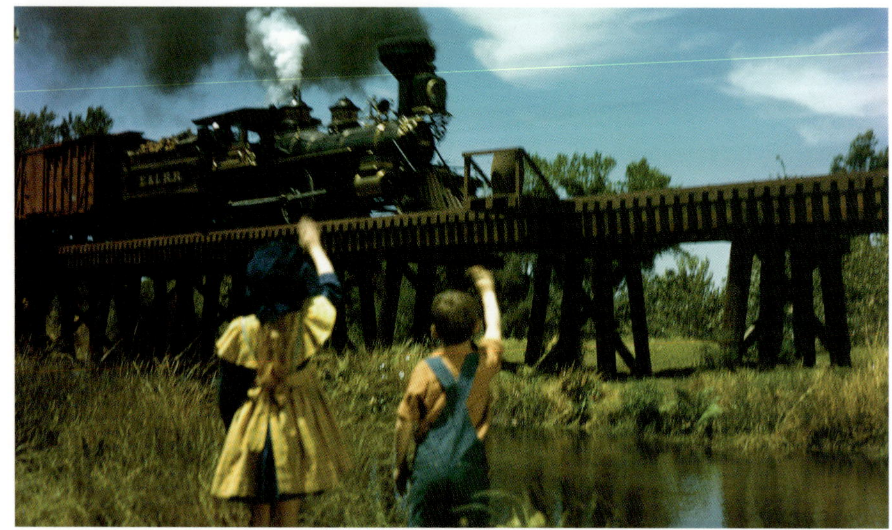

Walt, like most Americans, was enamored by the stories of "Westward Expansion." Here Luana Patten and Bobby Driscoll wave at "Old Number 99" in the feature *So Dear to My Heart*, released in January 1949.

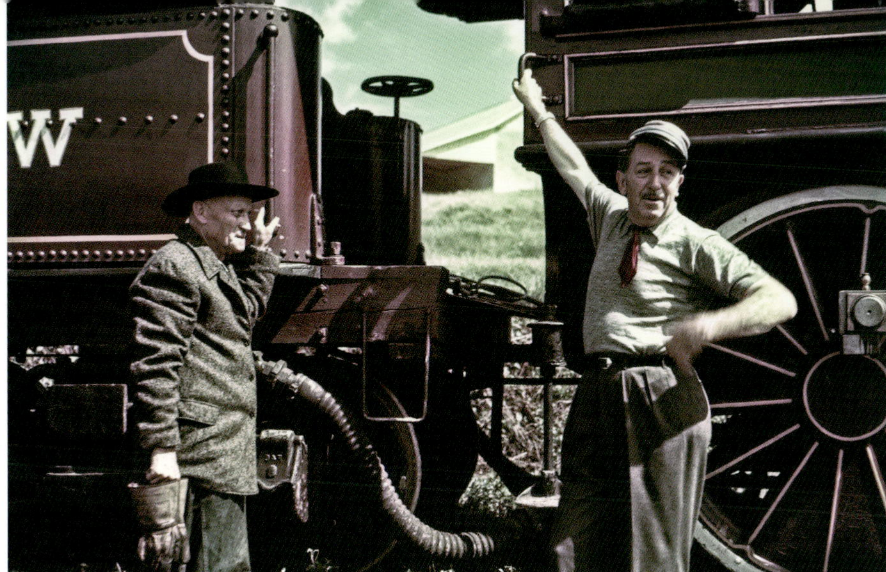

Walt with the 1856 steam locomotive *William Mason*, on the Georgia/North Carolina border location of *The Great Locomotive Chase*, released in June 1956.

Moving Westward

It's remarkable to think that a scant two centuries ago, the primary means of transportation was by self-ambulation, horse or other animal, and water.

The major population centers within the United States were located on natural harbors or navigable waterways along the Atlantic coast. As the population expanded, the addition of canals (the Erie Canal being the most successful example), increase in river traffic (the introduction of steam-powered boats to the Mississippi River system—the Mississippi, Ohio, and Missouri Rivers), and the persistent westward movement of wagon traffic further shaped the geography of settlements and created boundaries.

By the mid-nineteenth century, the expansion of the railroad brought a swiftness and efficiency to the movement of passengers and goods in a system that soon spread across the nation, with scheduled routes and year-round operation that interconnected the states and territories. The First Transcontinental Railroad in 1869 connected the existing Eastern US rail network from Omaha, Nebraska, and Council Bluffs, Iowa, with San Francisco.

In the regions, cities, and towns that were founded in the path of this expansion, more transportation options over shorter distances became a necessity. Intercity and interurban passenger networks of "street running" rail lines extended within communities and outward between many cities; they also interchanged passengers and freight with the long-route railroads.

This was the era of transportation advancement in which Walt Disney grew up.

Transportation in Transition

As Walt moved into his teen years, the ascent of the personal automobile and the greater route adaptability of motorized buses meant the beginning of a decline for all types and scales of rail systems across the United States. Interurban rail service waned, quickly followed by the intra-urban trolleys and streetcars. During World War II, a scarcity of materials slowed the growth of the personal automobile market—a situation that only emphasized how much of the nation's mass-transit rail networks had already declined.

By this time, Walt was a successful and renowned Hollywood studio head. Yet he observed and studied all these changes and transitions with the zeal of a true scholar. His fascination with technological advancement combined with his childhood love of the rails to increase and expand his interest and study.

Naturally, Walt's progress-focused mind-set also had a remarkable impact on his professional output and various endeavors. Animation ascended in technical proficiency under his watch (with Disney often leading the way) and brought a quality of visual sophistication that made it a new and more appreciated art form. The innovations of Technicolor photography and the development of the multiplane camera were part of that, as was the development of the first theatrical stereophonic sound system, created by the studio technicians for the road show release of *Fantasia* in 1940. Walt additionally experimented with wide-screen formats (he originally envisioned such a presentation for *Fantasia* but was limited by budget) such as CinemaScope and Technirama 70 in later animated features.

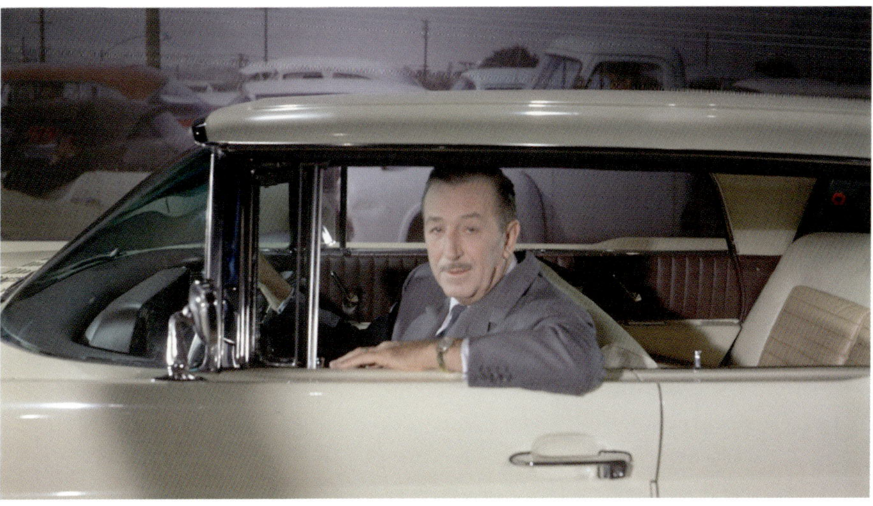

Walt at the wheel for an introduction to *Magic Highway, U.S.A.* on the May 14, 1958, episode of the weekly *Disneyland* television series.

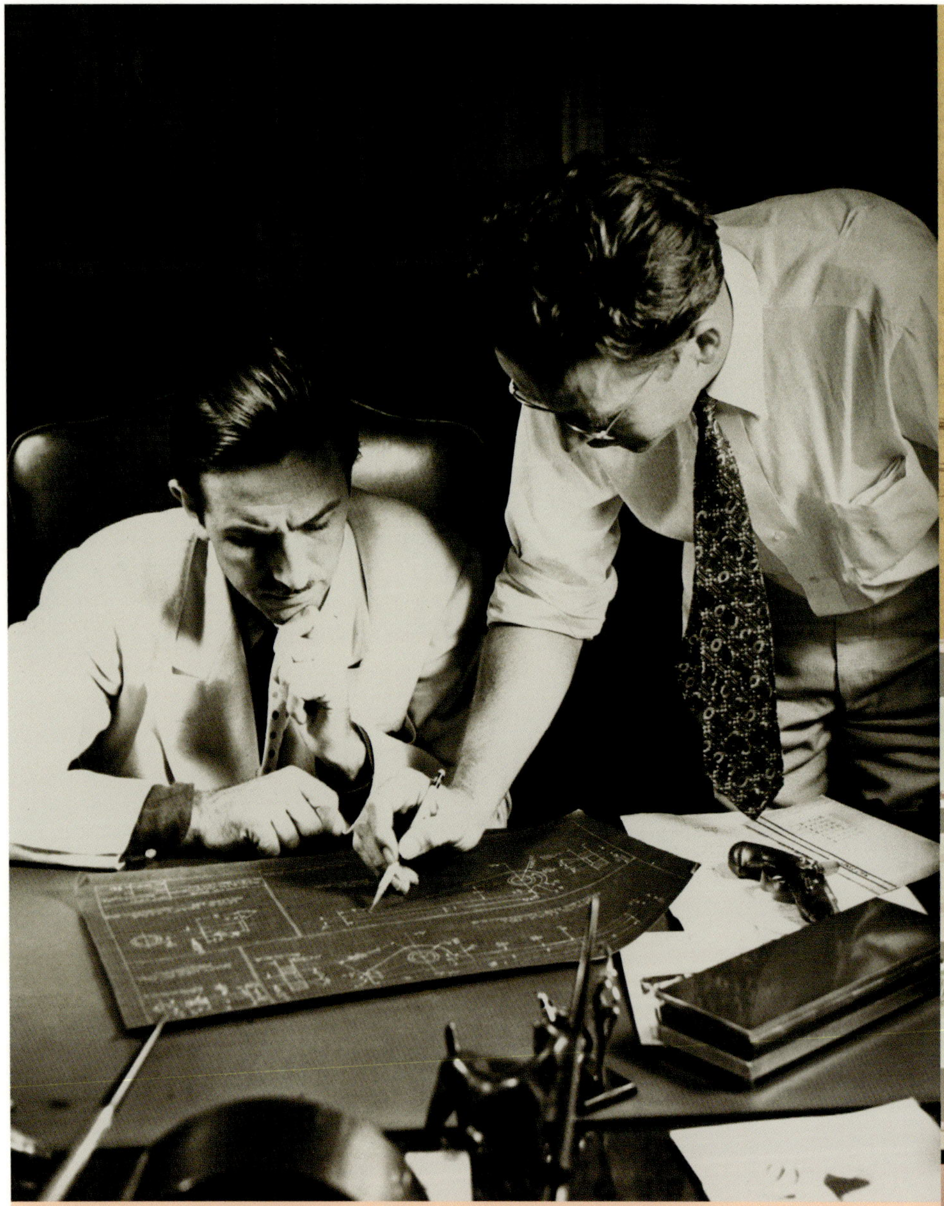

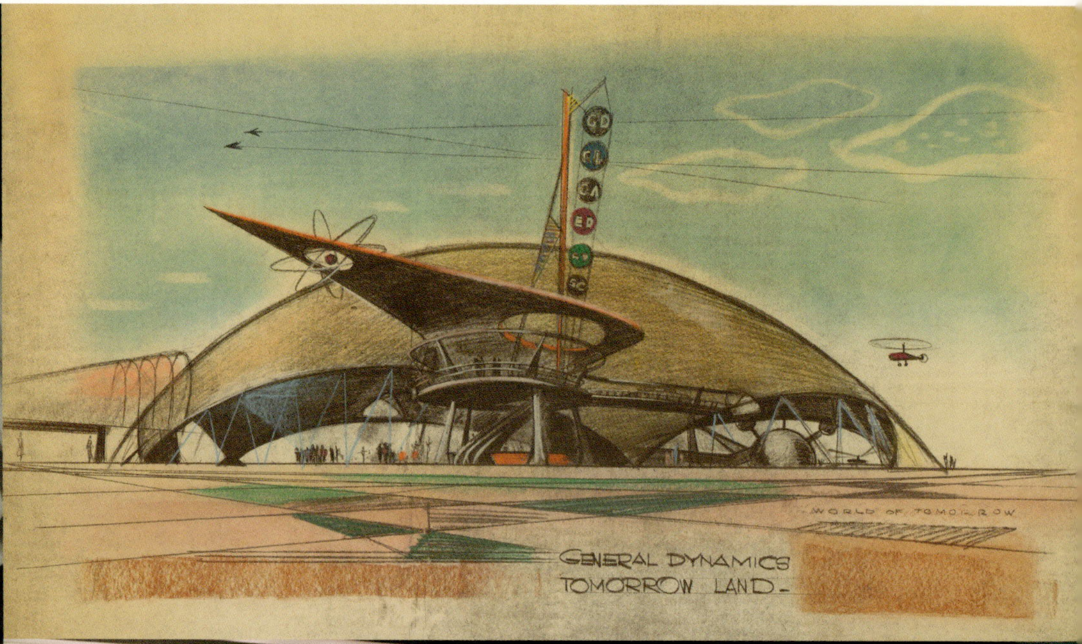

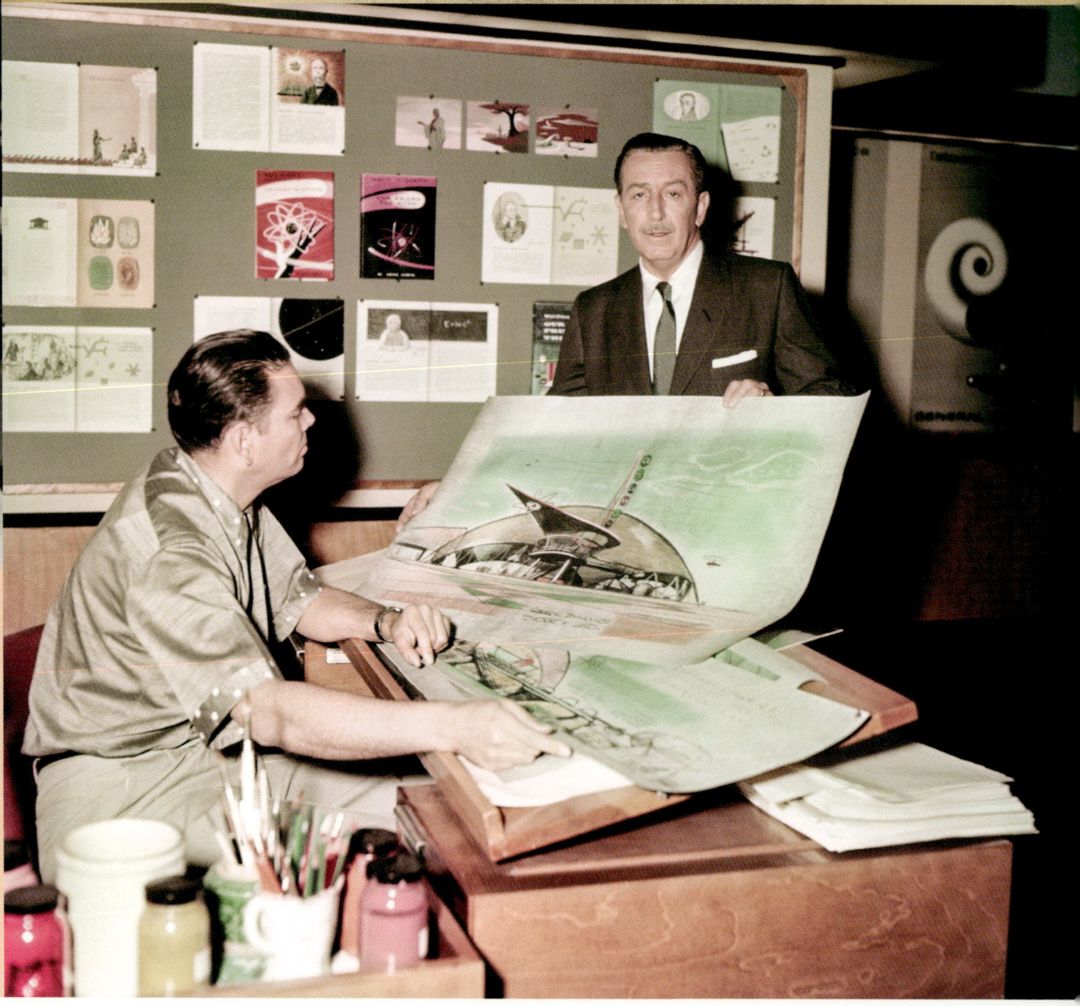

ABOVE: Walt's interest in "progress" was aided throughout his career by such talents as Disney Legend Bill Garity. Dave Smith, Disney's chief archivist emeritus and also a Disney Legend, once said, "With his pioneering efforts in sound and camera techniques, he helped set the Disney studio apart from others, while his planning and supervisory expertise resulted in the building of a highly efficient studio in Burbank."

RIGHT: For the lead-in to the January 23, 1957, *Disneyland* television broadcast of *Our Friend the Atom*, Walt Disney and Disney Legend Claude Coats collaborate on art to present the future to the public.

GENERAL DYNAMICS
TOMORROW LAND

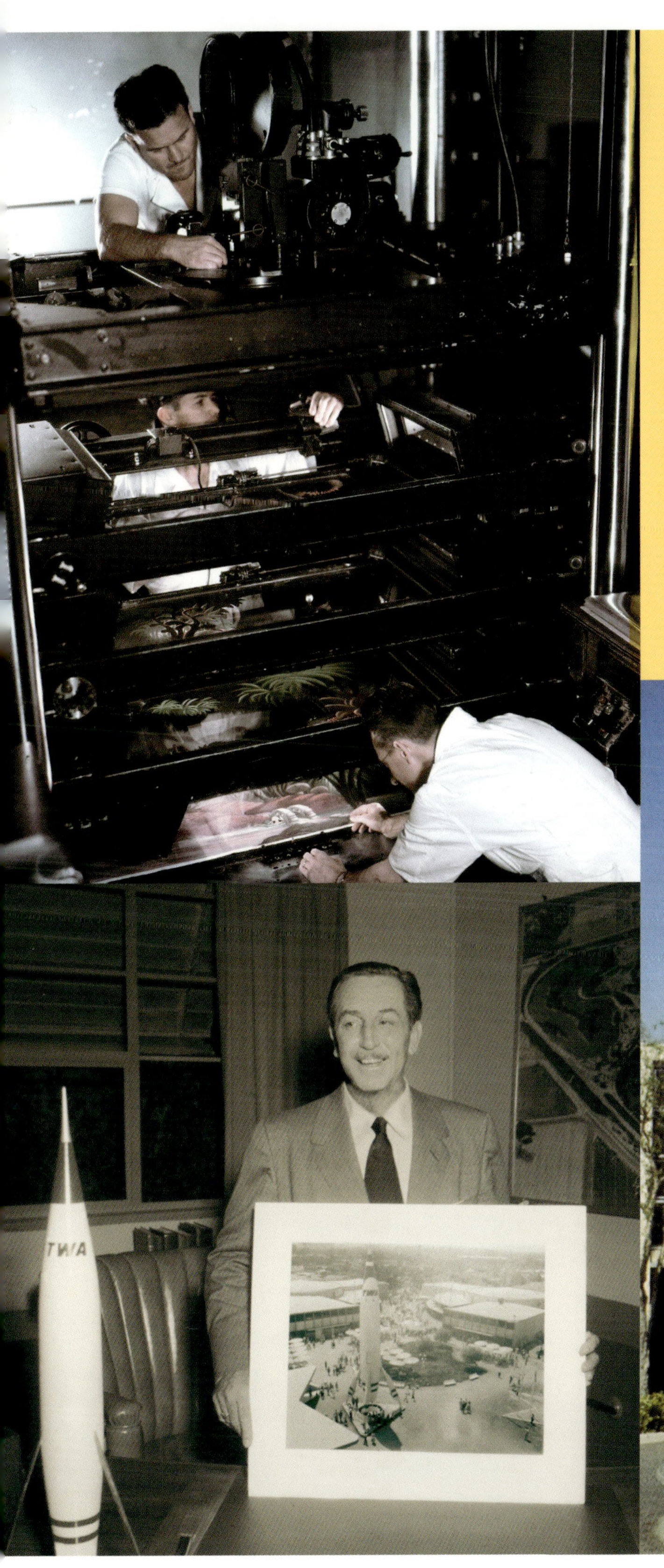

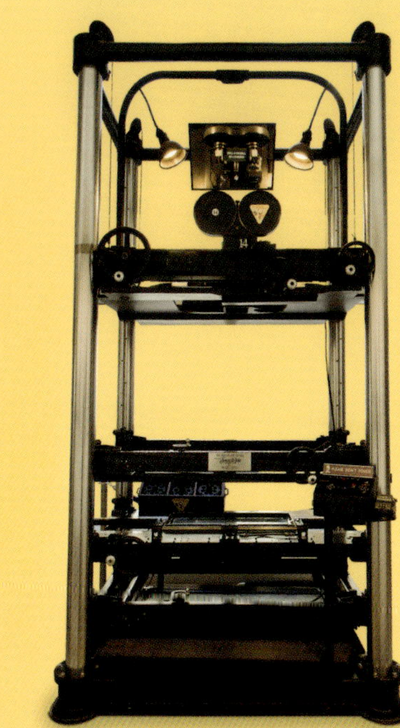

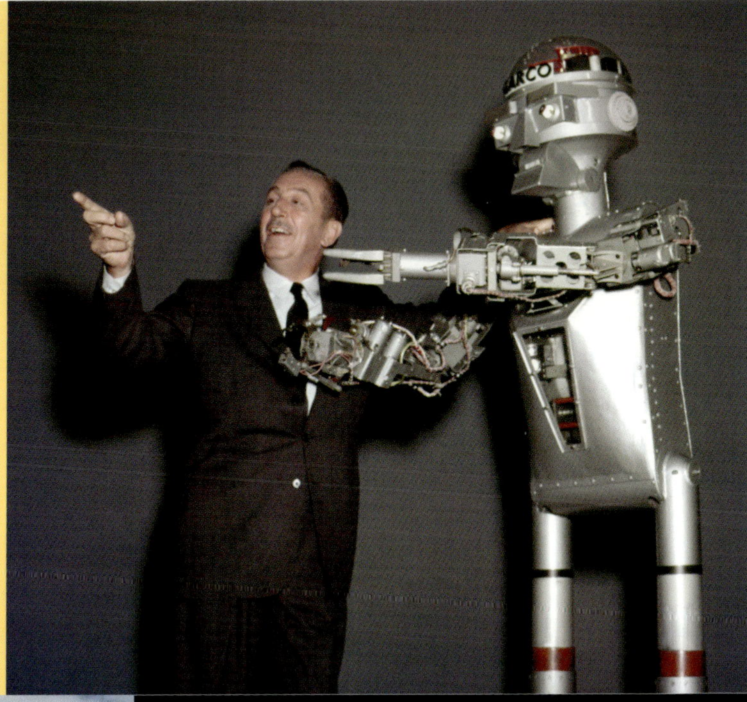

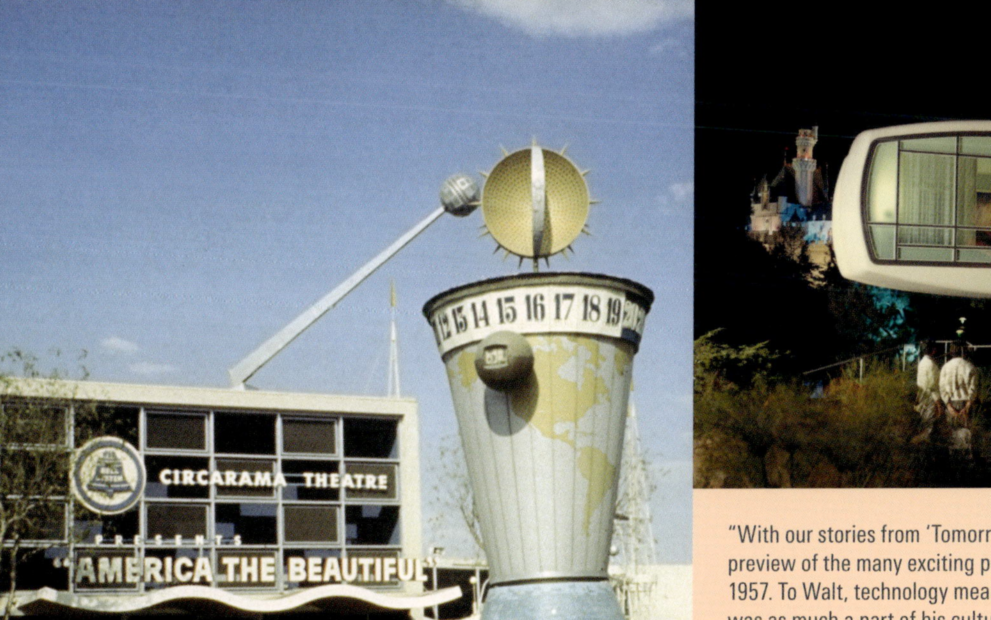

"With our stories from 'Tomorrowland' we try to give you a preview of the many exciting promises of science," Walt said in 1957. To Walt, technology meant a better life, and technology was as much a part of his culture as was art, music, and family.

CLOCKWISE FROM TOP LEFT: A multiplane camera in use and (years later) on display near the Walt Disney Archives on the Disney studio lot in Burbank, Walt engages with GARCO the robot in 1957, the Monsanto House of the Future at Disneyland, the Clock of the World icon at Tomorrowland in the early 1960s, and Walt with the TWA Rocket to the Moon.

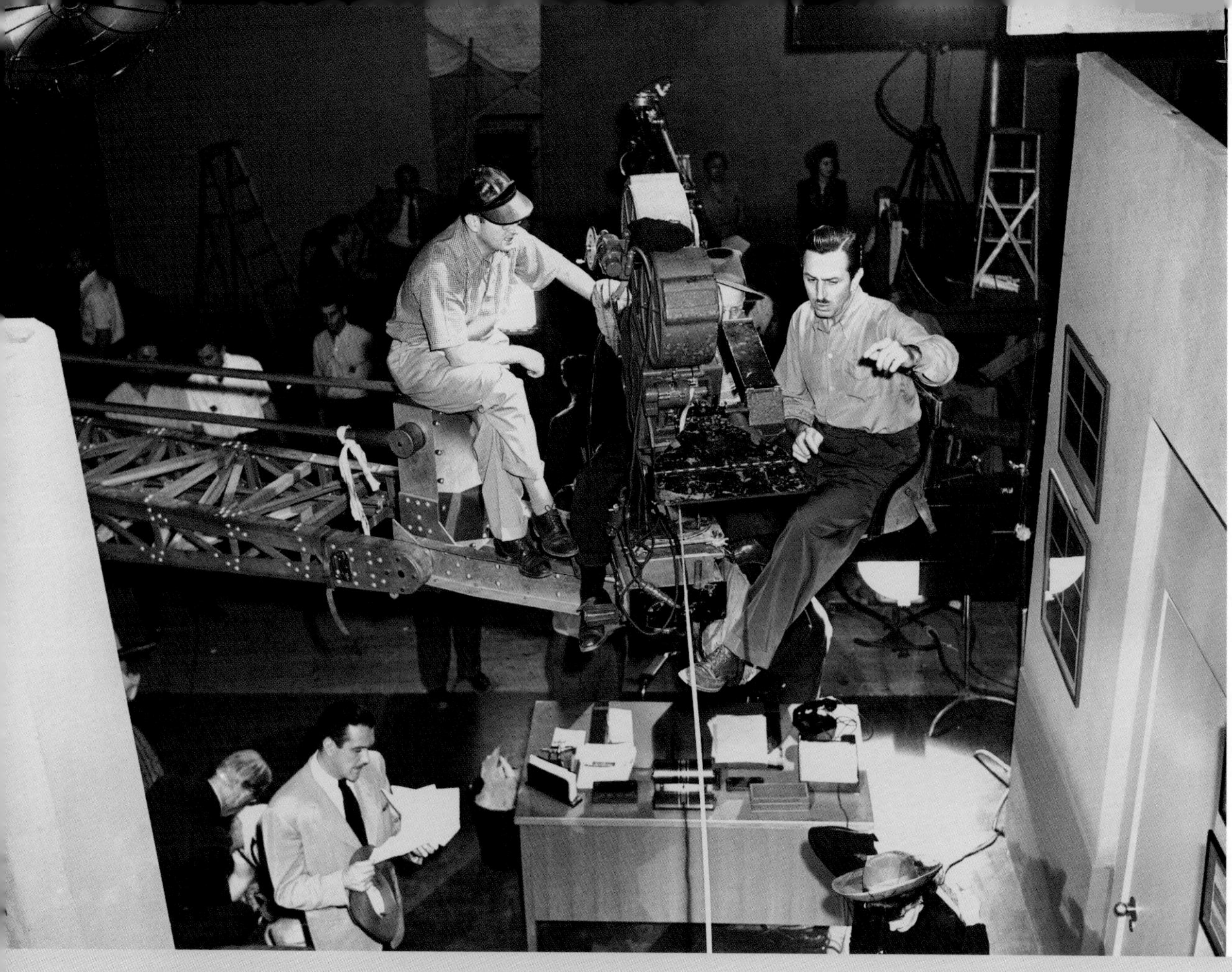

ABOVE: Walt rides the camera crane above the set for the live-action shooting of *Victory Through Air Power*, shot on Stage One at The Walt Disney Studios in Burbank.

Taking Flight

Of course, Walt was similarly interested in aviation technology. His curiosity intensified during World War II, when his studio focused almost entirely on supporting the military, producing several propaganda and training films. His passion for a military policy based on aviation strategies resulted in what is surely the most peculiar Disney feature in history, *Victory Through Air Power* (1943), based on the 1942 book of the same name by Alexander P. de Seversky. Walt felt that Seversky's ideas and message were so important, he created the film to express the aviator's theories and gain support for them with government officials, as well as the general public.

The strength of wartime aviation innovation resulted in a huge advancement in the public airline industry which by the 1960s dealt a huge blow to the flagging rail system, already suffering a deterioration of ridership that had begun even before the war. As air transportation expanded, many passenger railroad lines could no longer profitably operate. Passenger rail routes either closed down or drastically reduced service, greatly impacting the overall national rail network. By the early 1970s, almost all passenger rail operation and ownership had been transferred to one heavily subsidized federal passenger system, Amtrak.

Walt saw many of these changes as beneficial; some were even inspiring, though many were also vexing. He expressed these often-conflicting feelings in his work, typically with hope and optimism.

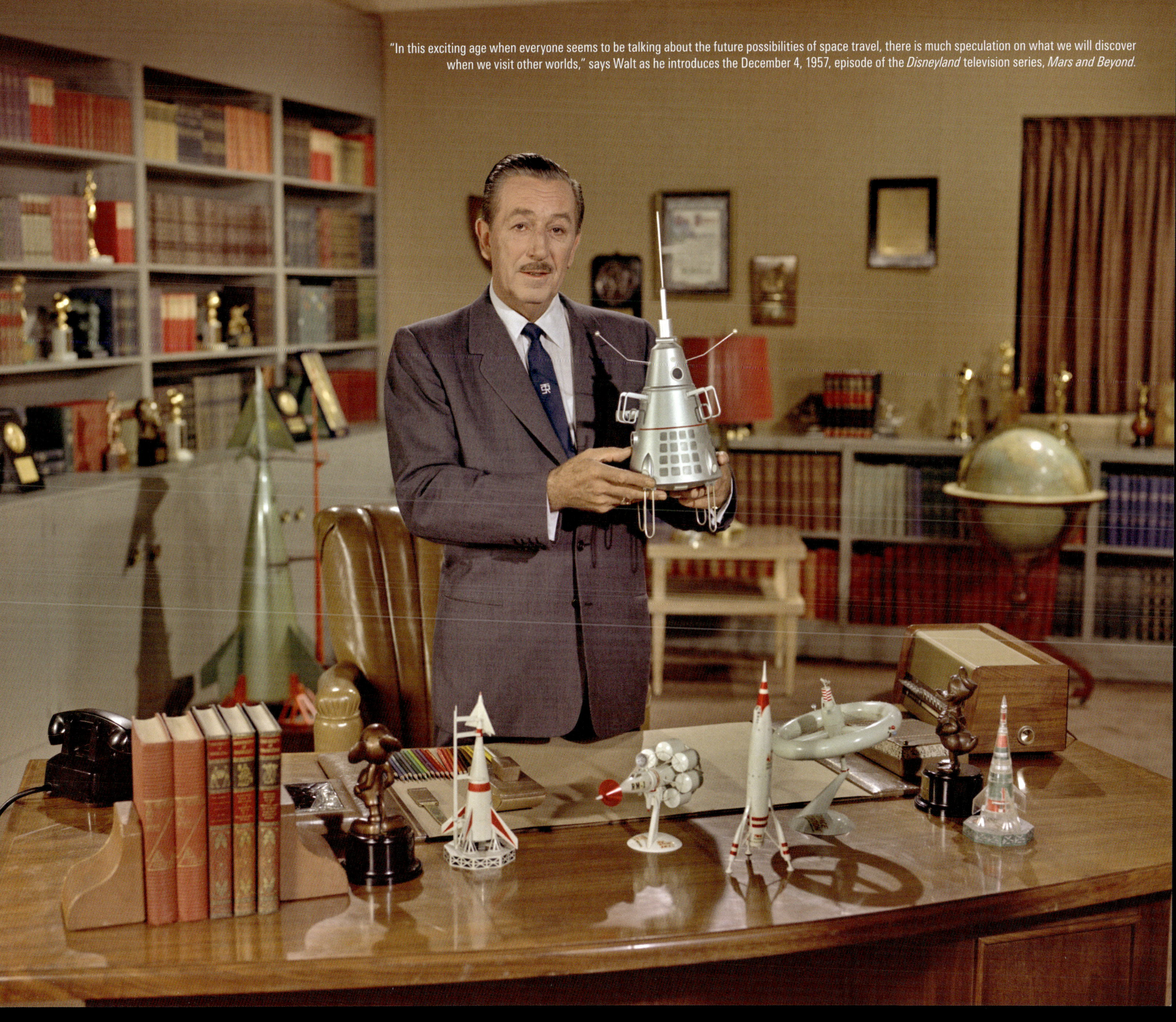

"In this exciting age when everyone seems to be talking about the future possibilities of space travel, there is much speculation on what we will discover when we visit other worlds," says Walt as he introduces the December 4, 1957, episode of the *Disneyland* television series, *Mars and Beyond*.

Look to the Stars

As Walt entered the television market in 1954, he saw the opportunity with his weekly network television hour not just to entertain, but also to enlighten and educate. In addition to realms of fantasy, adventure, nostalgia, and history, the program offered a unique venue for showcasing Walt's optimistic views of what he considered human potential through technology—a whole new perspective on a word he made sparkle and vibrate with its exciting ideas and limitless possibilities: "tomorrow."

"A vista into a world of wondrous ideas," reads the dedication plaque for Disneyland's Tomorrowland, "signifying man's achievements . . . a step into the future, with predictions of constructive things to come. Tomorrow offers new frontiers in science, adventure, and ideals: the Atomic Age . . . the challenge of outer space . . . and the hope for a peaceful and unified world."

Rather than create "space operas" that were simply retooled television Westerns, or sci-fi "kid shows" such as *Space Patrol*; *Rocky Jones, Space Ranger*; or *Tom Corbett: Space Cadet*, Walt found spaceflight and outer space exploration as genuine technological possibilities to be an idea much more interesting to share with the public.

Several television episodes in the *Disneyland* series were created under the supervision of producer, director, and co-writer, and Disney Legend, Ward Kimball. The first episode, *Man in Space*, aired on March 9, 1955. Nearly forty-two million people tuned in to the show, which was rebroadcast several times, while a slightly trimmed version had a theatrical release—resulting in *Man in Space* being nominated for an Academy Award for documentary short subject. It was followed by *Man and the Moon* (December 28, 1955), *Mars and Beyond* (December 4, 1957), and *Eyes in Outer Space* (June 18, 1959). Although three other "space" shows were developed (*The Vanguard Project*, *The UFO Show*, and *The NASA Show*), they were never produced.

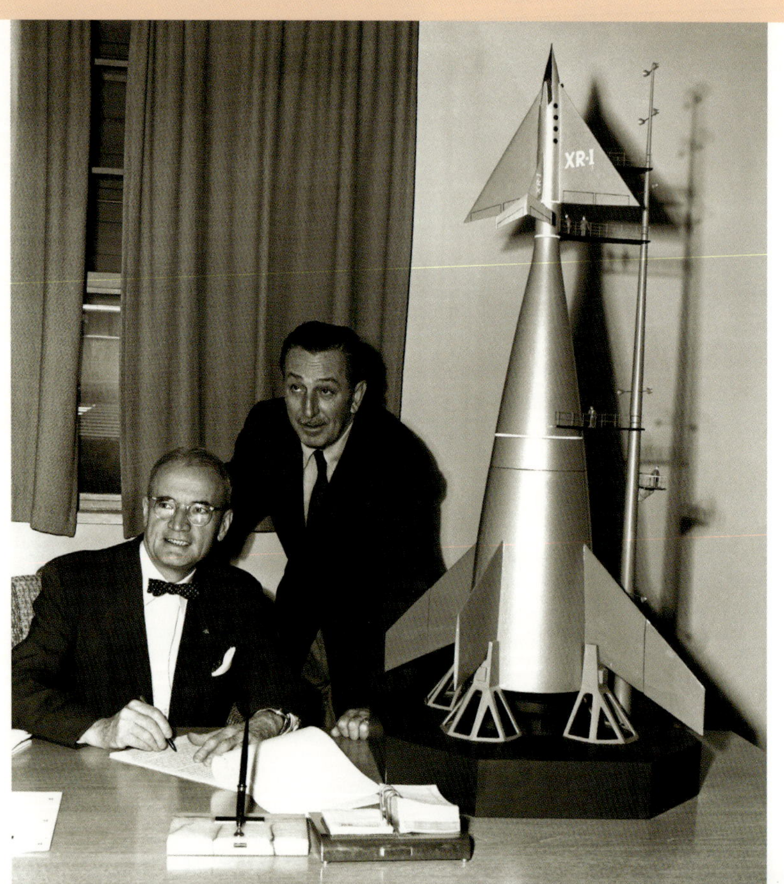

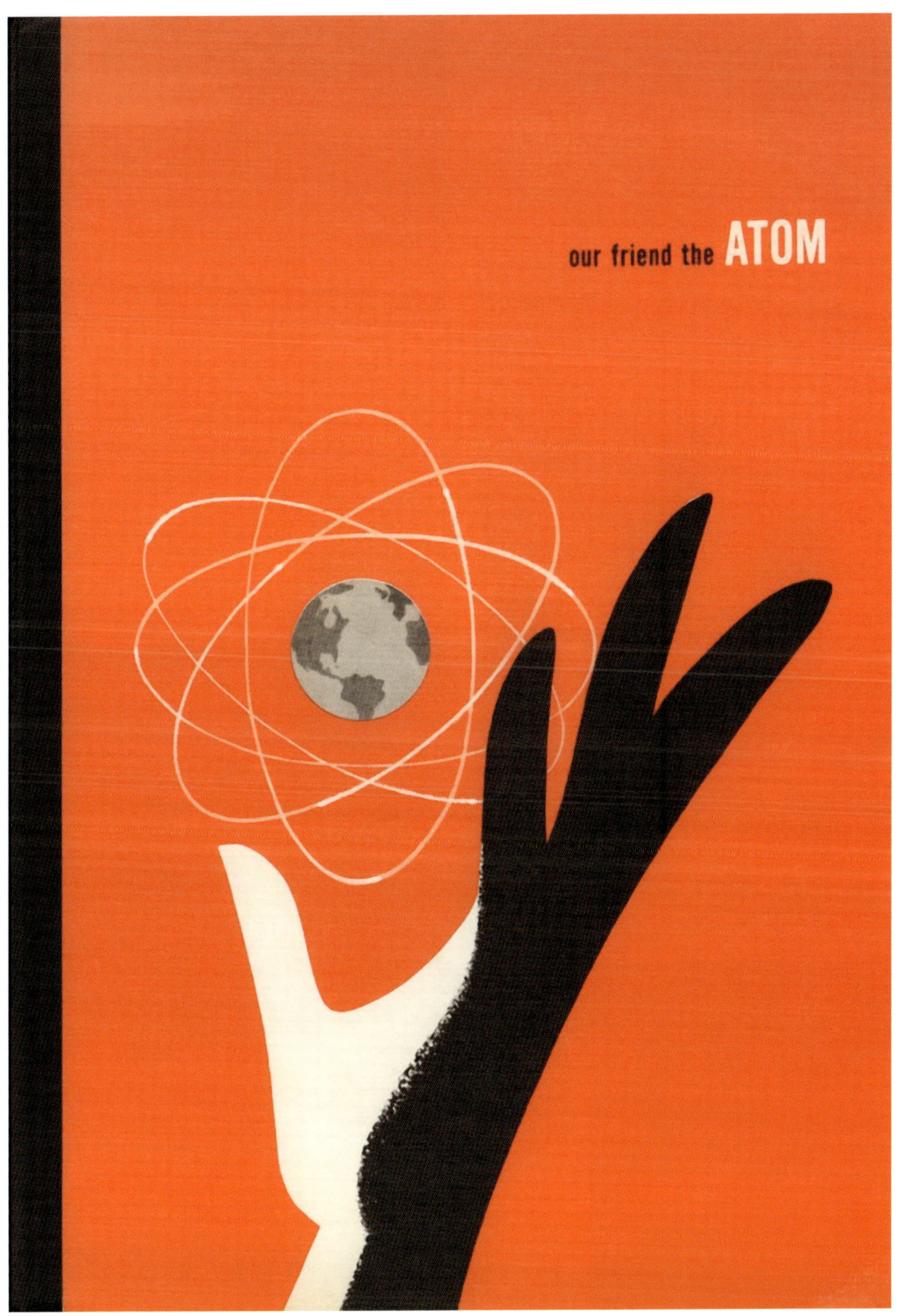

Walt Disney Presents Nuclear Physics

Walt's vision of the future was not just extraterrestrial, though. Perhaps one of the most unusual Disney television entries originated with Walt's interest in and study of nuclear energy. "I'm doing more on the Tomorrowland series where I'm going to do science more, future things," he said. "I have one in work right now that tells the story of the atom and this new era that we're living in. Nuclear energy. I'm working with scientists on it, and we're trying to put over the story of what it is, what it means to us. We're calling it *Our Friend the Atom.*"

Hosted by German physicist and science writer Dr. Heinz Haber, *Our Friend the Atom* aired on January 23, 1957. Even though only a little more than a decade had passed since the destructive force of nuclear energy had made a horrifying debut on the world stage, Walt chose to emphasize the technical, historic, and constructive aspects of nuclear physics.

"Now under our control, that thing can do anything for us, you see?" he said. "It can do all the different things. It's going to give us a new source of energy. It's going to conserve a lot of other resources for other purposes, you see? It's aiding medical science—and [may] even unite the world. That's the hope, that this atomic thing may be the very force which will unite the world. Wouldn't that be wonderful?"

The *Our Friend the Atom* program and a corresponding book were a staple of elementary education for a decade or more following their 1957 premiere.

OPPOSITE TOP RIGHT: Walt gazes at the Sea of Tranquility on a model of the moon created for his *Man in Space* series of television hours created in the 1950s for his *Disneyland* show.
OPPOSITE BOTTOM LEFT: Walt Disney and Ralph Damon, president of TWA, 1955.
OPPOSITE INSET: Dell Comics' 1958 title *Walt Disney's Man in Space: Satellites.*
LEFT: Cover of the 1956 book *Our Friend the Atom,* a companion to the January 23, 1957, *Disneyland* television episode; design by Paul Hartley.

Magic Highways and Freeway Trouble

At the time the *Disneyland* television series was at its most popular, the United States was building a network of high-capacity, high-speed highways to create a transcontinental thruway for personally operated vehicles. Skyrocketing automobile ownership made the personal car a standard of American living.

In 1958, Walt introduced a documentary program on his weekly television hour, *Magic Highway, U.S.A.* Produced and directed by Ward Kimball, the program told the story of transcontinental expansion by means of transportation, the development of the Interstate Highway System, and future developments— including mention of solar-powered and electric-powered vehicles.

A 1950 Goofy short, *Motor Mania*, had taken a somewhat more lighthearted (or perhaps pessimistic) view of the American motorist. Directed by Jack Kinney, the film stars Goofy as the passive pedestrian, "Mr. Walker," who transforms into the agitated "Mr. Wheeler" once he is in his car. This short inspired a pair of 1965 educational films also starring Goofy, *Freewayphobia* and *Goofy's Freeway Troubles.*

The highways of yesterday, today, and tomorrow were perpetual objects of Walt Disney's fascination.

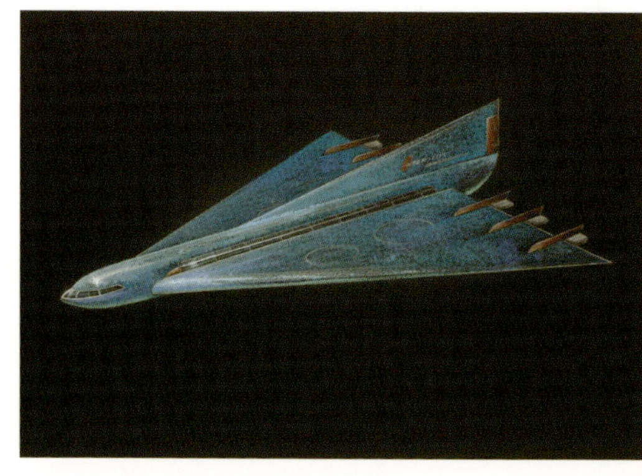

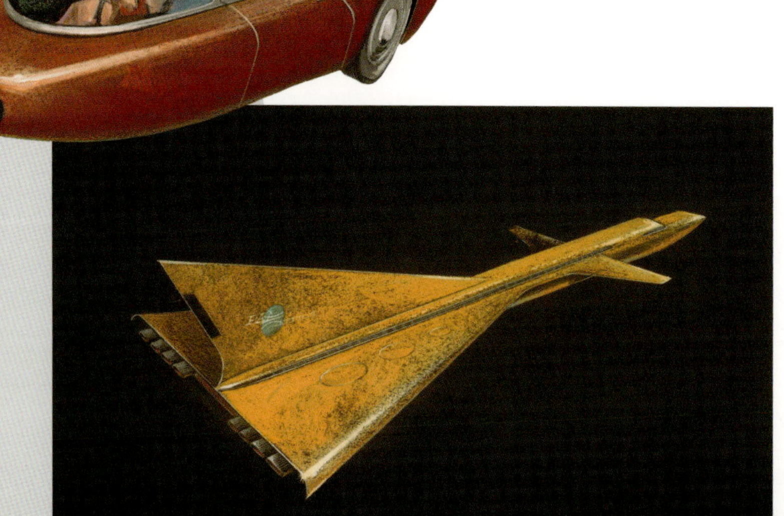

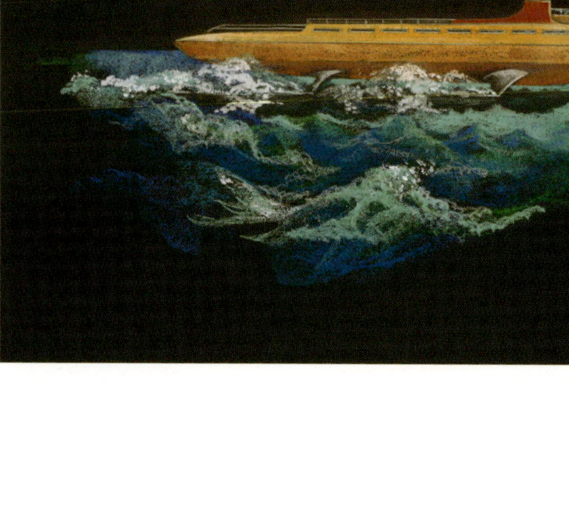

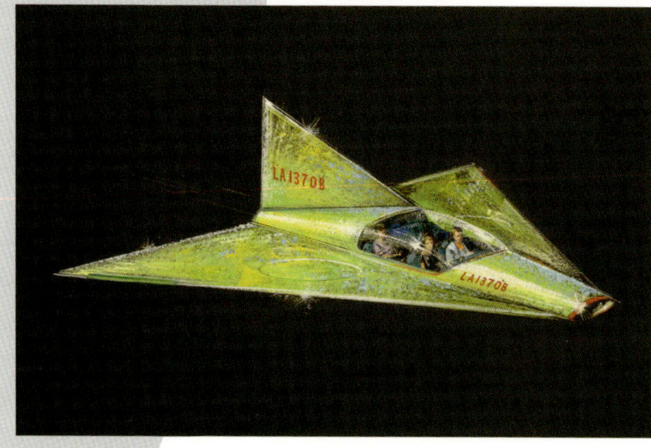

ABOVE AND LEFT: A series of futuristic vehicles conceived for the General Electric pavilion at the 1964–1965 New York World's Fair, by Sam McKim. Pastel and chalk on black paper, 1963.

Tomorrow at Disneyland

Disneyland, of course, offered Walt a physical, tangible, real place in which to showcase the past, present, and future. This constant attention to technology, innovation, and "progress" often led to frustration—since he tended to dream bigger and faster than the world could create.

But in Disneyland, Tomorrowland was the straggler in the development of attractions for opening day. Imagineer Randy Bright wrote of it as "the land that time (and budget) almost forgot." With less than six months remaining before the park's opening, there were many on the Disneyland team who felt that, with time and money running out, it might be best to put up an elaborate fence across the plaza entrance with artwork and promises of exciting attractions to come.

Naturally, that was an idea that Walt summarily dismissed, and on opening day, there was a place called "Tomorrowland," albeit somewhat anemic and underpopulated when compared to the more robust experiences in fantasy, history, and adventure.

Just a Dream Away

Over the next decade, Walt remained vexed by the lack of actual "tomorrow" in Tomorrowland. He continued to add attractions and exhibits, including the Astro-Jets and the Monsanto House of the Future, but a cohesive and complete Tomorrowland would evade Walt until he decided simply to demolish most of it and start over in 1966.

But one of Walt's earliest efforts to add more "tomorrow" to Tomorrowland endures today and has a fascinating and rich history as an idea, as an aspiration, and as a practical application of all the transportation history that Walt had been a student of his entire life: the monorail.

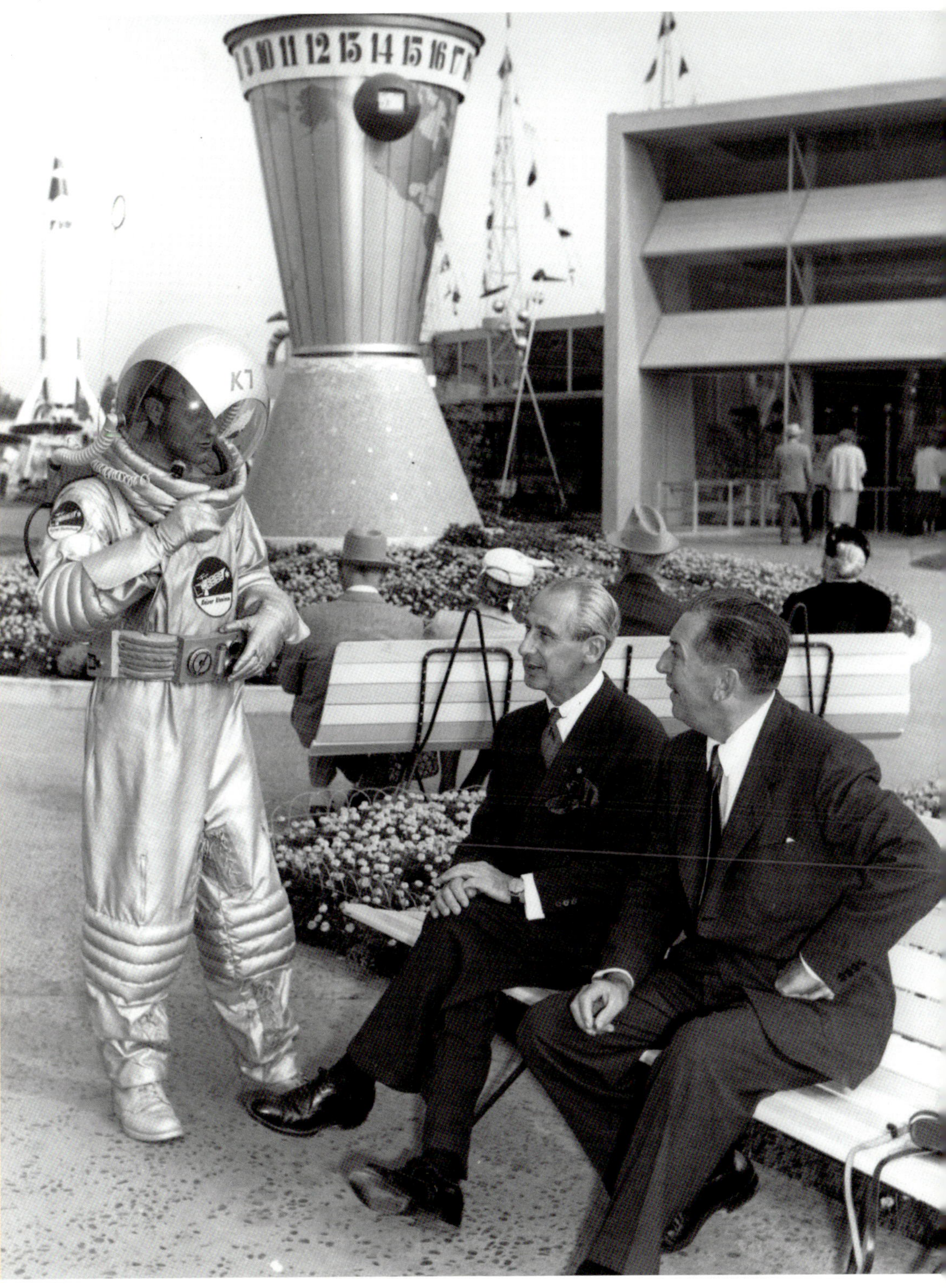

RIGHT: Walt Disney and German physicist and science writer Dr. Heinz Haber are greeted by Spaceman K7 during an October 1955 visit to Tomorrowland at Disneyland.

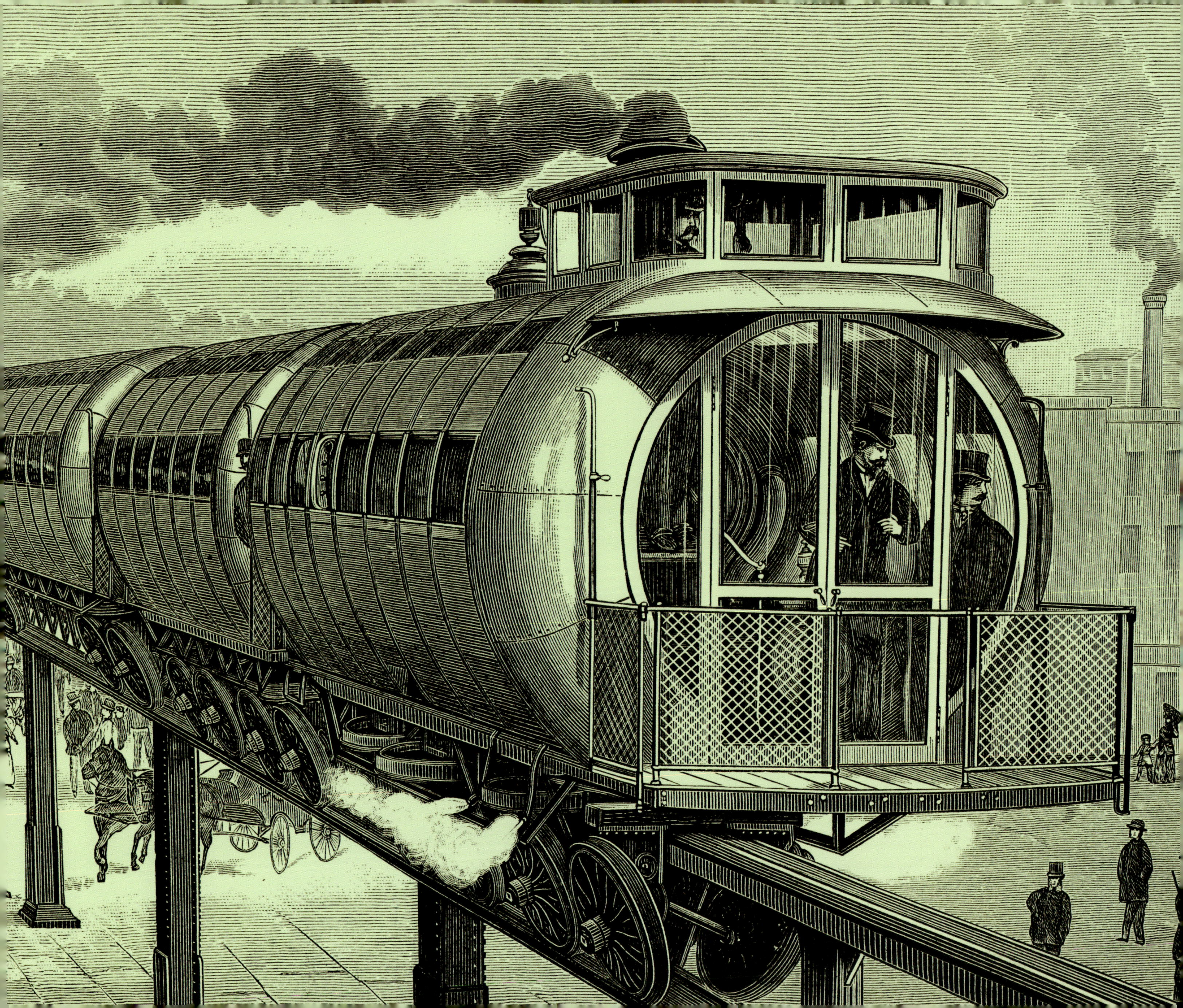

CHAPTER 2

Early Monorails: Imagination, Exploration, and Invention

"I am not an economist, but things are not as bad as they seem. I have a great deal of confidence in our future."

—Walt Disney

Monorails in History

Sleek and swift, traveling with speed and silence, expertly created with the absolute cutting edge in science and technology. That's a fairly succinct view of how monorails might be perceived in popular culture. The reality is, as is often the case, quite different than the perception.

An inventor named Henry Robinson Palmer filed the earliest patent for what we might today consider a monorail, or as the inventor described it, "a single line of rail, supported at such height from the ground as to allow the center of gravity of the carriages to be below the upper surface of the rail." Propulsion was by horse.

The patent (UK No. 4618) was dated November 22, 1821.

OPPOSITE: Engraving of the Meigs Elevated Railway, originally published in *Scientific American*, July 10, 1886.

Cheshunt Railway (1825)

This earliest known monorail was actually not very glamorous, or terribly futuristic. It wasn't even designed for passengers; it was engineered to carry bricks. It opened on June 26, 1825, in Cheshunt, England, a borough twelve miles north of central London, "running from Mr. Gibbs' Brick Pit, to the west of Gews Corner, to a wharf on the River Lea, not far from the site of the current Cheshunt Station," according to Nicholas Blatchley of Hertfordshire Community Archives. Although bricks were its primary cargo (the containers straddled the overhead rail on a yoke, like a pair of pannier baskets on a mule), people couldn't resist jumping into the carriers. Thus was born the first passenger monorail in the world.

This basic "Palmer design" evolved through the nineteenth century; the Palmer design was improved with the addition of stabilizing wheels and additional rails (rendering the term "monorail" a misnomer). In 1829, Maxwell Dick introduced "safety rails" below the running rails to reduce the likelihood of derailment. He also articulated the main advantage claimed for this class of vehicle: "The pillars or supports [are] of different heights as circumstances of the country may require." In other words, the system was better suited for crossing rough terrain.

Philadelphia Centennial (1876)

General LeRoy Stone's Centennial Monorail was a steam-driven system first unveiled at the first World's Fair ever held in the US—the United States Centennial Exposition, held in Philadelphia in 1876 celebrating the one hundredth anniversary of American independence.

The track for Stone's system, which connected the Horticultural Hall and the Agricultural Hall in Fairmount Park, was 170 yards long. Its "fleet" was a single double-decker railcar decorated in an utterly opulent high-Victorian style that even Captain Nemo would have found comfortable. The pilot's cabin was at the end, below which there was a pair of water tanks with a coal bin behind them. The system was propelled by a pair of load-bearing double-flange wheels, of which one was driven by a rotary steam engine.

A modified version of this prototype was used two years later on Bradford & Foster Brook in Pennsylvania.

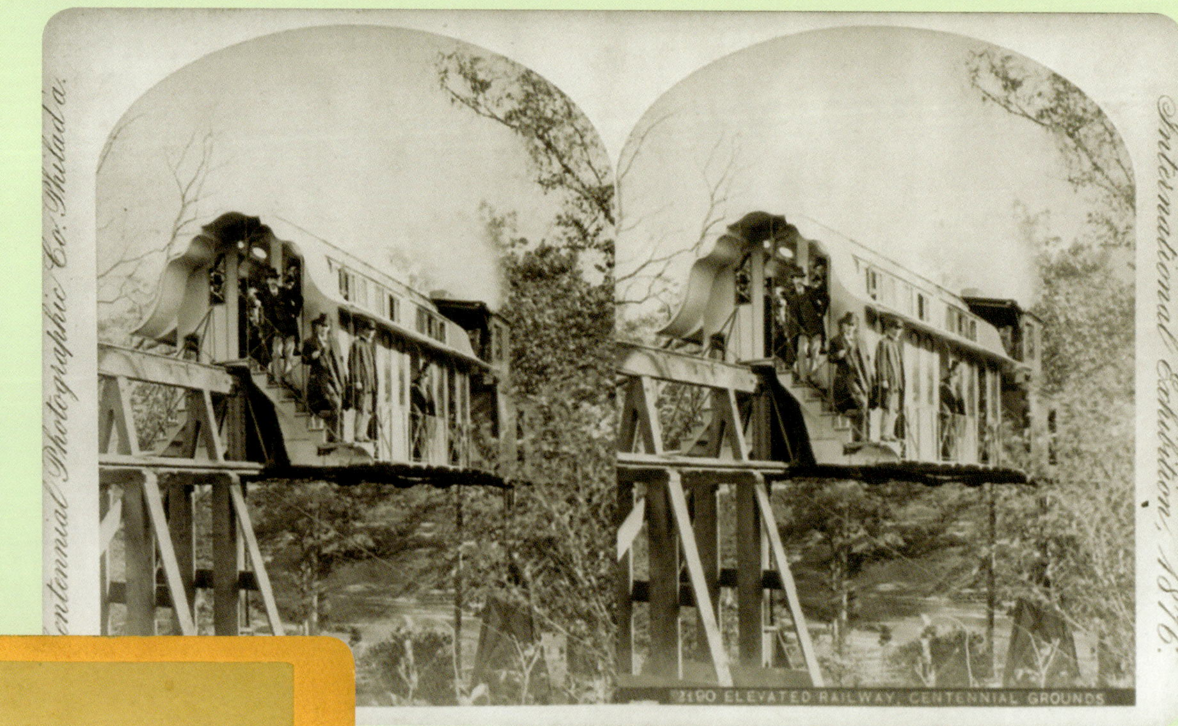

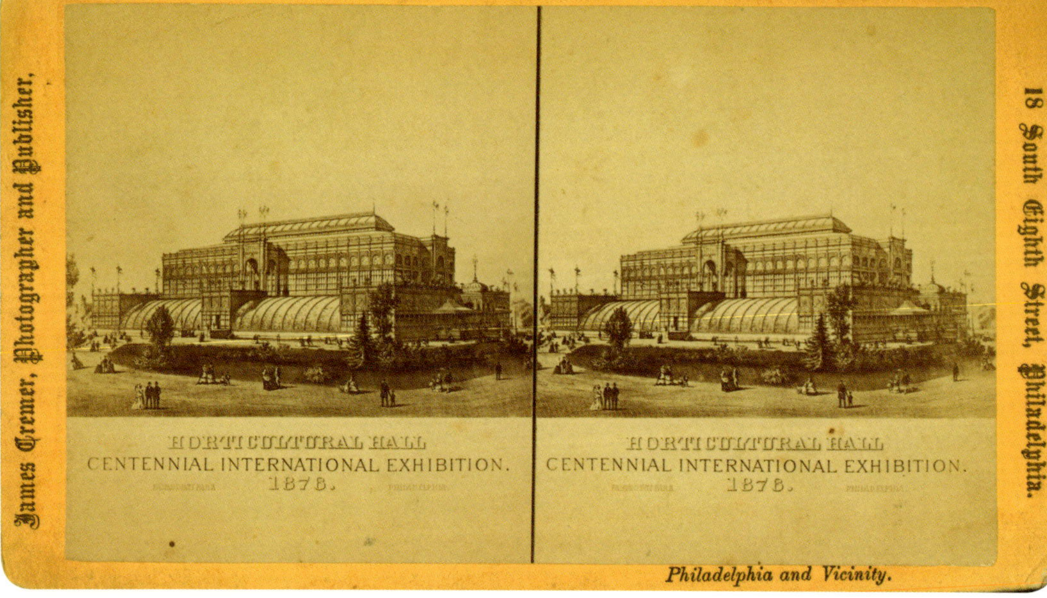

TOP: Stereopticon photo card of General LeRoy Stone's double-decker steam-powered monorail.
ABOVE: Stereopticon photo card of the Centennial International Exhibition in Fairmount Park in Philadelphia, where Stone's monorail debuted.

Sonoma Prismoidal (1876)

The Sonoma Prismoidal was a wooden monorail, intended to be a seven-mile line connecting the Northern California city of Sonoma with a steamship landing at San Pablo Bay, near San Francisco. Promoter Joseph S. Kohn's design utilized a track fifteen inches high with a base twenty-seven inches wide that cost only $4,500 per mile to build—half the cost of a contemporary narrow-gauge railroad. It had a single locomotive engine, a boxcar, and ten platform cars.

Only three and a half miles of the proposed route to the ferry landing at the mouth of the Petaluma River were built, between Norfolk (now Wingo) and Schellville, and the line operated for only six months before the company went into bankruptcy.

Kohn had also proposed an elevated version of this railroad to be built in San Francisco along Market Street, but merchants and property owners along the line protested, and it never moved forward.

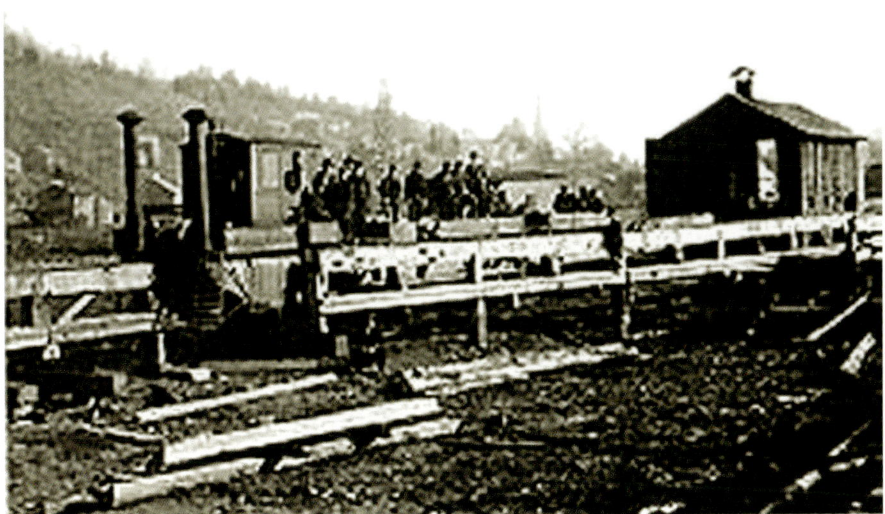

Bradford & Foster Brook Monorail (1878)

After the success of the Centennial Monorail at the Philadelphia Centennial Exposition of 1876, General LeRoy Stone thought that his prototype system might be adapted to solve transportation problems in Bradford, Pennsylvania. Bradford was then a booming oil town, and thousands of dollars' worth of machinery, supplies, and personnel required efficient conveyance. Roads in the area were insufficient, often impassable, and unable to handle the movement of heavy equipment.

The four-mile line was designed to transport oil workers and drilling apparatus to Derrick City, with additional stations at Tarport, Babcock's Mill, and Harrisburg Run. Once it began running, local residents also started to ride the line.

A number of different engines were tried on the railway. The rotary engines that had been suitable to the limited route and occupancy of the exposition lacked power, and two initial engine designs failed to function, and finally a third and larger locomotive, driven by conventional pistons (but built with secondhand boilers), was tested to specifications.

However, on the trial run of the new locomotive on January 27, 1879, the engine was coupled to a flatcar full of officials and dignitaries and—to demonstrate its power and capabilities—run at a high speed. One boiler ran dry, too much water was added too quickly, and the boiler exploded, sending the train careening into a creek and killing the driver, fireman, and three of the passengers. After this tragedy, the entire enterprise was abandoned.

RIGHT, TOP: Engraving depicting The Listowel and Ballybunion Railway (also see page 33).
RIGHT, BOTTOM: Five engravings of Lartigue elevated single rail railways as originally published in *Scientific American*, February 19, 1887. The publication's original caption stated, "1. Train of the Lartigue Railway at Tothill Fields, Westminster, ascending a Viaduct on an Incline of 1 in 10. 2. Train for the Transport of Wounded Soldiers, at the Russian Guards' Camp, near St. Petersburg. 3. Electrical Train at the Mines of Ria, in the French Pyrenees, carrying Copper Ore. 4. Section of Railway and Third-Class Open Passenger Carriage. 5. View of Carriage for the Transport of Troops at the Russian Guards' Camp, near St. Petersburg."

Lartigue Monorail (1881)

The Lartigue Monorail system was named for its creator, French engineer Charles Lartigue (1834–1907). He further developed a horse-drawn monorail system based on the designs of Henry Robinson Palmer's 1821 patents.

Oddly, *camel caravans* had been the key inspiration for Lartigue's evolution of the Palmer system. While in Algeria, he had seen camels carrying heavy loads balanced side to side in baskets connected by a yoke on their backs. In 1881, Lartigue developed a fifty-six-mile-long line to transport esparto grass across the Algerian desert; this design used mules instead of camels to pull trains of carriages and containers on an elevated rail.

The most famous Lartigue railway was the Listowel and Ballybunion Railway in Ireland (see page 33). Next, in 1895, Lartigue built another system, an eleven-mile line between Feurs and Panissières in the Loire Valley region of France.

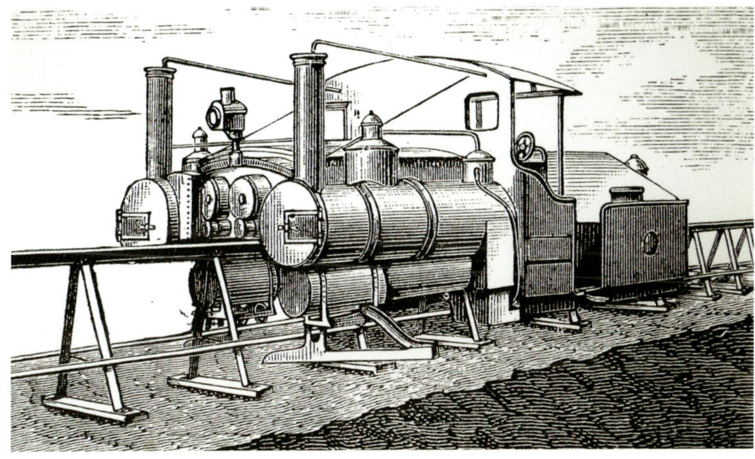

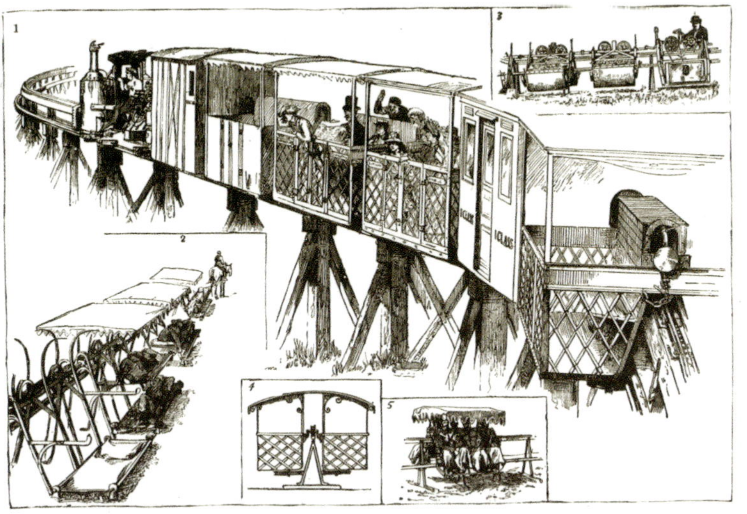

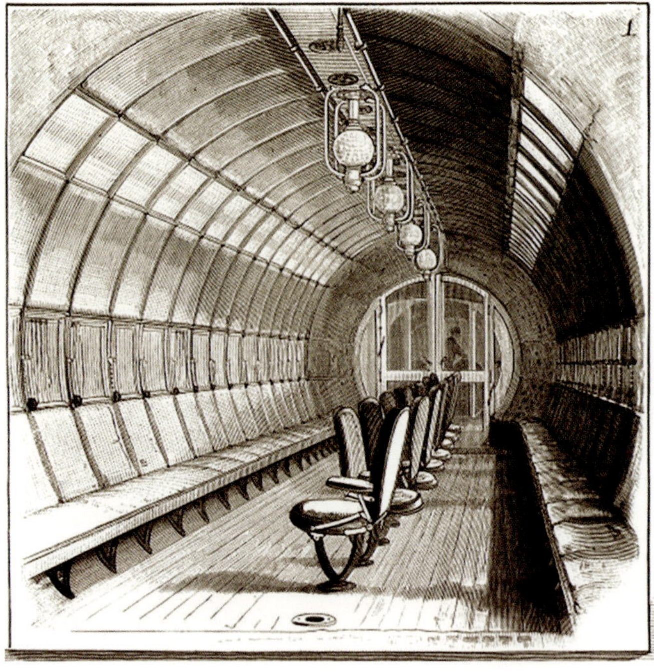

Meigs Monorail (1886)

Captain J. V. Meigs of Lowell, Massachusetts, invented and designed an elaborate and highly complex experimental steam-powered monorail in 1886. For his patent application, Meigs assembled an extensive explanation of how the railway worked, complete with illustrations, diagrams, and statistics, which was even published in *Scientific American* magazine.

A 227-foot-long prototype line was built in 1886 in East Cambridge, Massachusetts, on land adjacent to Bridge Street (now Monsignor O'Brien Highway). In addition to its scientific and engineering marvels, the train featured luxurious upholstered interiors and an aerodynamic car design that were easily half a century ahead of their time.

A fire, rumored to be of a suspicious nature, broke out the night of February 4, 1887, destroyed Meigs's car sheds along with the experimental coach and tender, and severely damaged the locomotive.

The Meigs prototype line was never expanded—but ran until 1894 before being dismantled.

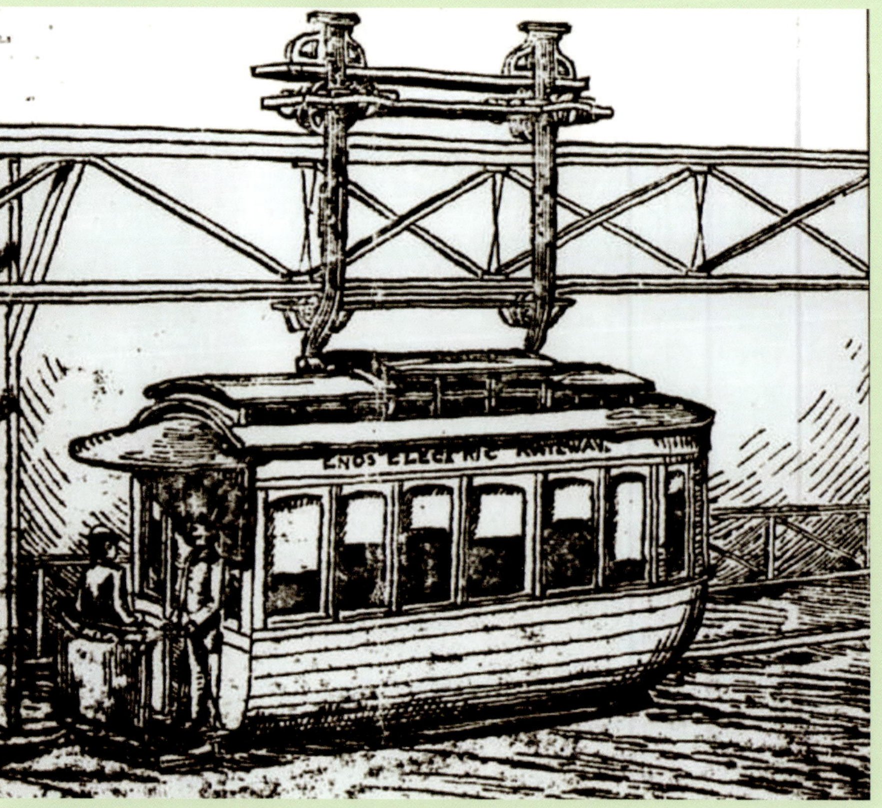

Enos Electric Railway (1888)

A group of St. Paul, Minnesota, businessmen petitioned for a franchise for the Enos Electric Railway Company in 1888. This company would build "an overhead monorail railroad to Minneapolis," ostensibly based on the 1826 Palmer plan. It would feature cars from the Enos Electric Railway Company of Boston, powered by four electric motors from the Thomson-Houston Company of Boston. Electricity was to be supplied by the Eureka Improvement Company of St. Paul.

Although the franchise was granted with the support of the St. Paul Chamber of Commerce and the *St. Paul Pioneer Press* (and a quarter-mile prototype line was built and operated), the company appears to have been quickly abandoned by 1889. But the design is said to have inspired the German engineer Eugen Langen—for the Enos monorail bears a remarkable likeness to the 1901 Wuppertaler Schwebebahn in Germany (see the next chapter).

ABOVE: Drawing of a car of the Enos Electric Railway system proposed for Winthrop, Massachusetts, in 1885.

BELOW: The design of the rail-frame appears to have influenced Wuppertaler Schwebebahn designer Eugen Langen's framing design, since it closely resembles the Enos construction. This image comes from the 1904 *Lexikon der gesamten Technik* (Dictionary of Technology) by Otto Lueger.

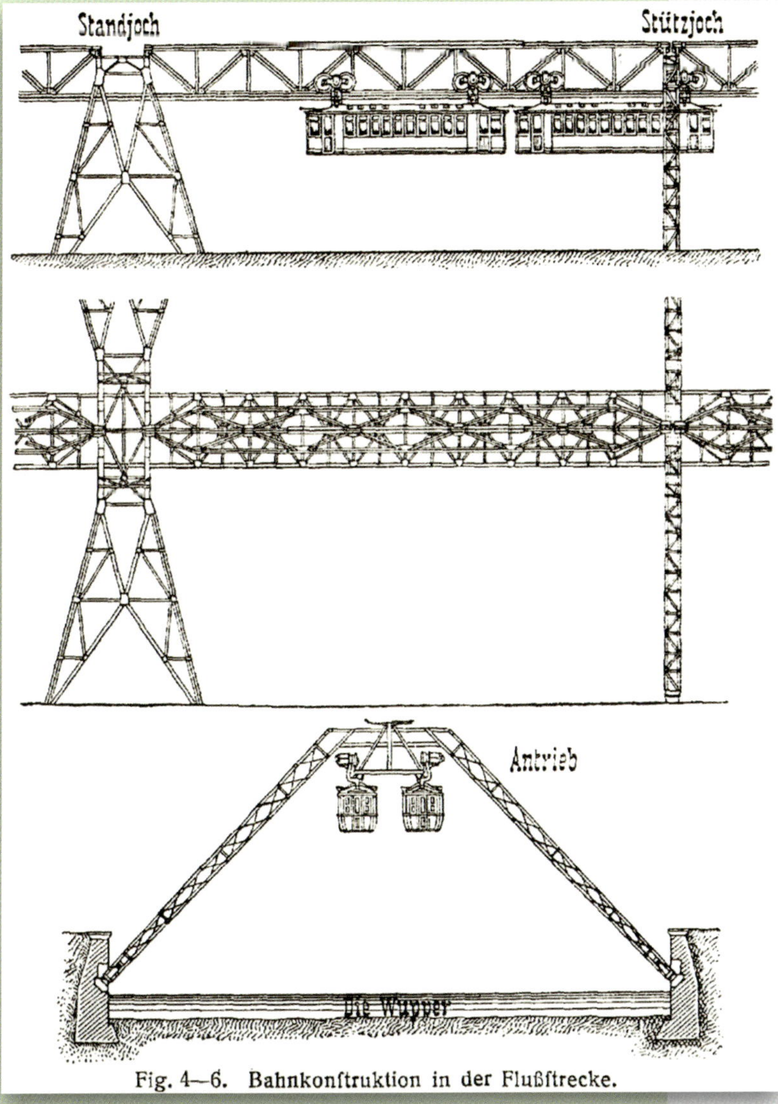

Fig. 4—6. Bahnkonftruktion in der Flußftrecke.

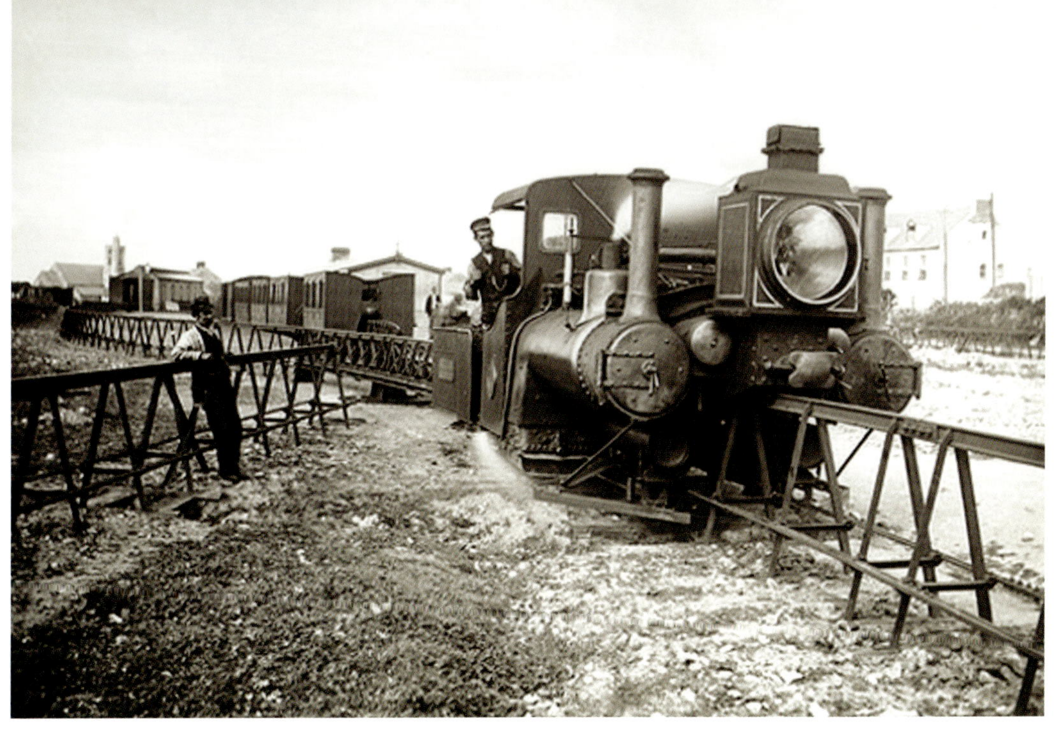

The Listowel and Ballybunion Railway (1888)

The seaside resort town of Ballybunion (on the west coast of Ireland), and the market town of Listowel were once linked by a nine-mile steel-rail monorail system operated by the Lartigue Railway Construction Company. It began operations March 1, 1888, and ran until 1924, carrying freight, passengers, and livestock. It was, for many years, the only passenger-carrying monorail in the British Isles, and the only commercially successful monorail of its type. (In 1899, Parliament rejected a proposal to build a thirty-mile version of the line in England between Manchester and Liverpool. The Lartigue company was dissolved in 1906.)

A decade of war and revolt prompted the demise of the Listowel and Ballybunion, keeping tourists away from the Kerry coast. Britain relinquished control of Irish railways in 1921, but the provisional Irish government excluded the Lartigue from the national railway system because the specialized equipment couldnot be used on any other lines. Rising operational costs and the ascent of road transportation, along with a major system breakdown, ultimately forced it out of business in 1924. Today, a visitor to Listowel can ride on a full-scale diesel-powered replica of the original monorail. There is also film of the original Lartigue monorail in action, as well as models, displays, and memorabilia tied to it at the Lartigue Museum in Listowel.

Tracking Progress

As time went by, the idea of monorails persisted. They did not die out, or fall out of favor as a notion, or a prototype. They didn't become quaint relics of an impossible optimism. Their implementation was certainly outpaced by more traditional transportation methods, yet something about this system of transportation was so attractive, so inspiring, and so exciting that engineers, inventors, city planners, and futurists kept returning to it through the next century—and beyond.

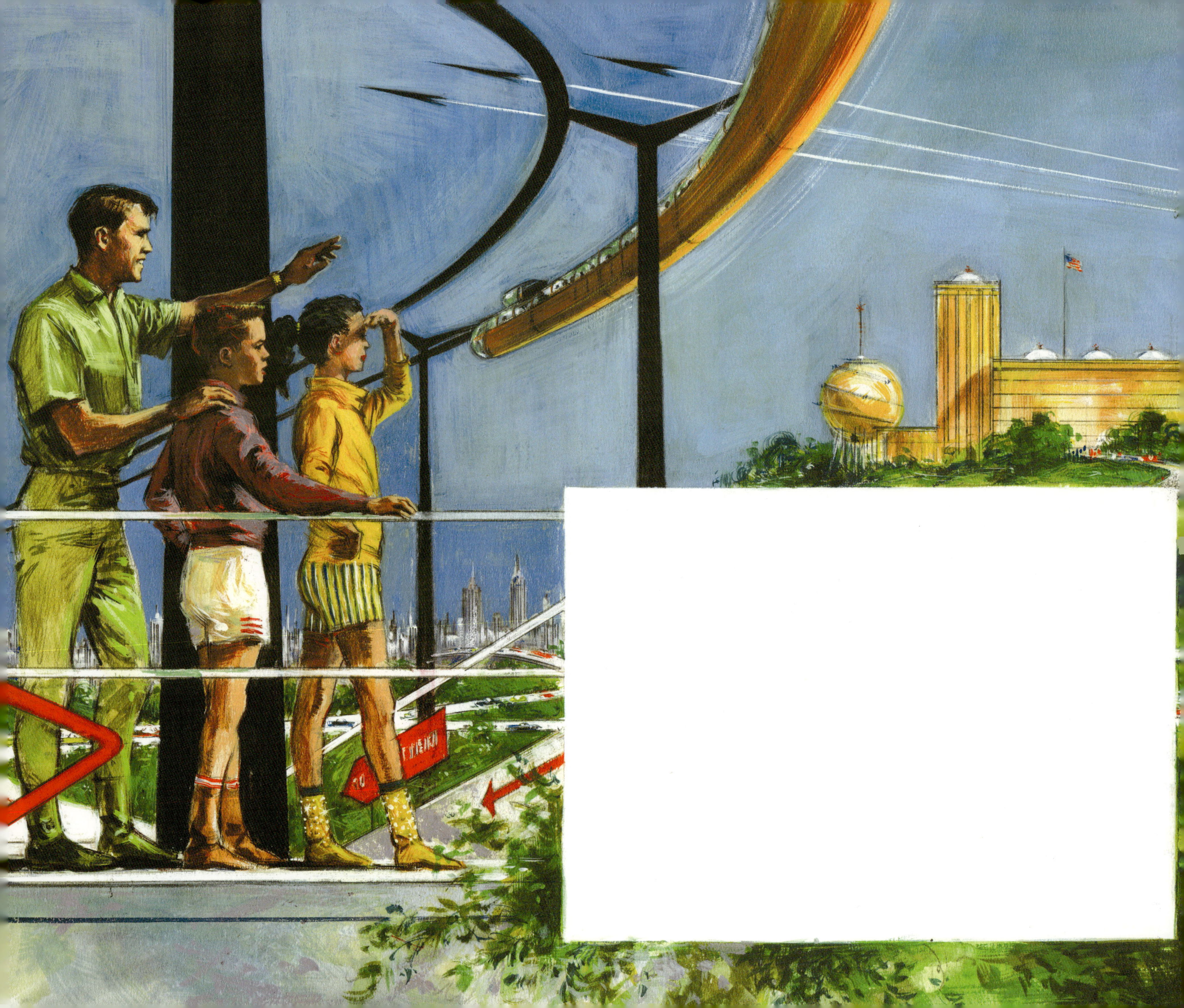

CHAPTER 3

The Twentieth Century: Science Fiction to Science Fact

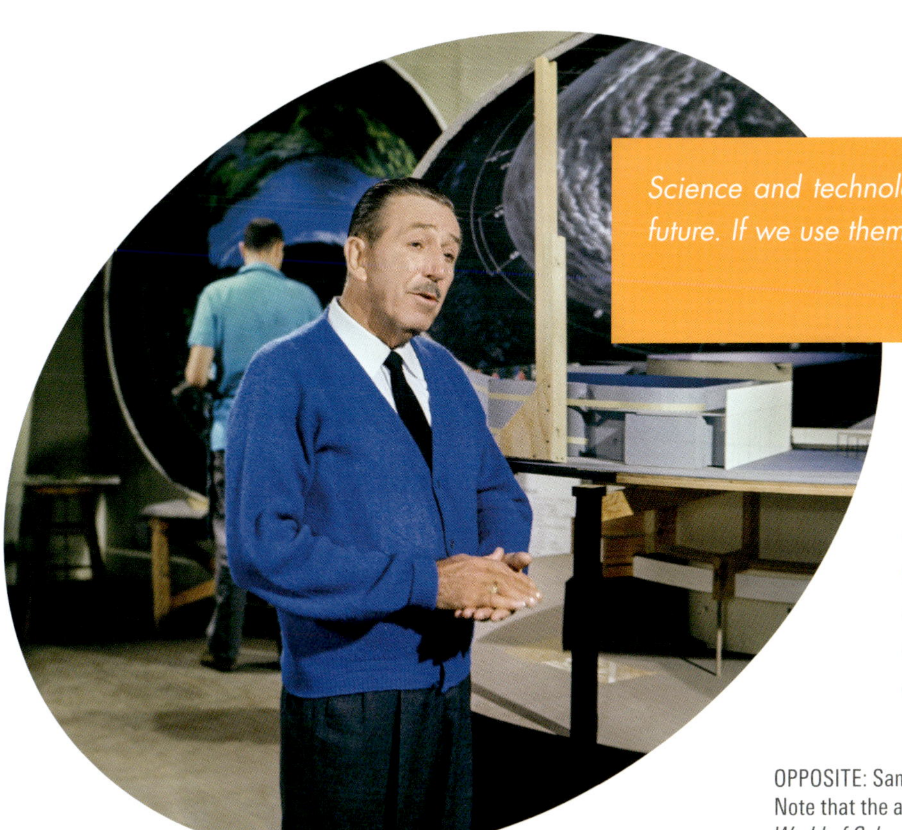

Science and technology have already given us the tools we need to build the world of the future. If we use them right now, we won't have to wait to know what tomorrow will bring.

—Walt Disney

Onward

The experimentation, demonstration, and innovation of the nineteenth century continued into the next. Even as monorails endured in the minds and laboratories of those involved in transportation, engineering, and science, they likewise established an ongoing presence in the new literary field of science fiction and its attendant incarnations in pulp magazines, comic books, and the movies. An efficient, accessible, efficient monorail system consistently seemed like it was "just a dream away."

OPPOSITE: Sam McKim's illustration for the article "Butch and Jan Meet the Atom," *Walt Disney's Magazine*, April 1957. Note that the article's text was laid into the white box in the lower right. ABOVE: Walt hosting a *Walt Disney's Wonderful World of Color* episode.

Wuppertal Suspension Railway, or Wuppertaler Schwebebahn (1901)

Electric Elevated Railway (Suspension Railway) Installation, Eugen Langen System (Anlage einer elektrischen Hochbahn [Schwebebahn], System Eugen Langen) is the official mouthful of a name for an enduring monorail—more commonly known as the Wuppertal Suspension Railway.

The brainchild of civil engineer Eugen Langen of Cologne, Germany, the system was originally designed for the city of Berlin. The suspension railway and its elevated stations were built in Barmen-Elberfeld (now known as Wuppertal) and Vohwinkel (now a section of Wuppertal) between 1897 and 1903; the first track opened in 1901.

It has operated successfully on an eight-mile route along the Wupper River between Oberbarmen and Sonnborner Straße, and about two miles above the valley road between Sonnborner Straße and Vohwinkel, for nearly 120 years. The Wuppertal Suspension Railway has survived two world wars and startling changes in transportation and technology, and (as of this book's printing) eighty-five thousand people still use it daily.

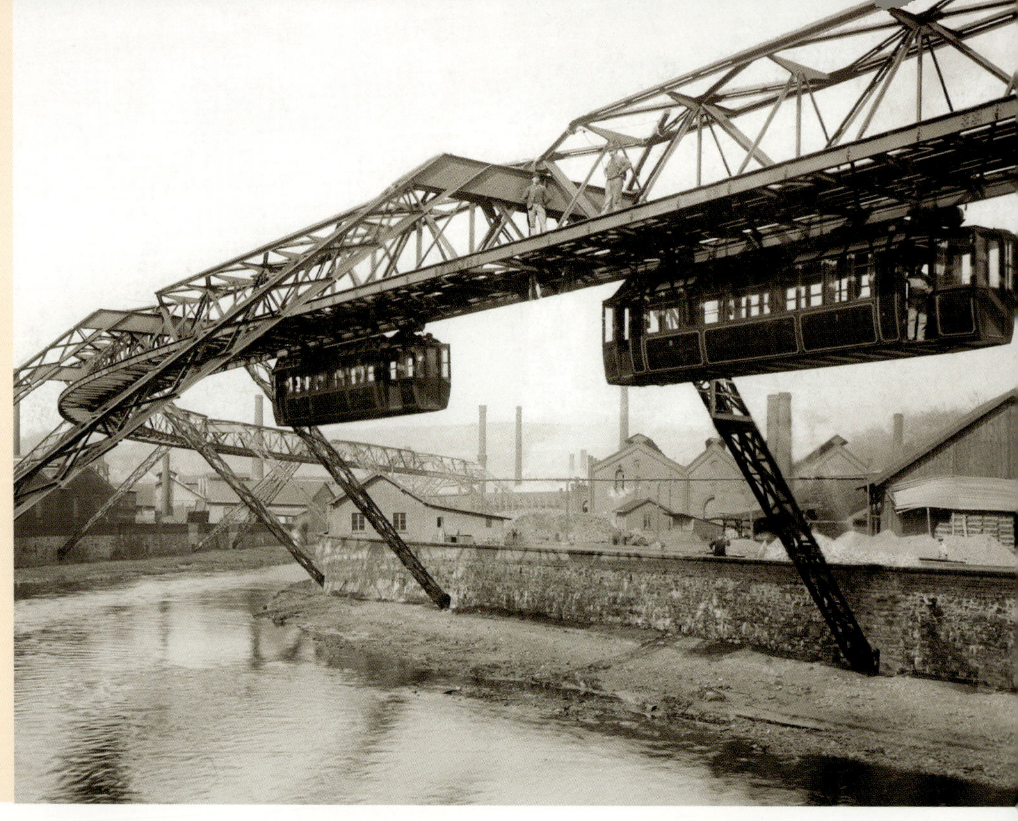

Brennan Monorail (1909)

Intended primarily as a military transport method, Louis Brennan's design for a gyroscopically balanced monorail was patented in 1903. The speed and efficiency with which track could be assembled was a primary appeal of Brennan's idea, and a full-scale demonstration was presented on November 10, 1909, in Gillingham, England. The vehicle's gyroscope system was a remarkable invention—even with all passengers loaded on one side of the vehicle, the two onboard gyroscopes would keep the cars level. Unfortunately, this great benefit was also the Brennan monorail's undoing; even after successful demonstrations to scientists, engineers, and the military, their fear that the gyroscopes *might* fail prevented this innovative system from being applied to practical uses.

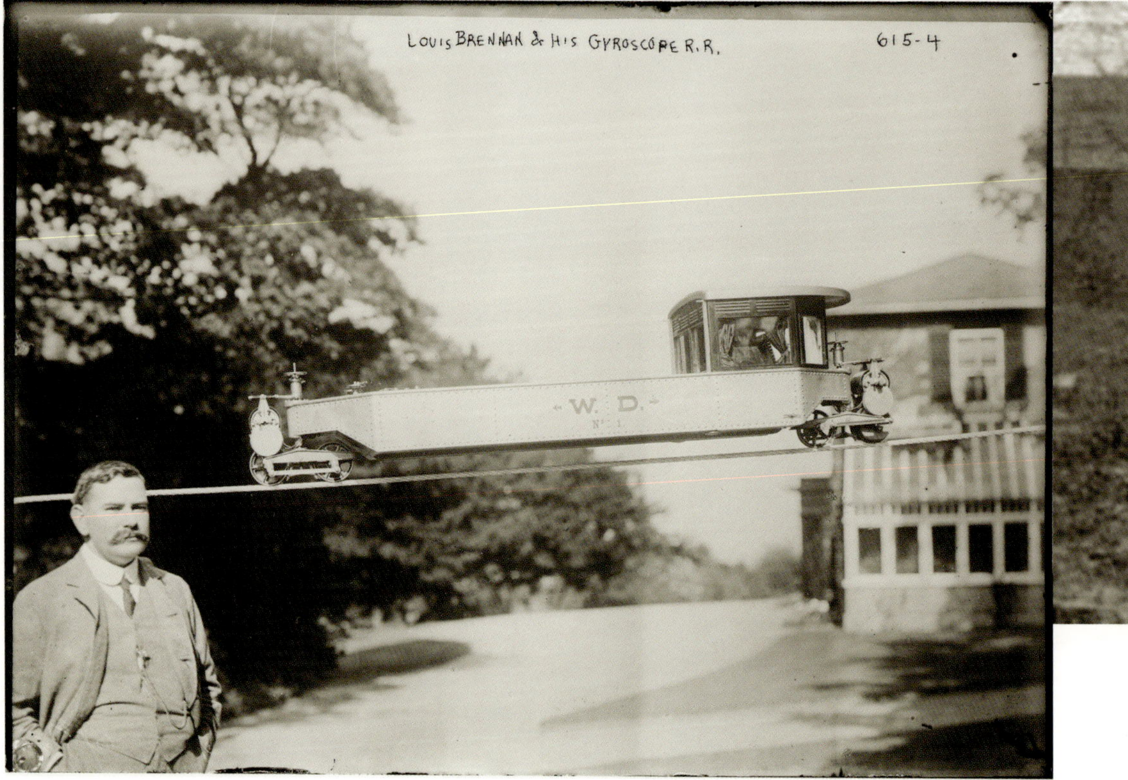

Pelham Park and City Island Railroad (1910)

This short route also had a short life span. The horse-drawn monorail designed by Howard H. Tunis was part of the Pelham Park and City Island Railroad in the Bronx, New York City. It connected City Island with the Bartow Station of the Harlem River and Port Chester Railroad. Between 1910 and 1914, the mainland section monorail had a single car, nicknamed the "Flying Lady." It was not a success, and the monorail ceased operation in 1914. The line was dismantled at the outset of World War I, when the terminal near City Island was requisitioned for military use.

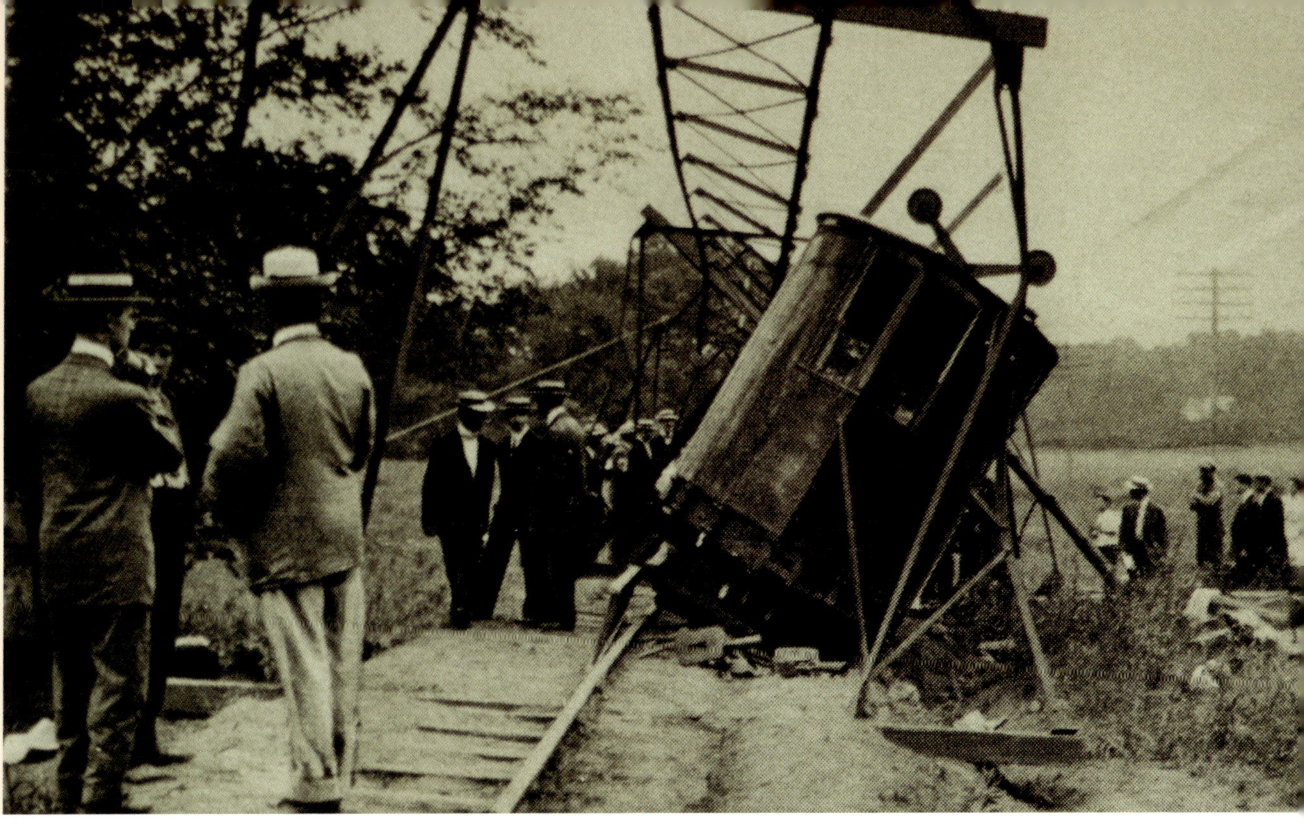

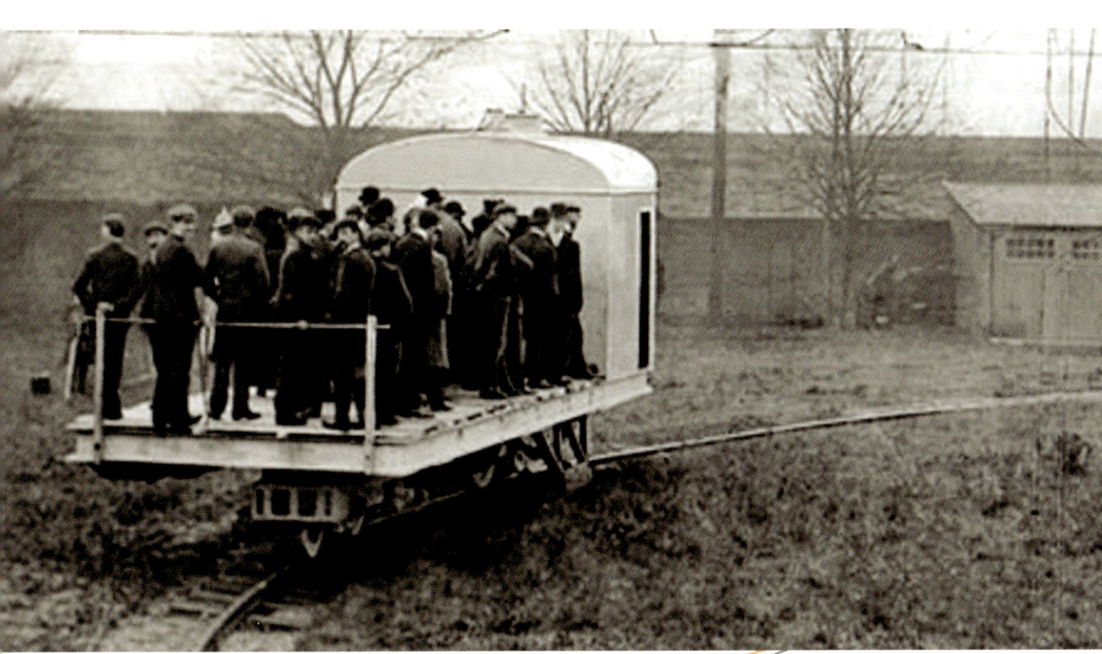

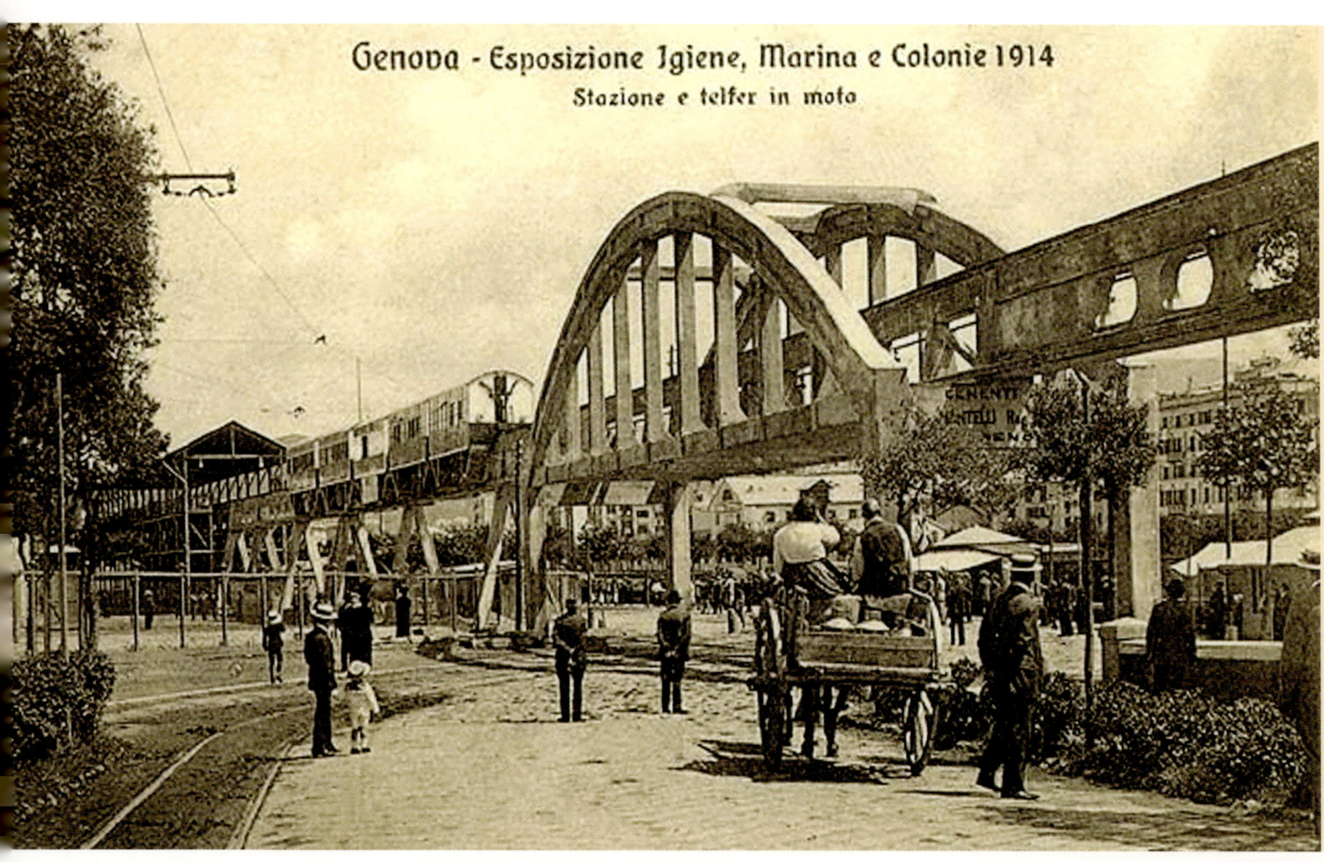

Genoa Monorail (1914)

Visitors to the Genoa, Italy, Esposizione Internazionale di Igiene, Marina e Colonie (International Exhibition of Marine and Maritime Hygiene) were able to experience a ride on a straddle-type monorail that bore a resemblance to the later Alweg-designed monorails. Along a line running from the exhibition site to the central city, passengers rode in four coaches that were similar to railroad cars, with an electric locomotive in the center. The Telfer Monorail was proposed as a mass transit system, but never garnered much interest. It ran in Genoa for four years, but was then abandoned and dismantled.

William H. Boyes Monorail (1911)

Most people know of the Seattle Alweg monorail built for the city's 1962 world's fair (Century 21 Exposition), but few know of the first Seattle monorail, built and exhibited by William H. Boyes in 1911 along the tideflats area of the city. The cost of the wooden rails and track was estimated at the bargain construction and installation cost of only $3,000 per mile. The *Seattle Times* cautiously enthused, "The time may come when these wooden monorail lines, like high fences, will go straggling across country, carrying their burden of cars that will develop a speed of about 20 miles per hour." But without the corresponding cautious enthusiasm of financial backers, there was no further development, and Boyes's monorail became an artifact of Seattle's perpetual "boom and bust" culture.

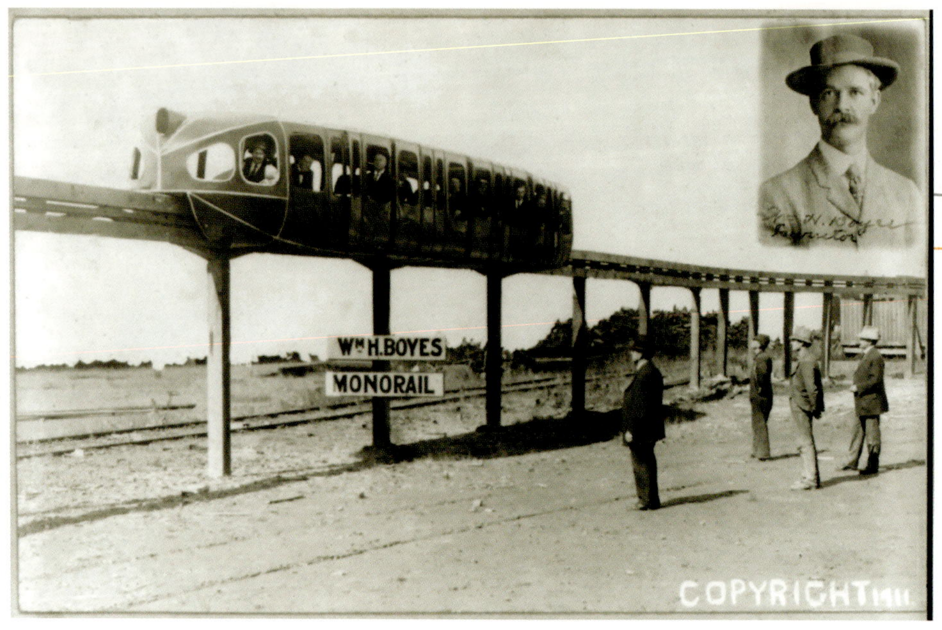

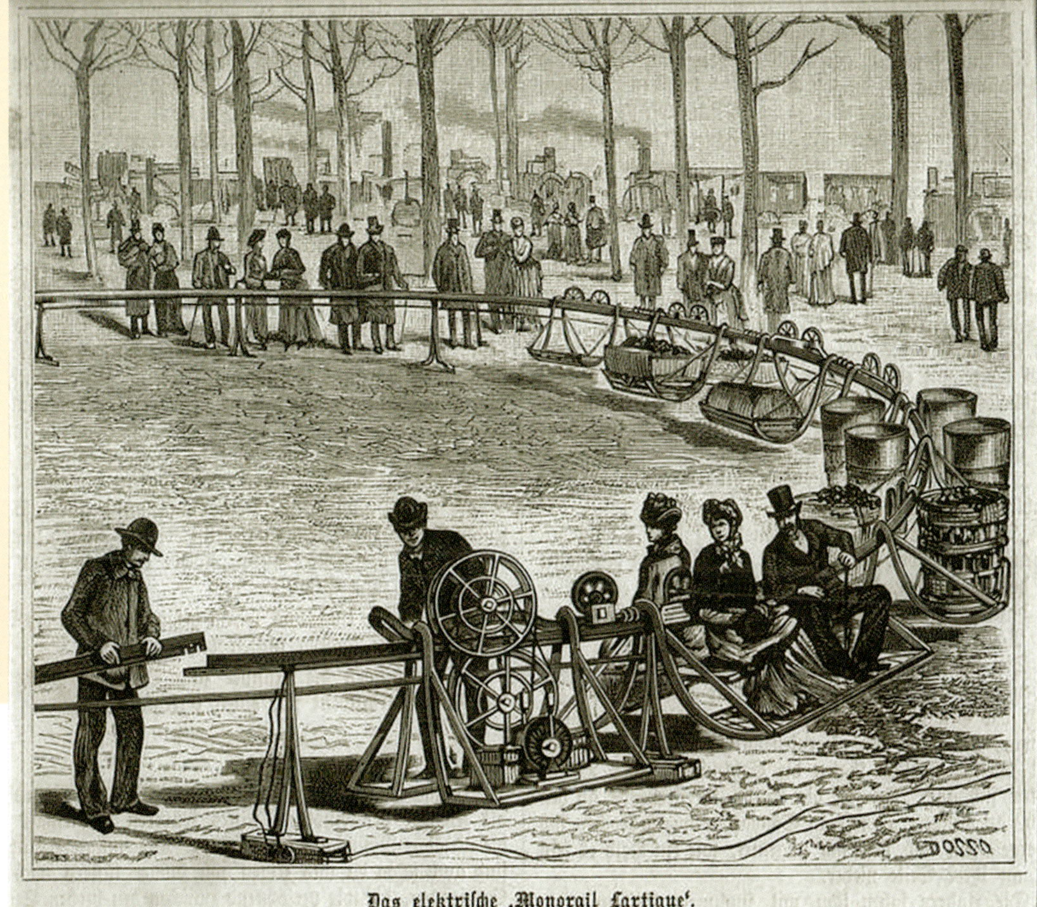

Das elektrische ‚Monorail Lartigue'.

The Magnesium Monorail (1924)

A lengthy twenty-eight-mile system featuring one of the last Lartigue-based monorails was built in San Bernardino, California, in 1924. It carried epsomite (hydrated magnesium sulfate) from a rich deposit in the Crystal Hills area of the Owlshead Mountains across the rugged terrain of the Saline Valley to the railhead of the Trona Railway. Built by the Sierra Salt Corporation, the line was efficient and cost-effective, but ran only until 1926, when more modern magnesium extraction techniques used by competitors put the entire mining company out of business.

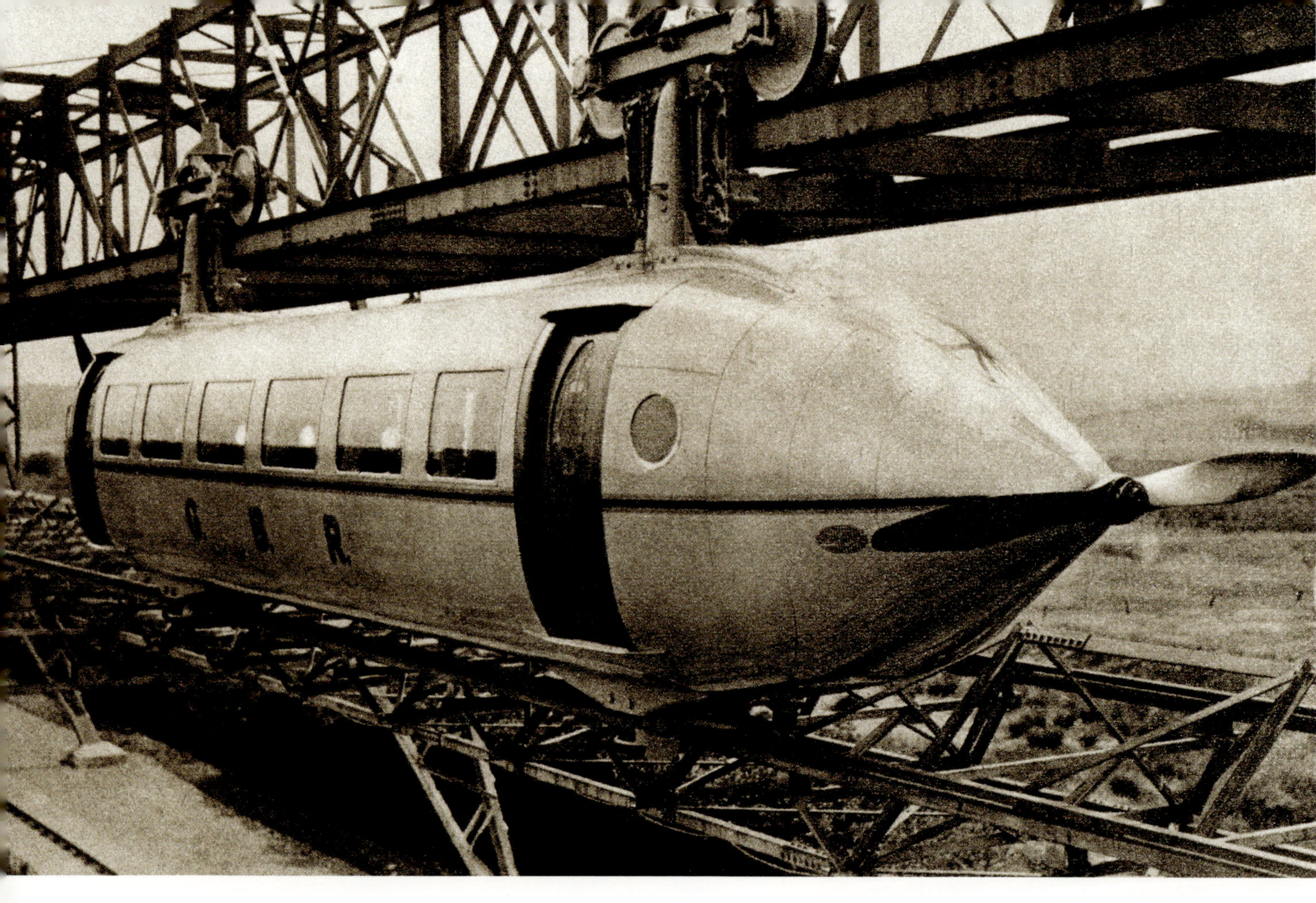

The Bennie Railplane (1929)

Perhaps the first designer to marry the romance and futurism of the monorail with engineering reality was Scottish engineer George Bennie, with the creation of the Bennie Railplane.

Looking every bit like the cover of a pulp science fiction magazine, the Bennie Railplane was a cylindrical rocket-shaped train car that sped along an overhead rail by means of two electrically powered propellers mounted on the front and rear nose cones.

Bennie had begun his development of his *railplane* in 1921, and by 1929 was able to fund and build a one-car prototype on a 130-yard-long track in Milngavie, Scotland, off the Glasgow and Milngavie Junction Railway. The railplane was not technically a monorail; it was suspended on an overhead rail, but stabilized by guide rails beneath the car.

Bennie's design was not only sleek and powerful (it could safely reach a speed of 120 mph), its design *intent* was also ingenious. Bennie's idea was to run his lines along the easements of conventional railways. Faster traffic for passengers, mail, and perishable goods would speed along above; heavy and less immediately needed goods and shorter local passenger traffic routes could continue on the slower ground-based line.

Bennie's innovation elicited interest from all over the world, but the economic conditions of the 1930s prevented his gaining the financial backing he needed. Proposed routes from Edinburgh to Glasgow in Scotland and between Southport and Blackpool in England were never built. Having financed almost all of the development and prototyping personally, Bennie was bankrupt by 1937.

The fantastical Bennie Railplane lay abandoned and decaying in a field in Milngavie for nearly twenty years, before being sold for scrap in 1956.

Department Store "Kiddie" Monorails

After World War II, an influential but now-forgotten monorail system began to make its appearance in cities across the United States. Though not transit systems by any stretch, they were nevertheless still monorails, for these closed-loop train tracks carried enchanted juvenile passengers by the thousands—suspended high above the floor of department store toy departments and Santalands!

The inspiration for these "Kiddie Monorails" came from a farming monorail developed by Louden Machinery in Fairfield, Iowa. The Louden system appears to have been adapted and the monorail cars built in collaboration with a company called Rocket Express Systems in Oak Park, Illinois.

The monorails were typically seasonal, and circled the ceilings of Wanamaker's in Philadelphia; Meier & Frank's in Portland, Oregon; E.W. Edwards & Son department store in Syracuse, New York; the Midtown Plaza mall in Rochester, New York; Herpolsheimer's department store in Grand Rapids, Michigan; and Rich's department store in Atlanta (where it was known as the "Pink Pig").

These systems are now long gone, having outlived the relevance of their hosts—and outgrown the safety codes that permitted them!

Alweg Monorail (1952)

There is perhaps no more familiar name associated with the modern monorail than "Alweg," an acronym of the name of Swedish industrialist Dr. Axel Lennart Wenner-Gren, the first person to further develop the monorail after World War II. His first design concept was intended as an efficient high-speed intercity system, but he subsequently reduced that scale in a new design that was tested in Fühlingen, Germany, at speeds close to a hundred miles per hour.

Skyway Monorail (1956)

A firm known as Monorail, Incorporated, built a prototype suspended monorail system in 1956 as a demonstration of mass transit solutions. Known as the "Skyway Line," the 1,600-foot-long track was built at Arrowhead Park in Houston. A driver was seated above the fifty-one-passenger vehicle on one of the two wheel trucks, with the carriage supported by eighteen standards shaped like inverted "Js." The system was powered by a pair of Packard gasoline engines.

After eight months of service, the Skyway Line was dismantled and rebuilt at the Fair Park near Dallas. Renamed the Trailblazer, the line remained a popular attraction, running during the annual fair and on weekends all year before being decommissioned in 1965. No further Skyway transit installations were built, and one of the original passenger vehicles is now part of a private home in Willis, Texas!

Tokyo Ueno Zoo Monorail (1957)

Post World War II, Japan's people were ready and eager to move on and modernize their entire culture and way of life. Toward that end, development of transportation systems became something of a craze. (Japan would later build more transit monorails than any other country in the world.) The first Japanese monorail debuted in 1957, at the Ueno Zoo in Tokyo. The two-station, single-track, thousand-foot-long suspended railway is still operated by the Tokyo Metropolitan Bureau of Transportation (Toei). It is a variation of the Wuppertaler Schwebebahn system, with rubber tires instead of steel wheels.

Alweg Monorail (1957)

After the success of their prototype test track in 1952, the Alweg organization continued to develop and modify their already robust monorail concepts. In 1957, at their site in Fühlingen, Germany, Alweg revealed what would become their most successful monorail design—the first full-scale Alweg monorail.

This remarkable futuristic design was being tested when a visitor from the United States, a renowned filmmaker and showman who had just branched into outdoor recreation, happened to drive past and see the Alweg monorail sweep by in a blaze of space-age glory. The rest, as the saying goes, is history.

SAFEGE Monorail (1958)

Although the Bennie Railplane was rotting in a Scottish meadow in 1947, the promise of its design and intent spoke to renowned French bridge builder Lucien Chadenson, who combined the idea Bennie had developed with the rubber tires he saw on vehicles running on the Paris Metro Route 11.

The result was a suspended monorail concept with fully enclosed passenger cars suspended under a steel and concrete box beam with an opening in the bottom. The rubber wheels ran *inside* the track, with the cars supported by flanges on the bottom of the beam—better protecting the wheel systems and track from harsh weather, and making the system more suitable for continuous operation in changing conditions.

Chadenson built a test track that was just under a mile in length in Châteauneuf-sur-Loire, France, in 1959, underwritten by SAFEGE (an acronym for the French consortium Société Anonyme Française d' Etude de Gestion et d' Entreprises, which in English is the French Limited Company for the Study of Management and Business). The monorail line was a "featured player" in François Truffaut's 1966 film adaptation of Ray Bradbury's *Fahrenheit 451*, but was dismantled not long afterward.

In the end, the French never used the SAFEGE system—but the Japanese built two successful SAFEGE lines.

1964–1965 New York World's Fair AMF Monorail

Based on the success of the Disneyland-Alweg system, WED Enterprises had originally been under consideration to build an encircling monorail system to surround and give access to the entire fairgrounds for the 1964–1965 New York World's Fair at Flushing Meadows in Queens, New York. Cost, schedule, and other complexities scuttled that ambitious plan.

AMF (American Machine and Foundry), at the time one of the largest recreational equipment companies in the United States, proposed a one-station I beam dual-rail monorail system that was confined to the amusement area of the fairgrounds. Although today known primarily for bowling equipment and recreation centers, AMF at the time was expanding into projects and products as diverse as garden equipment, yachts, and even atomic energy. AMF had licensed the SAFEGE monorail technology, and installed and operated the New York World's Fair monorail for the run of the fair.

Italia '61 Alweg Monorail (1961)

The Exposition Internationale du Travail—Turin 1961 (International Labor Exhibition—Turin 1961), known colloquially as Italia '61, was a modern world's fair, which the Italian government expanded to include a celebration of the centennial of Italian unity.

At Italia '61, visitors could hop on an Alweg monorail for a mile-long ride between the north expo entrance and the Palazzo del Lavoro at the south end of the exposition grounds. The thirty-eight-ton train was composed of three passenger cars and could reach a speed of fifty-five miles an hour; during the expo (May 1 to October 31, 1961), the line carried a total of five hundred thousand passengers.

Plans to continue the operation of the monorail permanently and extend the line five miles to the town of Moncalieri never came to fruition, and an act of arson destroyed the Turin monorail in the late 1970s. The remains of the system were finally scrapped in 1981. The north station has since been repurposed as an office building.

Tokyo Monorail (1964)

Opened in September 1964, just in time for the 1964 Summer Olympics in Japan, the Tokyo Monorail (officially the Tokyo Monorail Haneda Airport Line) connects Haneda Airport in Ōta, Tokyo, Japan, to the Monorail Hamamatsuchō Station in Minato, Tokyo, along an elevated railway that follows the coast of Tokyo Bay. Originally built by Hitachi Monorail, the first cars were made in Japan from Alweg designs, but have been replaced and updated over the decades as the line of service has been extended.

Seattle World's Fair Monorail (1962)

The 1962 world's fair in Seattle, known as the Century 21 Exposition (April 21 to October 21, 1962) saw the innovation of an Alweg *dual-rail* monorail line. Running between the core of the downtown business district at Westlake Center to the fairgrounds in the Denny Regrade neighborhood, the Alweg monorail and the Space Needle became icons of an exposition whose entire theme was about progress and science moving mankind into the twenty-first century. The monorail remains a beloved attraction in Seattle today.

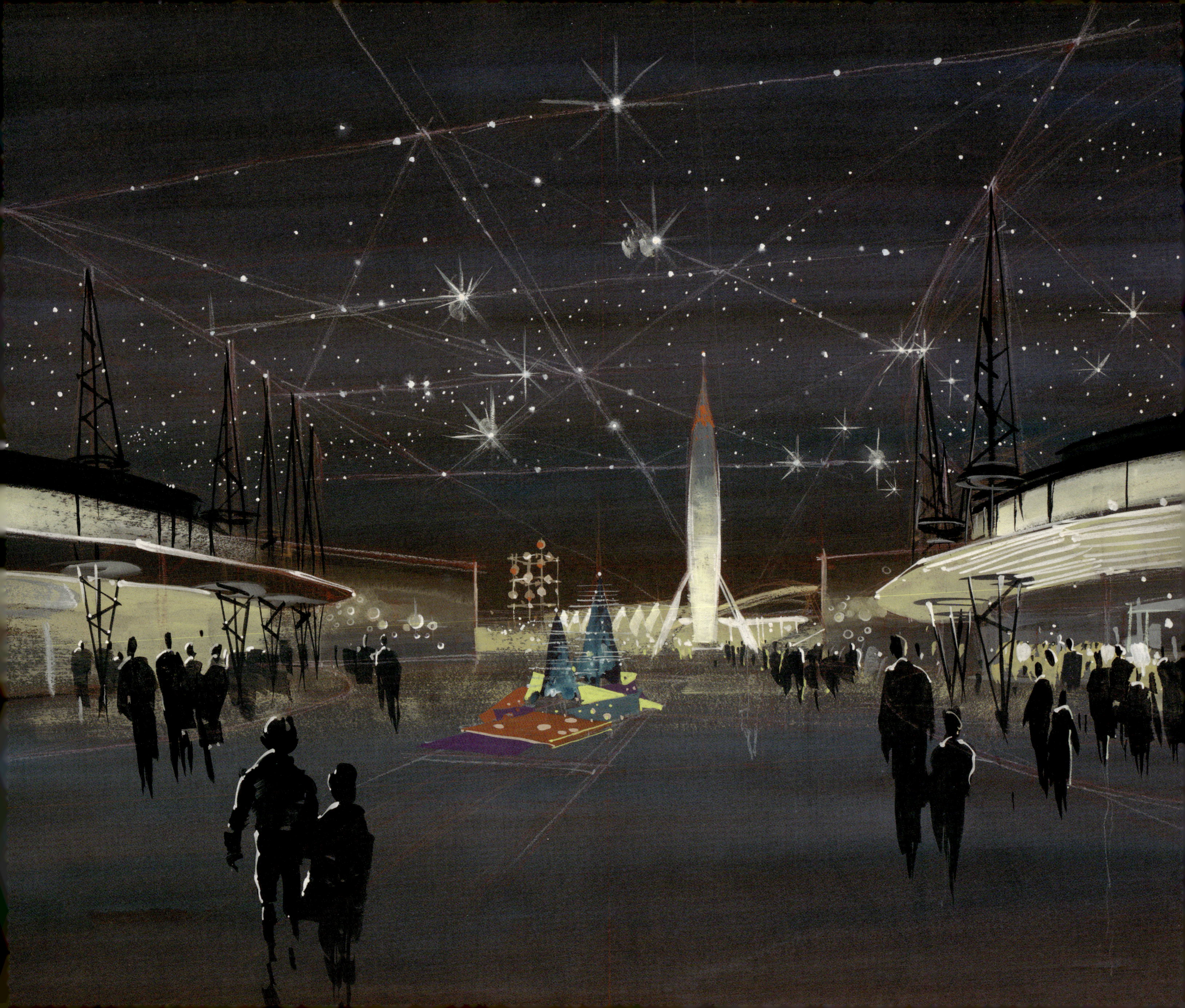

CHAPTER 4

Disney's Early Tomorrows

Recalling Yesterdays, Dreaming of Tomorrows

"Today we are shapers of the world of tomorrow. That is the plain truth. There is no way we can duck the responsibility; and there is no reason, except sloth and cowardice, why we should."

—Walt Disney

With the conception and development of Disneyland in the early 1950s, the key story elements of "Walt Disney's Magic Kingdom" began to coalesce. Walt and his team of Imagineers began to create fantastic living realms.

Shared memories of Midwestern small-town roots, along with Walt's inspirations from Henry Ford's Greenfield Village and a booming postwar Victorian revival design trend created the nostalgia of Main Street, U.S.A. A royal palace courtyard was imagined as a home for Disney's beloved characters and film properties to come to life in Fantasyland. A wilderness realm inspired by the successful and popular nature film series, True-Life Adventure, evolved into the vaguer but no less exciting Adventureland. The contemporary popularity of all things Western—in movies, television, pulp magazines, comic books, and the prolific paperback novels of Louis L'Amour (featuring his alter ego, Jim Mayo)—resulted in a somewhat "tamed" version of the Wild West in Frontierland.

LEFT: Tomorrowland entrance, Herb Ryman, 1954. This opaque watercolor and conté crayon rendering was one of many explorations in presenting futuristic ideas in a permanent form.
FOLLOWING SPREAD: This loose gouache painting, a striking nighttime view with a "water wall" and "molecular fountain" dispenses with architectural details and instead delivers an alluring mood. Herb Ryman, 1954.

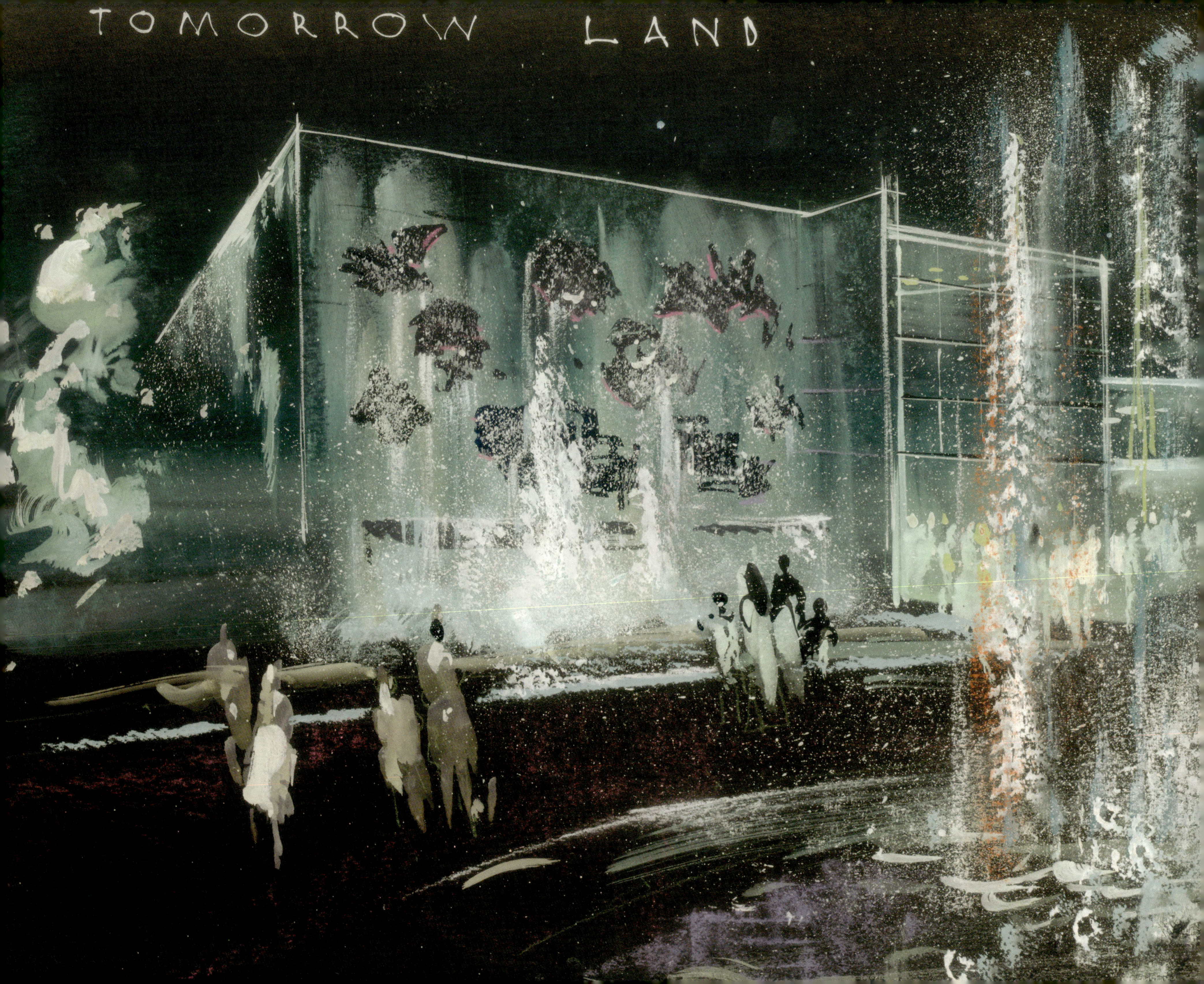
TOMORROW LAND

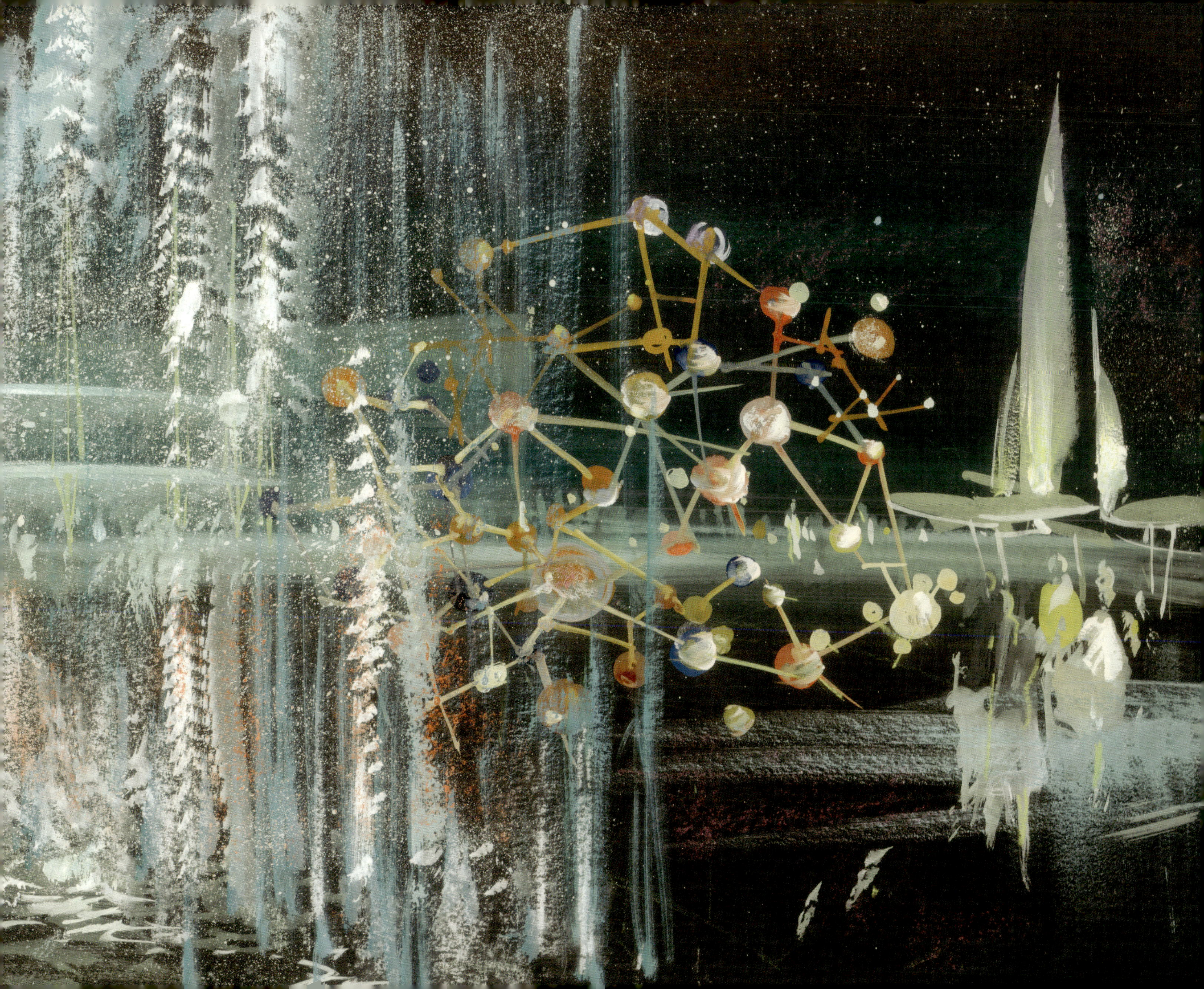

Where We've Been, Where We're Going

Disneyland was a microcosm of a postwar cultural yearning for a *definition* of the American identity. Americans celebrated their national ethos, looked through a rose-colored rearview mirror at their history, and treasured the fantasies of childhood; far too many had recently returned from unwanted adventures in far-flung corners of the world—often under great peril. But the nation, as it sought to redefine itself, looked forward to where that characterization would lead—and people such as Walt Disney had an optimistic view of things to come, a notion of America's progress and mankind's destiny as parallel ideas. To reflect this, Disneyland also needed a future.

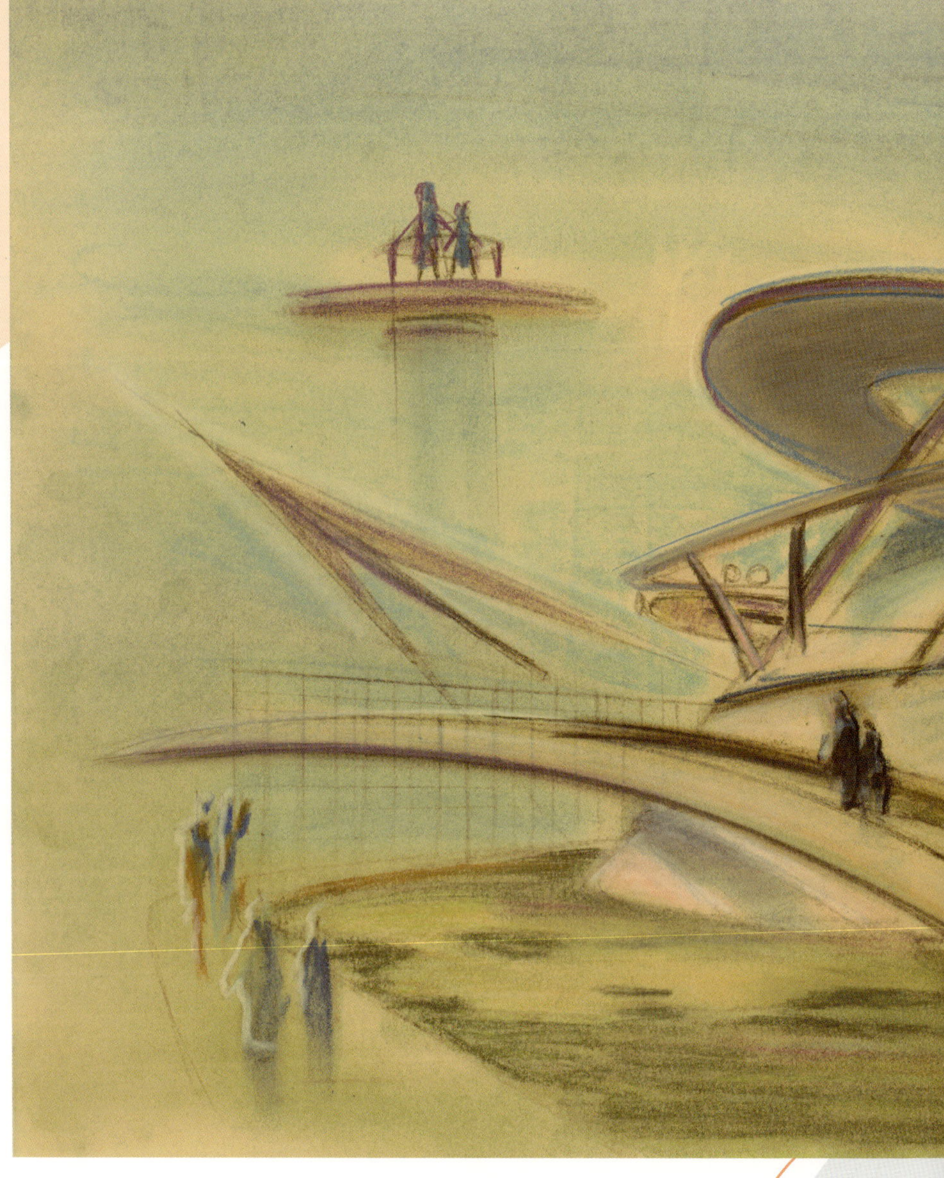

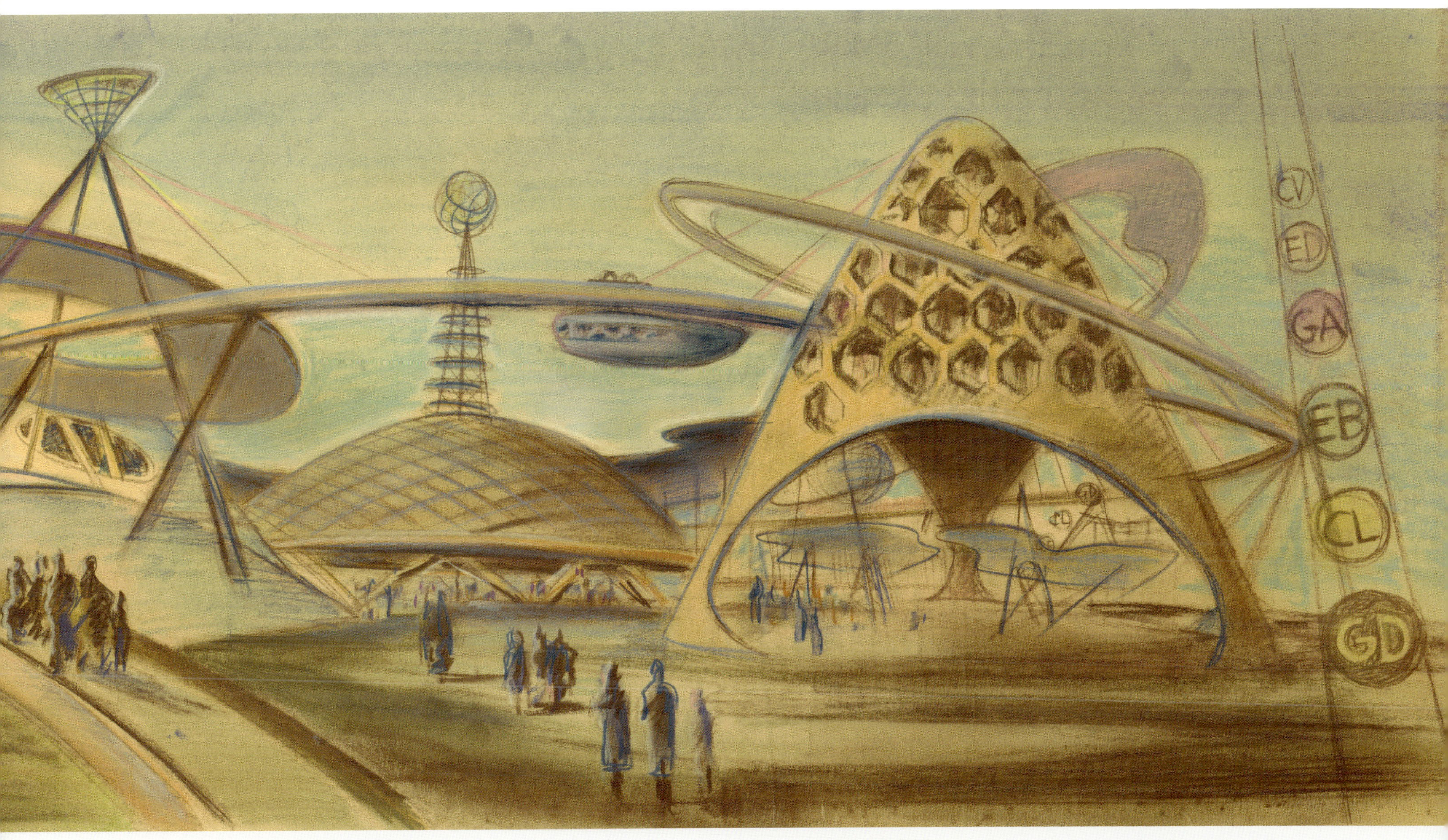

A Tomorrowland concept by Claude Coats, c. 1955, carries forward more of the past decades' futurism of softer spheres and optimistic curves as seen in such applications as the 1939 New York World's Fair.

"I didn't truly enjoy trying to delineate something for this 'Land of the Future.' That's what we called it, at that time," artist and Disney Legend Herb Ryman once said.

Ryman preferred visualizing realms, regions, epochs, and personalities that he had the ability to study deeply. He was not a futurist, and he did not, like Walt, consume and study the coverage and literature of science and technology.

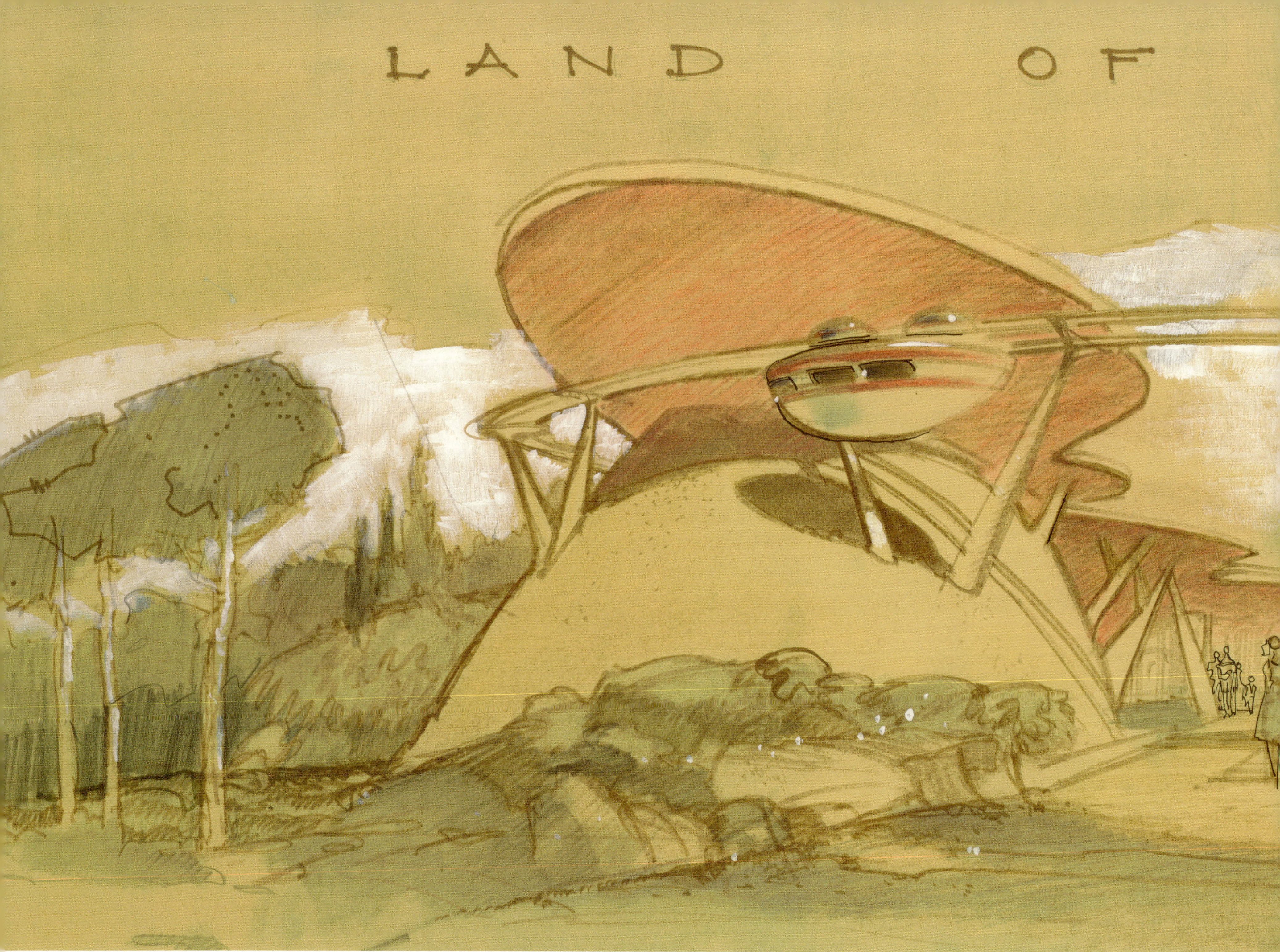

It is interesting to see Herb Ryman's futuristic vernacular change from this almost-regressive 1954 watercolor and colored pencil on diazo print, a "Buck Rogers" concept that seems rooted in the 1930s to the more visionary concepts created by him seen on the preceding and following pages.

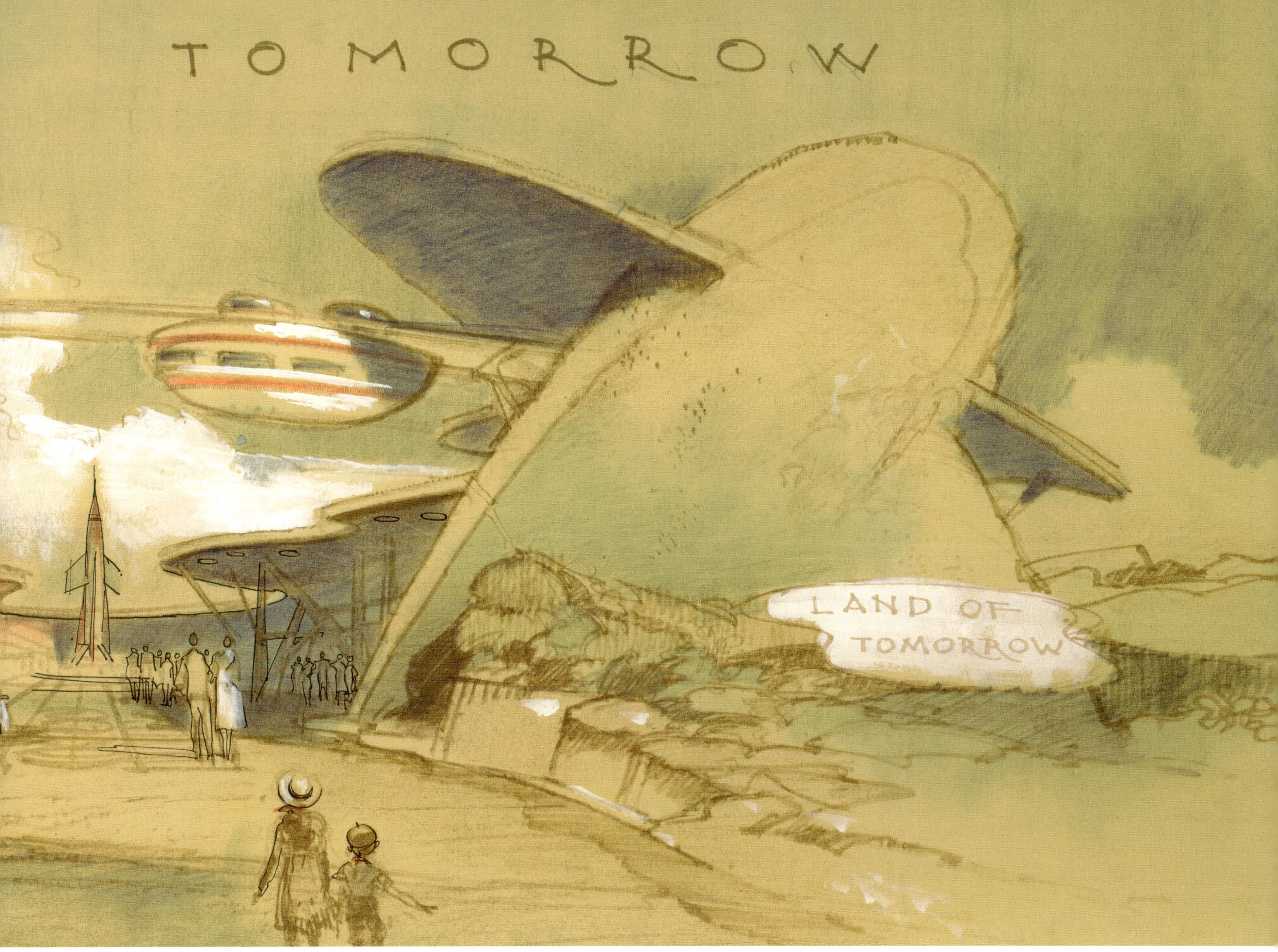
TOMORROW
LAND OF
TOMORROW

Ryman also realized that there were ideas the boss had taken a shine to that just weren't hitting the mark, so he devised a sly strategy. Early ideas and art for Disneyland's Tomorrowland seemed too much like the pulp magazine stuff of yesterday, or rehashed visual styles from old Buck Rogers and Flash Gordon film fictions. Ryman realized that these past fictions were tripping up Walt's futuristic realities.

Certainly, if Ryman could deliver as a concept *designer*, perhaps he could be a concept *extinguisher*. "Another usefulness I served was to 'unsell' an idea. There were certain things I disapproved of, which I persuaded Walt's disapproval of by doing a drawing to show what it would look like. You couldn't disagree with him, but you could make a drawing. He'd say, 'Why, that's terrible. We can't do anything like that.' Naturally, I'd agree."

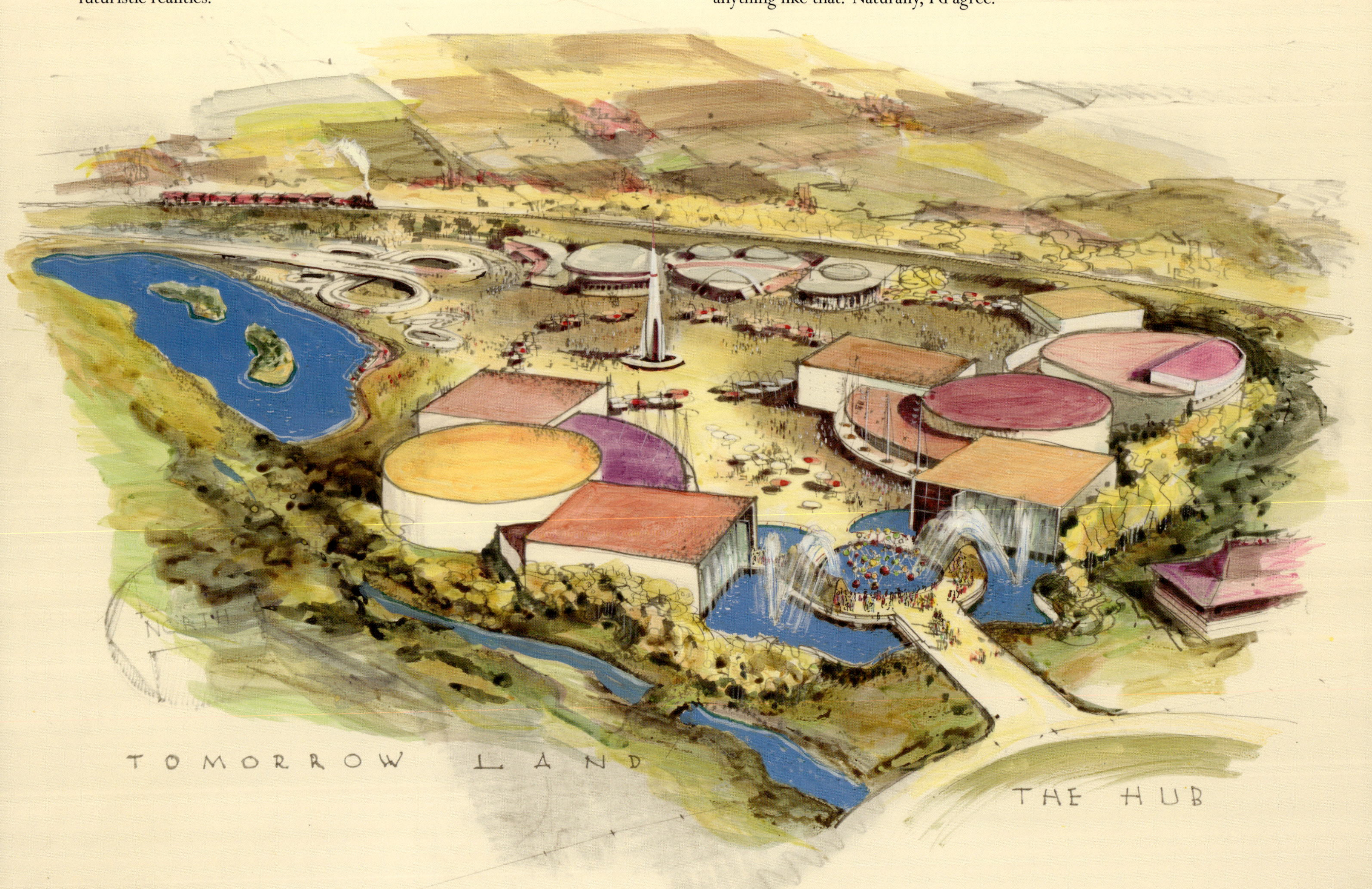

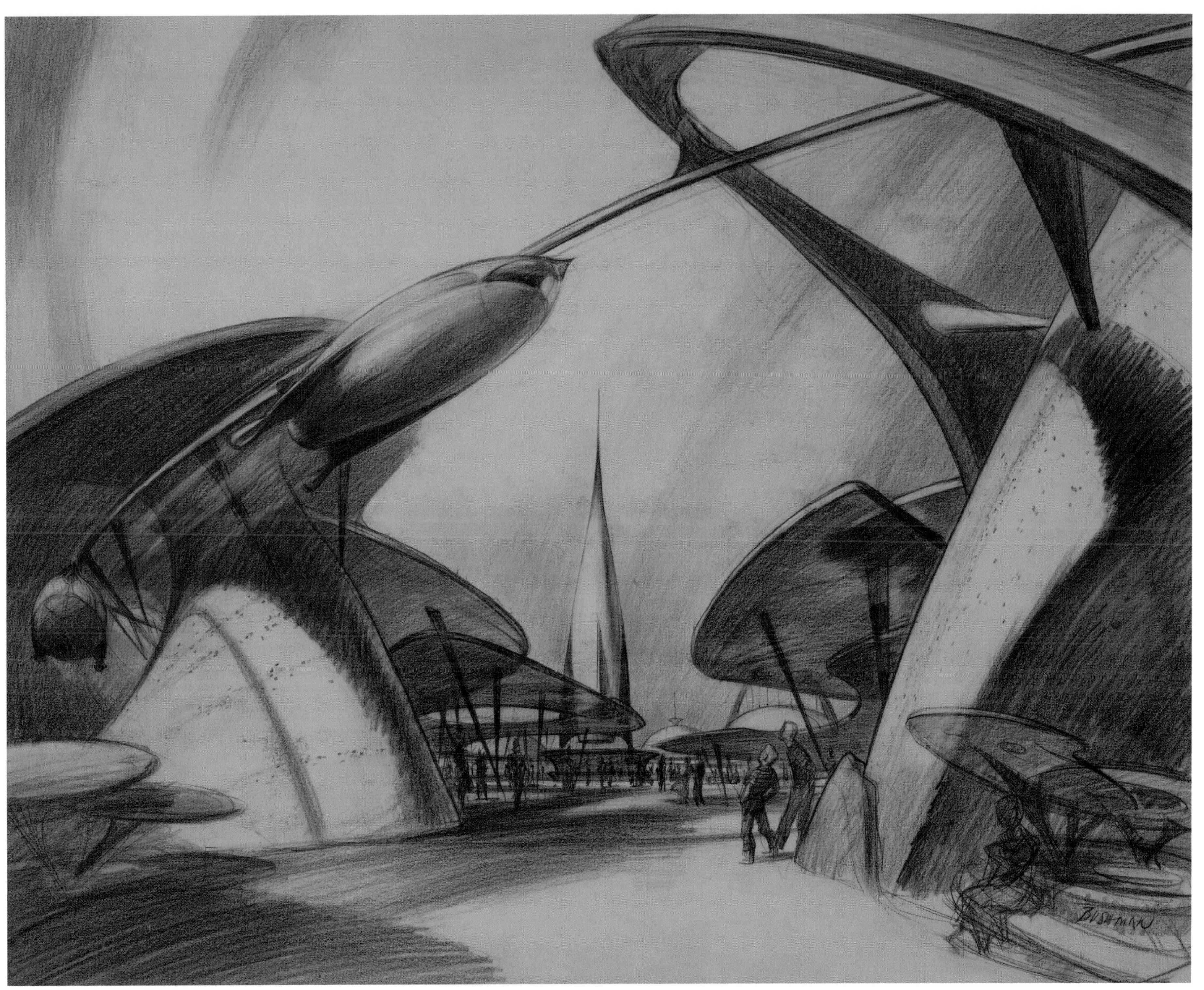

OPPOSITE: Overview of Tomorrowland created by Herb Ryman in 1954 for a Disneyland prospectus presentation book. ABOVE: Conté crayon rendering of Tomorrowland, created in 1954 by Bruce Bushman, used on the opening episode of the *Disneyland* television show. FOLLOWING SPREAD: Colored pencil, pen and ink, and acrylic rendering of a Tomorrowland Fountain of the 48 States, by Herb Ryman, 1954.

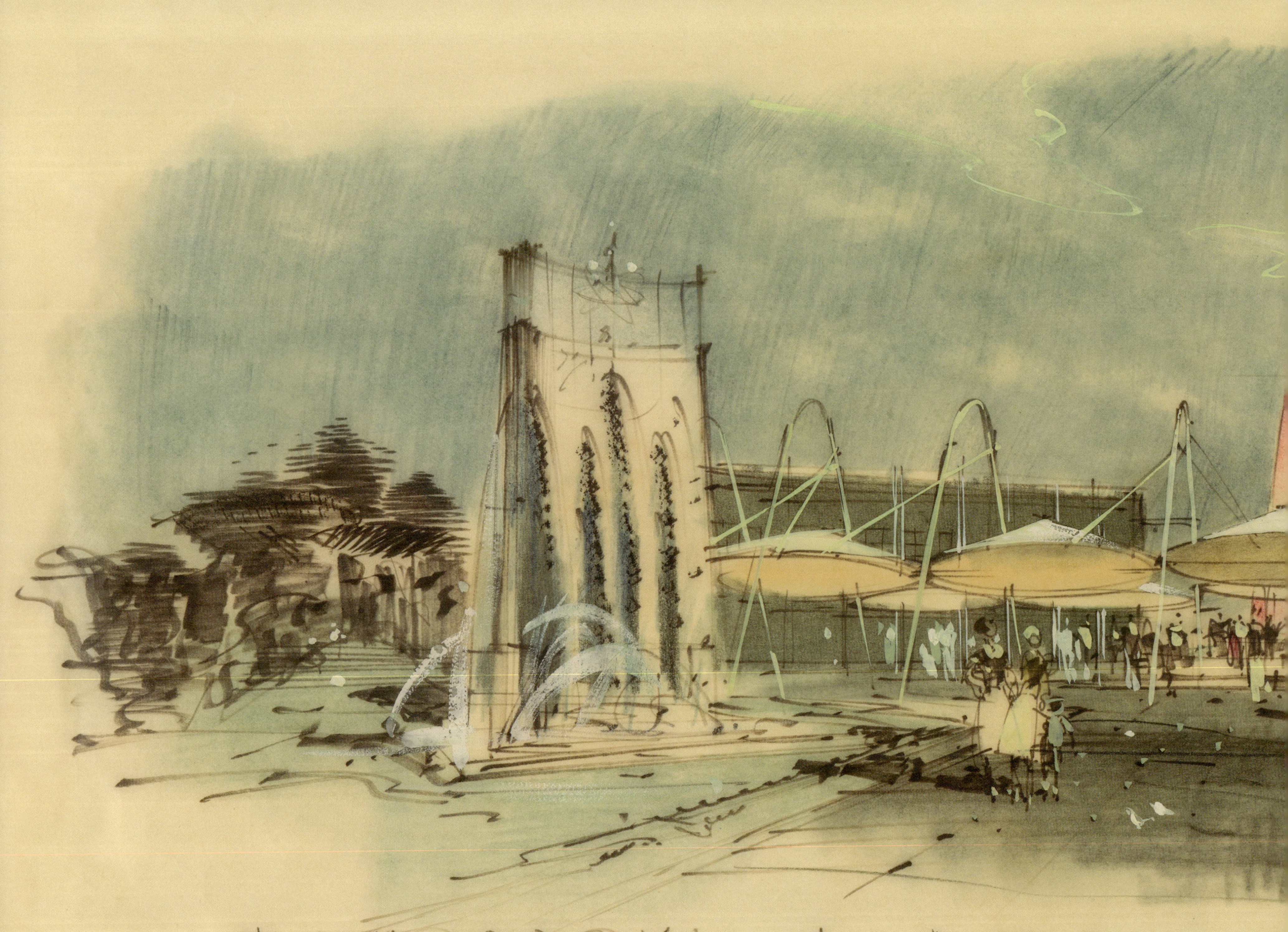

TOMORROW LAND

DESIGNED BY W.E.D. ENTERPRISES INC.

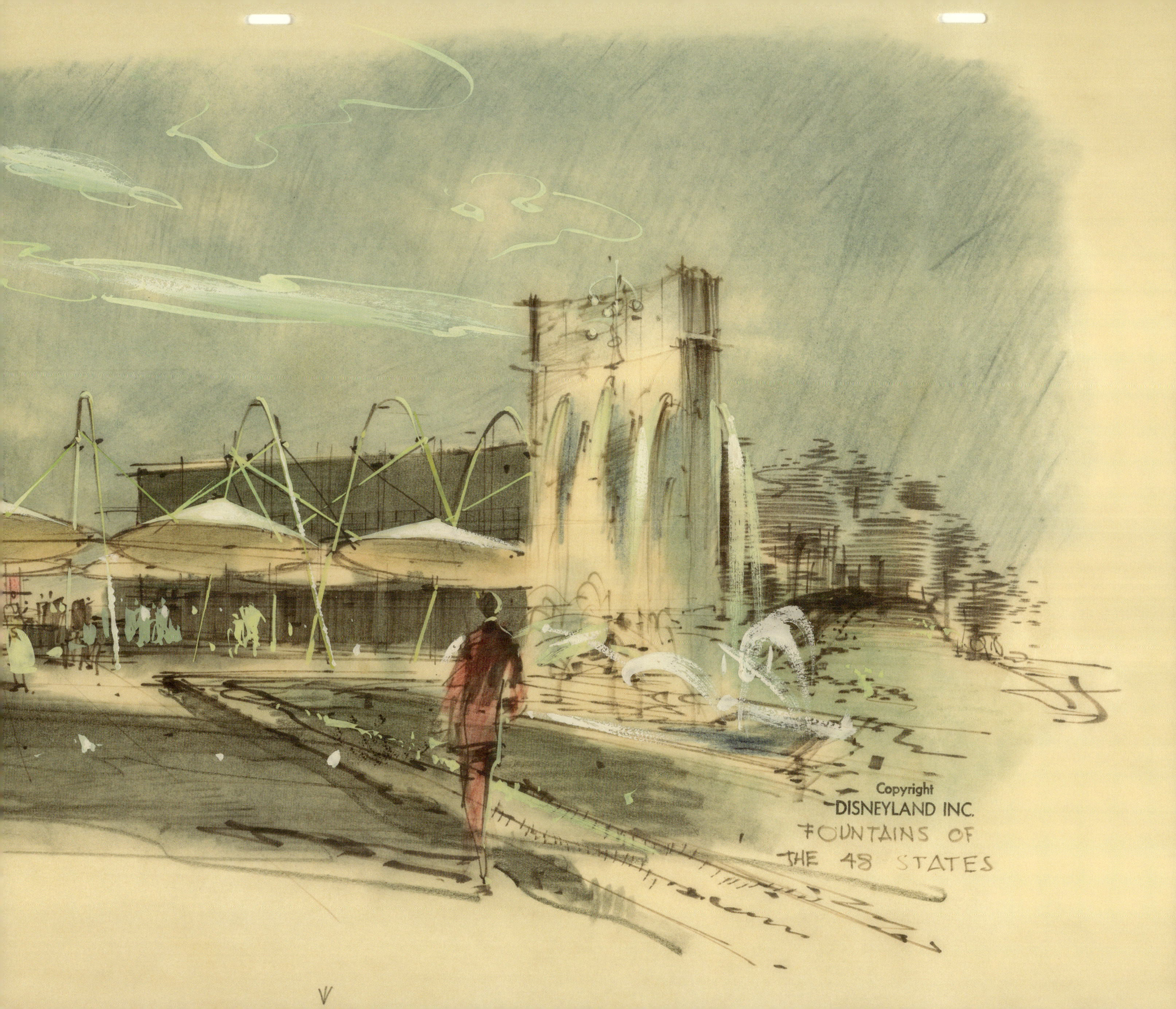
Copyright
DISNEYLAND INC.
FOUNTAINS OF
THE 48 STATES

Todayland

Tomorrowland was the last land opened, and had the least cohesion of vision—a last-minute assembly of space-fillers combined with repurposed attractions and commercial trade shows.

The Clock of the World (a fanciful dimensional sculpture/timepiece that showed the time anywhere in the world) greeted Guests at the entrance to Tomorrowland. Drawing visitors into the area was the towering Moonliner (at seventy-six feet tall, it was the tallest structure in the new park). Circarama, U.S.A. presented the 360-degree film *A Tour of the West*, Space Station X-1 presented a thrilling satellite view of Earth, *The World Beneath Us* explained the origin of fossil fuels in an exhibit and twelve-minute Disney-made CinemaScope film (which liberally used footage from "The Rite of Spring" segment of *Fantasia*), and the Tomorrowland Boats (later the Phantom Boats) and the Tomorrowland Autopia created kinetics and movement through the somewhat barren Tomorrow-*landscape*.

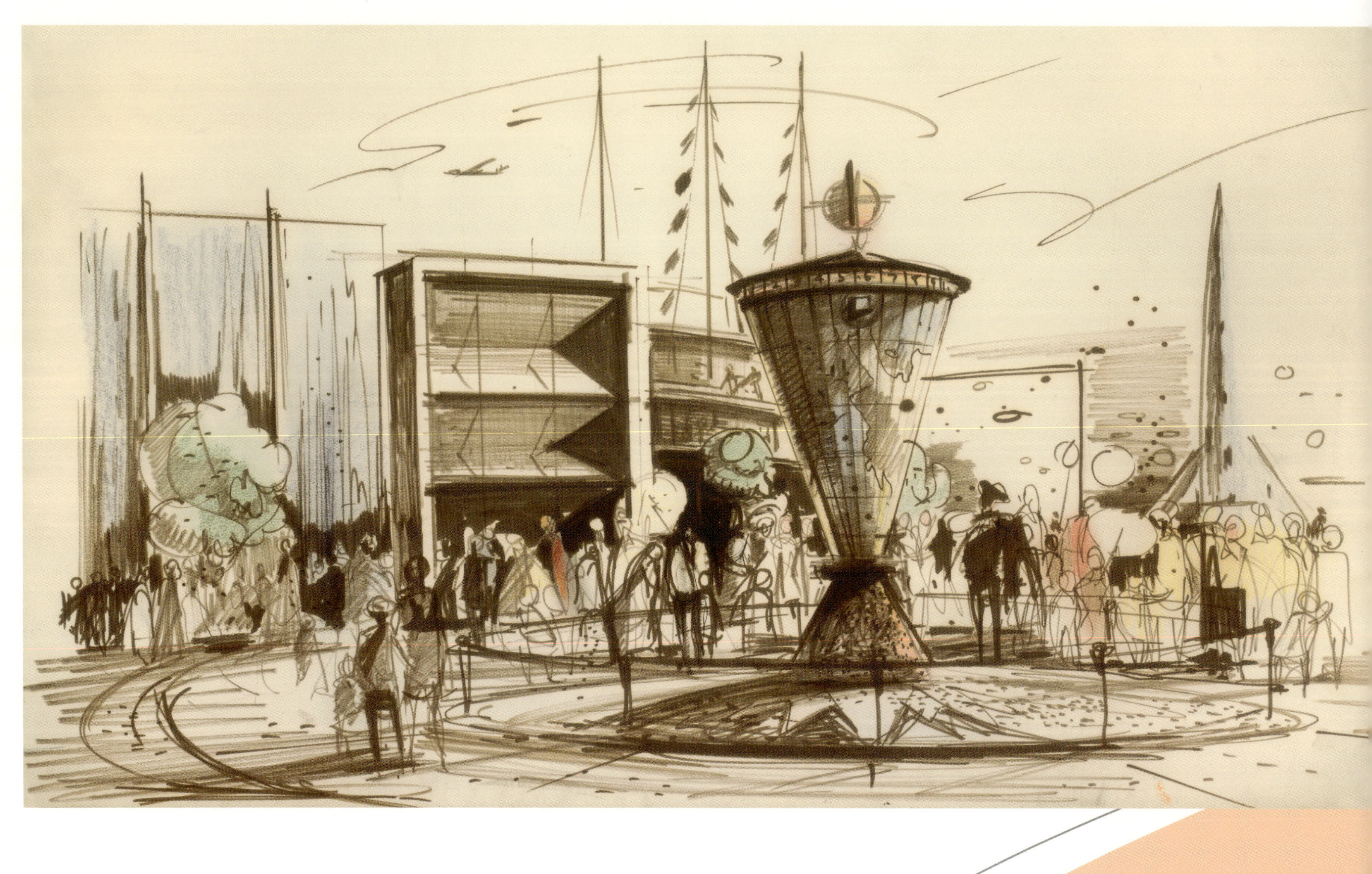

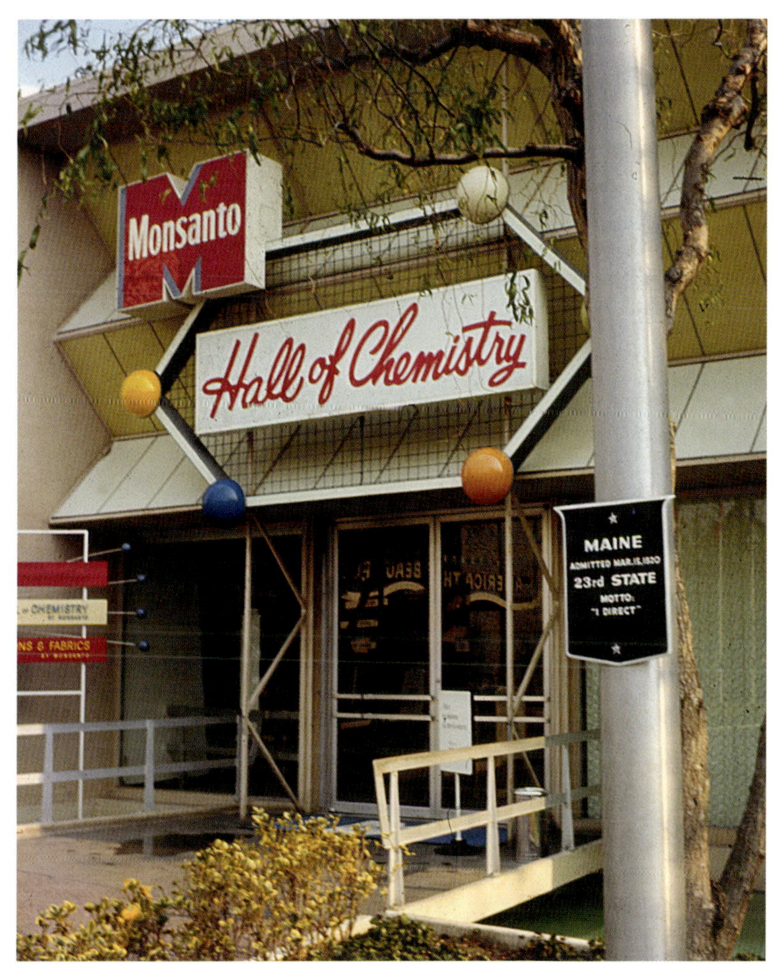

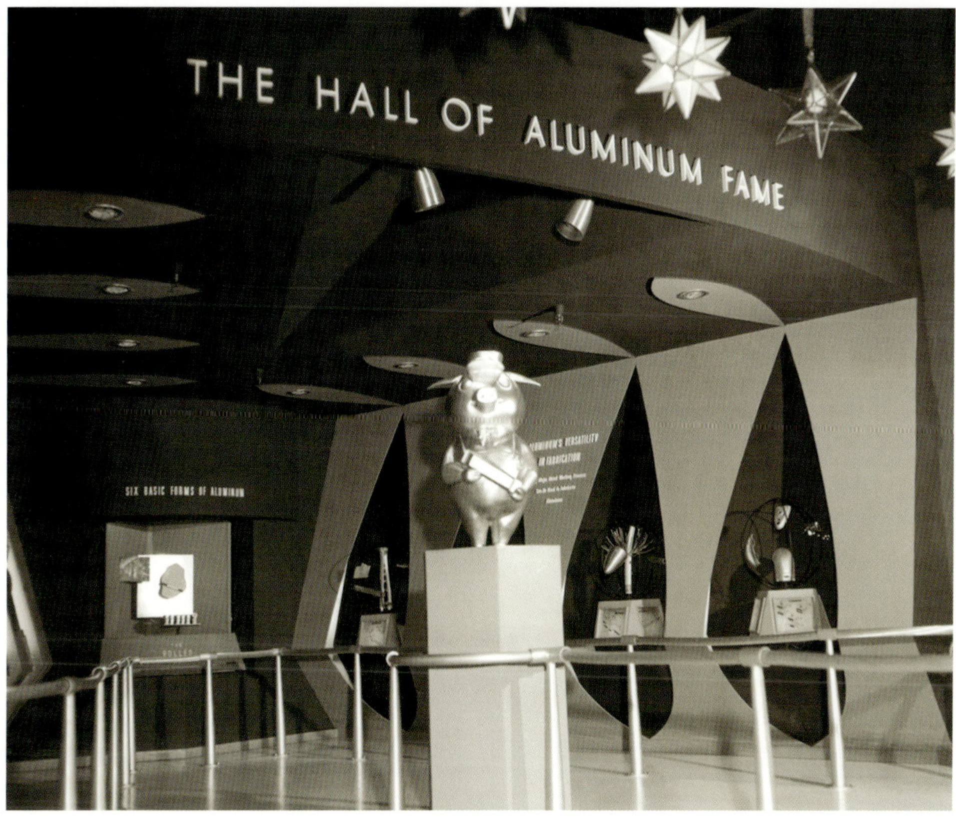

OPPOSITE: Tomorrowland entrance and the Clock of the World by Herb Ryman. "At a glance, this elaborate chronometer tells you the exact minute and hour anywhere on the face of the planet Earth," a contemporary advertisement said. BELOW: Examples of some corporate county-fair-type exhibits that populated buildings of Tomorrowland.

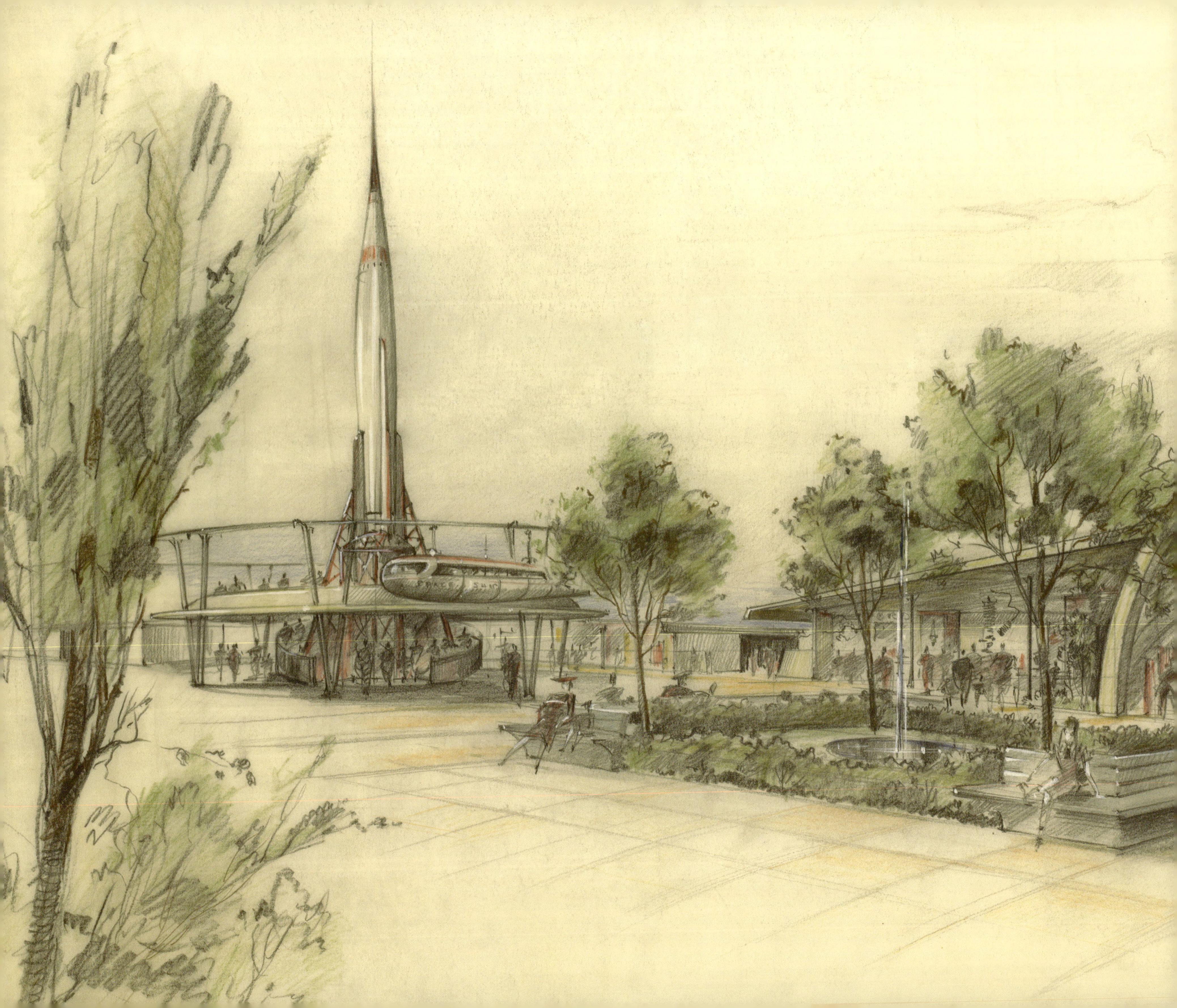

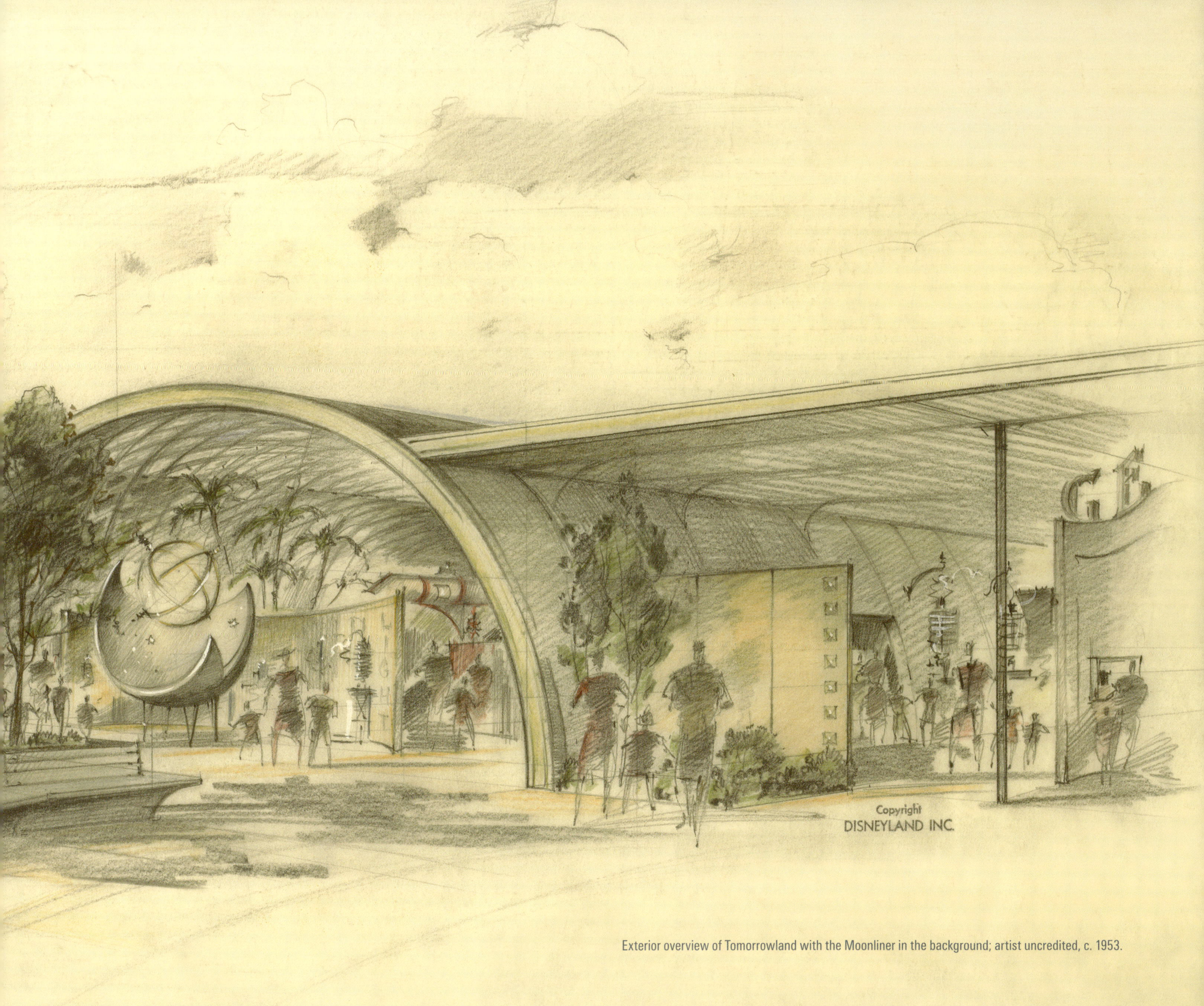

Exterior overview of Tomorrowland with the Moonliner in the background; artist uncredited, c. 1953.

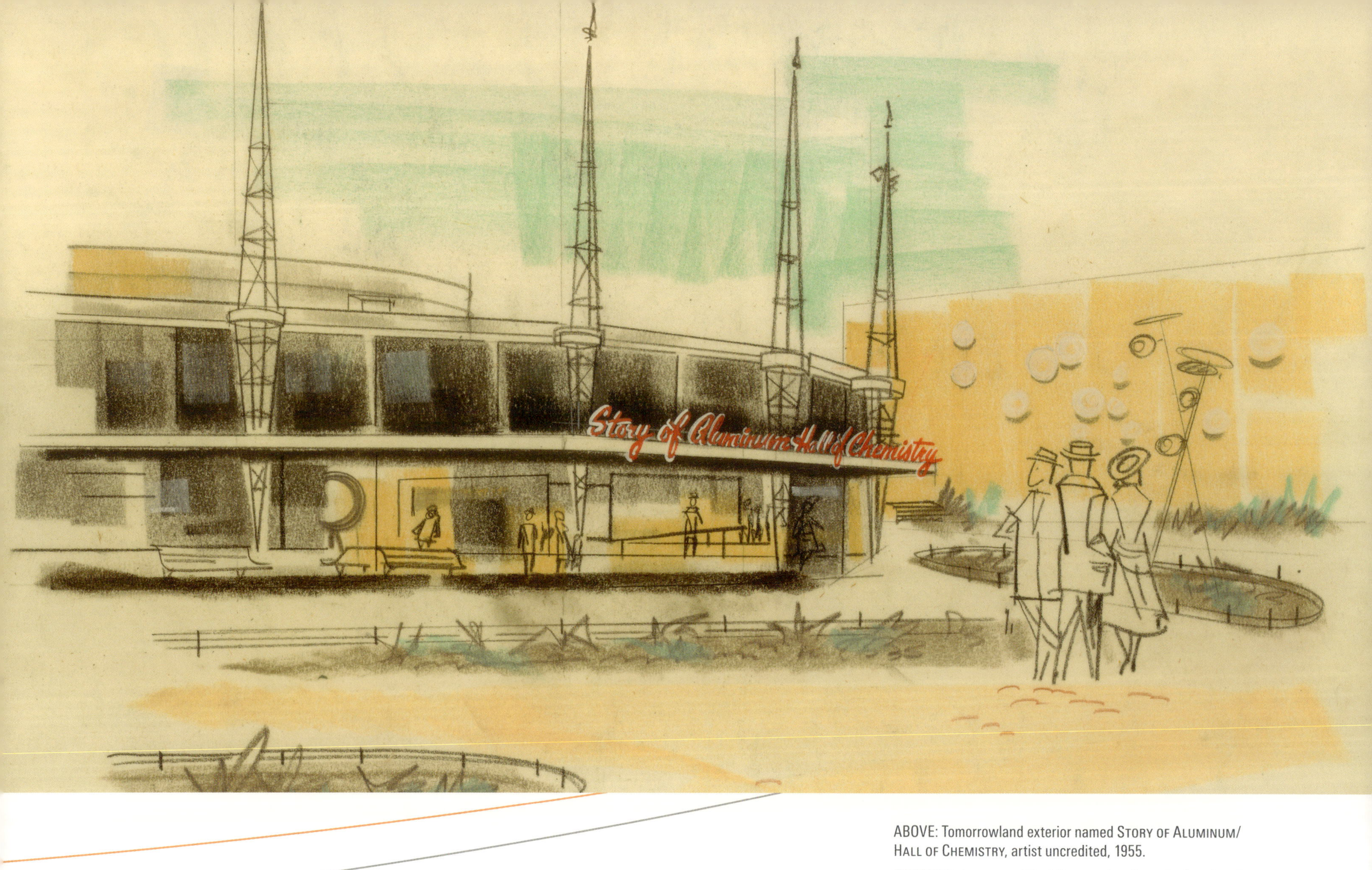

ABOVE: Tomorrowland exterior named Story of Aluminum/ Hall of Chemistry, artist uncredited, 1955.

OPPOSITE: An unusual Herb Ryman view from the interior of Tomorrowland toward the plaza; charcoal and pencil on paper, c. 1954.

In addition, as Imagineer Randy Bright wrote, ". . . Before the opening of Tomorrowland, Walt had been forced to accept several corporate county-fair type exhibits to populate the buildings. The Monsanto 'Hall of Chemistry,' the Dutch Boy Paints 'Color Gallery,' and Kaiser's 'Hall of Aluminum Fame' [and even a bit later, in 1956, the Crane Company Bathroom of Tomorrow] did little more than promote the companies themselves, and even less to promote the future."

But even the earliest misfires and never-built concepts always contained the seeds of ideas, concepts that Walt envisioned and insisted upon.

"I knew, of course, that Walt was always interested in having a monorail in the park," Disney Legend Bob Gurr says. "If you look at the original sketches made up for Disneyland, it was kind of an overhead hanging type of monorail. But it was there. In the very first batch of ideas, it was there."

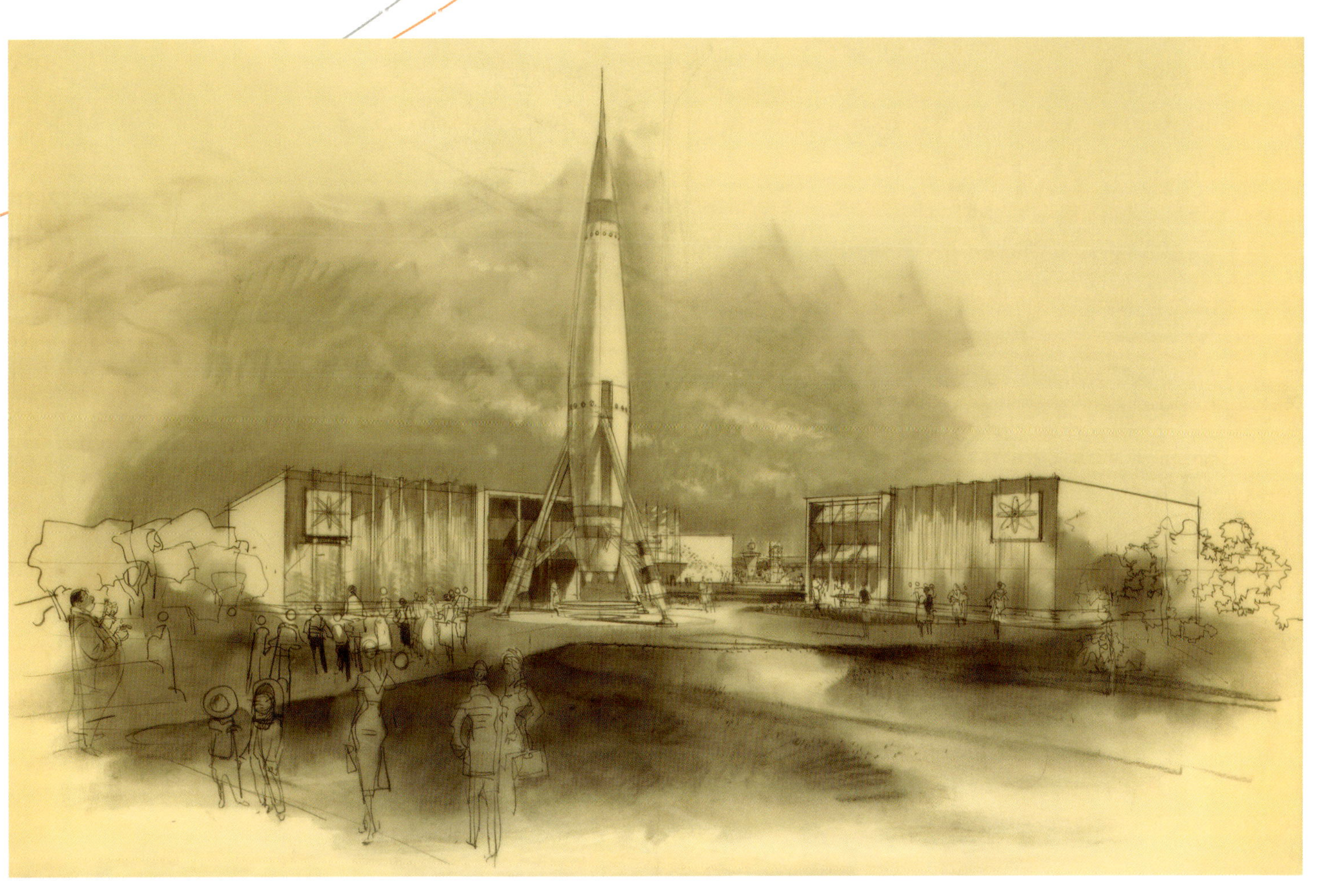

Herb Ryman, 1954: Tomorrow Land Main Avenue; pen and ink, colored pencil on paper.

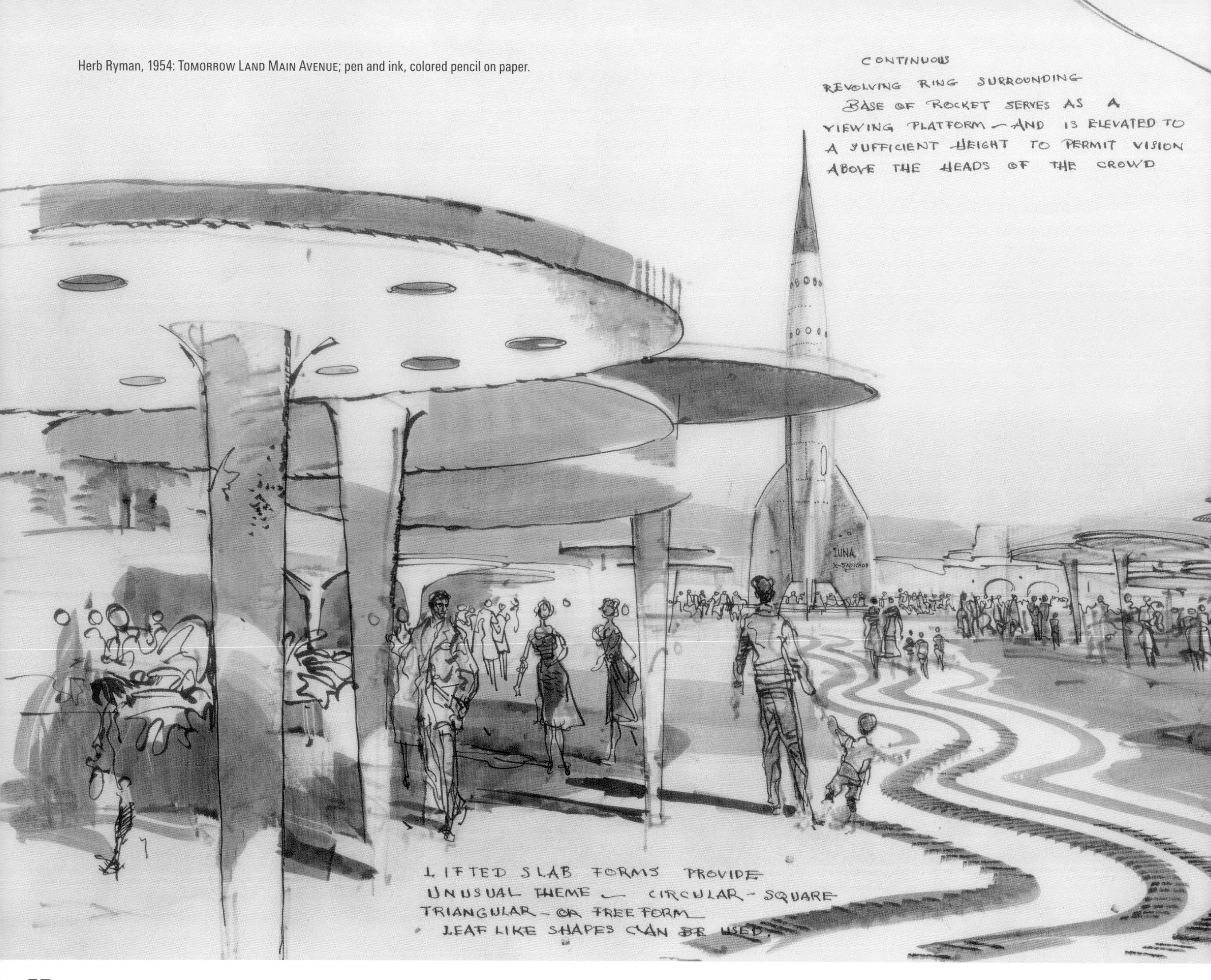

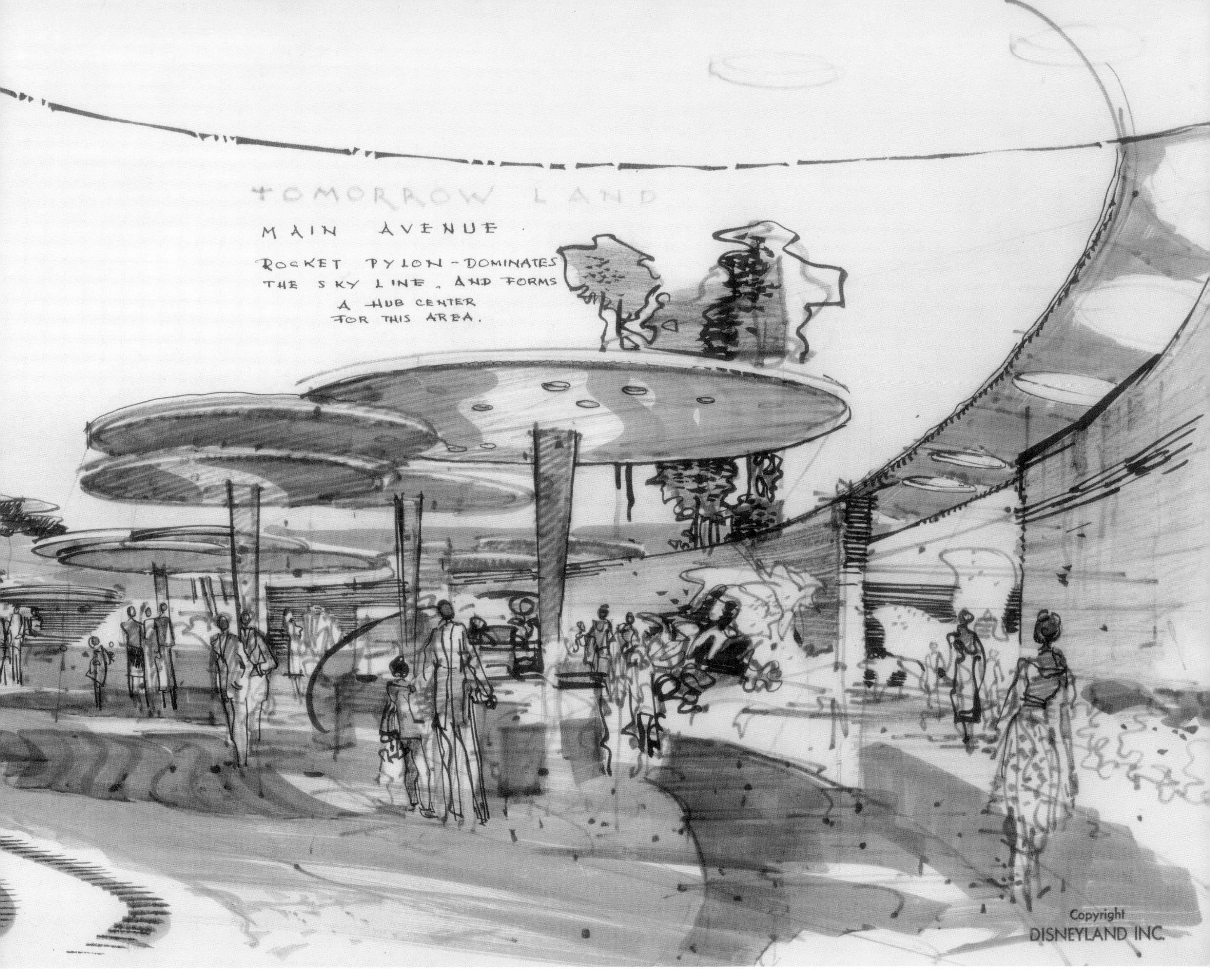
TOMORROW LAND
MAIN AVENUE.
ROCKET PYLON - DOMINATES
THE SKY LINE, AND FORMS
A HUB CENTER
FOR THIS AREA.
Copyright
DISNEYLAND INC.

BELOW AND RIGHT: Two 1954 monorail concepts for Disneyland by Disney Legend Marvin A. Davis. His background in both architecture and motion picture art direction made him a perfect fit as one of the primary Disneyland designers.

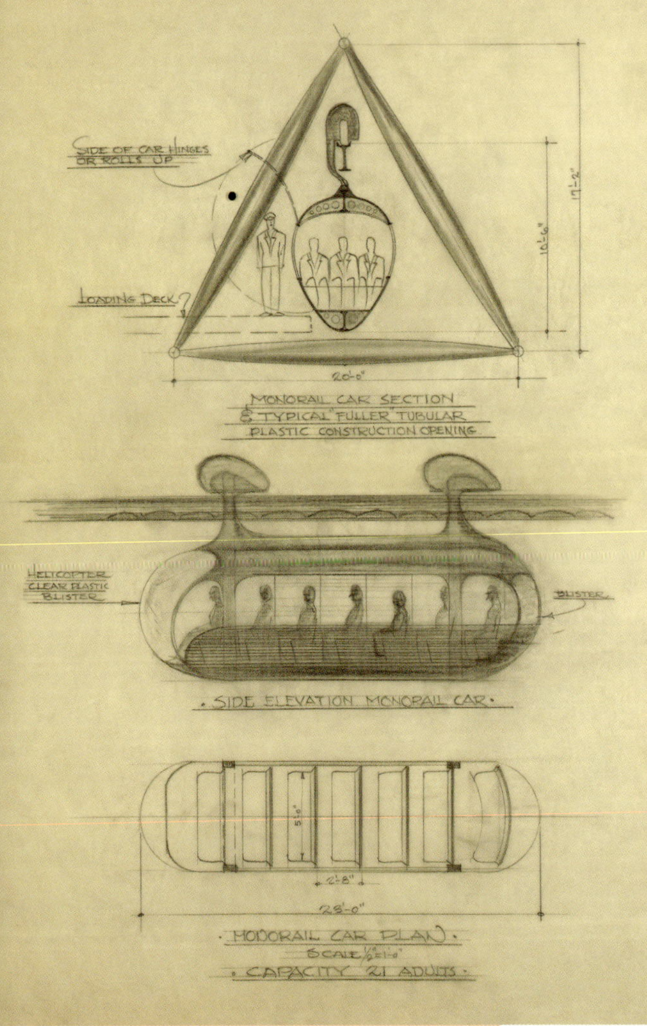

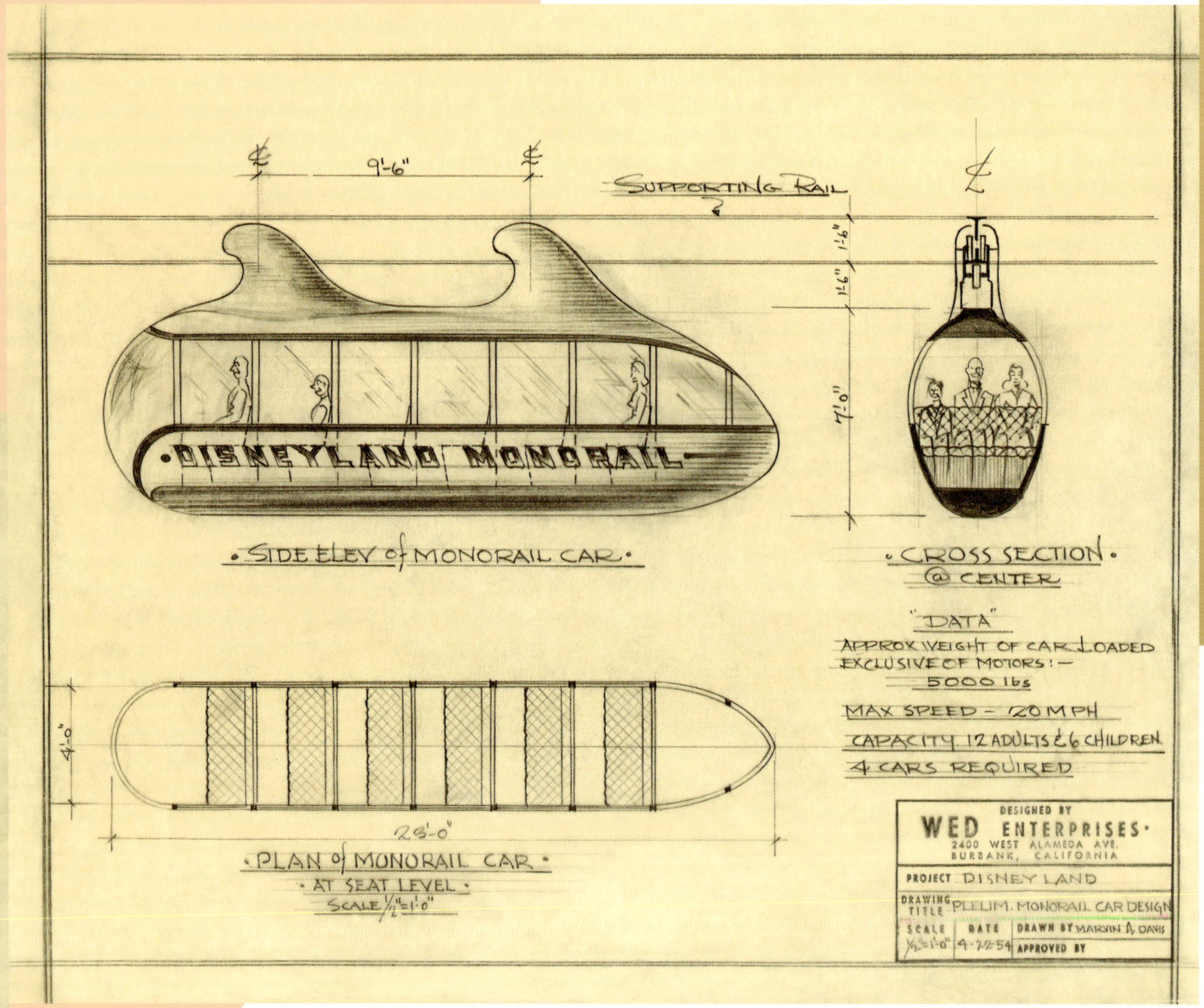

9'-6"
SUPPORTING RAIL
1'-6"
1'-6"
7'-0"
DISNEYLAND MONORAIL
· SIDE ELEV of MONORAIL CAR ·
· CROSS SECTION ·
@ CENTER
"DATA"
APPROX WEIGHT OF CAR LOADED
EXCLUSIVE OF MOTORS: —
5000 lbs
MAX SPEED – 120 MPH
CAPACITY 12 ADULTS & 6 CHILDREN
4 CARS REQUIRED
4'-0"
28'-0"
· PLAN of MONORAIL CAR ·
· AT SEAT LEVEL ·
SCALE 1/2"=1'-0"

DESIGNED BY
WED ENTERPRISES ·
2400 WEST ALAMEDA AVE.
BURBANK, CALIFORNIA
PROJECT DISNEY LAND
DRAWING TITLE PRELIM. MONORAIL CAR DESIGN
SCALE 1/2"=1'-0"
DATE 4-22-54
DRAWN BY MARVIN A. DAVIS
APPROVED BY

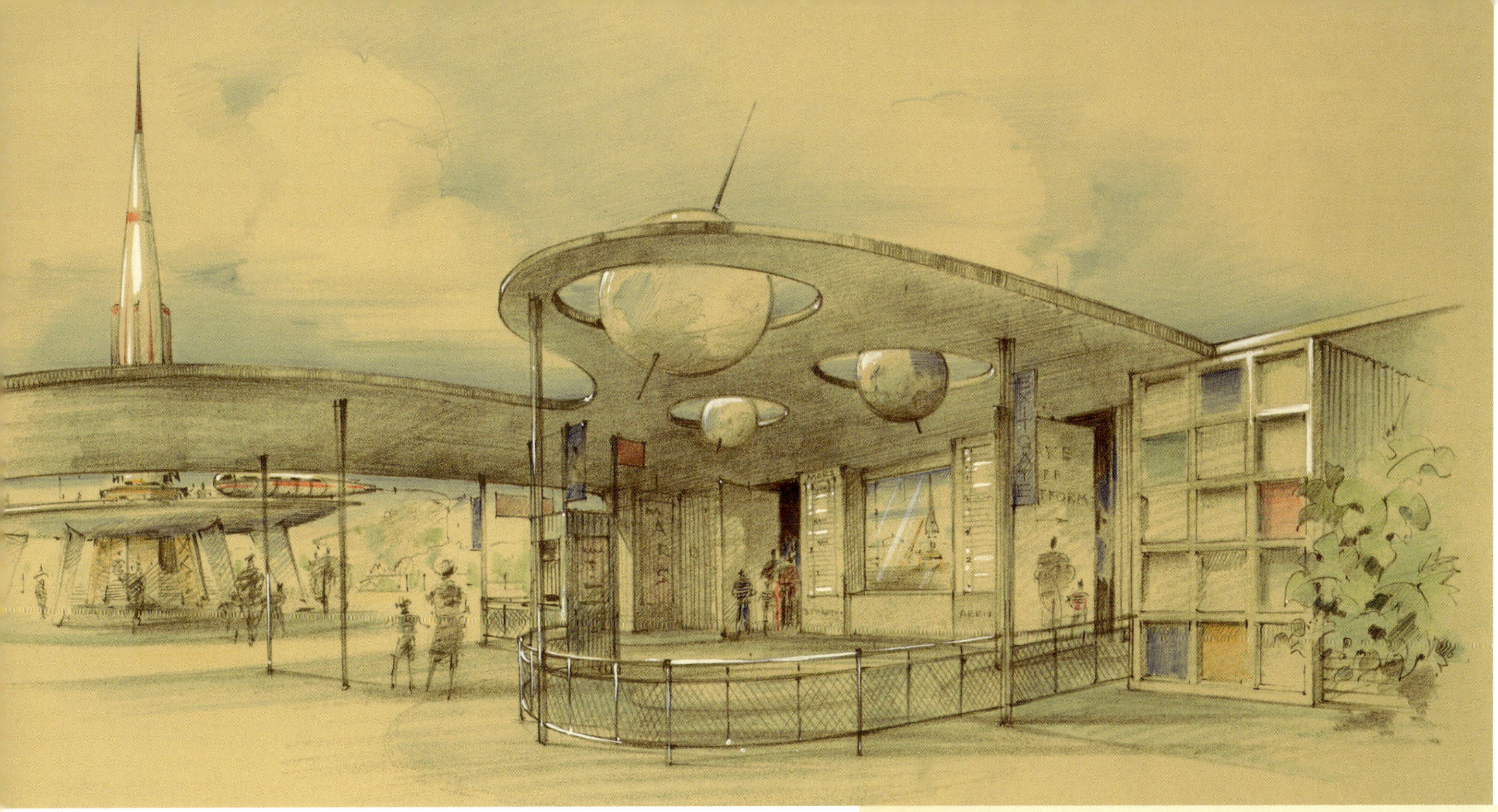

BELOW, LEFT: Multimedia interior rendering by John Hench for the Rocket to the Moon attraction, 1955.

LEFT: Colored pencil on paper view of Tomorrowland's southeast area and Moonliner rocket; artist uncredited, 1954.

BELOW: Tomorrowland exterior view and Rocket to the Moon interior, created by Herb Ryman in 1954 for a Disneyland prospectus presentation book.

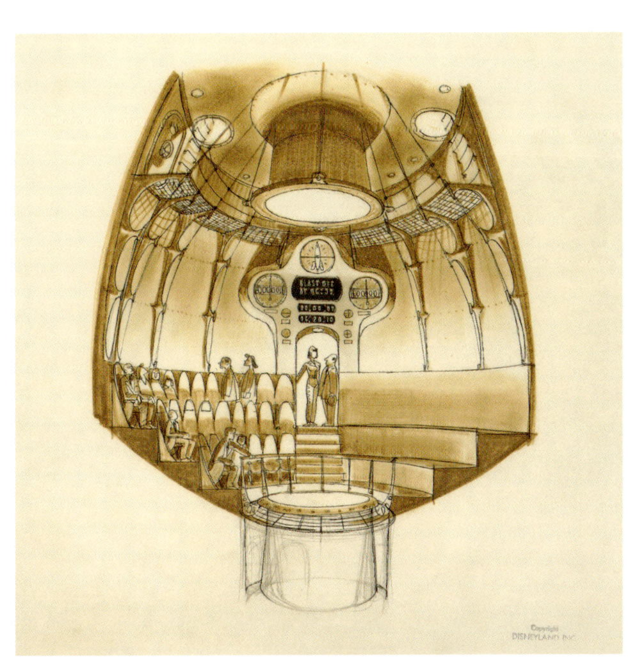

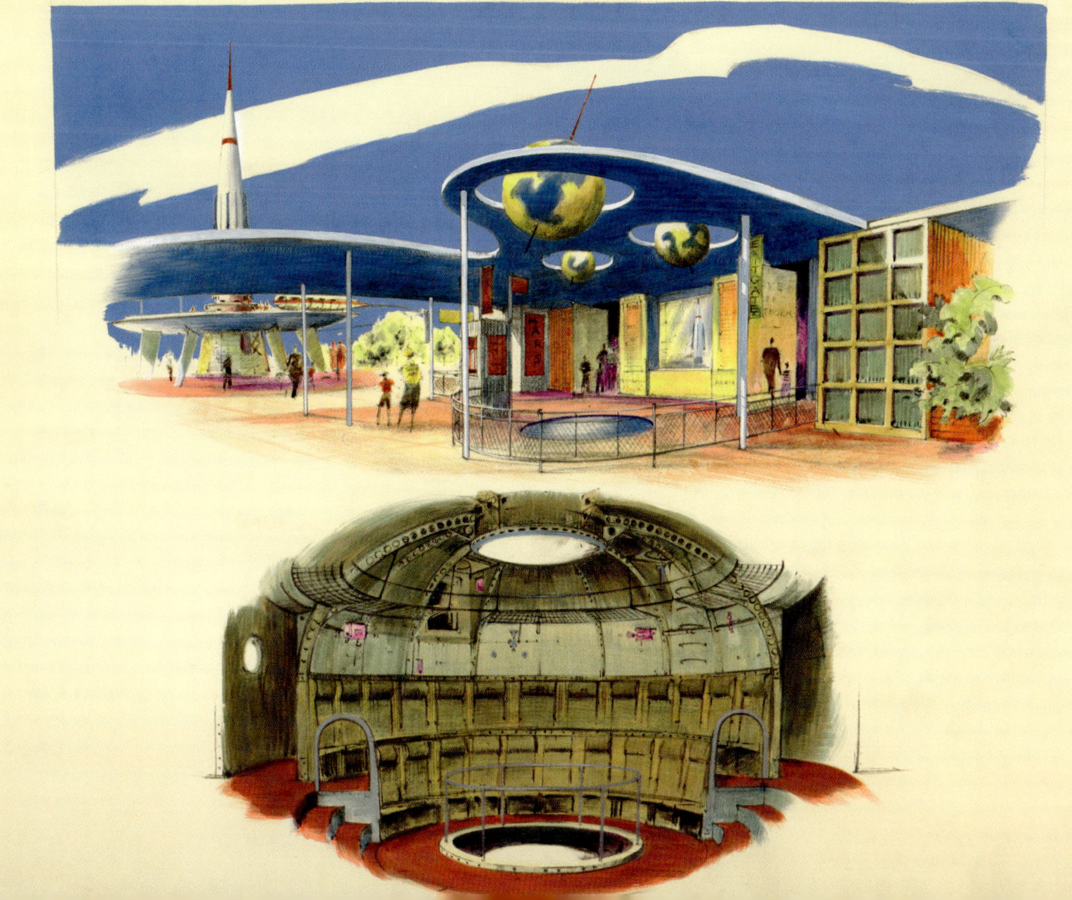

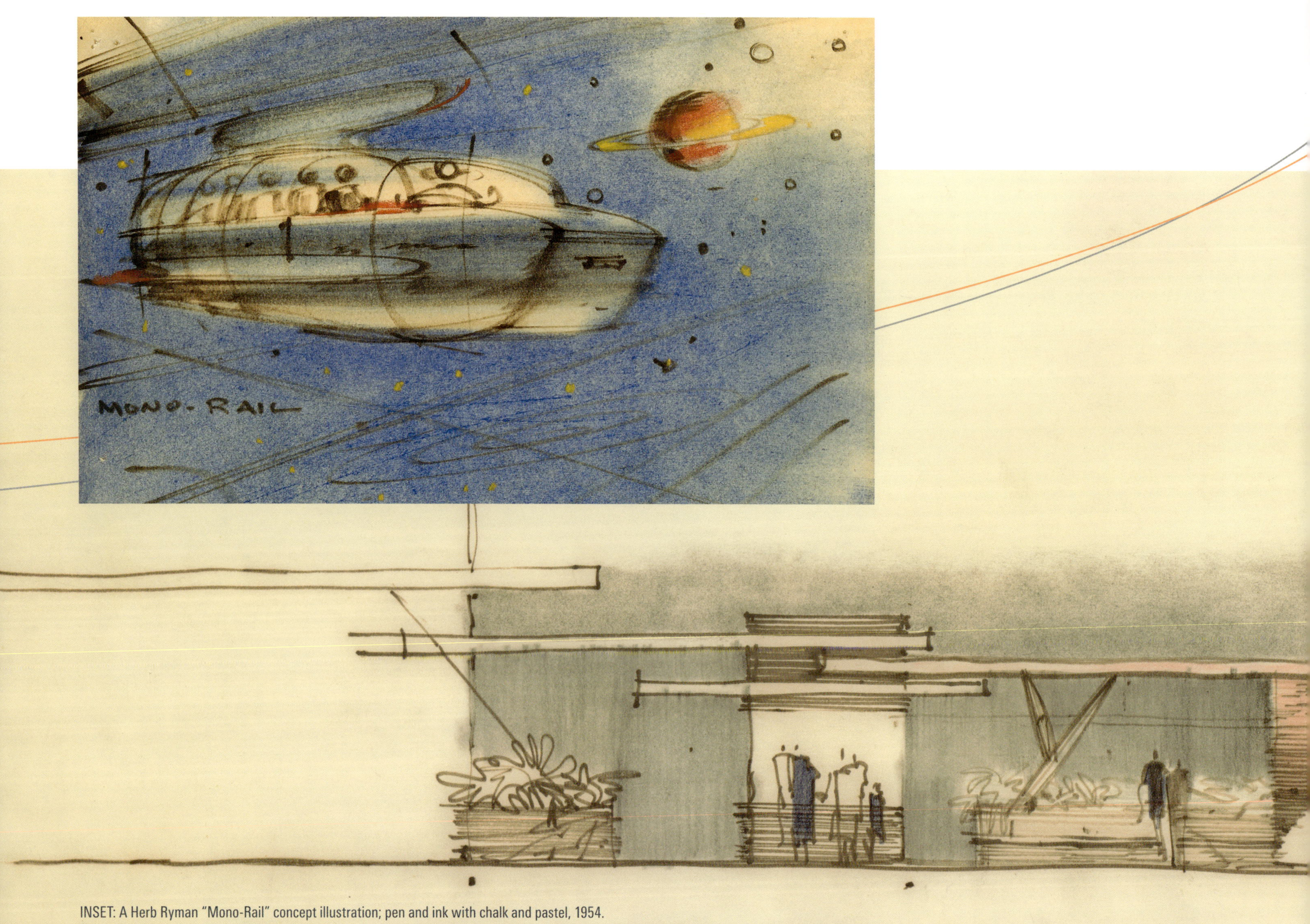

INSET: A Herb Ryman "Mono-Rail" concept illustration; pen and ink with chalk and pastel, 1954.
This colored pencil exterior elevation of a Tomorrowland concept by Ryman, c. 1954, notes that a "Miniature Monorail on Endless Track Spans Entrance."

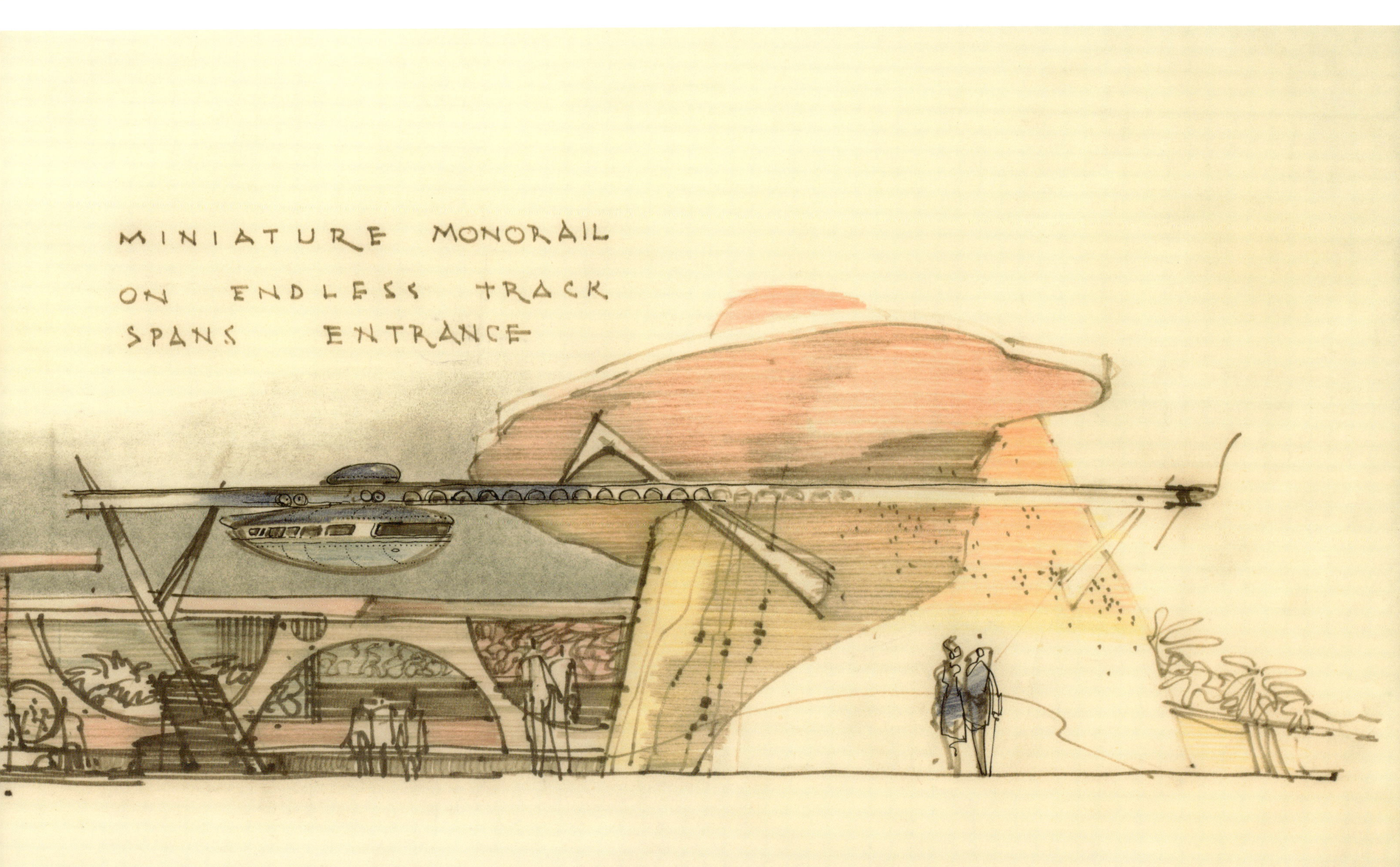
MINIATURE MONORAIL
ON ENDLESS TRACK
SPANS ENTRANCE

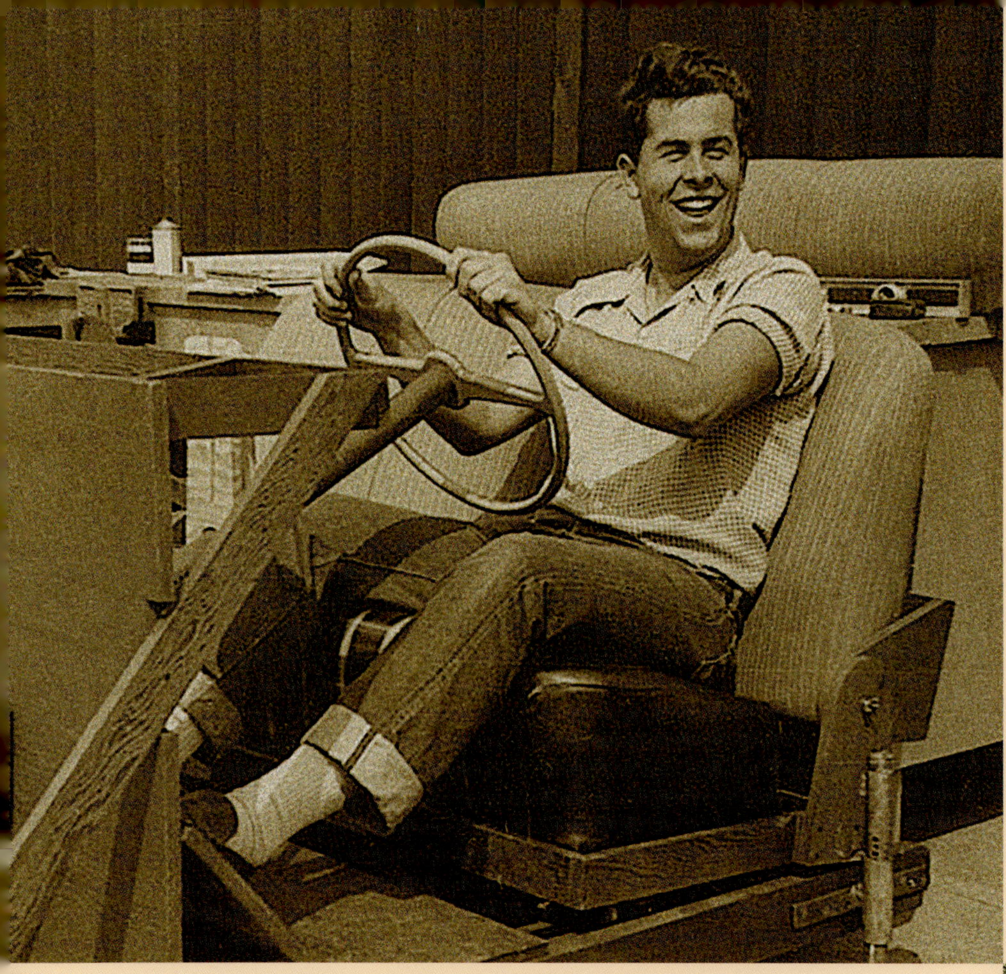

ABOVE: Bob Gurr takes the wheel in an automotive design class at the Art Center School (now known as the ArtCenter College of Design), 1951. OPPOSITE RIGHT: Still on the job in 2000, on-site, for a new and improved Autopia at Disneyland. RIGHT: Still moving forward, foot on the gas, 2019. (2000 and 2019 photos by Stephen Russo.)

Bob Gurr

"Director of Special Vehicle Development"

There is probably no single person more associated with Disney transportation design than Disney Legend Bob Gurr. As he's often said of himself, "If it moves on wheels at Disneyland, I probably designed it."

For more than forty years, he helped move millions of Disney Guests on board vehicles and ride conveyances of his own conception. During his Disney career, Bob developed more than a hundred designs for attractions ranging from the Autopia and Matterhorn Bobsleds to the Disneyland and Walt Disney World Monorails—and beyond.

As Amy Boothe Green explained on D23's web site for Gurr's official Disney Legend biography:

> *But it seems Bob Gurr has always been "a man on the move." Born in Los Angeles on October 25, 1931, young Bob was fascinated with tools, mechanical devices, and cars. He often crawled through a hole in the fence of the nearby Grand Central Air Terminal in Glendale to sneak into the cockpits of idle airplanes; and while at school he decorated his test papers with sketches of automobiles.*

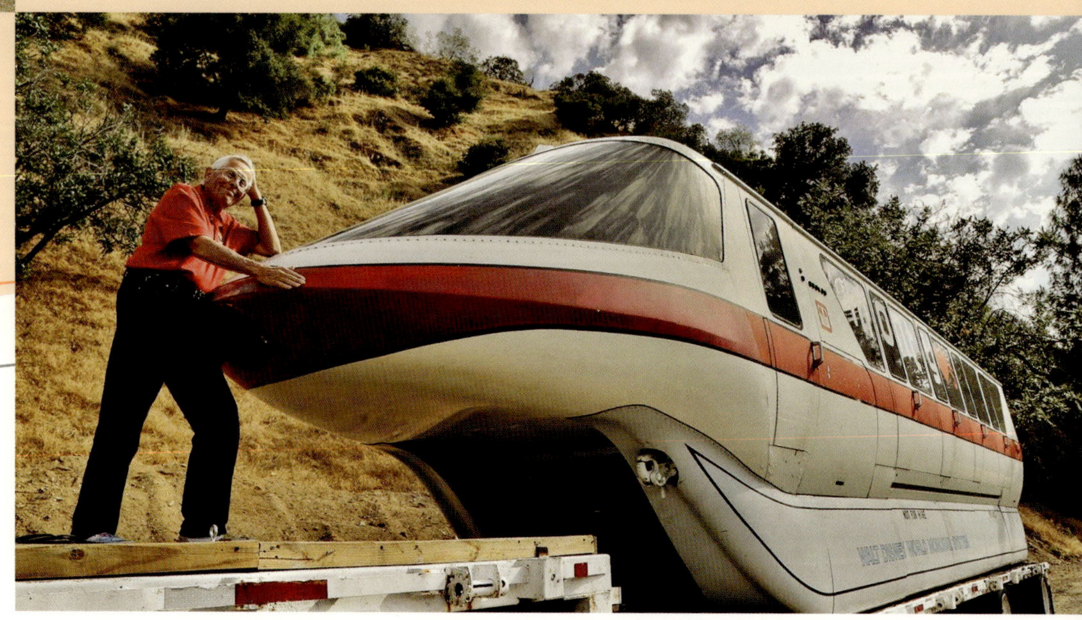

Later, he attended ArtCenter College of Design in Los Angeles on a General Motors scholarship, where he studied industrial design. Upon graduation in 1952, he was hired by the Ford Motor Company, but soon purchased a rubber stamp marked "R. H. Gurr Industrial Design" and went into business for himself.

Soon after, WED Enterprises, today known as Walt Disney Imagineering, hired Bob to consult on the design of miniature cars for Autopia. Walt Disney was so impressed with Bob's knowledge and skill that he invited him to become an Imagineer, when that small team was solely dedicated to the design and construction of Disneyland.

Over the years, Bob developed a remarkable portfolio of vehicles and systems, including the Flying Saucers attraction in Tomorrowland, the antique cars and double-decker buses of Main Street, U.S.A., Ford Motor Company's Magic Skyway, which premiered at the 1964–1965 New York World's Fair, and more. Bob also helped design the mechanical workings of Disney's first Audio-Animatronics human figure, Abraham Lincoln, featured in Great Moments with Mr. Lincoln.

In 1981, Bob retired early from Imagineering to launch Gurr Design, Inc., and, three years later, joined creative forces with two former Imagineers to form Sequoia Creative, Inc. The firm, which specialized in "leisure-time spectaculars" and "fantastical beasts," developed a full-scale physical King Kong and Conan's Serpent figures for Universal Studios Hollywood.

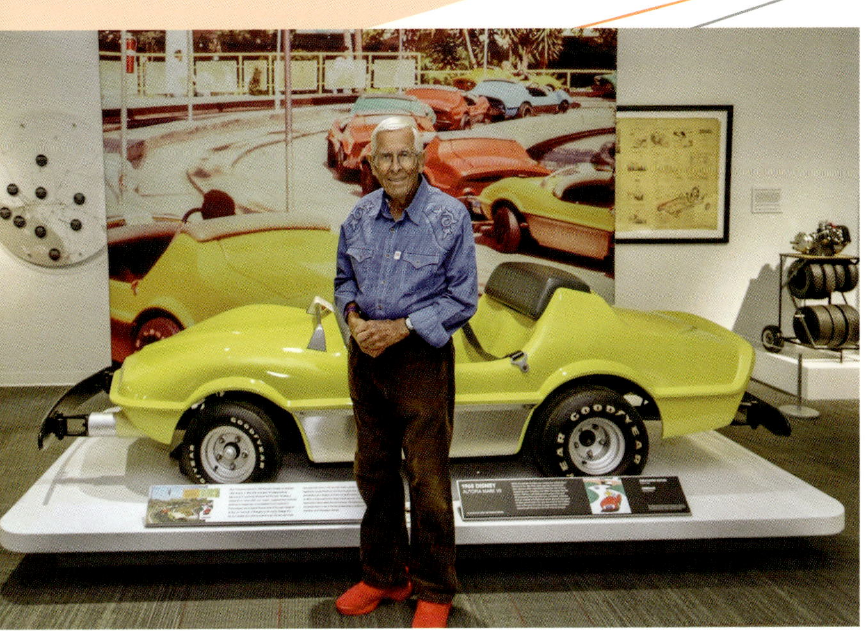

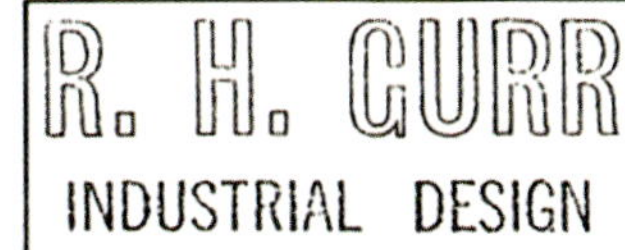

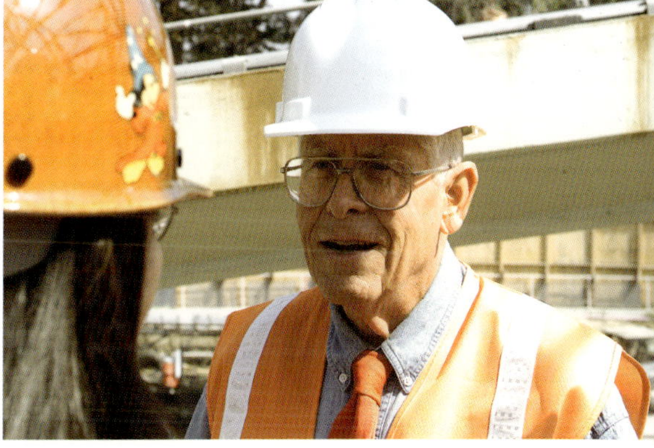

Among his other mechanical feats, Bob was instrumental in creating the mysterious UFO that soared over the closing ceremonies of the 1984 Los Angeles Summer Olympic Games. He also consulted on the animated physical T-Rex figure featured in Steven Spielberg's 1993 motion picture Jurassic Park.

Bob continued to consult on Disney projects, including the giant Ursula creature featured at Tokyo DisneySea. In 1999, he was honored with the Themed Entertainment Association's Lifetime Achievement Award. He released his memoir, Design: Just for Fun, *in 2012.*

Bob continues to educate new generations in lectures and personal appearances, while living his favorite philosophy, which in the words of [the late entrepreneur] Malcolm Forbes were, "While alive, live!"

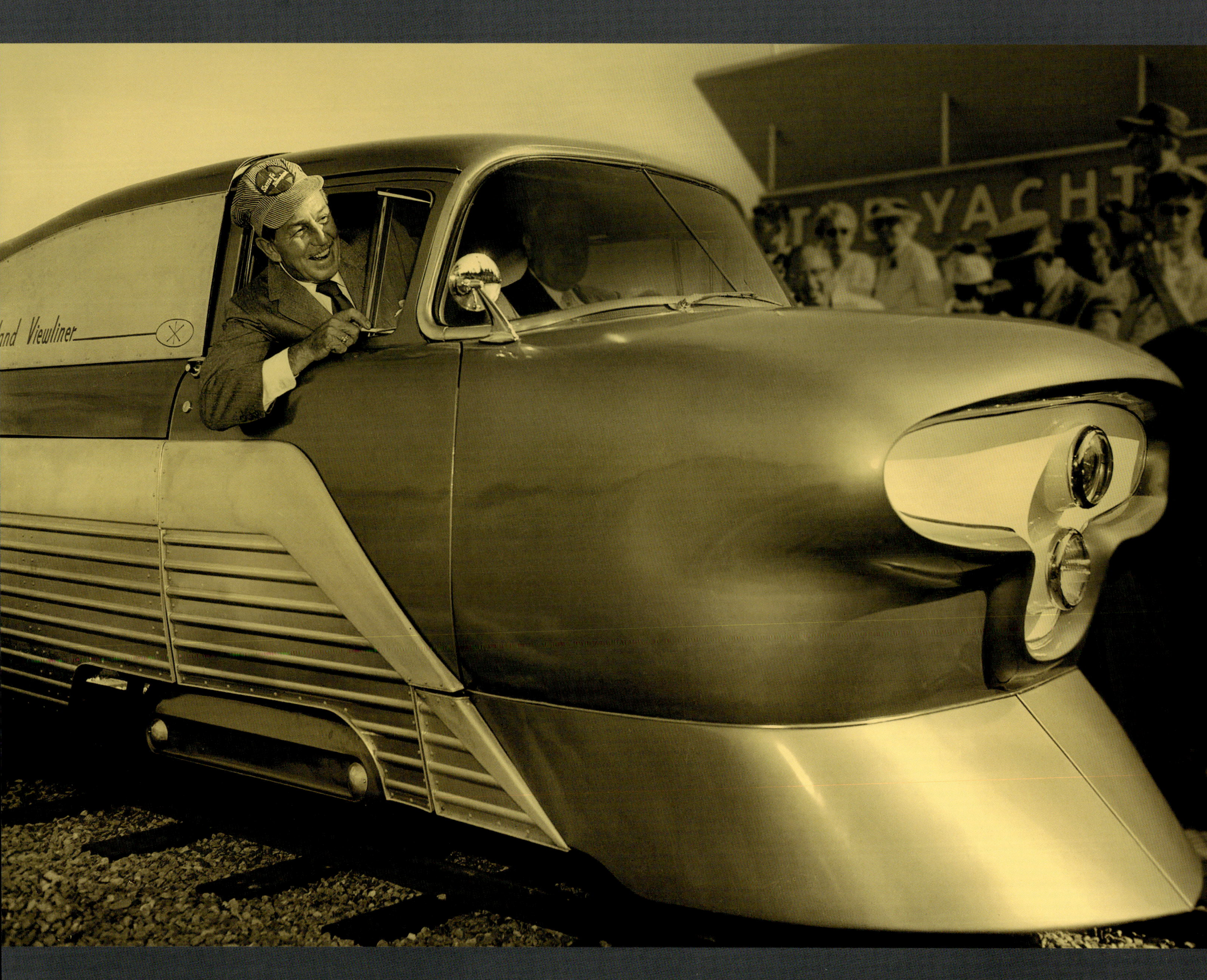
land Viewliner

CHAPTER 5

Inspirations and Prototypes: Walt and the Alweg Connection

"Tomorrow is a heck of a thing to keep up with." —Walt Disney

A Peculiar Side Trip for the Disney Monorail

Imagineer and Disney Legend John Hench observed, "Walt was always looking for inventive new ways of moving Guests around."

Although a practical monorail still eluded him, Walt had a need in 1957 to fill space and create some excitement in Disneyland, and an unusual sightseeing train that would come to be known as the Viewliner was created.

"I guess it was [Disney Legend and chief of engineering design] Roger Broggie who talked Walt into making a miniature version of General Motors' 'Train of Tomorrow' [a 1947 futuristic train prototype]," Bob Gurr recalls.

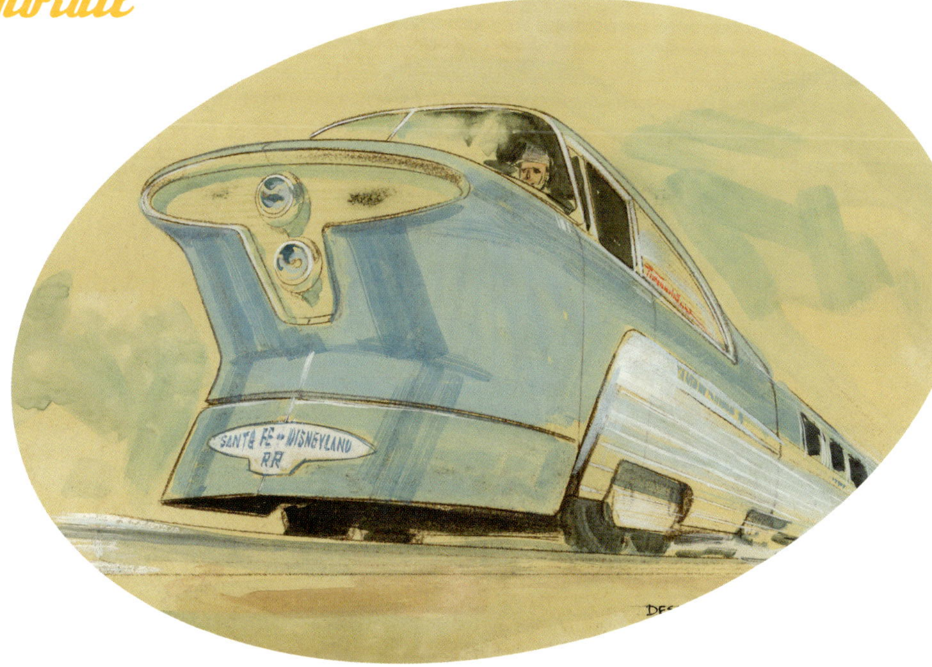

OPPOSITE: Walt pilots the Viewliner, "Train of Tomorrow," 1957. His copilot is Leo E. Sievert, executive representative of the president of the Santa Fe Railway.
RIGHT: A pencil and gouache illustration of the Viewliner by Bob Gurr and Sam McKim, 1956.

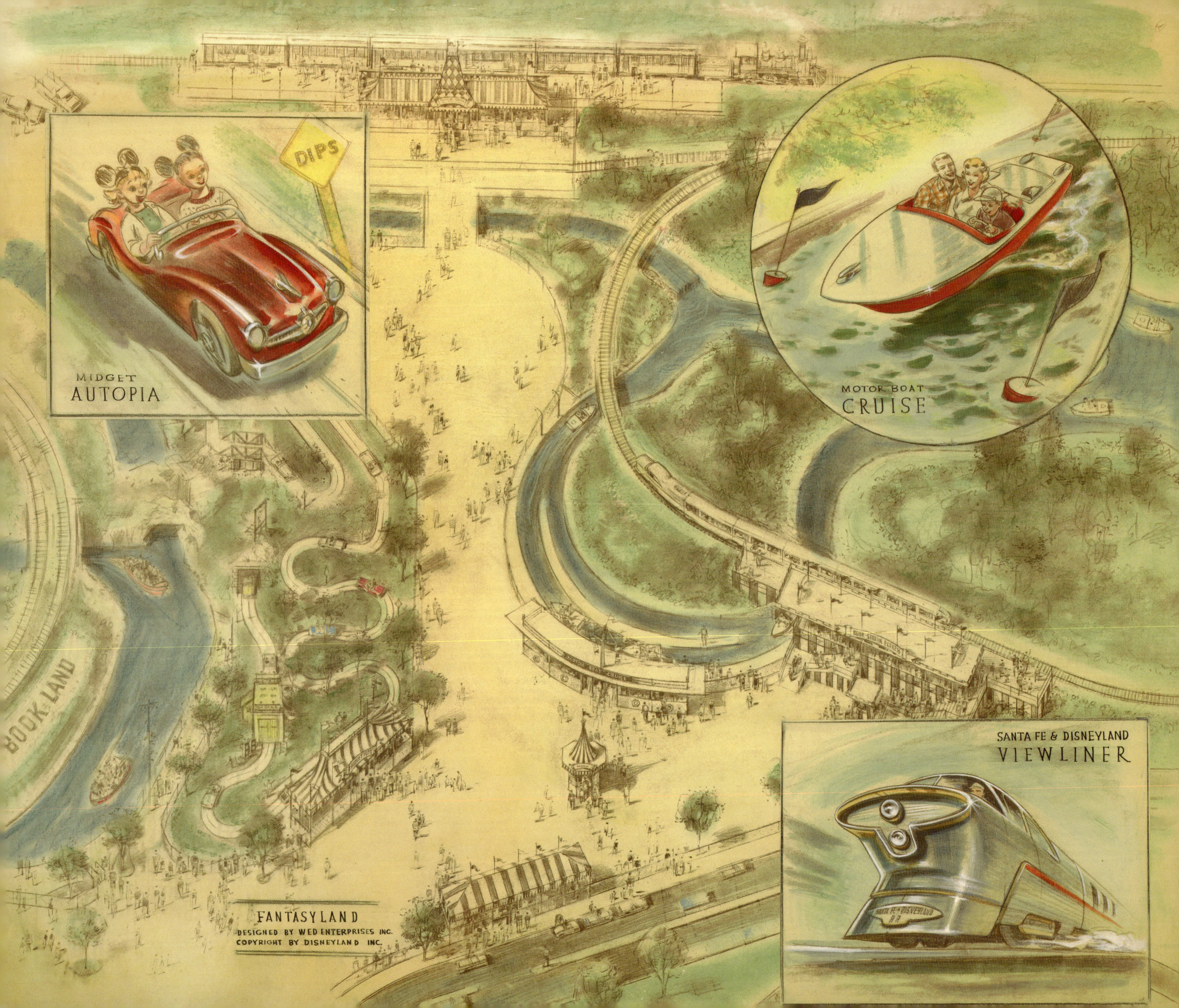
DIPS
MIDGET
AUTOPIA
MOTOR BOAT
CRUISE
BOOK LAND
SANTA FE & DISNEYLAND
VIEWLINER
FANTASYLAND
DESIGNED BY WED ENTERPRISES INC.
COPYRIGHT BY DISNEYLAND INC.

The trains were designed by Gurr, who ultimately based his vehicles on General Motors' futuristic Aerotrain instead; that prototype was then running daily between Los Angeles and Las Vegas. Walt's locomotives were built in the shops and soundstages at The Walt Disney Studios; the passenger coaches were constructed by Standard Carriage Works in downtown Los Angeles.

Although they looked sleek and space-age, the Viewliners were actually an oddly cobbled-together pair of miniature excursion trains. By and large, it was actually a rail-bound automobile, much of it built from salvaged and repurposed automotive parts. "I started looking for an old car I could transform into a train," Gurr said. "I finally settled on a 1954 Oldsmobile 88, which had a perfectly symmetrical dashboard."

It was important that the passenger and driver's sides match, since the train had to have a right-hand drive. The Oldsmobile, like other cars of the time, was far too large for the narrow-gauge Viewliner track, which, at thirty inches wide, was the same size as the Casey Jr. Circus Train track in Fantasyland.

This was resolved by cutting the cab in half and removing the fourteen-inch center section where the radio went. It's also why the aerodynamic Viewliner locomotives had an uncharacteristic seam in their windshields.

Although promoted by Disneyland as "the fastest miniature train in the world," the Viewliner trains revealed their automotive heritage with standard-issue car steering wheels, gas pedals, brake pedals, stick shifts—and reverse gear. The means of propulsion was hardly futuristic—a Chevy Corvette V-8 engine was the power source, coupled with a Jeep transfer case powering driveshafts to front and rear wheel trucks. But there were also some innovative engineering features, such as articulated cars and a low center of gravity, enabling greater maneuverability on curves and at higher speeds.

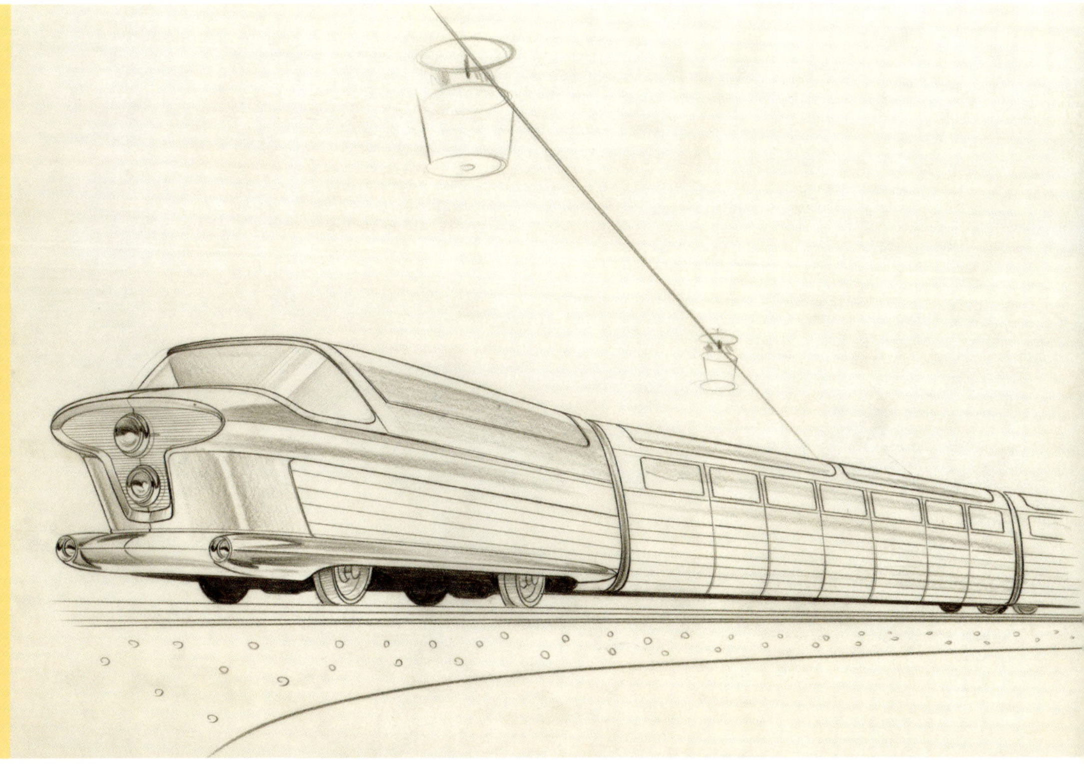

OPPOSITE: Area overview concept and vehicle insets by Sam McKim; pastel and watercolor on diazo print, 1956. RIGHT: Viewliner pencil line art by Bob Gurr, 1956.

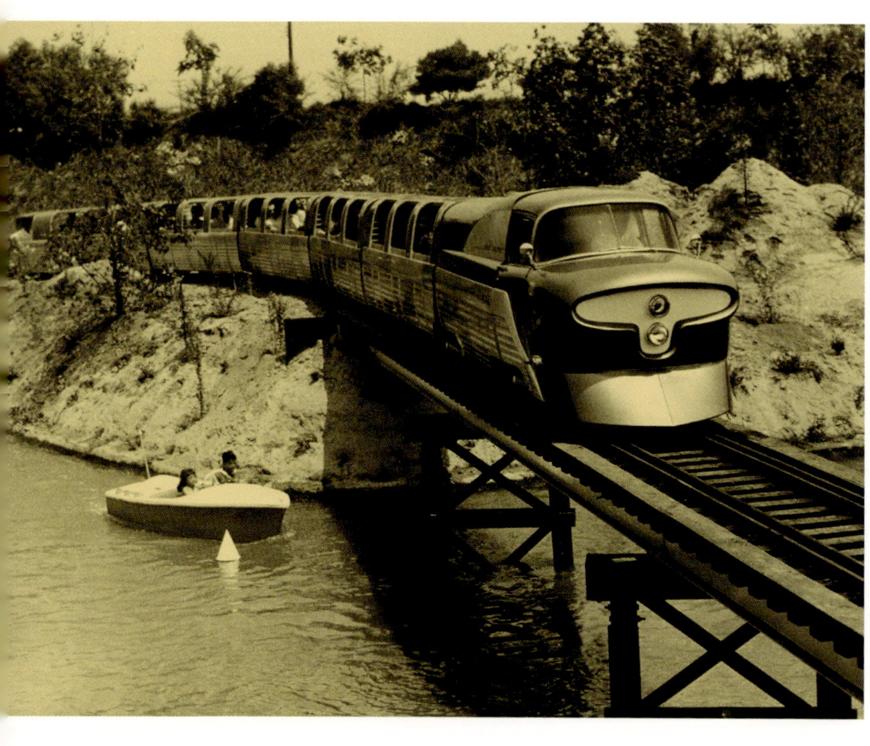

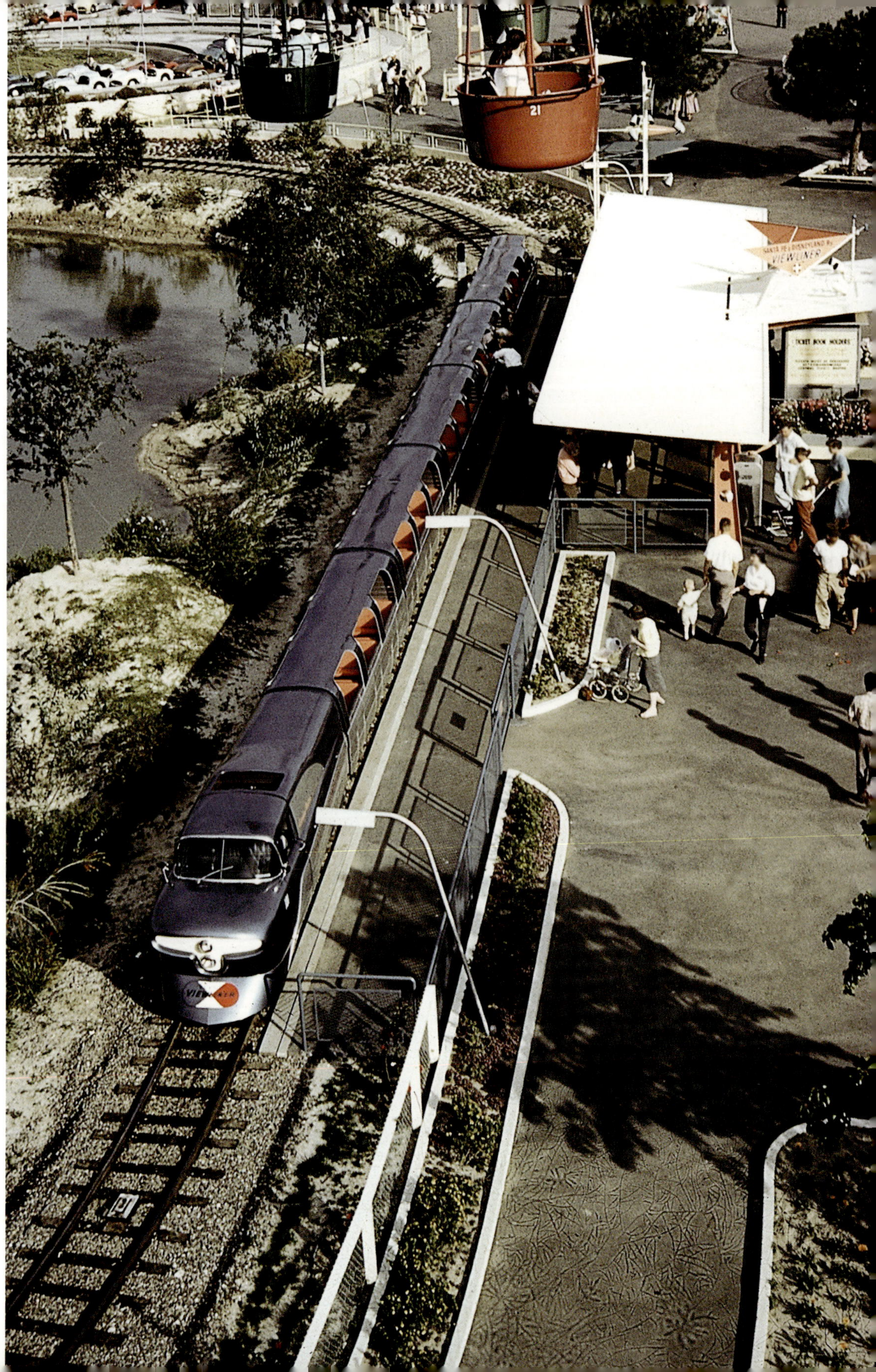

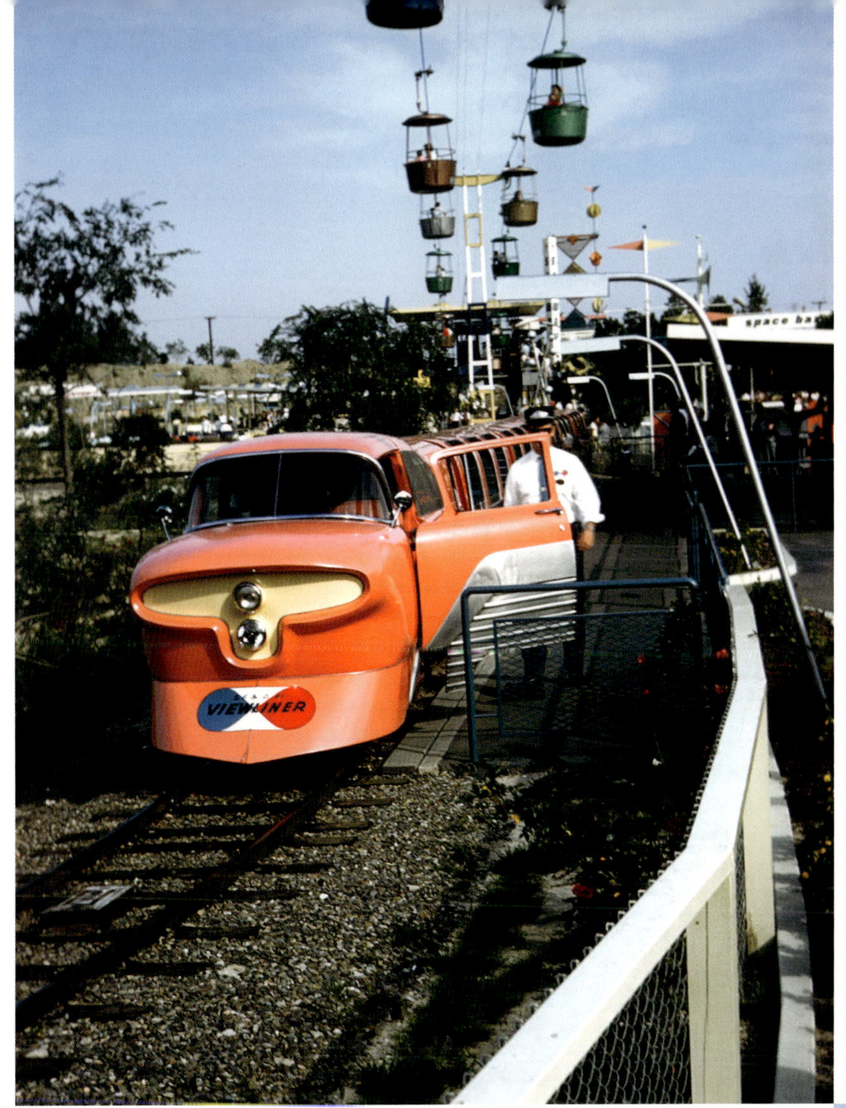

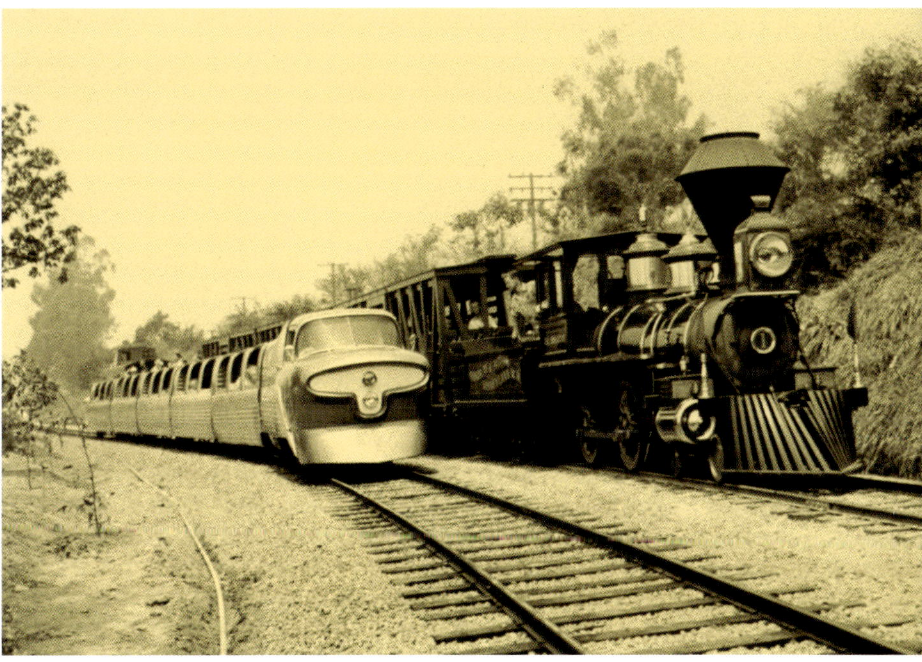

The Viewliner debuted June 26, 1957, as the Santa Fe & Disneyland Viewliner, running two passenger trains through parts of Tomorrowland and Fantasyland along a figure eight or "dog-bone" track. The red Tomorrowland train featured cars that were named for the planets, while the cars of the blue Fantasyland train were named after Disney characters.

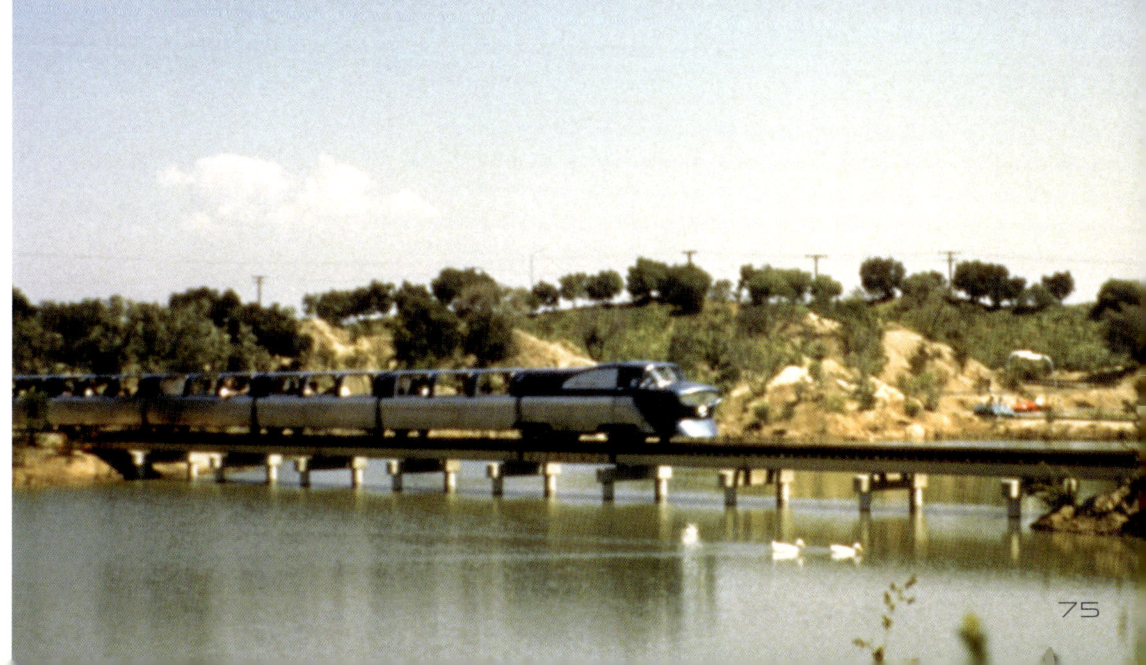

While not without design ingenuity and beauty, plus appearing as sleek and futuristic as it seemed, the Viewliner was all space-age show and little Tomorrowland substance. It only operated until September 15, 1958, before shutting down to make way for the construction of updates to Tomorrowland for 1959—including adding the Disneyland-Alweg Monorail System.

The Contemporary Monorail

The prevailing notion of a monorail at this time was typically one of either an industrial or agricultural conveyance, or based upon the longest-running and most successful passenger system, the Wuppertaler Schwebebahn, all of which had their carriages suspended beneath the rail. In 1952, while on a European excursion, Walt and his wife, Lillian, had a chance to ride the Schwebebahn. The swaying motion was reported to have made Mrs. Disney queasy, leading her to wonder aloud, "Why can't they run the cars on top of the track?"

It was clearly a simple notion, but one that stayed in Walt's mind.

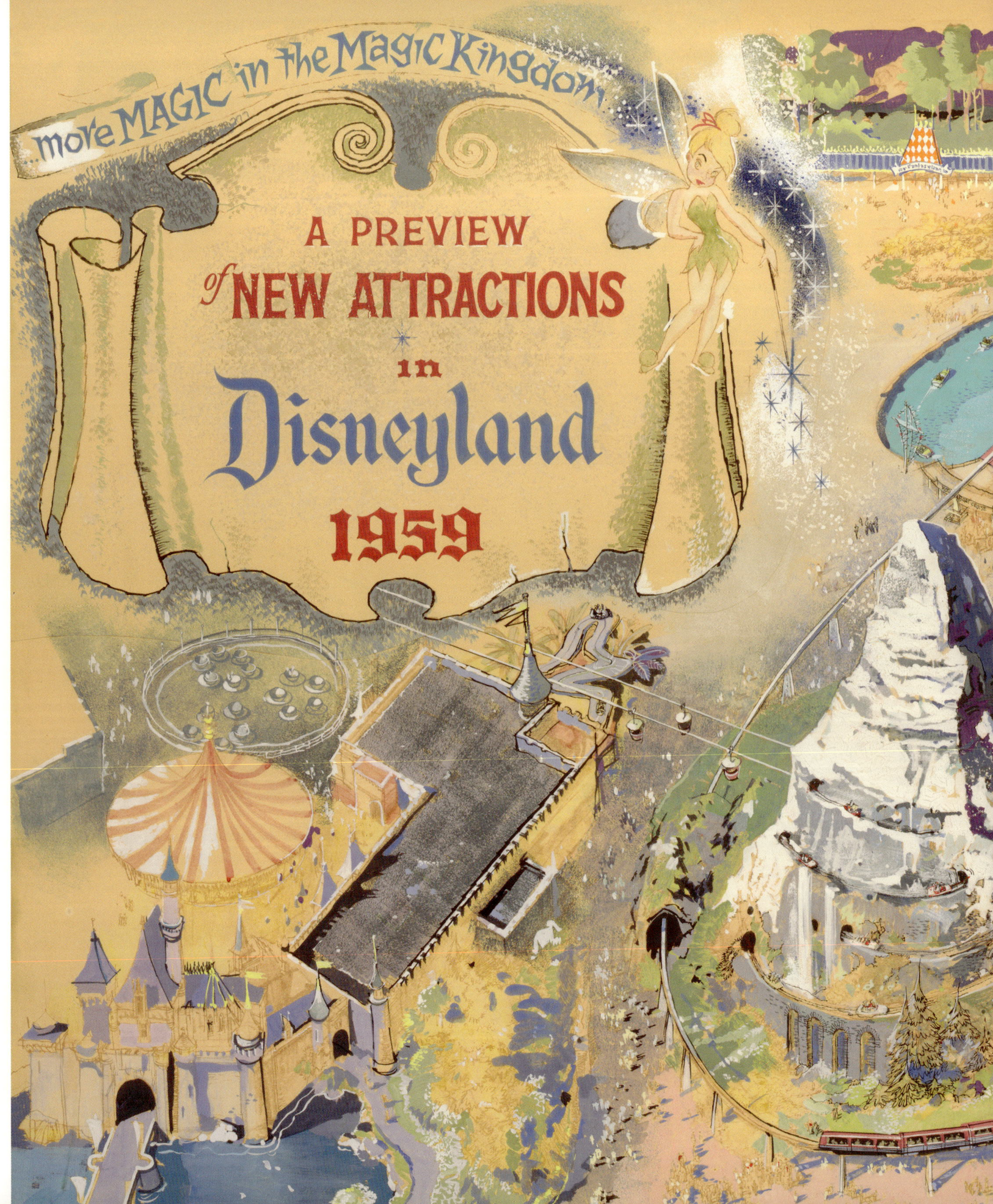

"A Preview of New Attractions in Disneyland 1959" by Herb Ryman, done in 1958, included a "Viewliner"-nosed monorail.

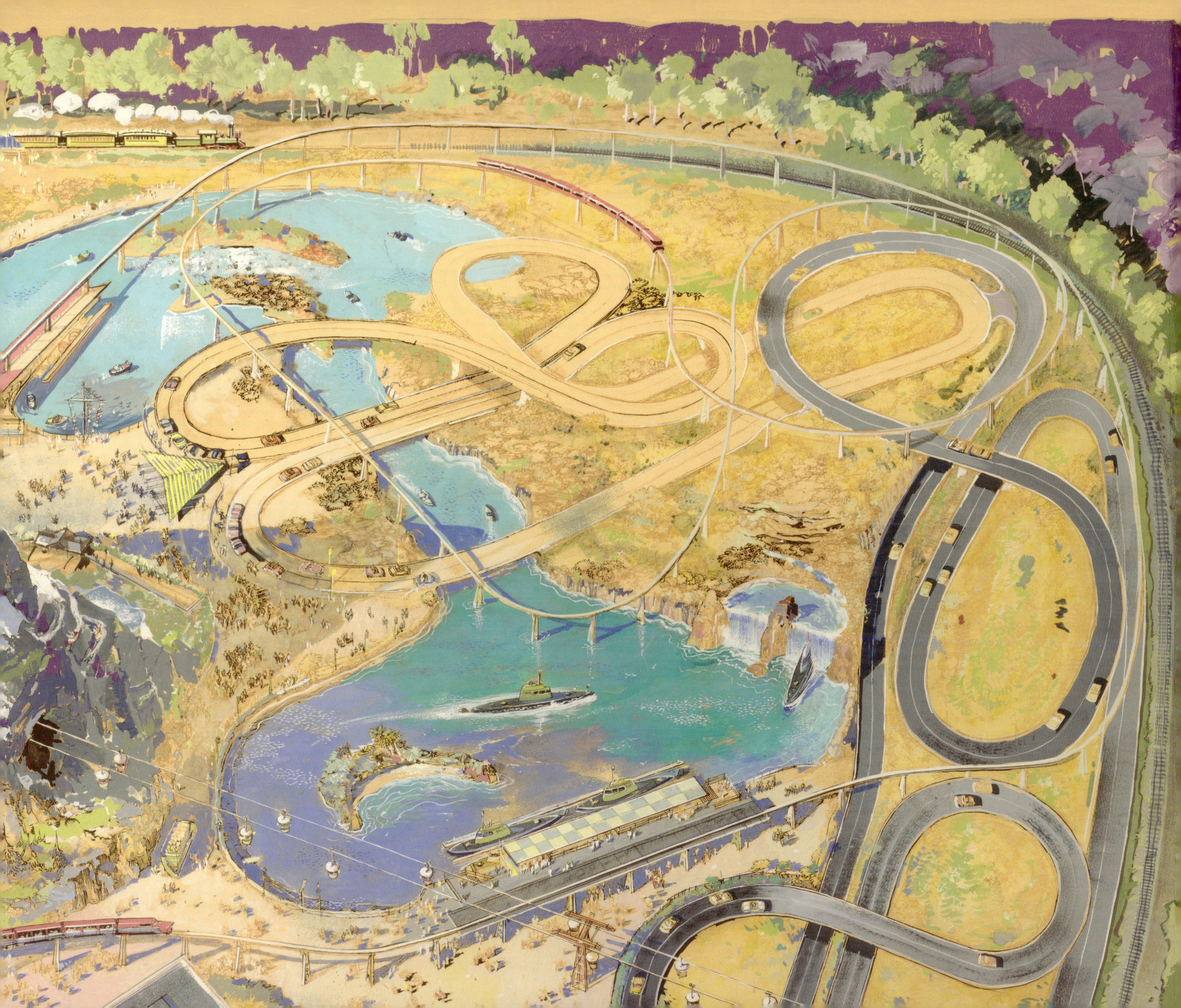

A Chance Meeting

A few years later, in the last days of June and first days of July 1958, Walt and Lillian were on another European trip. As they occasionally did during their travels, they decided to forgo a rigid schedule of planned events and went driving. This time, on a country road in Fühlingen, outside of Cologne, Germany, Walt finally met his elusive monorail—as legend has it, completely by happenstance.

"As the story goes," as chronicled by Bruce Gordon and David Mumford in their authoritative book, *Disneyland: The Nickel Tour*, "Walt rounded a bend into a clearing just as the monorail train passed above the road right in front of him. Walt must have found it almost as hard to believe then as we do now."

By chance, Walt and Lillian had driven onto a road that ran between the grounds of two campuses of the Alweg Research Corporation (Alweg-Forschung, GmbH). Spellbound by the remarkable train, Gurr says, "[Walt] stopped and chased the monorail over to a service yard where nobody spoke English. They sent him back across the road to the administration building—and Walt walked in through the front door of a company that builds monorails."

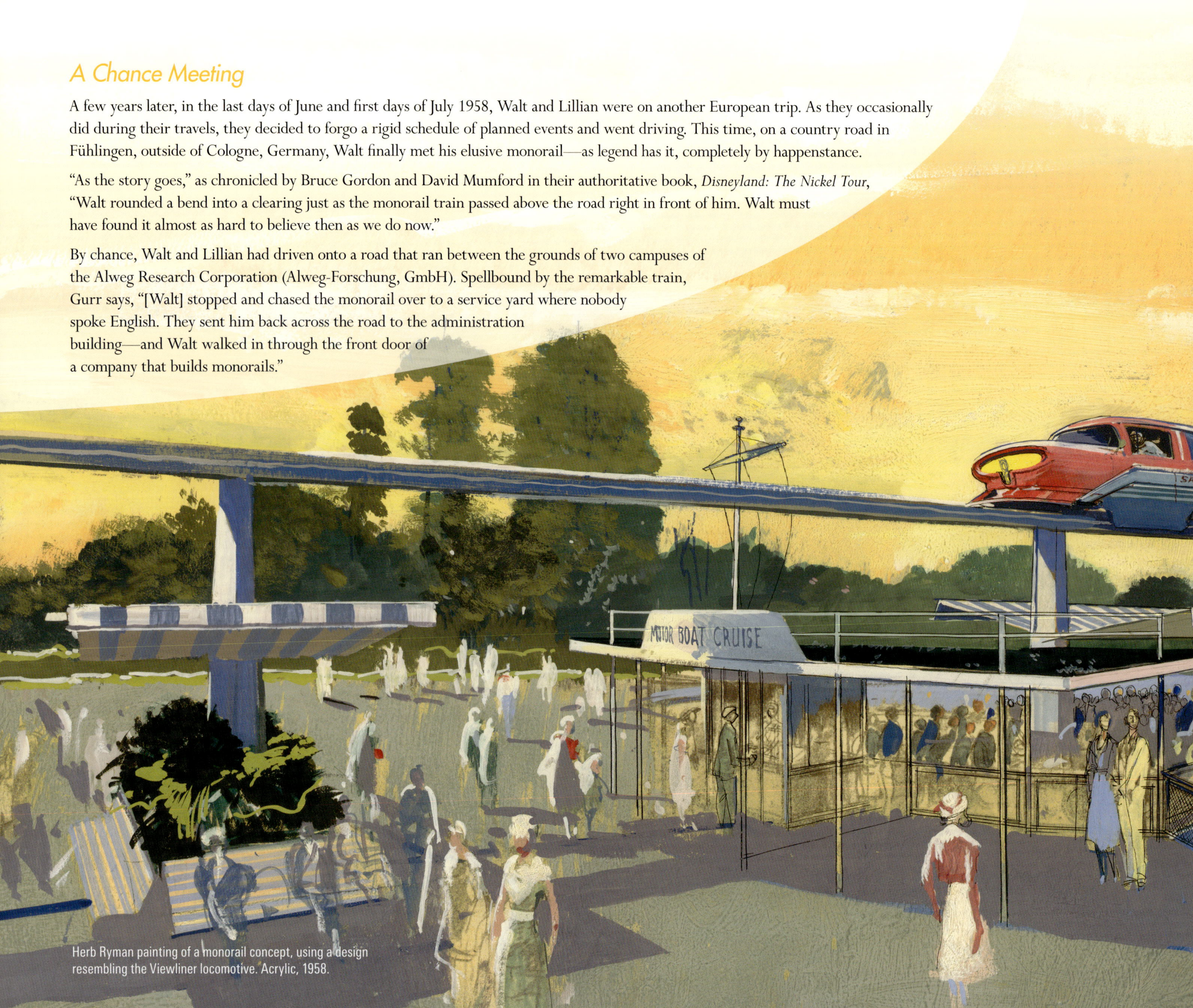

Herb Ryman painting of a monorail concept, using a design resembling the Viewliner locomotive. Acrylic, 1958.

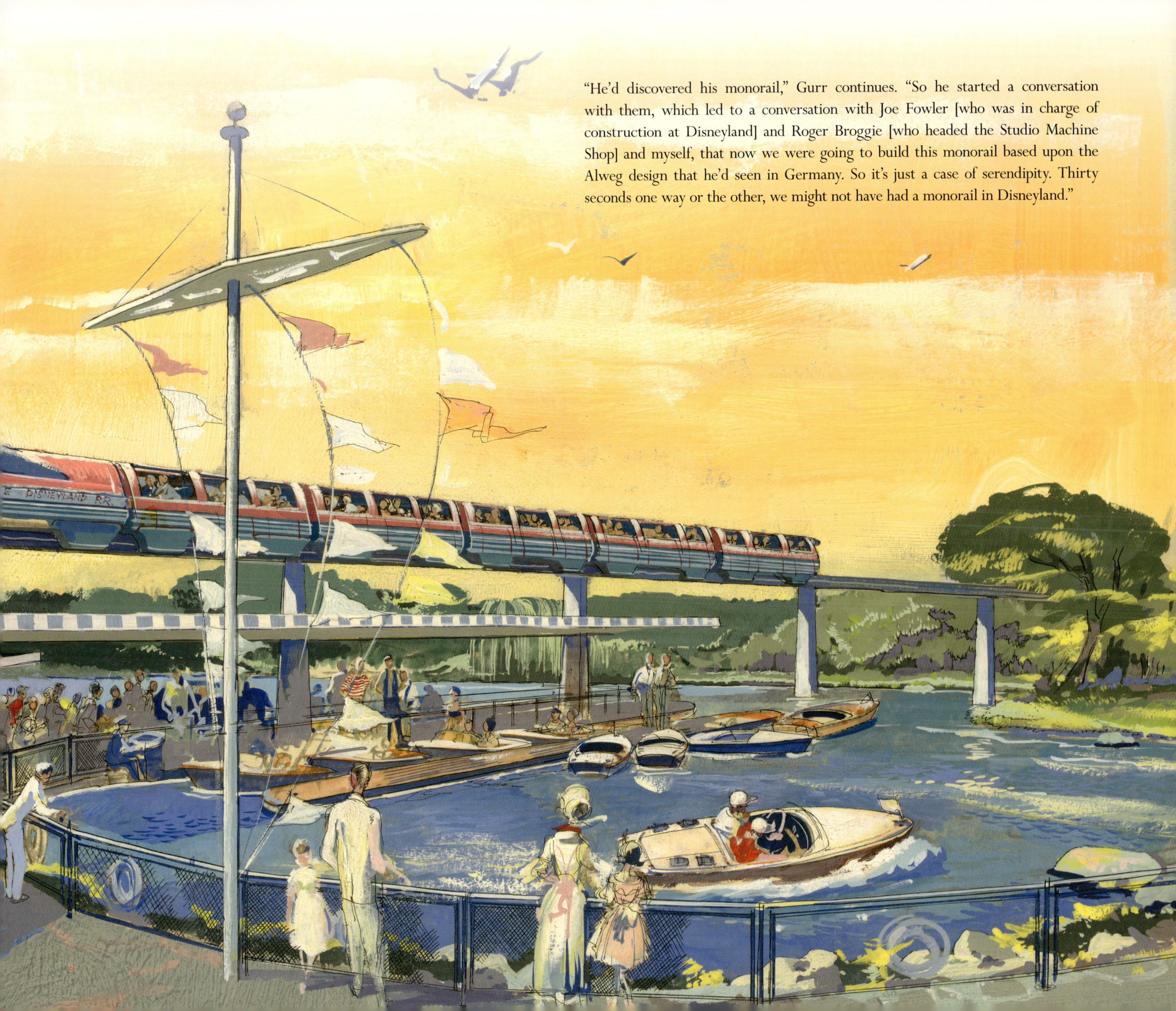

"He'd discovered his monorail," Gurr continues. "So he started a conversation with them, which led to a conversation with Joe Fowler [who was in charge of construction at Disneyland] and Roger Broggie [who headed the Studio Machine Shop] and myself, that now we were going to build this monorail based upon the Alweg design that he'd seen in Germany. So it's just a case of serendipity. Thirty seconds one way or the other, we might not have had a monorail in Disneyland."

From Alweg to Disney

"When he saw the German Alweg train in Germany . . . he was really excited," Bob Gurr recounts. "He got hold of Roger Broggie and myself and said, 'Fellows, I just found the monorail, and I would like to have you get started and see if you can figure out, how we can do this.'"

Disneyland vice president and director of construction Joe Fowler, also a Disney Legend, and Broggie were dispatched to Germany to meet with the Alweg group. In examining how to apply the Alweg technology to practical daily use in Disneyland, Broggie recalled an immediate divergence. "It was between engineering people who wanted to go in a straight line forever with no grades, and the Disney art directors who wanted to draw tight turning radii and plot an interesting ride that climbed maximum grades in order to thrill the Guests."

In the meantime, Gurr was assigned to transform the boxy and practical Alweg vehicles into something more in keeping with the Tomorrowland ideals Disney envisioned.

"I needed a way to hide the wheel of our train, and at the same time create a distraction so you wouldn't notice the concrete beamway underneath," Gurr says. "I sketched out the old Flash Gordon spaceship—an arrow-shaped cylinder with a big swept-back wing on top and one on the bottom. Then I erased the wing from the top, drew in the old Viewliner cars along the back, and there it was. The Monorail.

"So I sketched that up, made illustration of it, took it over to the Animation Building. Walt took one look at that thing, tapped on it, and said, 'Bobby, can you build that?' And stupidly I said, 'Yes.' Then I found out later I had drawn some parts that were almost impossible to fabricate. So that was a lesson—don't say yes too quickly unless you are quite sure that you can make these things work!"

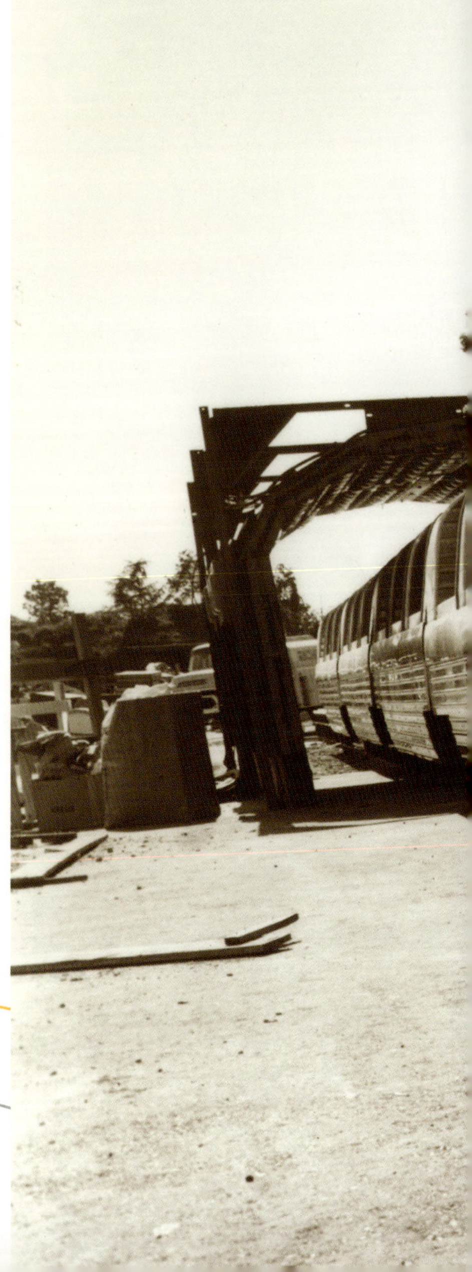

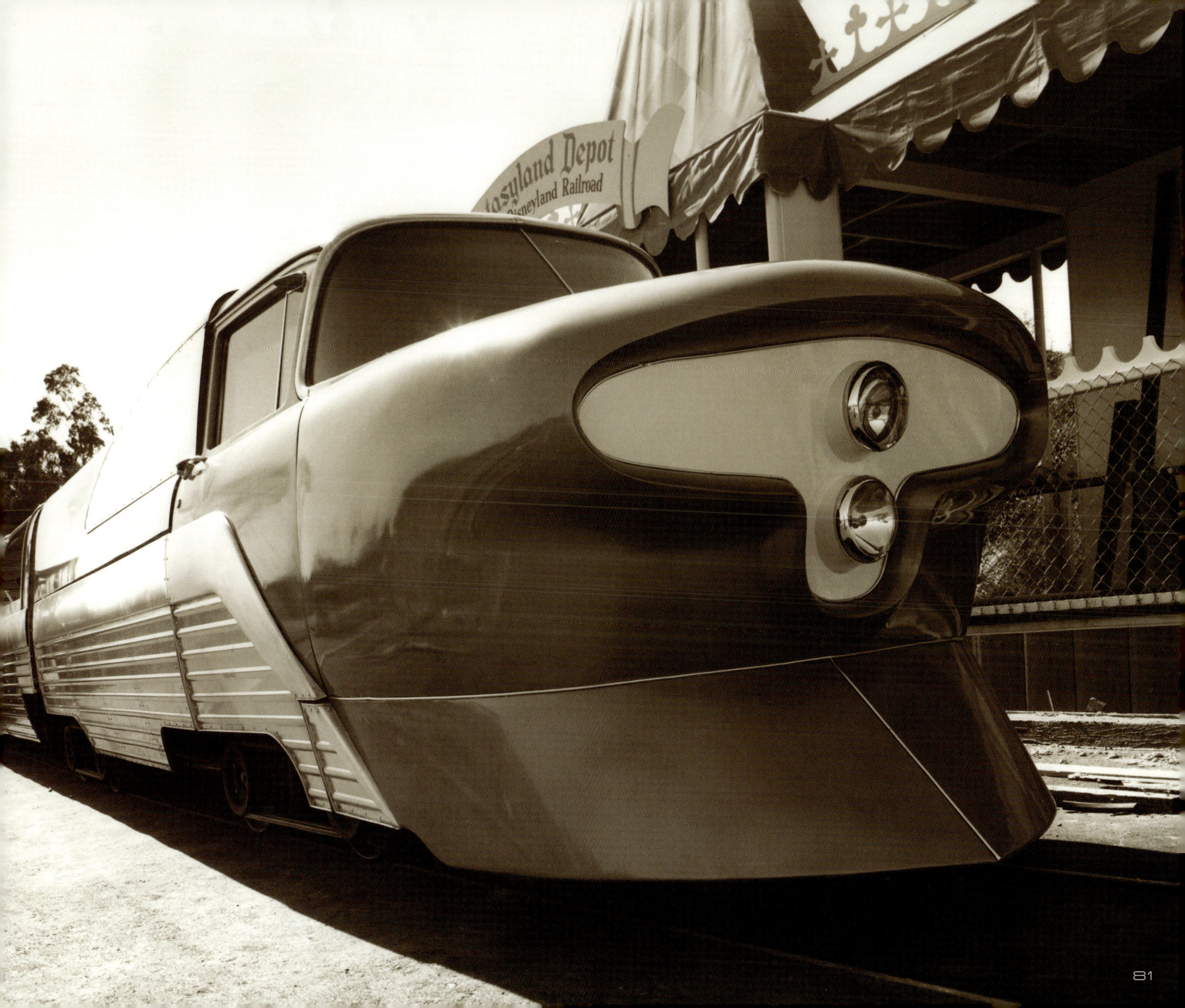

Disneyland Railroad

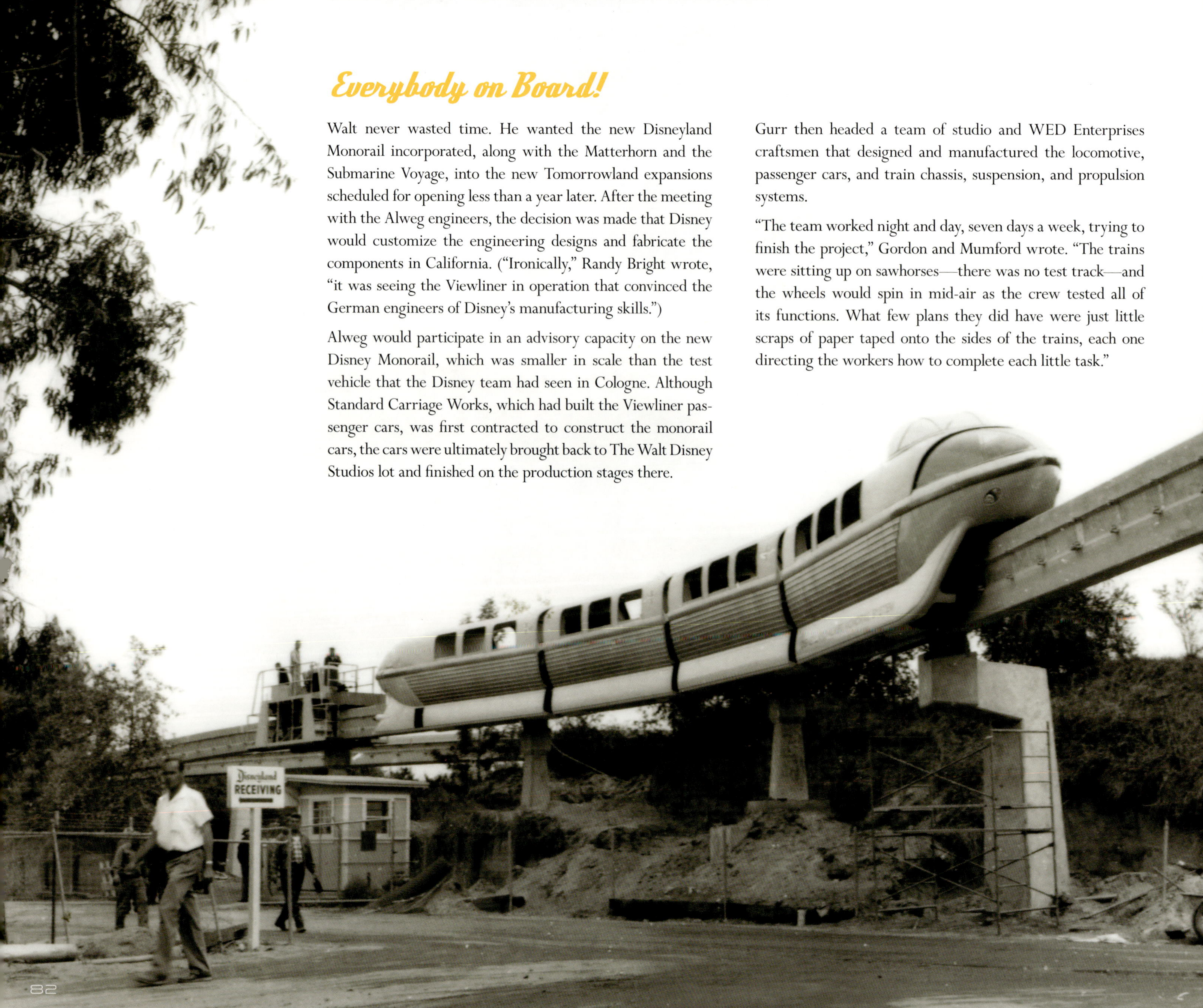

Everybody on Board!

Walt never wasted time. He wanted the new Disneyland Monorail incorporated, along with the Matterhorn and the Submarine Voyage, into the new Tomorrowland expansions scheduled for opening less than a year later. After the meeting with the Alweg engineers, the decision was made that Disney would customize the engineering designs and fabricate the components in California. ("Ironically," Randy Bright wrote, "it was seeing the Viewliner in operation that convinced the German engineers of Disney's manufacturing skills.")

Alweg would participate in an advisory capacity on the new Disney Monorail, which was smaller in scale than the test vehicle that the Disney team had seen in Cologne. Although Standard Carriage Works, which had built the Viewliner passenger cars, was first contracted to construct the monorail cars, the cars were ultimately brought back to The Walt Disney Studios lot and finished on the production stages there.

Gurr then headed a team of studio and WED Enterprises craftsmen that designed and manufactured the locomotive, passenger cars, and train chassis, suspension, and propulsion systems.

"The team worked night and day, seven days a week, trying to finish the project," Gordon and Mumford wrote. "The trains were sitting up on sawhorses—there was no test track—and the wheels would spin in mid-air as the crew tested all of its functions. What few plans they did have were just little scraps of paper taped onto the sides of the trains, each one directing the workers how to complete each little task."

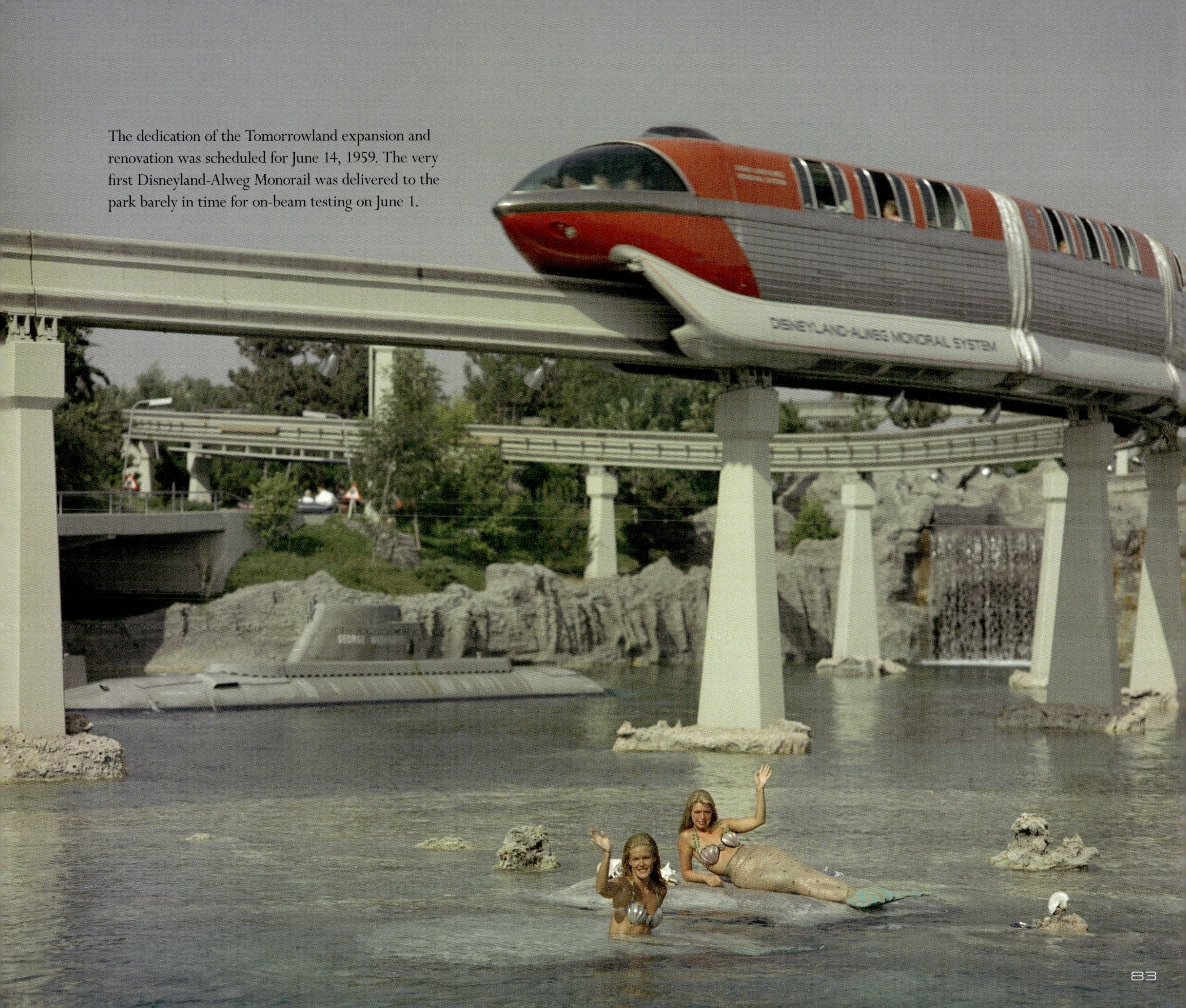

The dedication of the Tomorrowland expansion and renovation was scheduled for June 14, 1959. The very first Disneyland-Alweg Monorail was delivered to the park barely in time for on-beam testing on June 1.

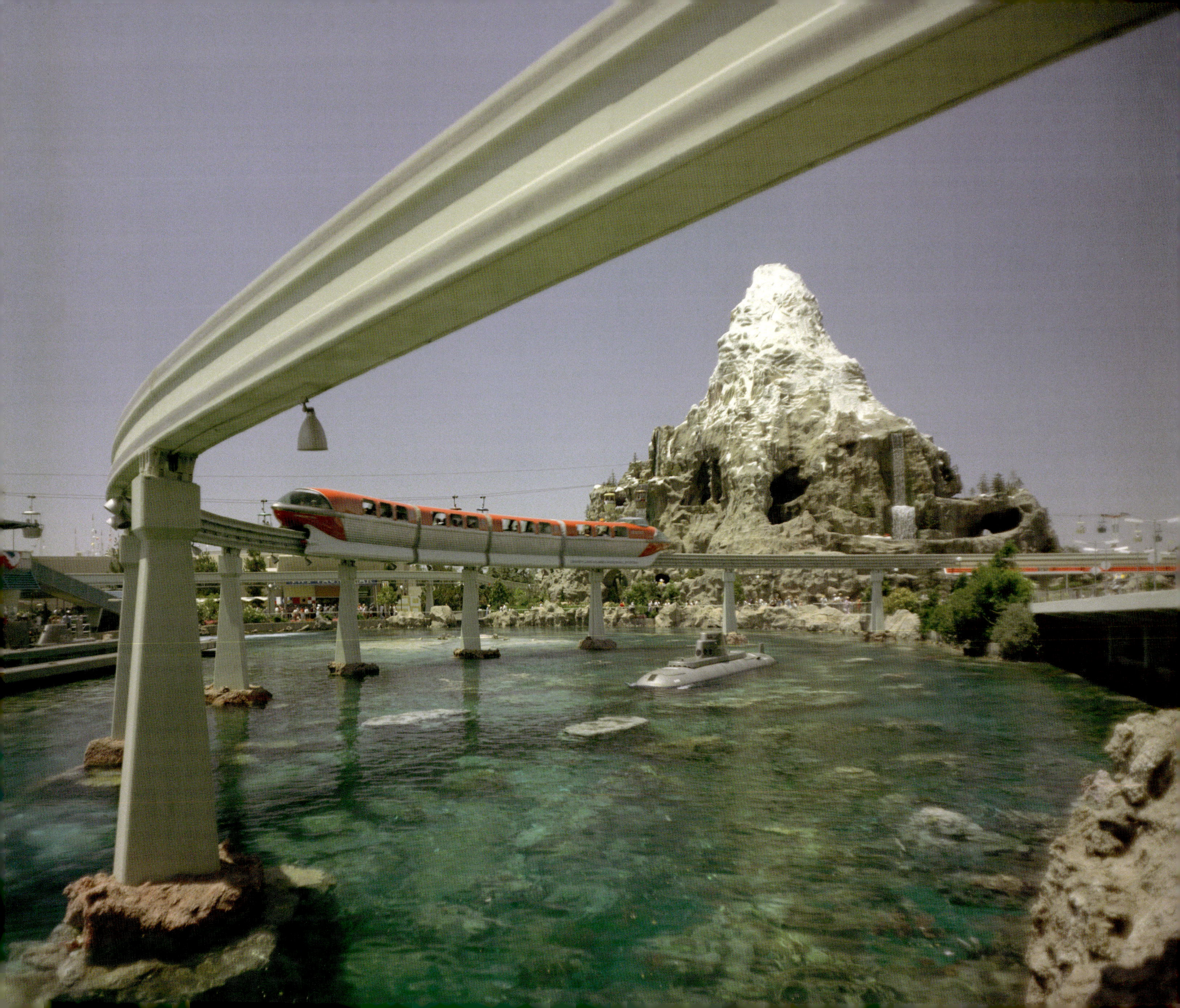

CHAPTER 6

A "Highway in the Sky" in a World on the Move

"Keeping on the move is an old American custom—and a good one." —Walt Disney

Disneyland '59

It's well known that Walt always saw Disneyland as a work in progress.

"Well, the park means a lot to me, in that it's something that will never be finished," he said. "Something that I can keep developing, keep plussing and adding to. It's alive. It will be a live breathing thing that will need changes. A picture is a thing [that] once you wrap it up and turn it over to Technicolor, you're through. *Snow White* is a dead issue with me. A live picture—I just finished the one I wrapped up a few weeks ago—it's gone, I can't touch it. There's things in it I don't like, I can't do anything about it. I wanted something live, something that could grow, something I could keep plussing with ideas, you see? The park is that. Not only can I add things, but even the trees will keep growing. The thing will get more beautiful each year!"

Opening day for Disneyland in 1955 wasn't the completion of the park, but rather the beginning of the creative evolution Walt intended. Immediately, additions and expansions were imagined, and once Disneyland proved a successful and viable enterprise, Walt had several choices—there were ambitious plans for the colonial-era Liberty Street, and a turn-of-the-century celebration of "progress through electricity" called Edison Square. Or he could develop, update, and improve his underpopulated and anemic Tomorrowland.

OPPOSITE: Tomorrowland's vehicular interrelationships were designed for kinetic interest, "A World on the Move."

A Second Grand Opening

Four short years after its debut, Disneyland had what Walt called a "second opening," including a vastly expanded Tomorrowland that featured an all-new expansion of Autopia, Submarine Voyage, and the Matterhorn Bobsleds, plus the nearby Fantasyland Motor Boat Cruise. On June 14, 1959, Disneyland Guests received a flyer with the following announcement:

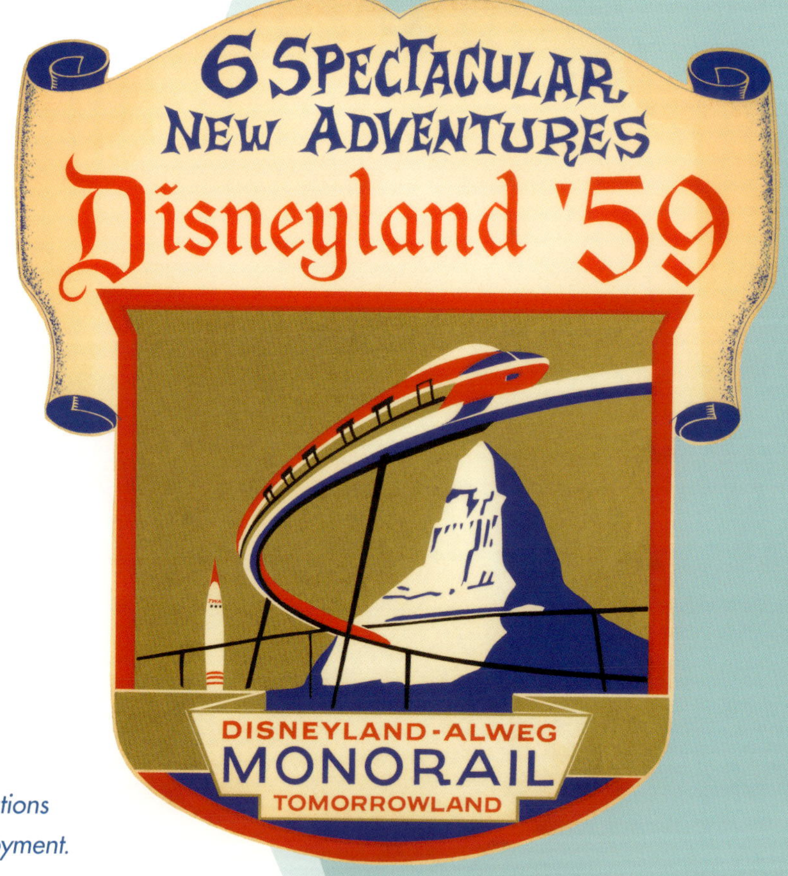

Yes, today is a special day at Disneyland . . . the occasion of our Press Preview and Dedication Ceremonies for Disneyland '59 and all its new adventures.

TODAY, all of these new adventures, including the Matterhorn Mountain and its bobsled runs; the Submarine Fleet on the Underseas Voyage; the Disneyland-Alweg Monorail Trains; the new Fantasyland Autopia, and the Motor Boat Cruise have been reserved for the press, celebrities and dignitaries who are taking part in the actual dedication ceremonies being staged for Press and Television cameras.

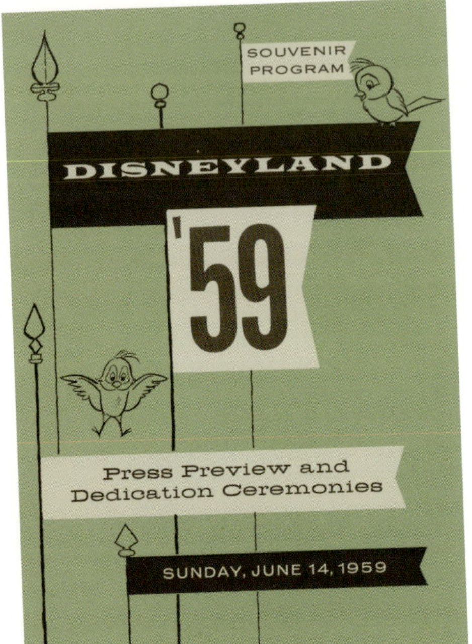

Of course all of Disneyland's other wonderful attractions will be open today for your entertainment and enjoyment.

TOMORROW, Monday, June 15th, all of the new Disneyland '59 attractions will officially open to the public.

A special Disneyland '59 Dedication parade will take place today beginning promptly at 1:30 p.m. on Main Street, and you are cordially invited to view this pageant which will start in Town Square, and follow a parade route down Main Street and around the Hub area.

Today's Parade and Dedication Ceremonies will all be on television tomorrow night over the ABC network in a special 90 minute program Kodak Presents—Disneyland '59. *In the Los Angeles area, this program will be shown over KABC, Channel 7 from 7:30–9 p.m.*

The Disneyland summer of 1959 was as much ballyhooed as the park's opening had been in 1955.

LEFT: A souvenir program for the Disneyland '59 opening gala.
ABOVE: Graphic detail, Disneyland '59 display element, artist uncredited.
RIGHT: Cover art for special newspaper color supplement advertising section, 1959.

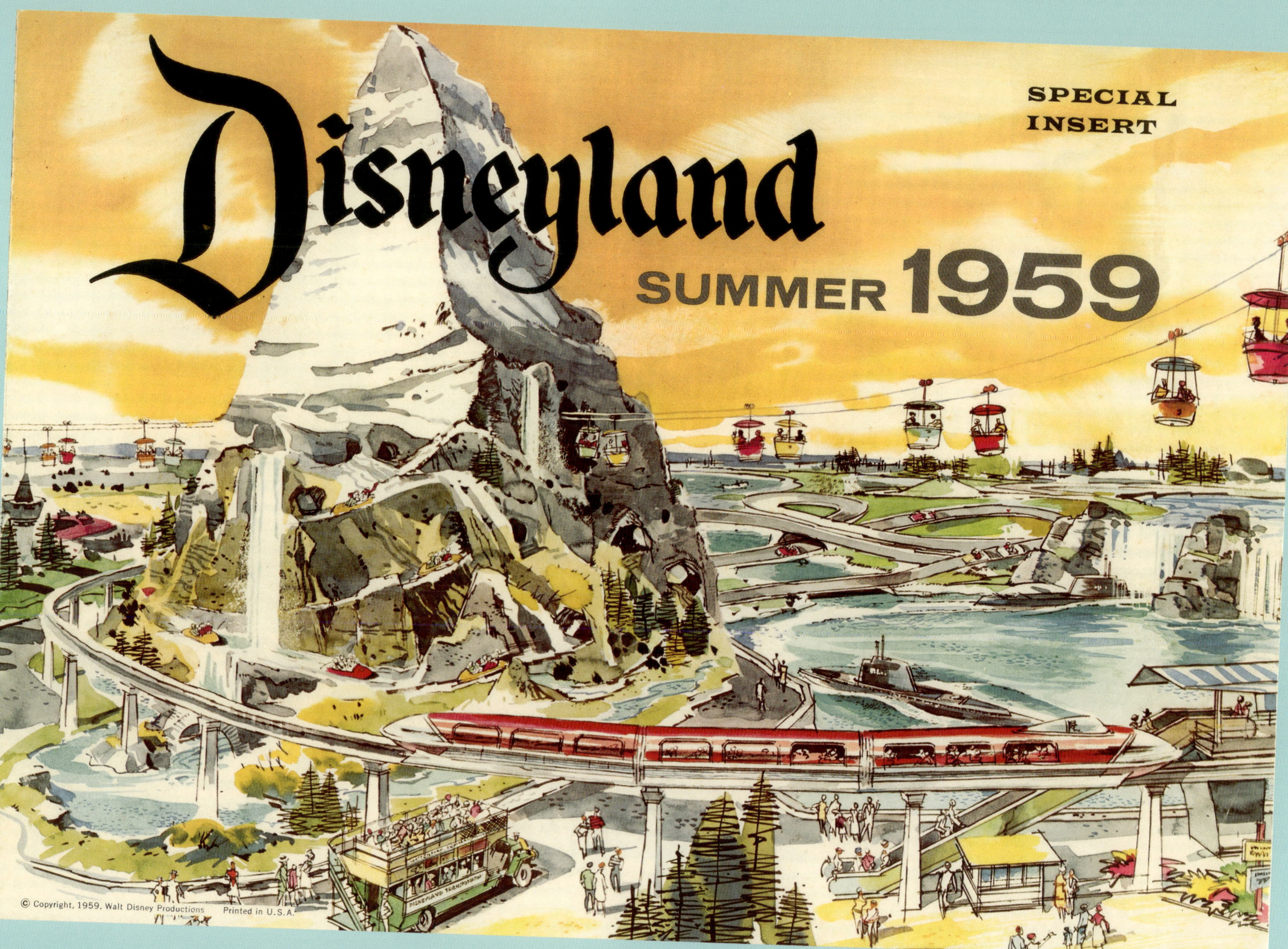
Disneyland
SPECIAL
INSERT
SUMMER 1959
© Copyright, 1959, Walt Disney Productions
Printed in U.S.A.

A Long Step Forward into the Future

The amiable master of ceremonies for the aforementioned television broadcast, Art Linkletter, proudly hailed the premiere of the newest Disneyland attraction: "You're about to see the debut of a revolutionary new form of transportation: the Monorail."

Linkletter introduced a filmed segment about the Monorail that made it clear that Walt wasn't slapping in a simple kiddie ride, or just looking for an entertaining excursion for Disneyland Guests. The new Disneyland-Alweg Monorail would demonstrate daily an innovative and immediately applicable solution to urban mass transportation problems. Alongside and above the congested motorways, a fleet of efficient, easy-to-build electric train lines could race, swiftly and silently.

"That's the Monorail," Linkletter said, "a long step forward into the future. Today you're seeing the first scheduled monorail system in operation. Soon, others will follow, heralding the day when such rapid transit systems will relieve America's crowded streets, and perhaps bring back the original meaning to the word 'freeway.'"

Past Walt Disney Imagineering executive and Disney Legend Marty Sklar recalled, "An executive of a major transportation company said later, 'You've built this entire system in less time, and for about the same money, that my company would allocate for a *feasibility* study.'"

That sunny Sunday afternoon, US Vice President Richard M. Nixon; his wife, Pat; and his daughters, Julie and Tricia, officially dedicated and were then the first passengers on the all-new Disneyland-Alweg Monorail System.

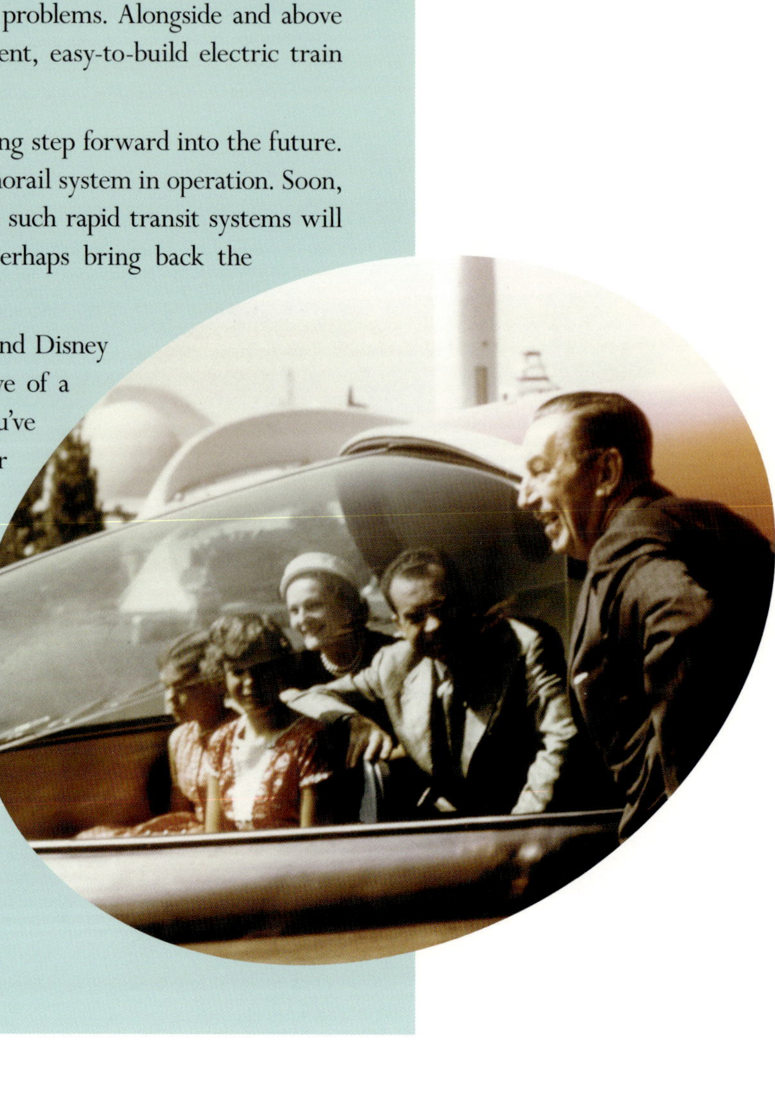

RIGHT: Vice President Richard Nixon and family at the June 14, 1959, grand opening of the Disneyland-Alweg Monorail System, Matterhorn Bobsleds, and Submarine Voyage at Disneyland.

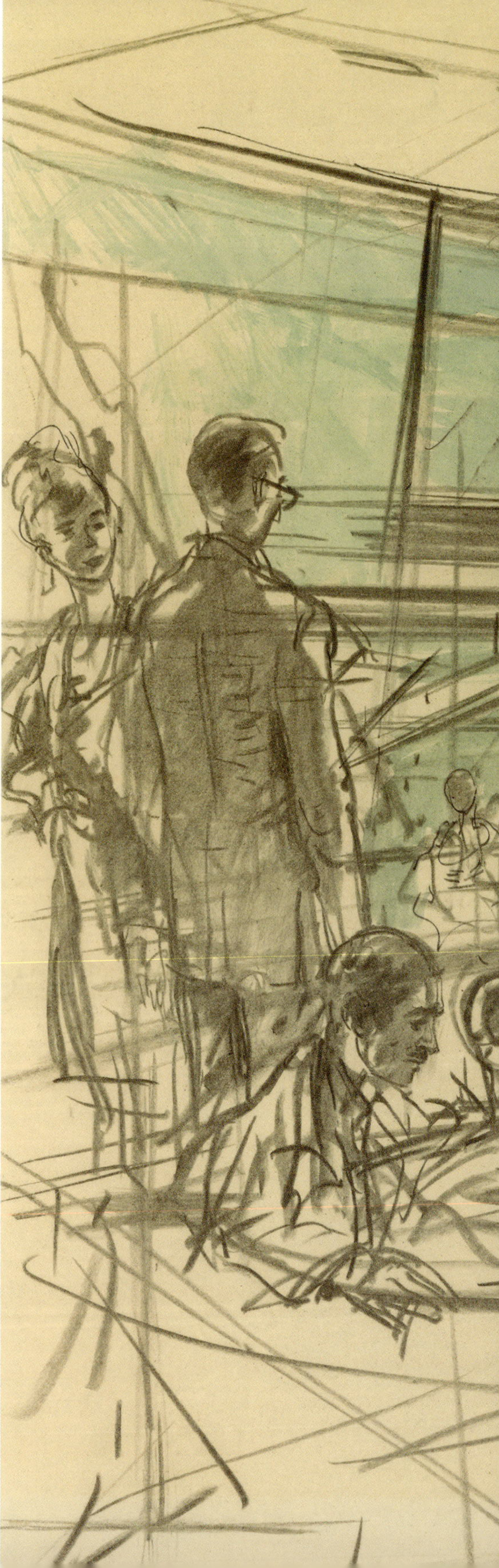

FAR RIGHT: Herb Ryman, "Dining Terrace Overlooking Monorail and Sub Ride," 1966.

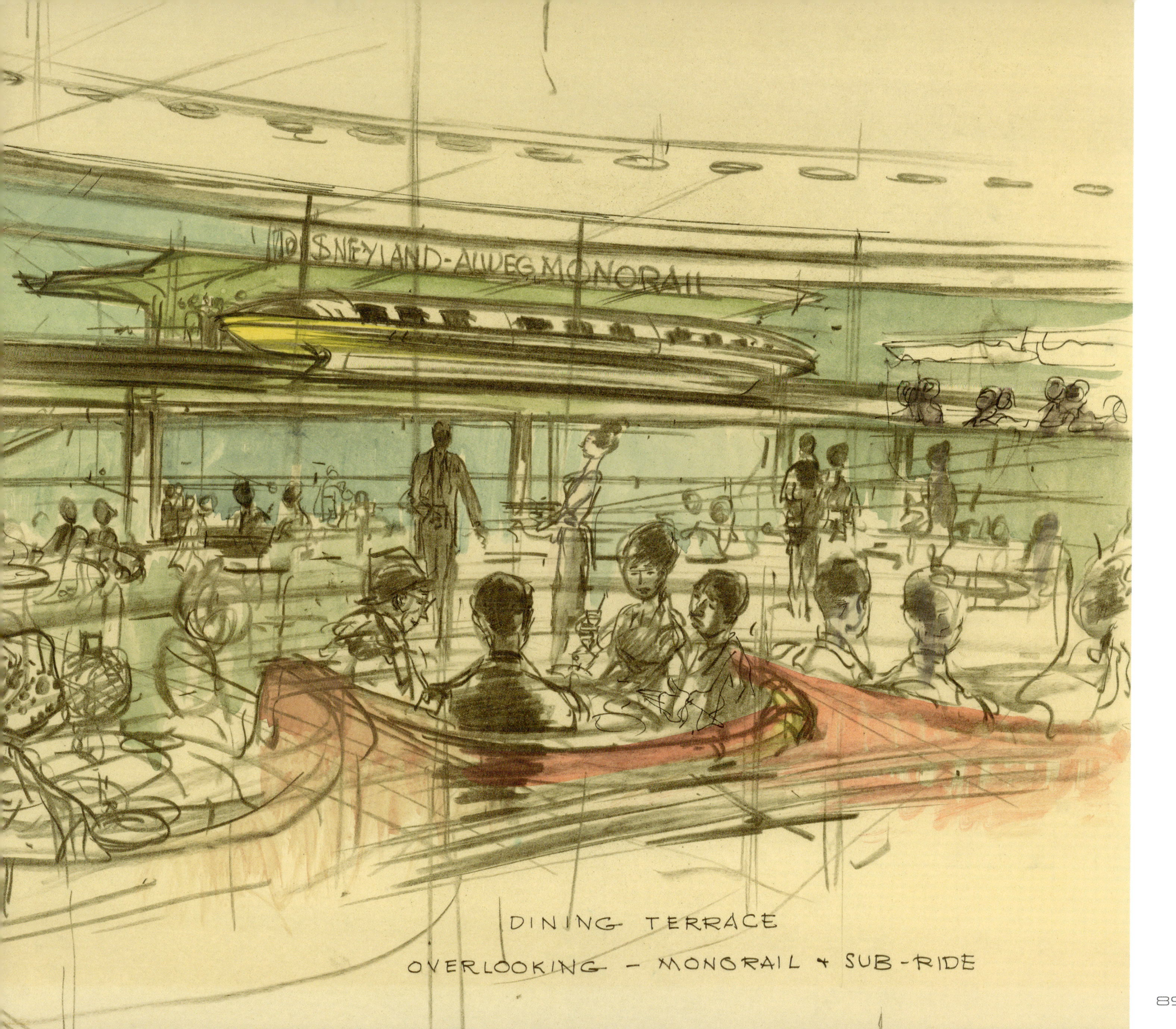
DISNEYLAND-ALWEG MONORAIL
DINING TERRACE
OVERLOOKING - MONORAIL + SUB-RIDE

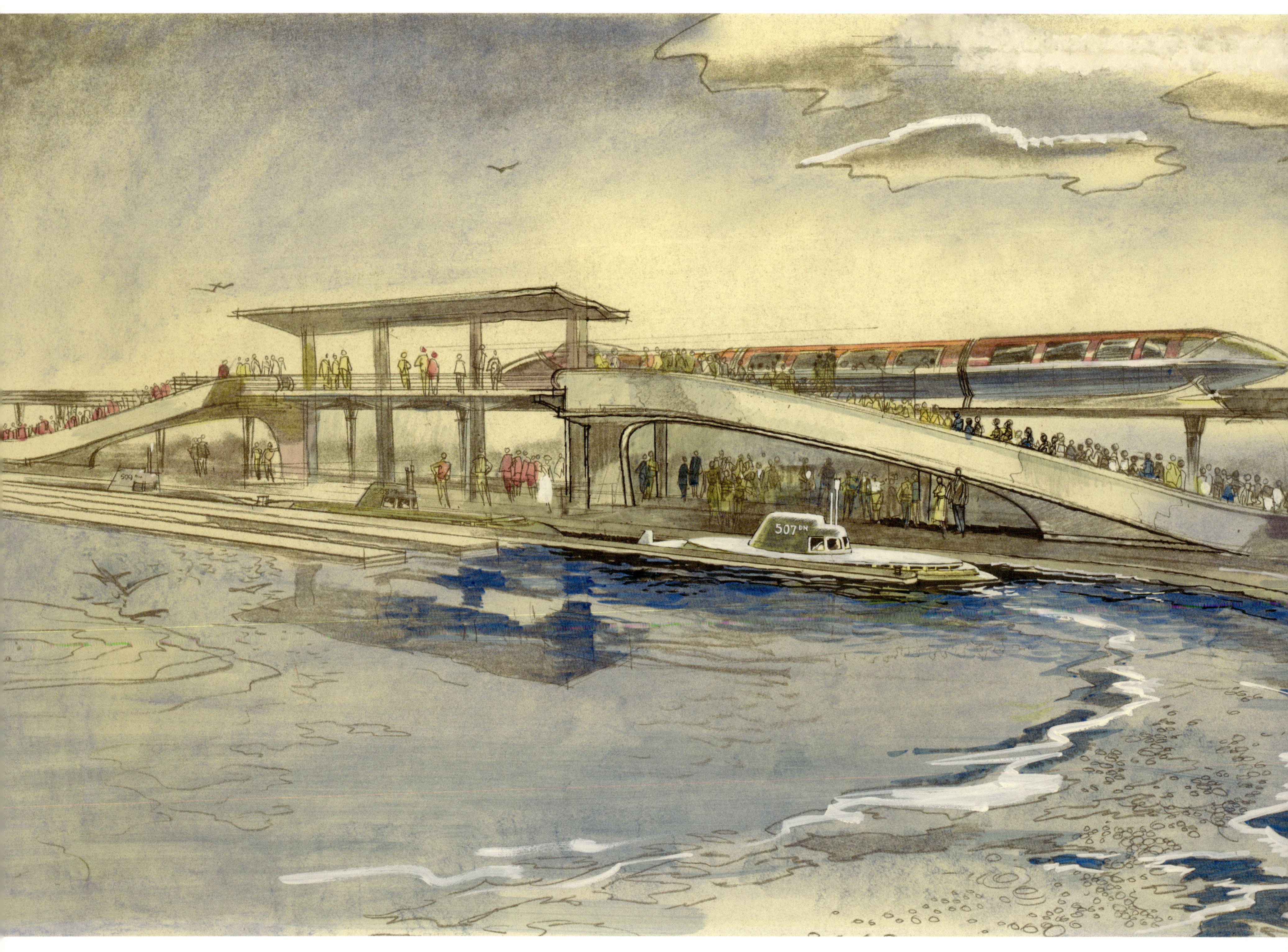
507DN

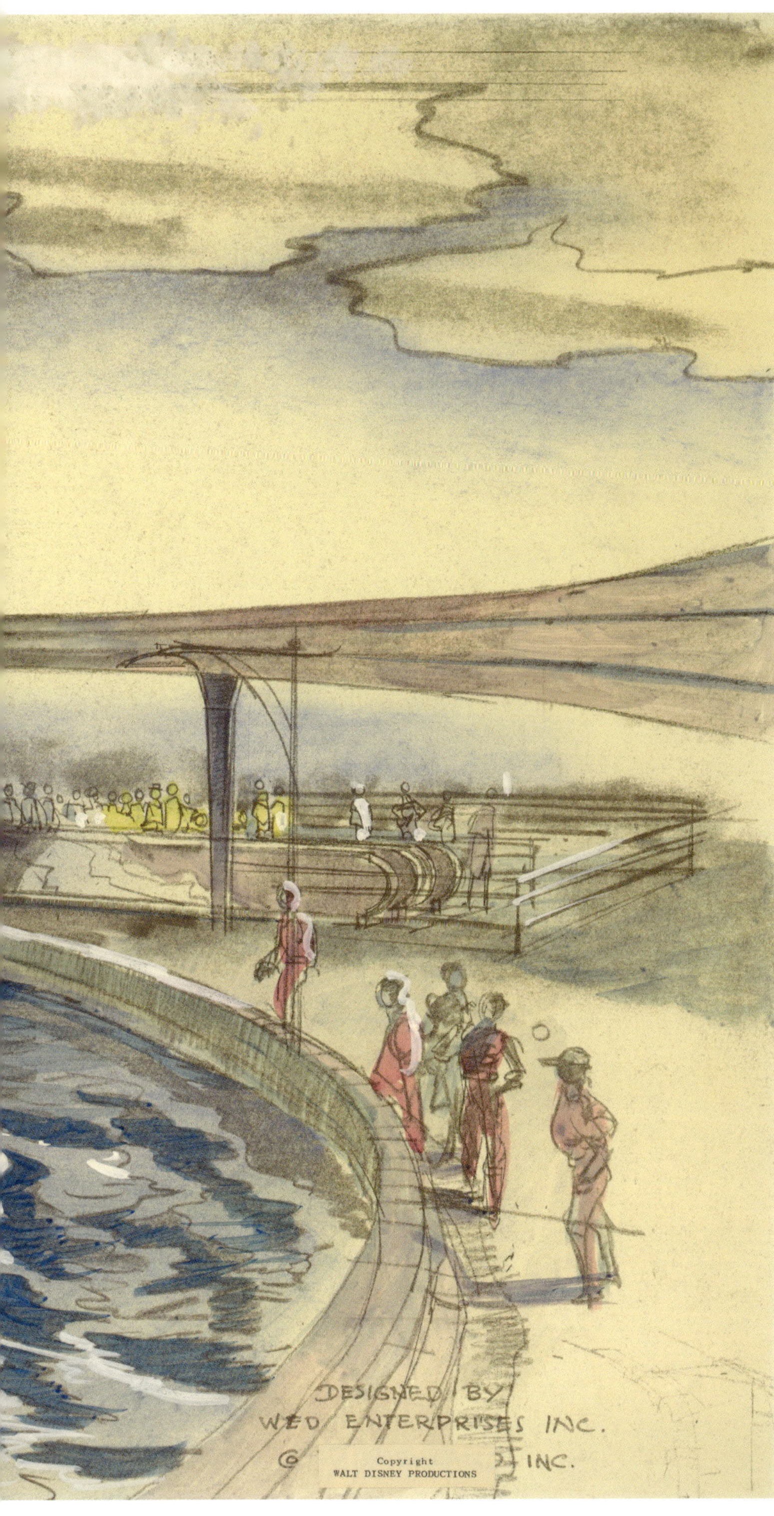

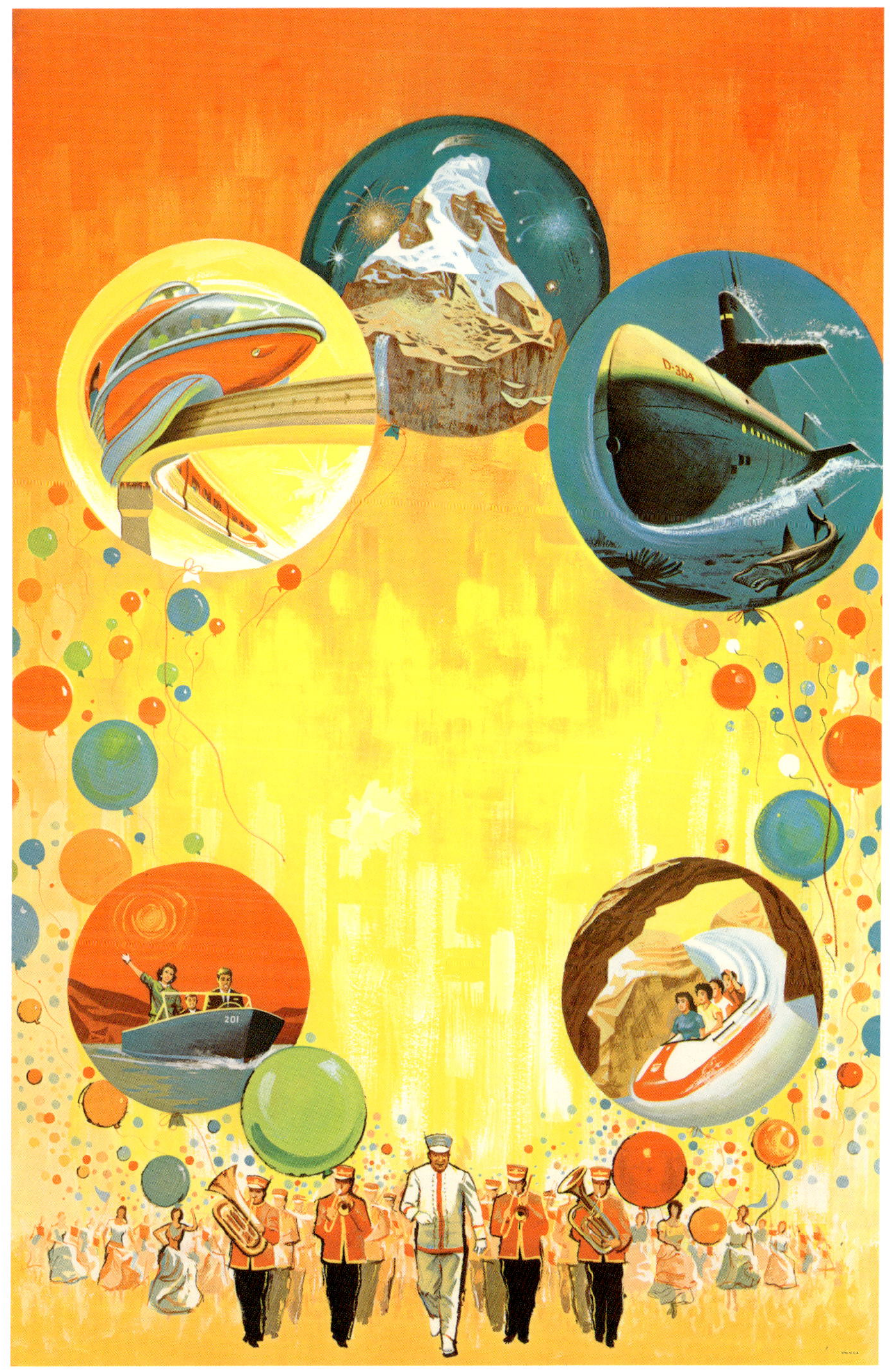

LEFT: Herb Ryman's elegant and serene Monorail Station concept, acrylic and pastel on diazo print, 1958.
ABOVE: Key art by John Hench for the 1960 featurette *Gala Day at Disneyland*, a color documentary covering the June 14, 1959, grand opening of the Monorail, Matterhorn, and Submarine Voyage.

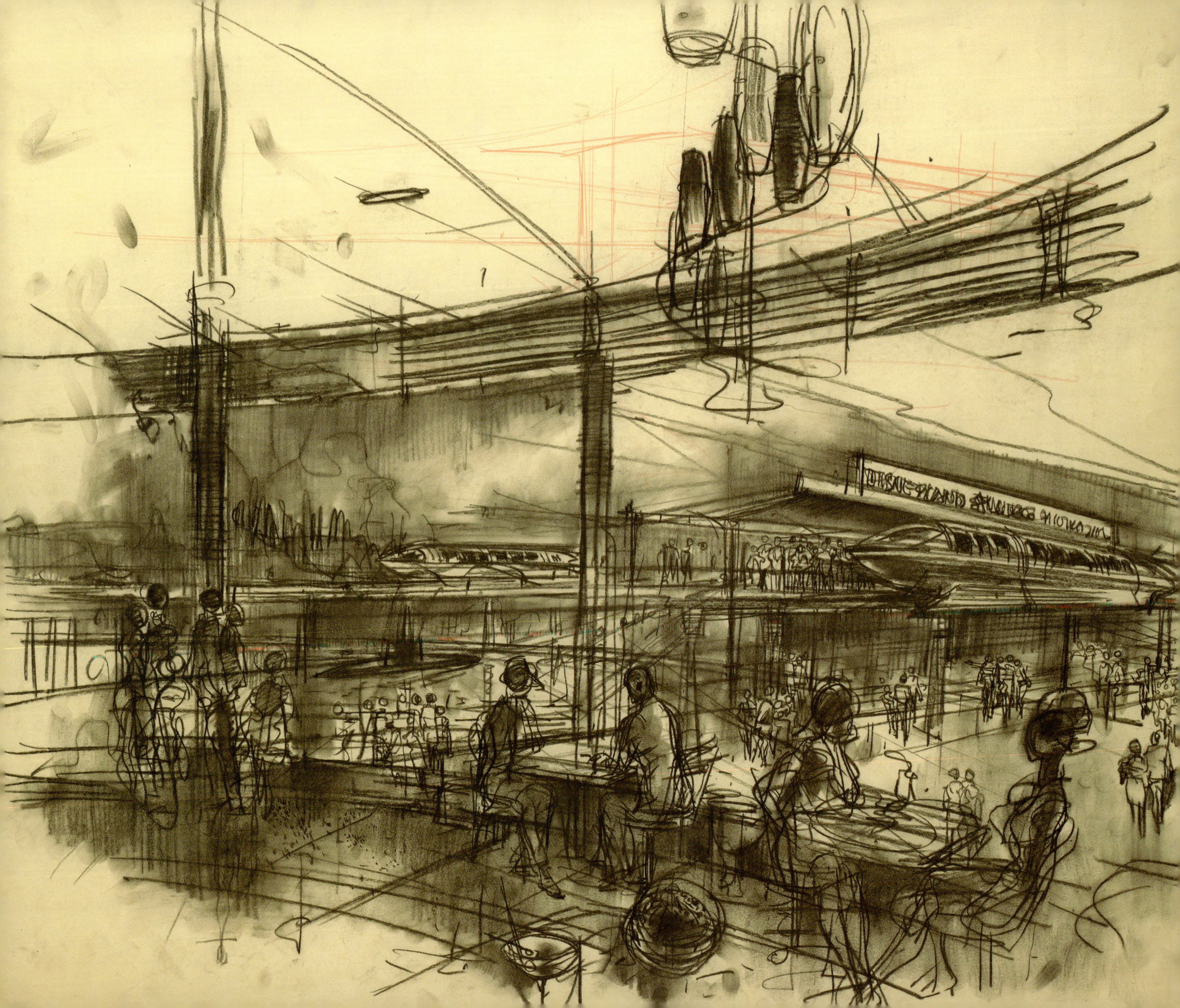

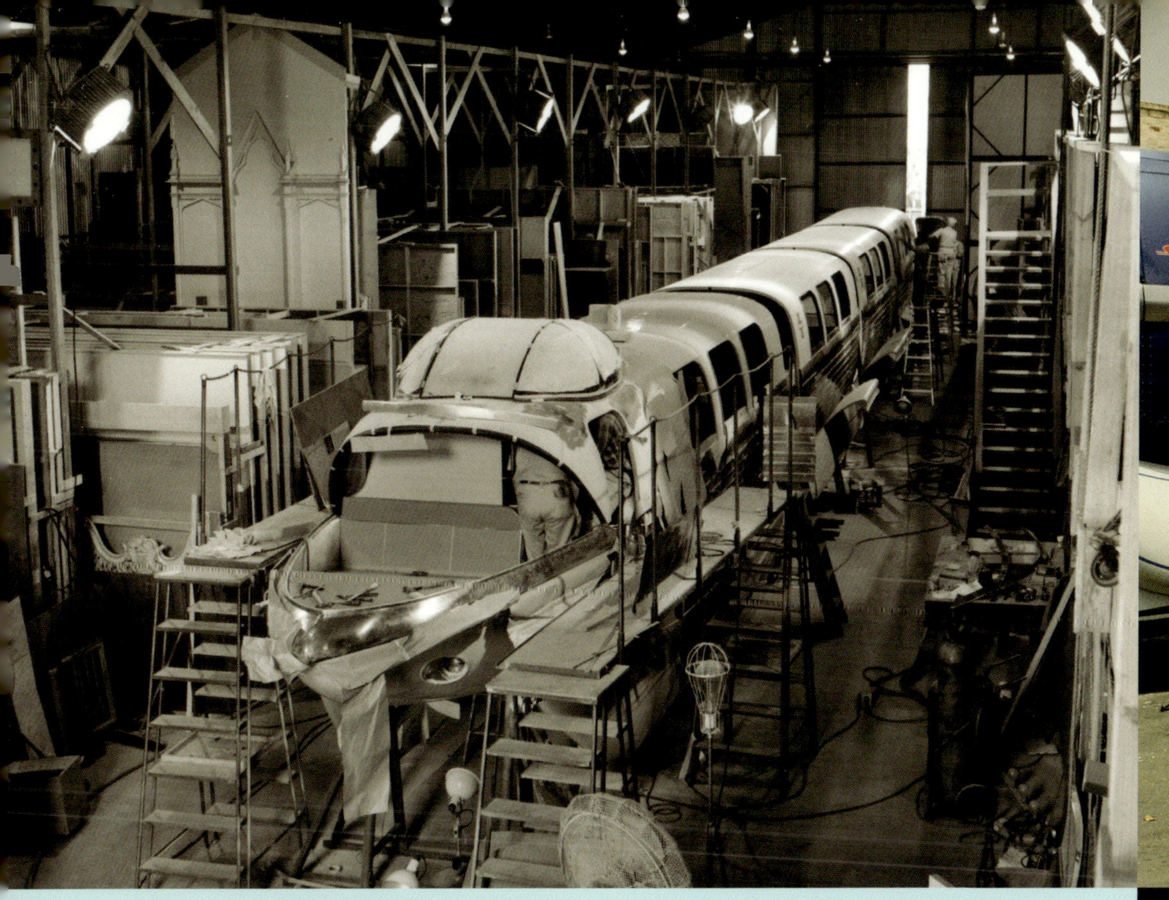

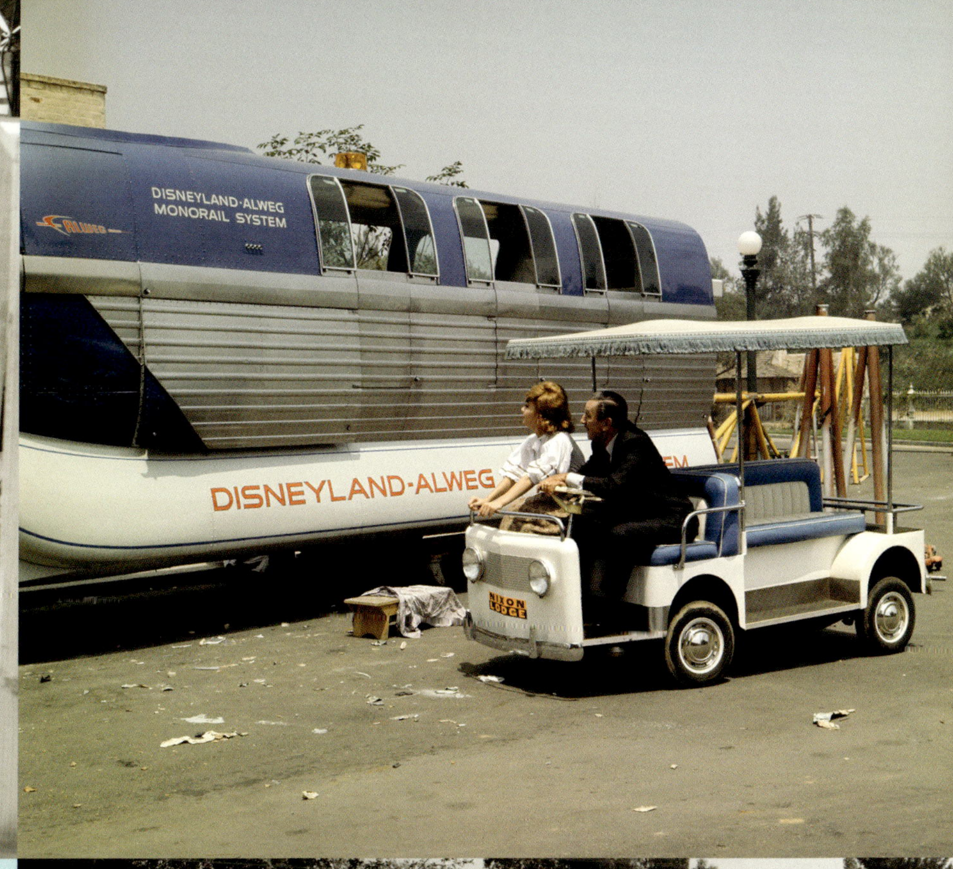

OPPOSITE: Herb Ryman rendering of an alternate angle of a dining terrace overlooking the Monorail and Submarine Lagoon, colored pencil and charcoal, 1966. ABOVE: Until the mid-1980s, the Disney Monorails were designed and built by Disney, in Disney facilities on the studio lot (in Burbank) and in nearby Glendale. TOP RIGHT: Walt gives Dany Saval, the ingenue of his 1962 comedy *Moon Pilot*, a look at a Mark II Monorail under construction. (For a breakdown of each Mark series within the Monorail fleets, see pages 130–131.) BOTTOM RIGHT: Any available space was useful and used when new trains were being built and placed in service, including the Residential Street set on The Walt Disney Studios lot.

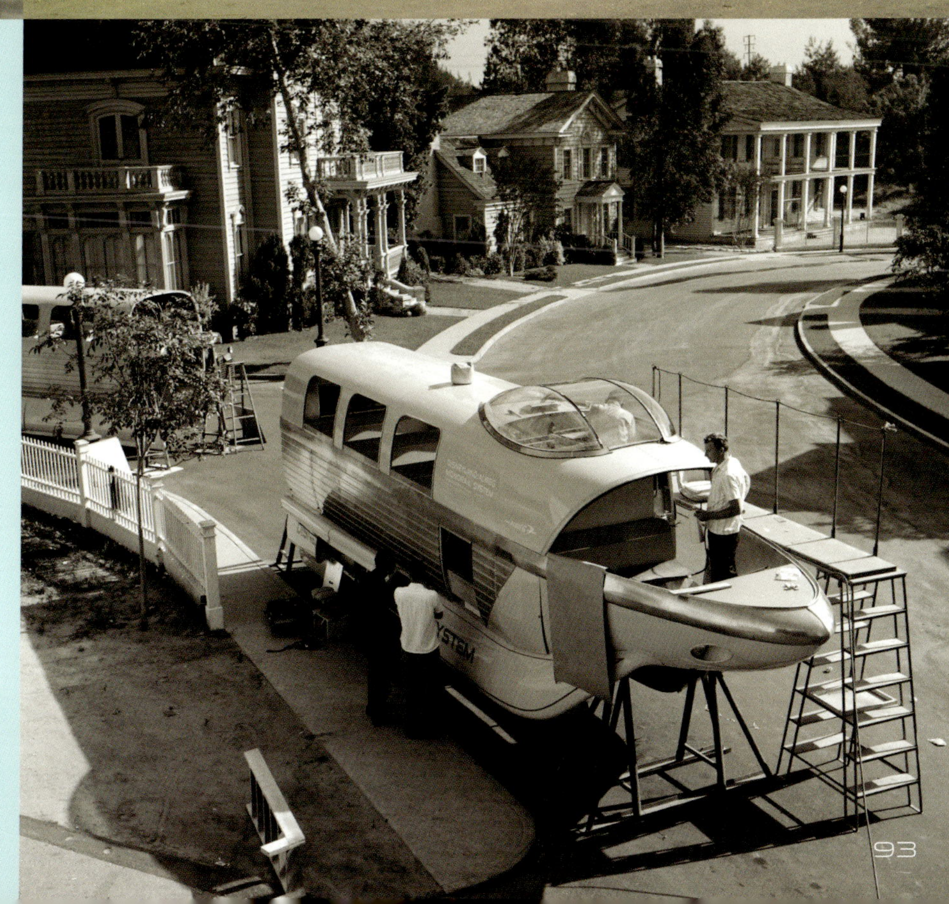

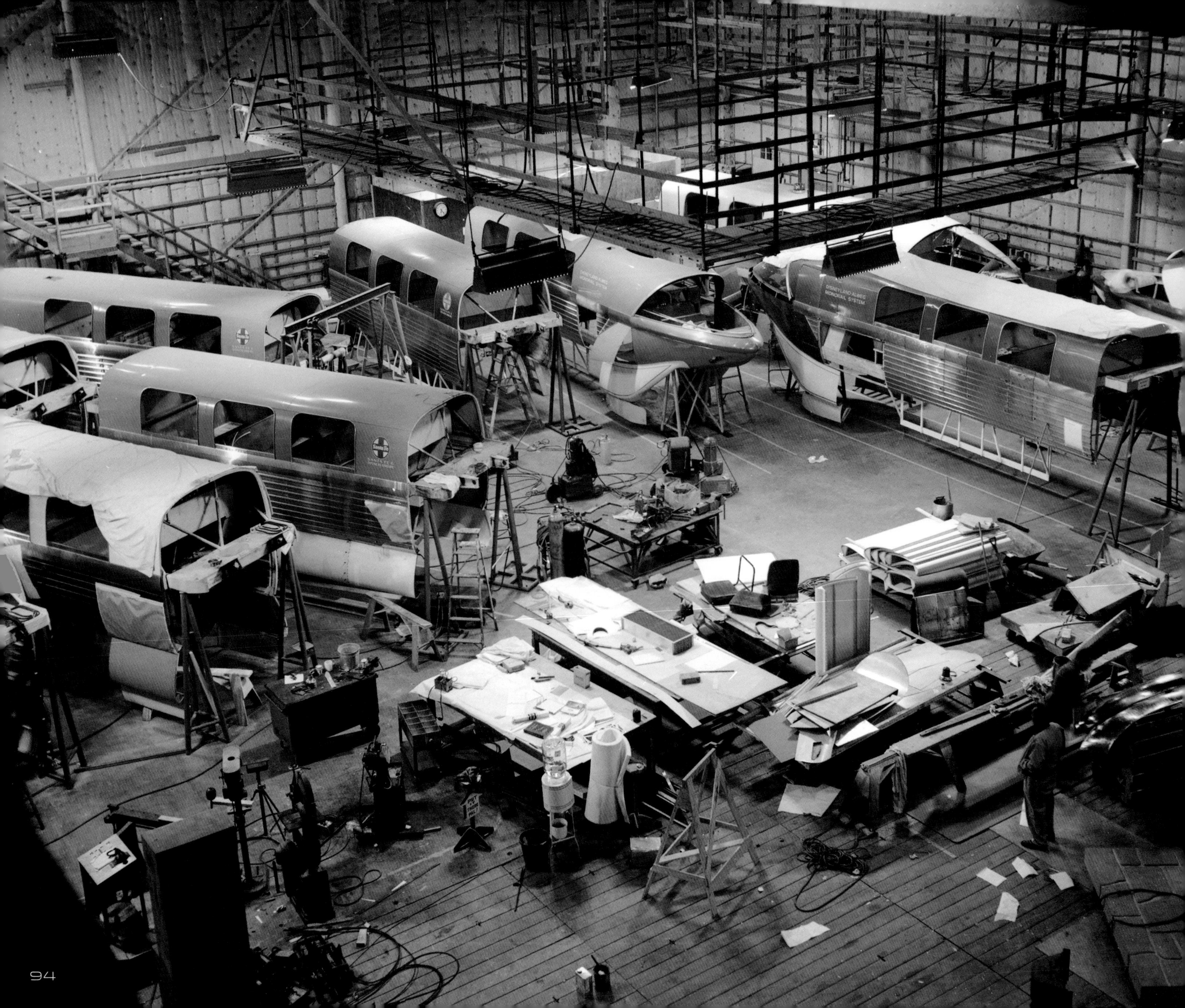
DISNEYLAND-ALWEG
MONORAIL SYSTEM

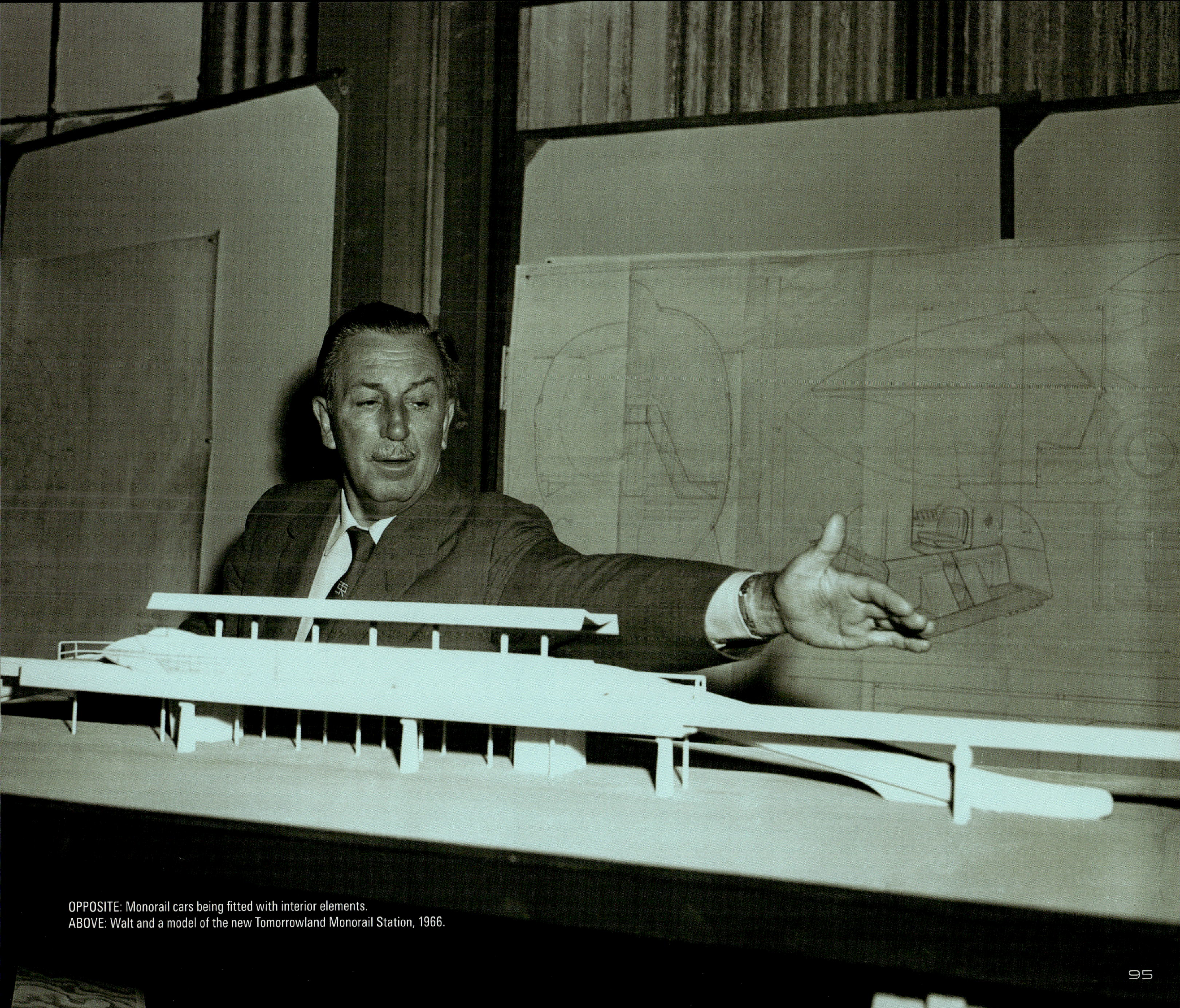

OPPOSITE: Monorail cars being fitted with interior elements.
ABOVE: Walt and a model of the new Tomorrowland Monorail Station, 1966.

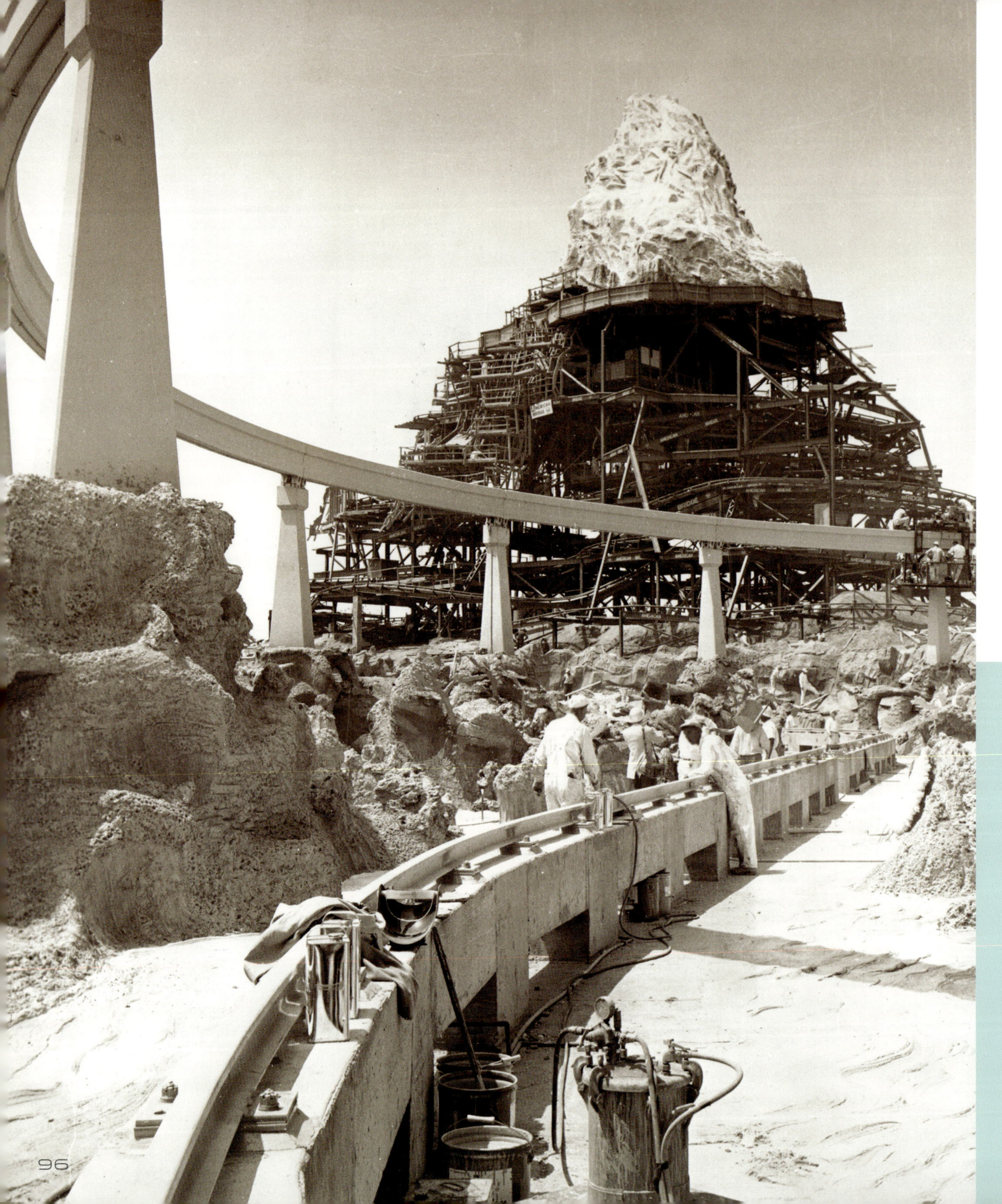

Although the Disney Monorail had been developed with Alweg, Disneyland had an exclusive agreement with the Santa Fe Railroad for *all* Disneyland railway attractions. So, until 1974, the Monorail was, officially, the "Disneyland-Alweg Monorail System, presented by the Santa Fe Railroad." Santa Fe logo medallions were located on the passenger cars, and park literature referred to the sponsorship. The participant agreement with the Santa Fe ended in 1974, and the Alweg name remained on the Disneyland Monorails until 1976—even though by that time the company had been defunct for a decade or more.

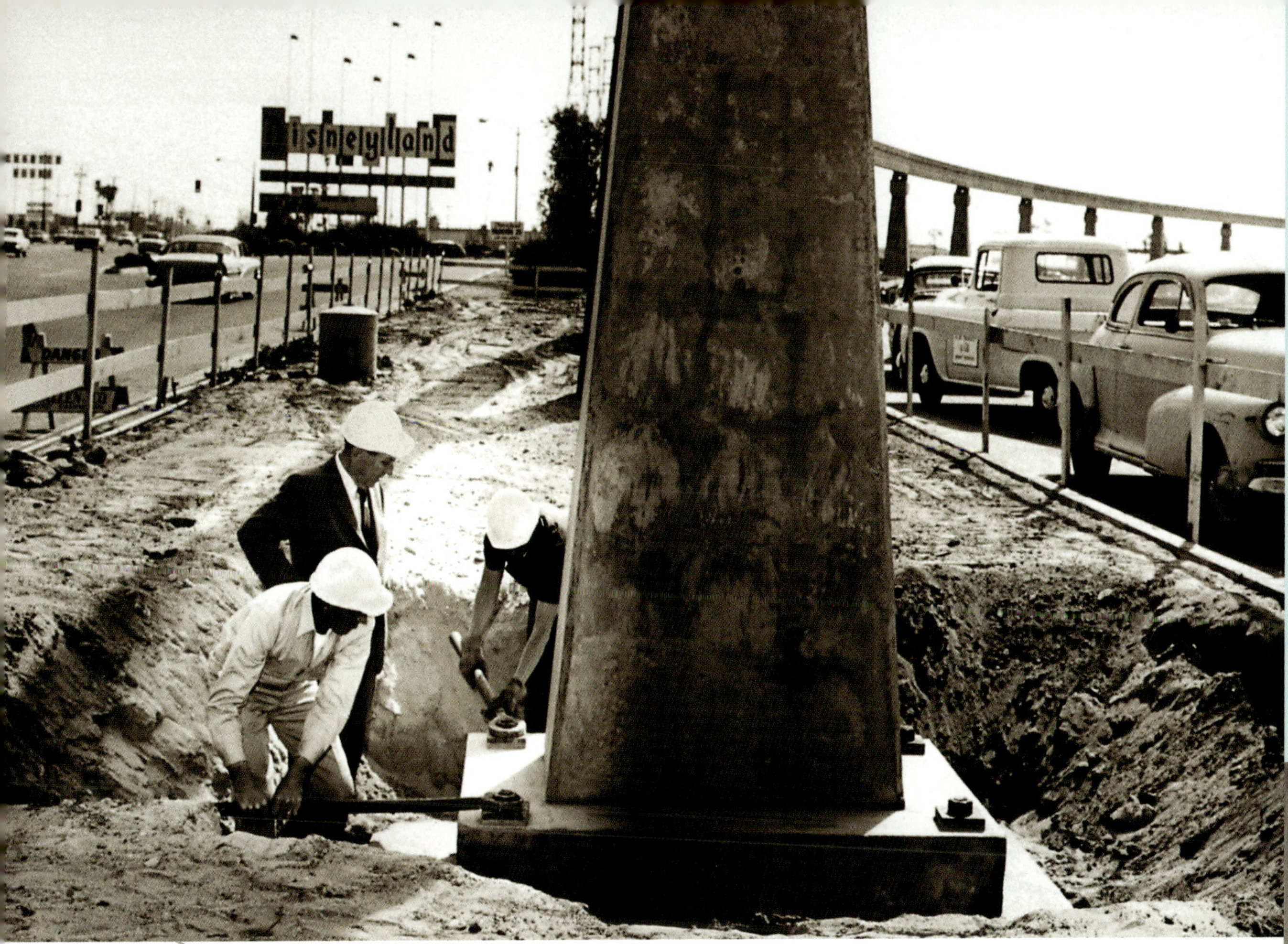

As such, the Monorail experience offered beautifully designed views of the Tomorrowland area, elegant vistas from both inside and outside the trains, and thrilling kinetics to ground-level pedestrians and other observers as the graceful trains glided on their elevated "Highway in the Sky."

The red Mark I Disneyland-Alweg Monorail that debuted in June 1959 was joined the following month by a companion Mark I vehicle in a complementary blue. Both three-car trains plied an elegant circular route of just eight-tenths of a mile, beginning and ending at the Tomorrowland Monorail Station. (For a breakdown of each Mark series within the Monorail fleets, see pages 130–131.)

The track layout was meticulously engineered to include curvatures 120 feet in radius, over- and underpasses, and grades up to 7 percent, in order to demonstrate the practicality and applicability of the system under all manner of real-world construction and topographic conditions. The beams and pylons as constructed for the park, although smaller than the original Alweg system, were of a scale that could be applied to use for any urban single-track monorail system.

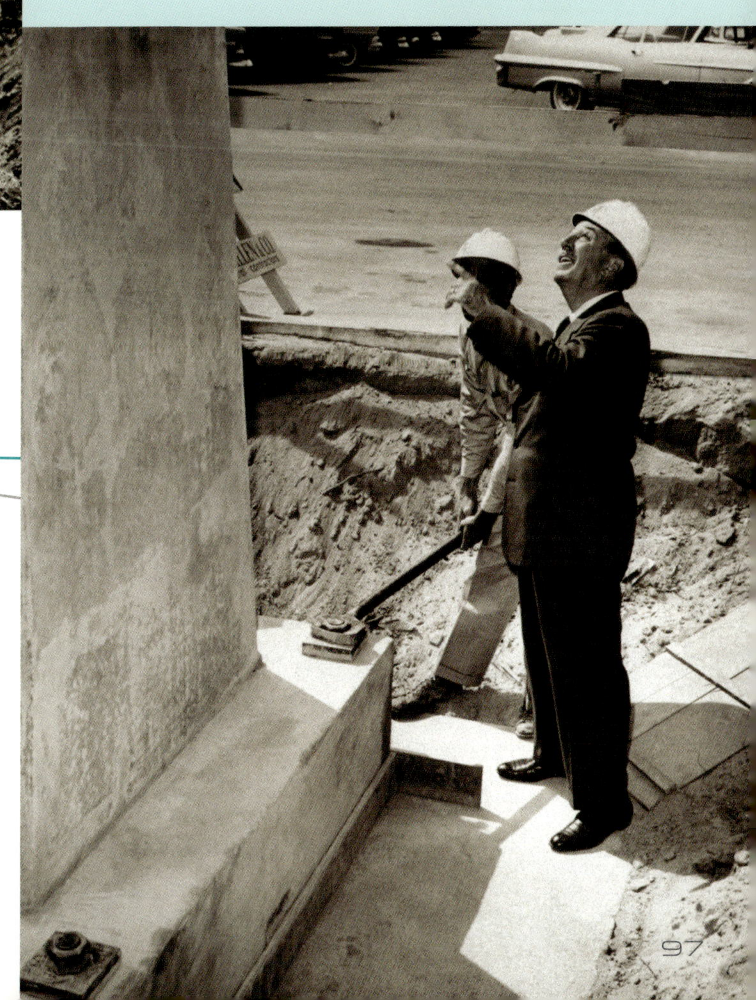

The 1967 renovation of Tomorrowland was promoted and celebrated as "A World on the Move." The variety of innovative and one-of-a-kind vehicles in daily operation vividly supports that theme. RIGHT: Vehicle scale and clearance elevation by John Hench, 1966.

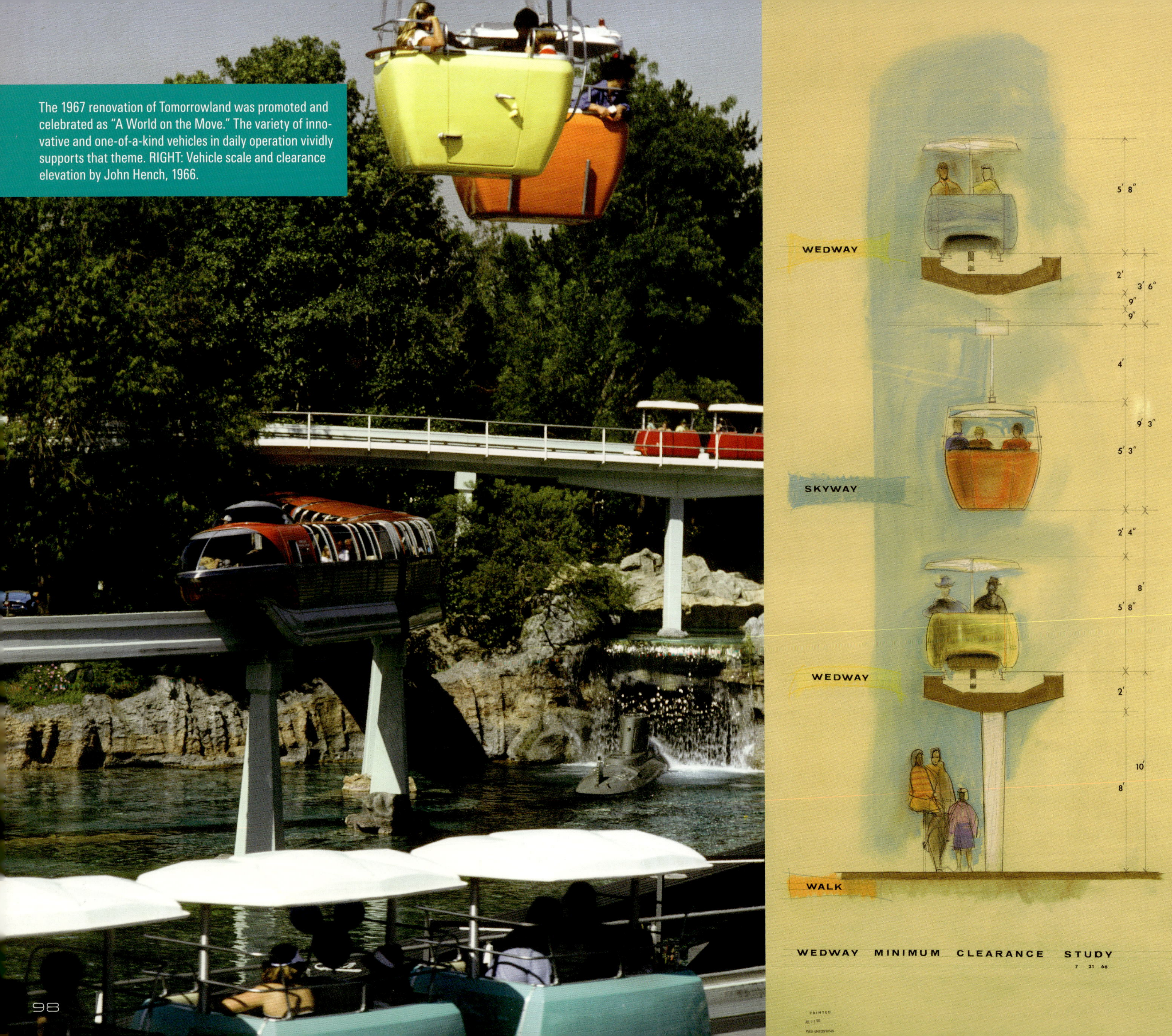

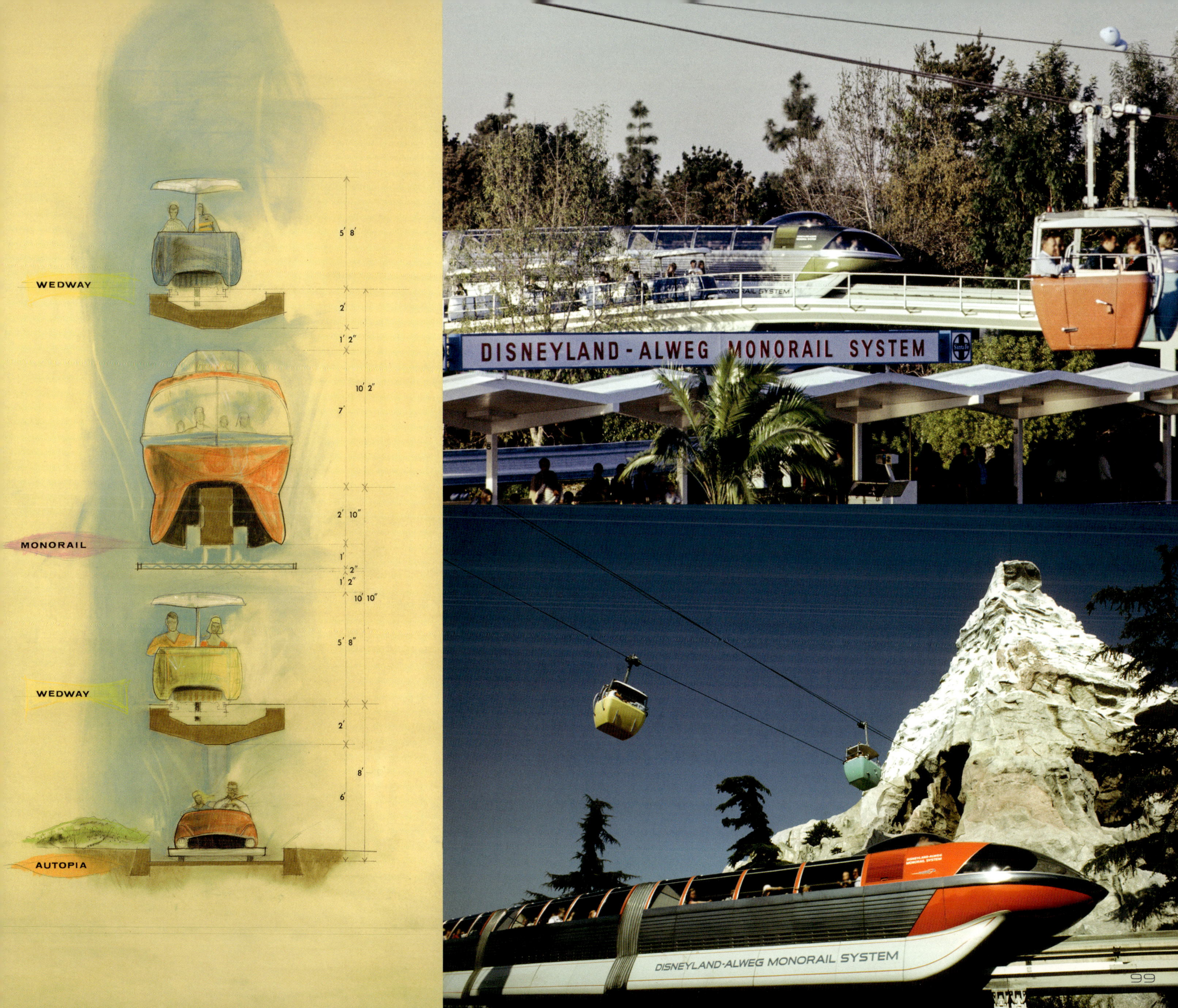
WEDWAY
5' 8"
2'
1' 2"
10' 2"
7'
2' 10"
MONORAIL
1'
2"
1' 2"
10' 10"
5' 8"
WEDWAY
2'
8'
6'
AUTOPIA
DISNEYLAND - ALWEG MONORAIL SYSTEM
DISNEYLAND-ALWEG MONORAIL SYSTEM

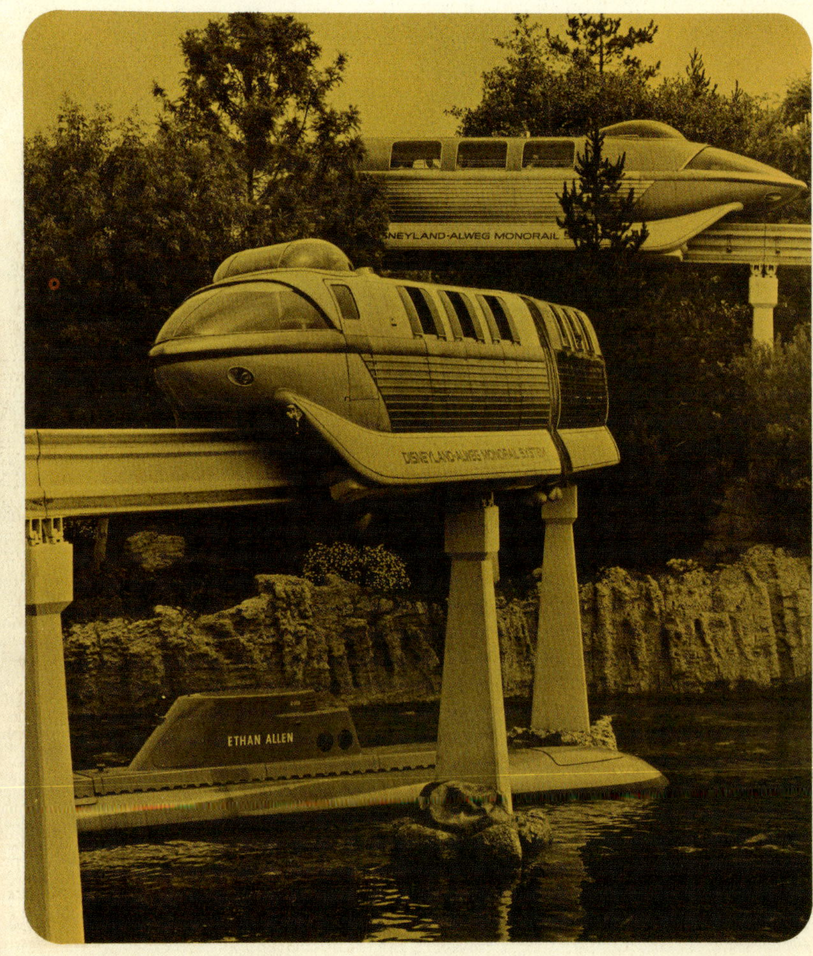

The Highway In The Sky

Story Guide and Operating Procedures

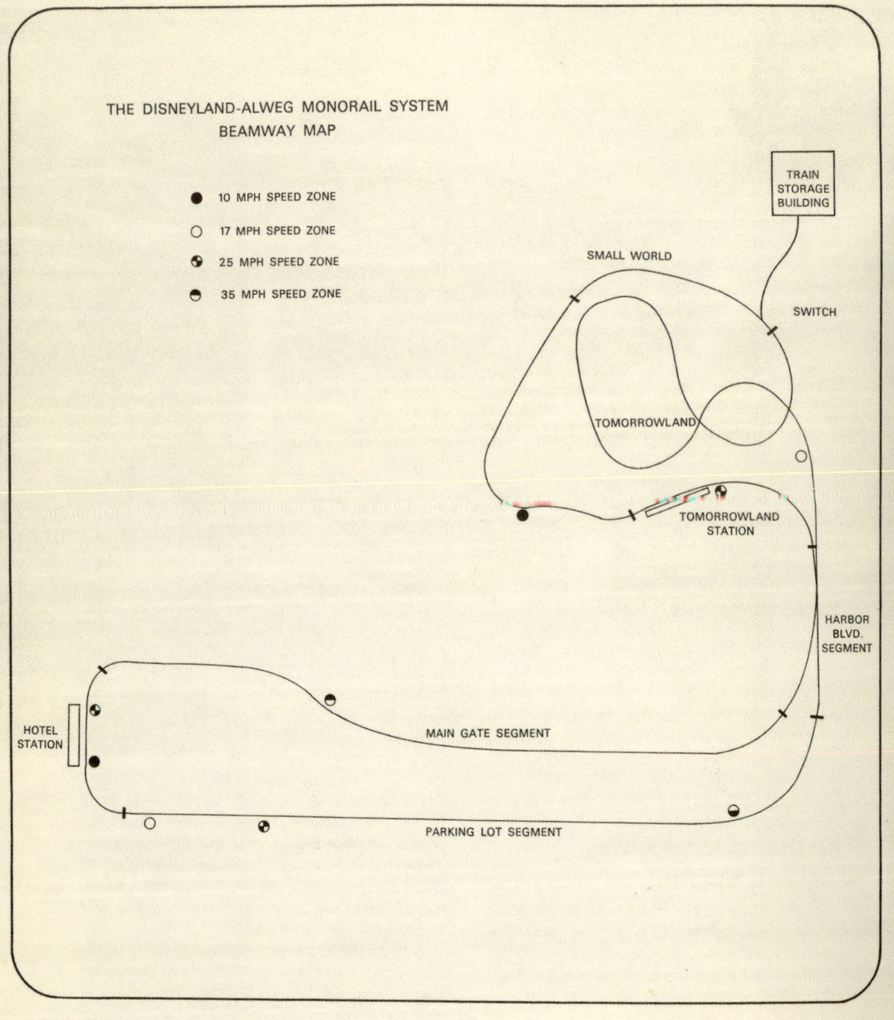

THESE PAGES: Page selections from a 1966 Cast Member training handbook for the Disneyland-Alweg Monorail System.

"Training was fundamental to issues such as operations and safety," Disney Legend Jim Cora says. "But also key to the value employees placed on their roles, and an understanding of the story they were part of telling."

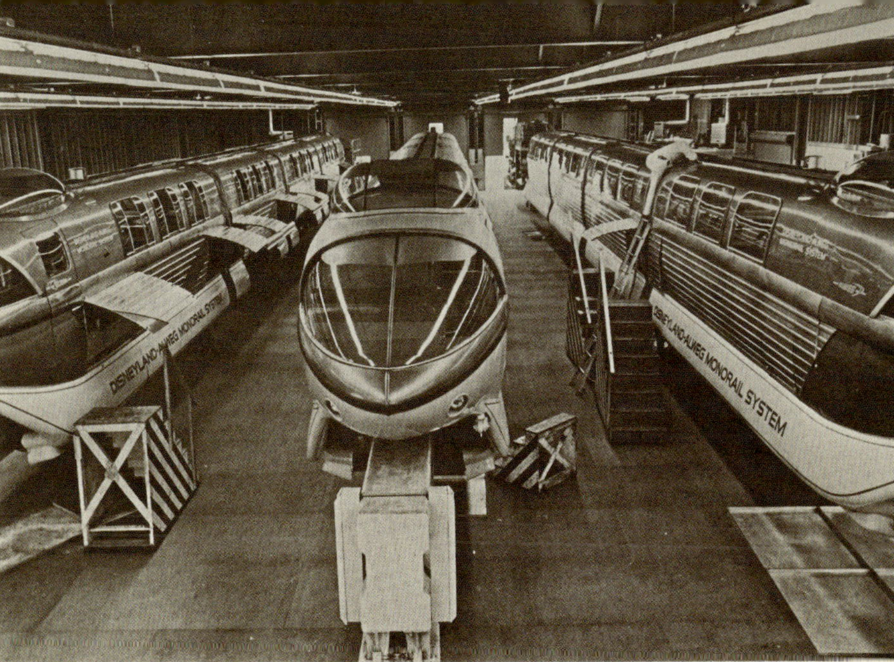

DISNEYLAND-ALWEG MONORAIL SYSTEM FACT SHEET

OPENING DATE: June 14, 1959.

REOPENING: June, 1962.

TOTAL LENGTH: 12,300 feet—almost 2½ miles.

NUMBER OF TRAINS: Three.

SEATING CAPACITY: 108 passengers per train.

POWER FROM TRACK: 600 DC volts.

MOTORS IN TRAIN: Four 55 horsepower motors.

LENGTH OF TRAIN: 110 feet.

HEIGHT OF BEAMWAY: Lowest point—5 feet; highest point—31 feet; average height—20 feet.

LENGTH OF BEAMS: 32 feet to 60 feet.

DESIGN STRENGTH OF BEAMS: 5,000 pounds per square inch.

TIRES USED IN TRAINS: Pneumatic rubber tires (960 per train).

TRIPS PER HOUR WITH THREE-TRAIN OPERATION: 19.5.

THEORETICAL HOURLY CAPACITY: 2,100.

LENGTH OF TOMORROWLAND LOADING PLATFORM: 100 feet.

LENGTH OF HOTEL LOADING PLATFORM: 112 feet.

TRIP TIME: 6 minutes and 45 seconds.

CYCLE TIME: 9 minutes and 20 seconds.

MANPOWER: One shift during peak operation—13.

29

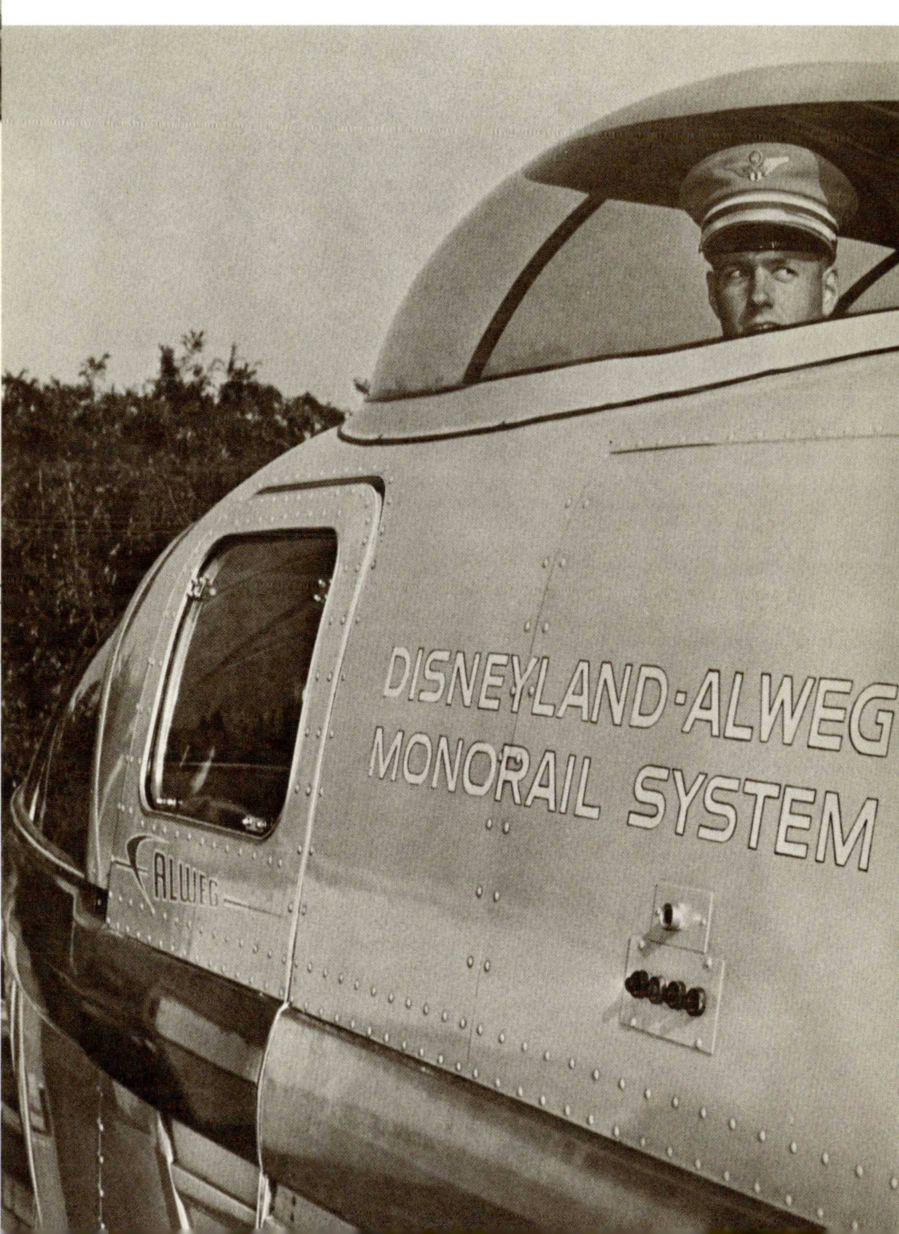

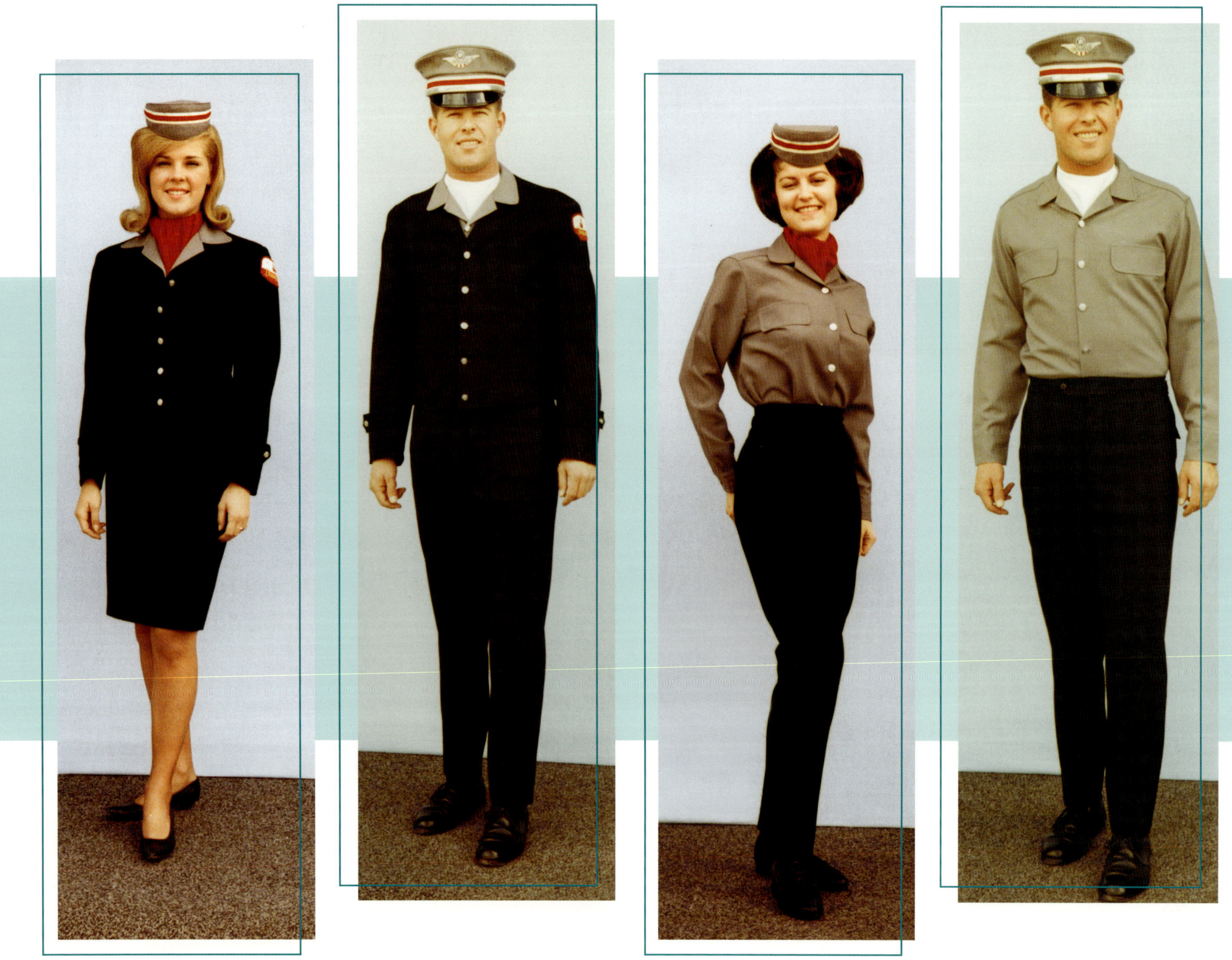

"Uniforms are for the Army," a decades-old Disneyland Cast Member handbook says, "where things must be, well . . . uniform. We wear costumes." Although in the case of the Monorails, those costumes intentionally resemble very stylish and snappy . . . uniforms.

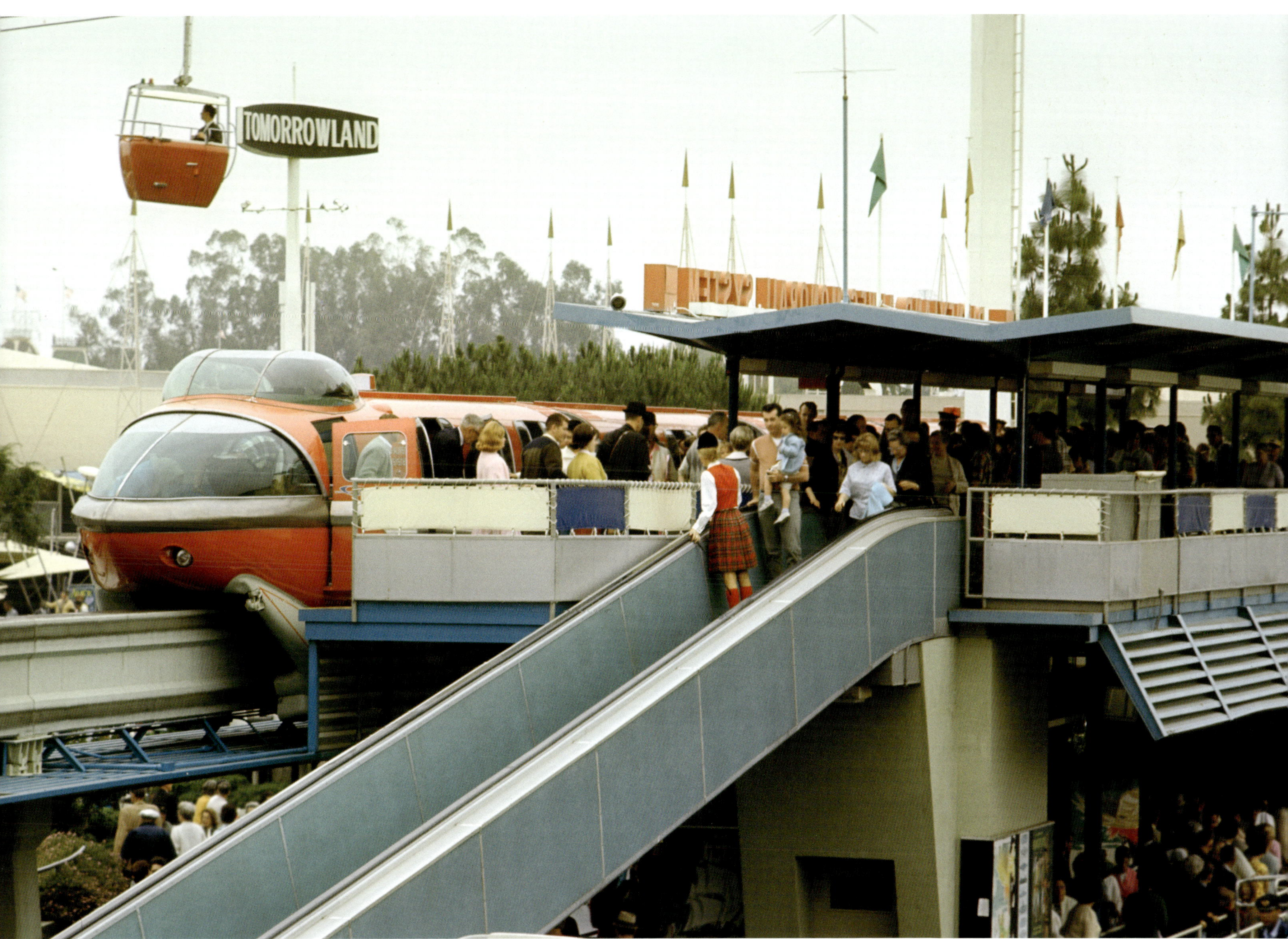
TOMORROWLAND

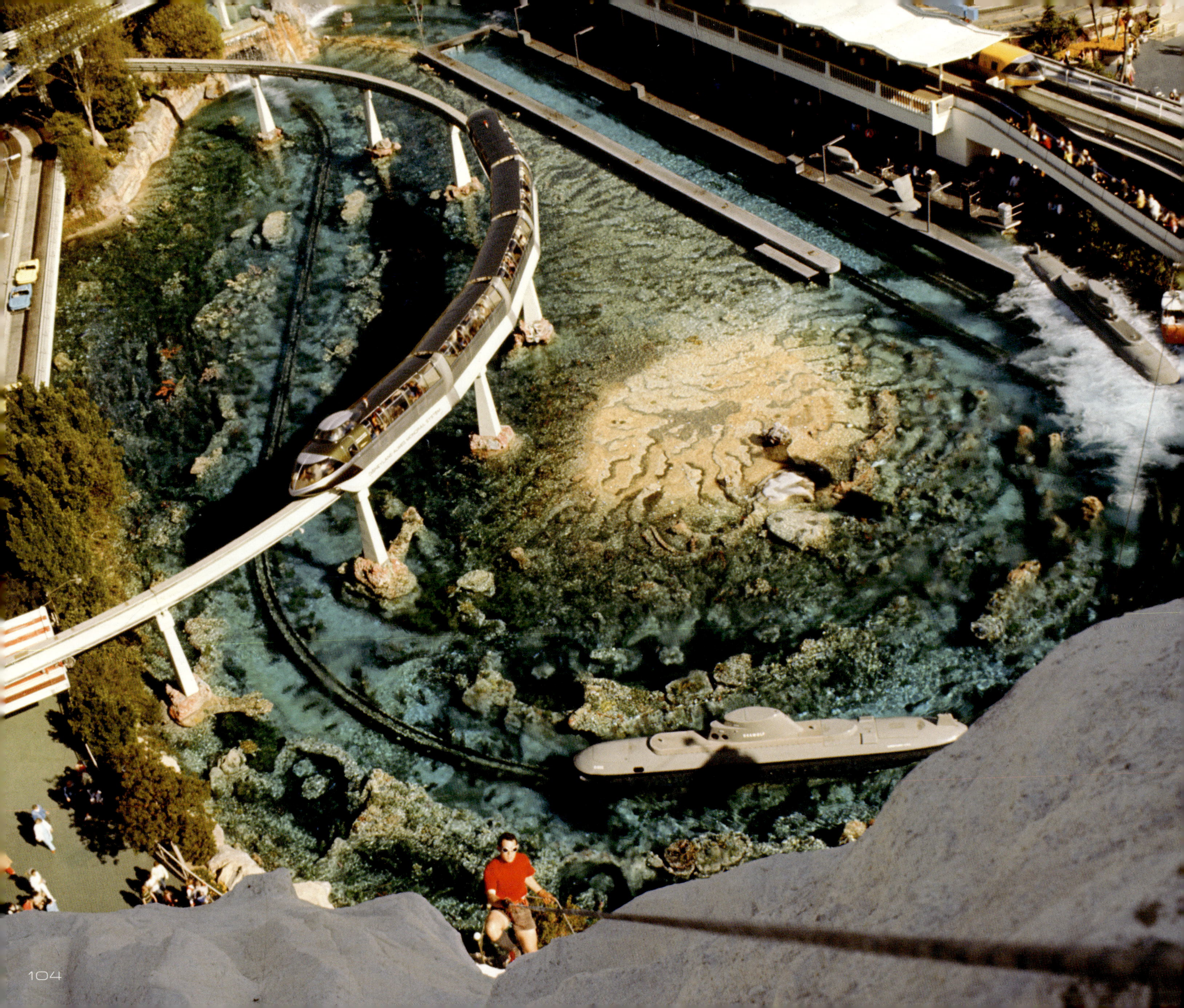

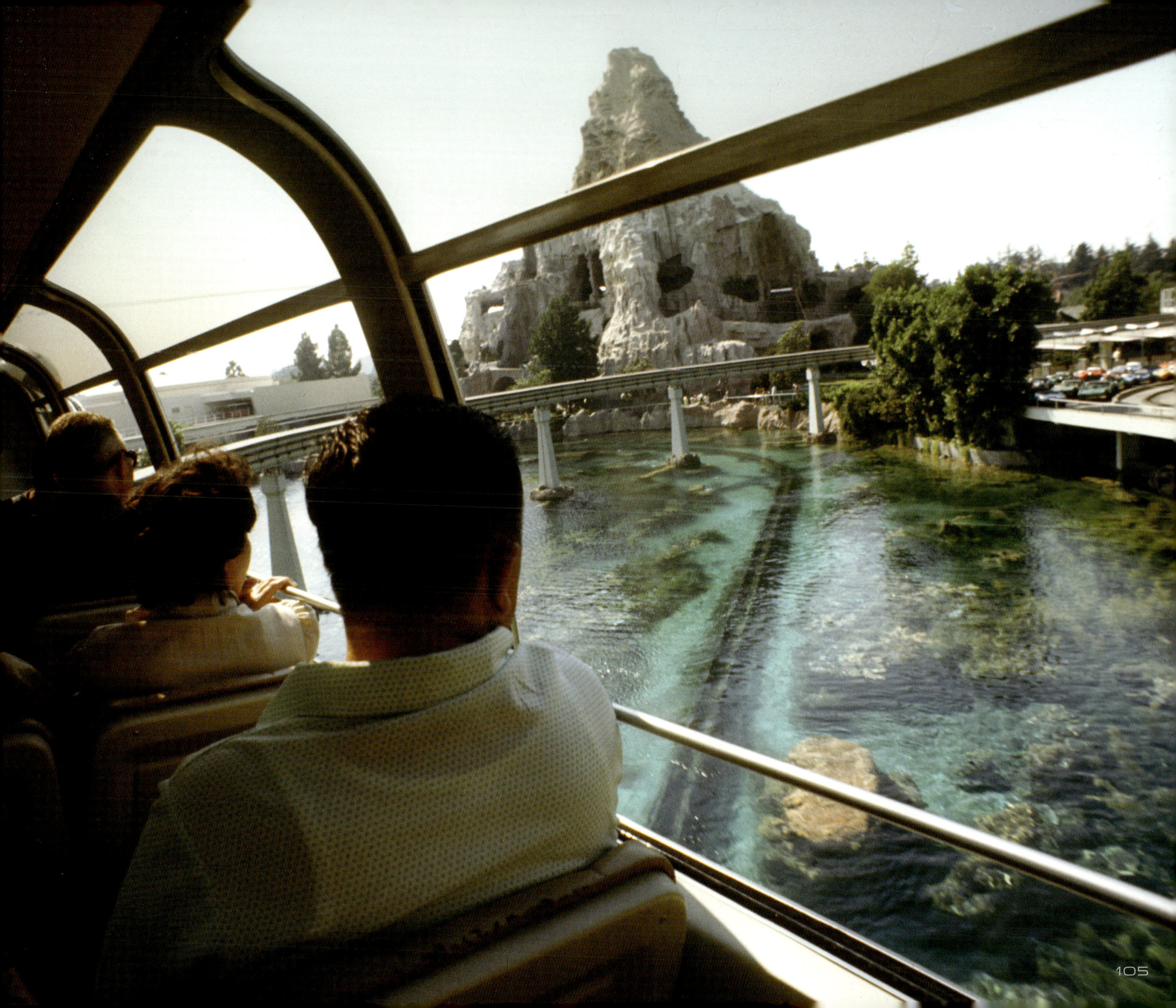

The Retlaw Connection

Something not widely known is that Disneyland was not the owner of the Disneyland Monorail—Walt Disney owned it *personally*. Walt had formed a privately held company called Retlaw Enterprises to control the benefits from his professional role, royalties, and the rights to his name and likeness—and to manage two Disneyland attractions that he personally owned: the steam trains and the Monorail. (The name "Retlaw" is "Walter" spelled backward.)

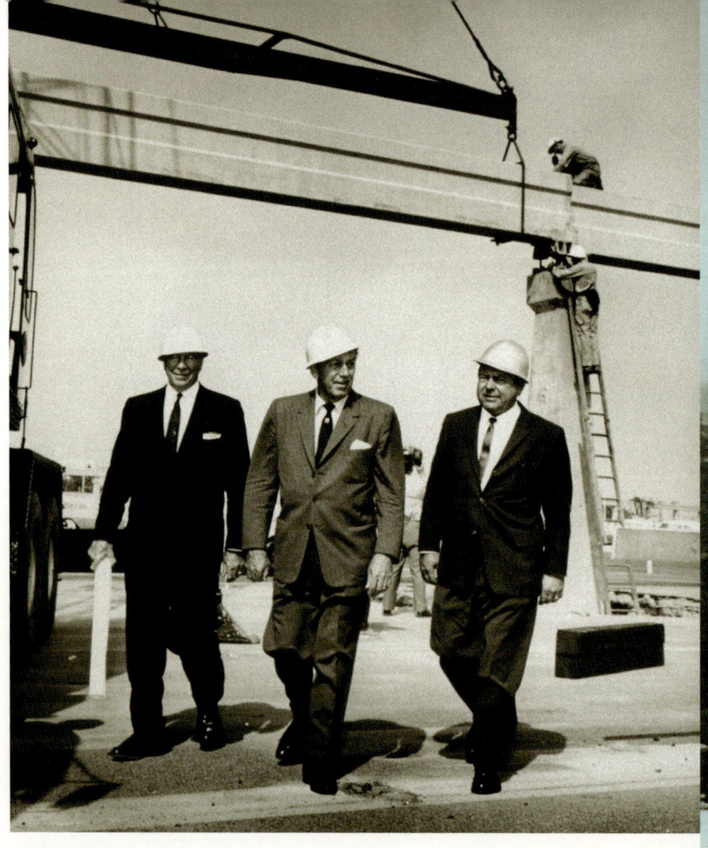

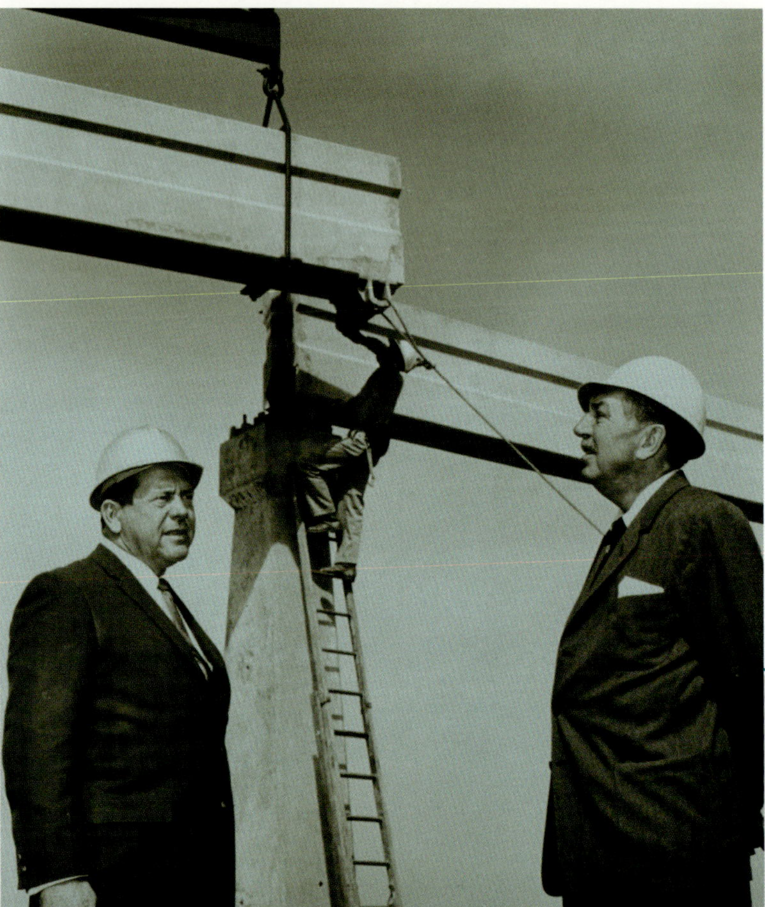

Retlaw paid fees to Disneyland for the attraction rights-of-way and employed those that worked at the attraction. Walt had also owned the Viewliner and the horse-drawn streetcars on Main Street, U.S.A. All of these assets were sold to Walt Disney Productions in 1982.

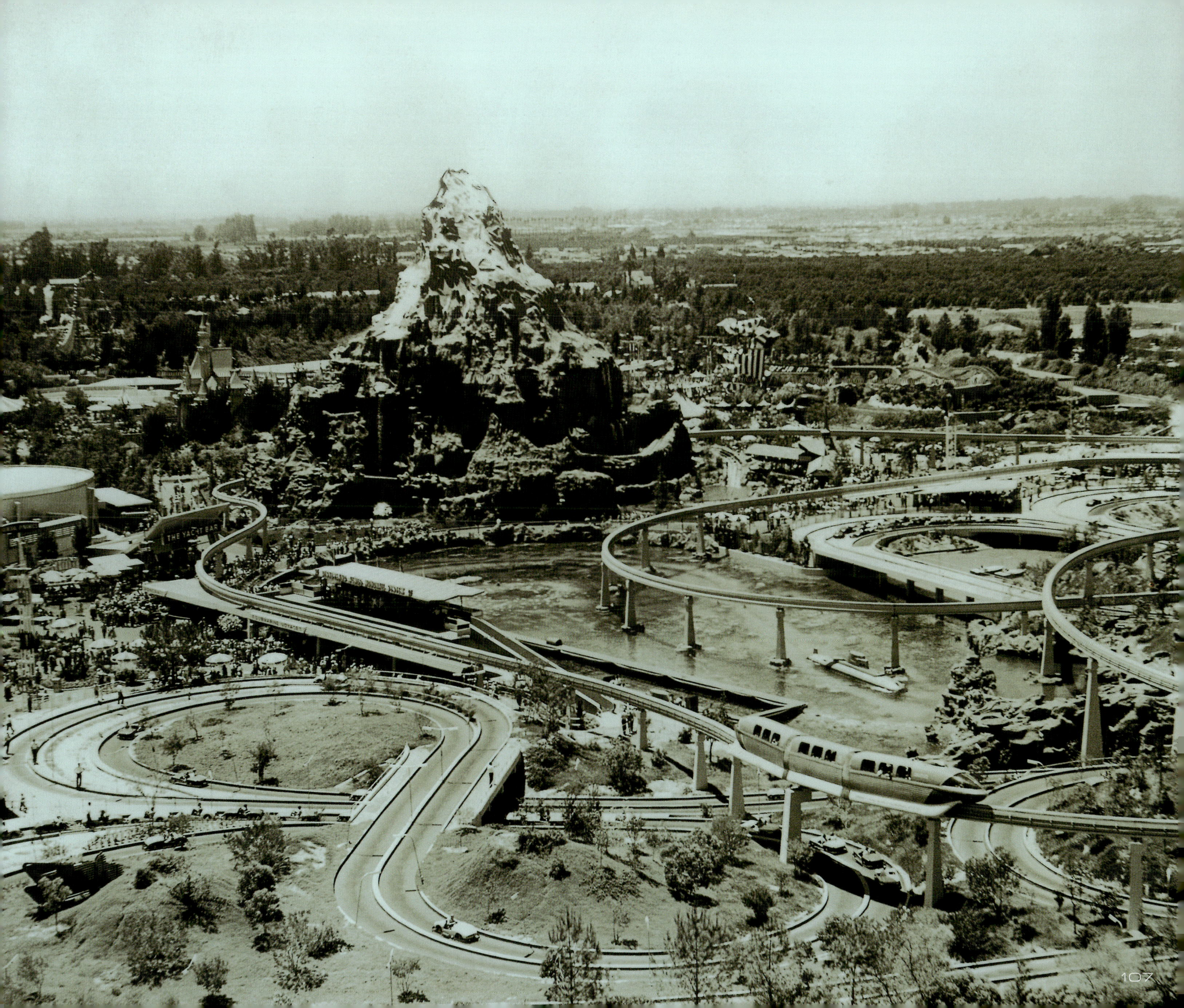
THE YACHT BAR

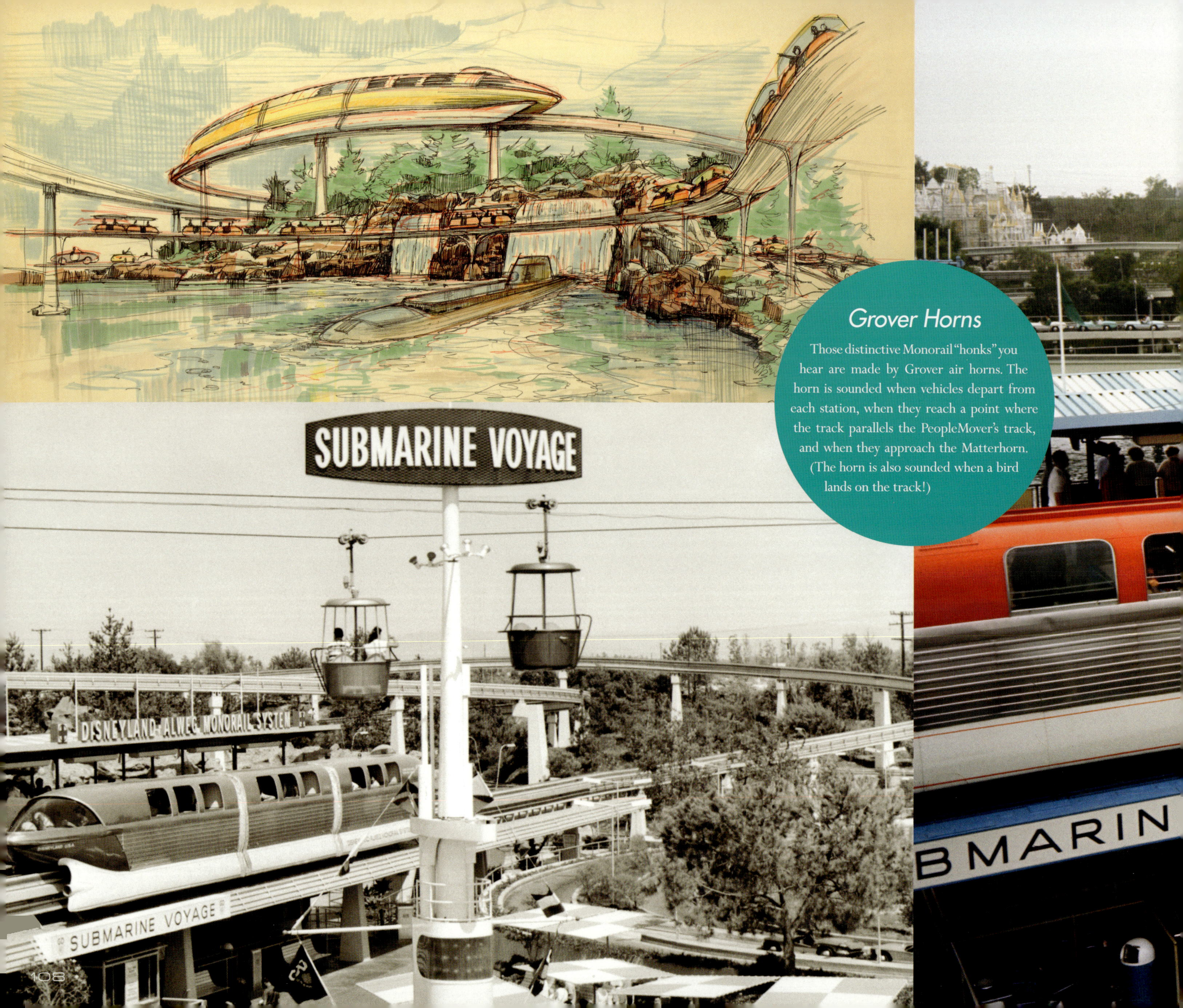

Grover Horns

Those distinctive Monorail "honks" you hear are made by Grover air horns. The horn is sounded when vehicles depart from each station, when they reach a point where the track parallels the PeopleMover's track, and when they approach the Matterhorn. (The horn is also sounded when a bird lands on the track!)

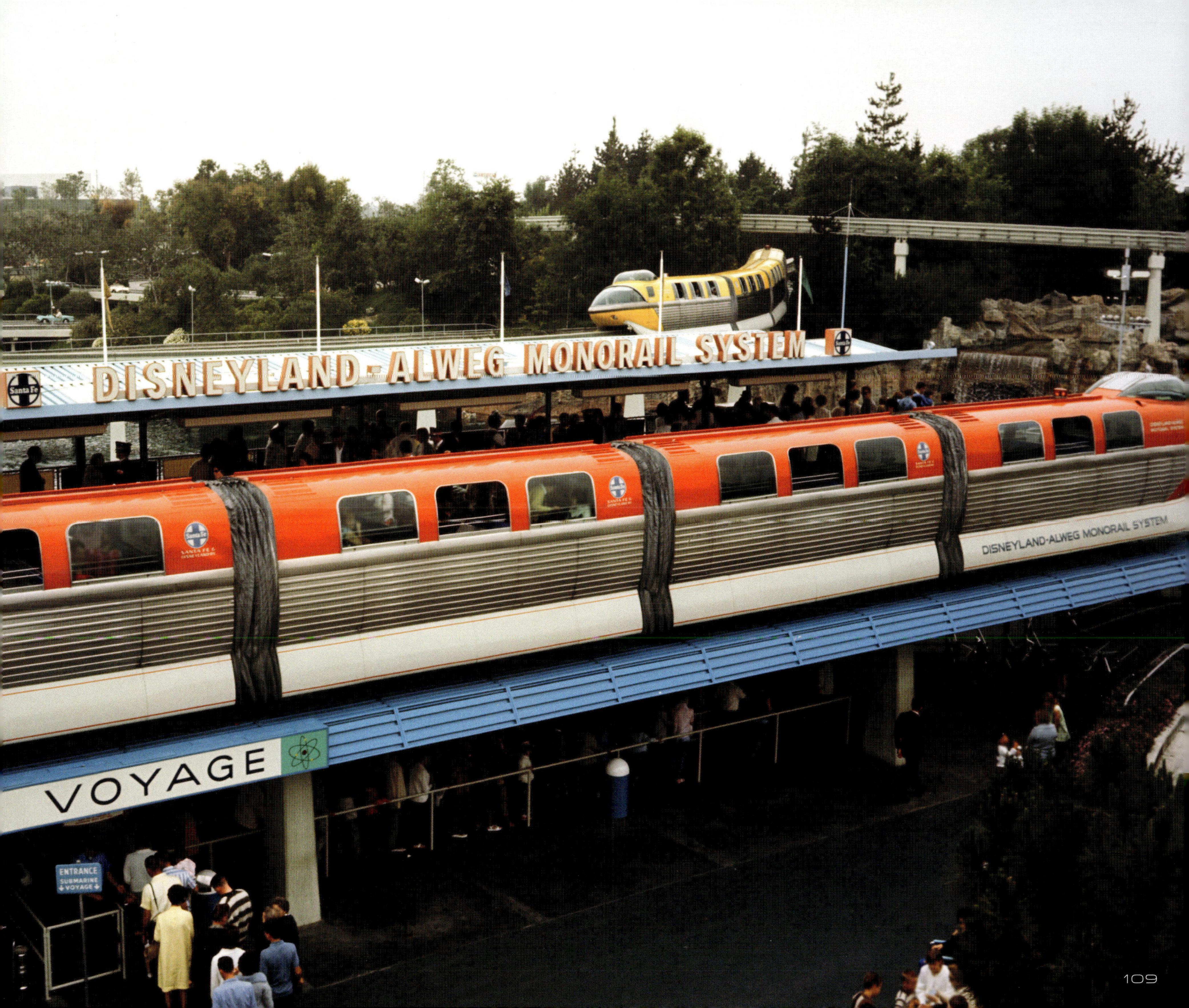
DISNEYLAND-ALWEG MONORAIL SYSTEM
DISNEYLAND-ALWEG MONORAIL SYSTEM
VOYAGE
ENTRANCE
SUBMARINE
VOYAGE

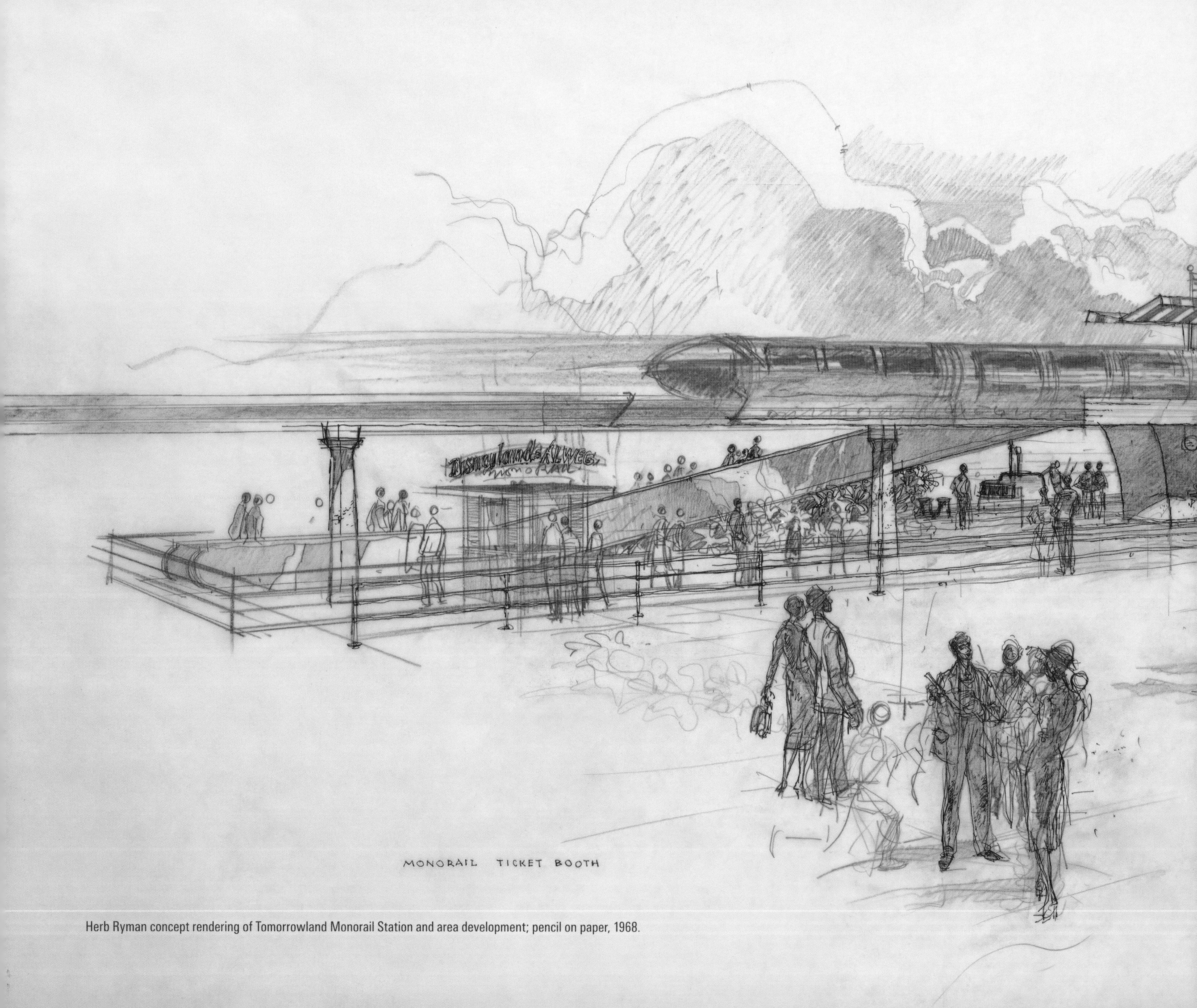

Herb Ryman concept rendering of Tomorrowland Monorail Station and area development; pencil on paper, 1968.

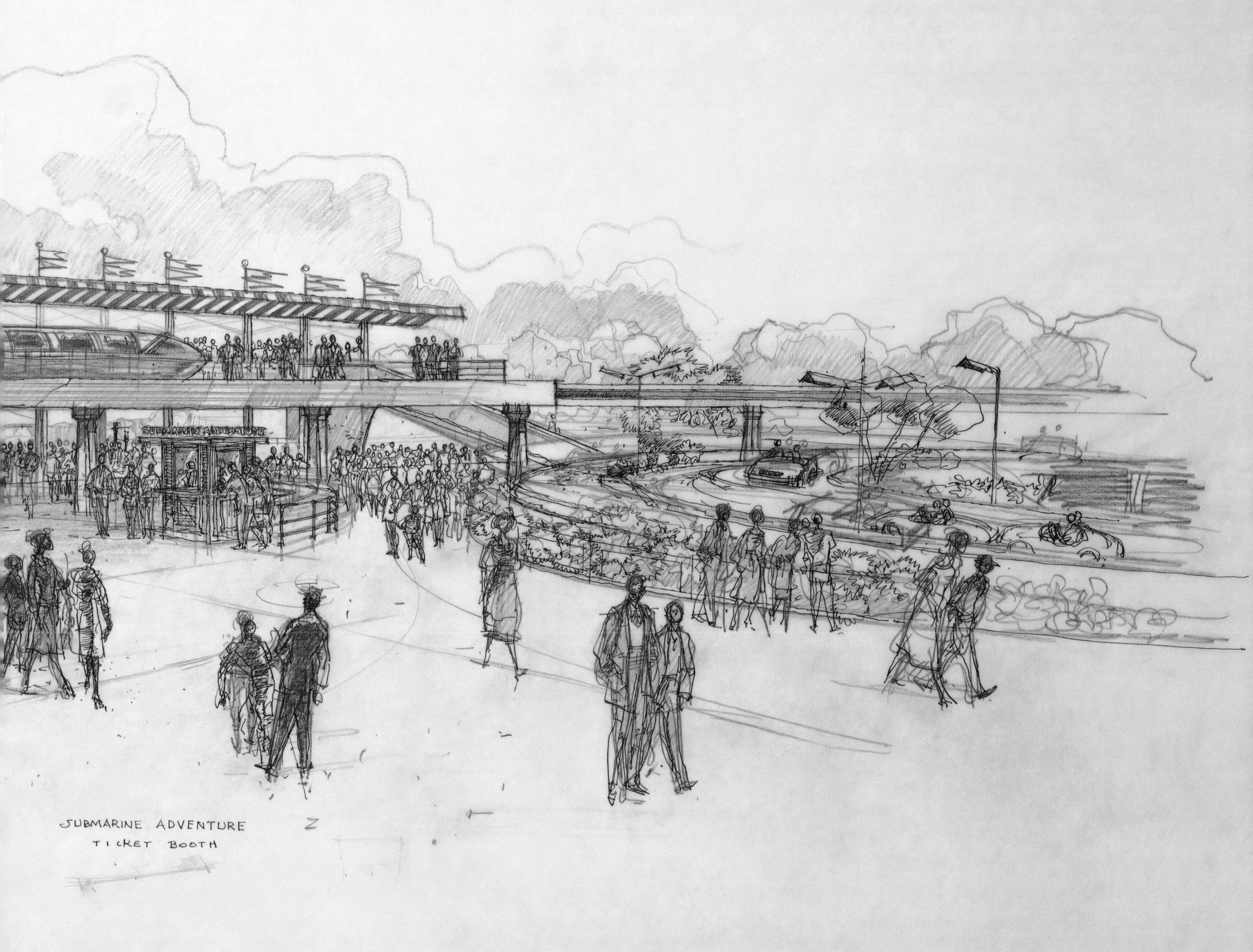
SUBMARINE ADVENTURE
TICKET BOOTH

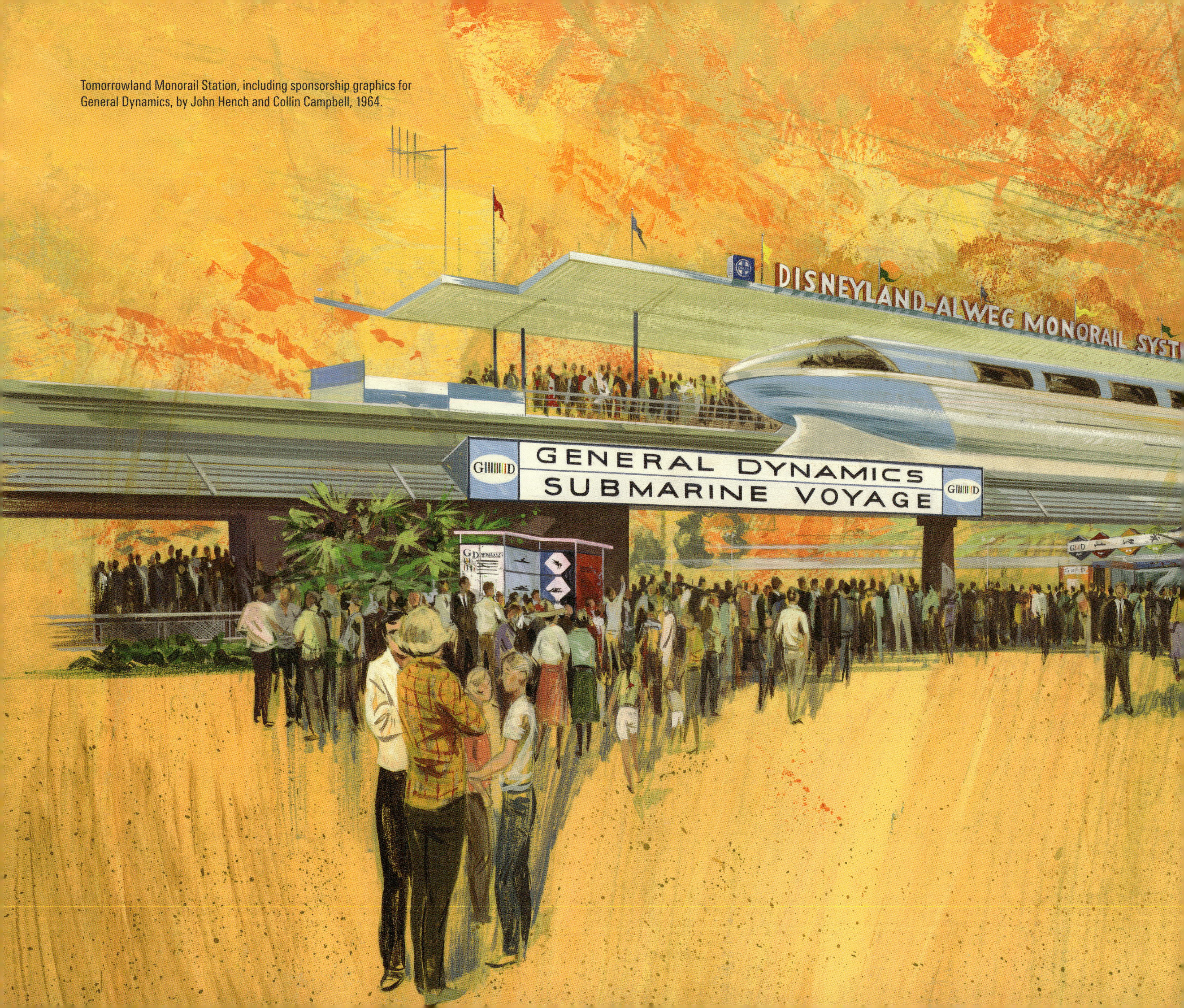

Tomorrowland Monorail Station, including sponsorship graphics for General Dynamics, by John Hench and Collin Campbell, 1964.

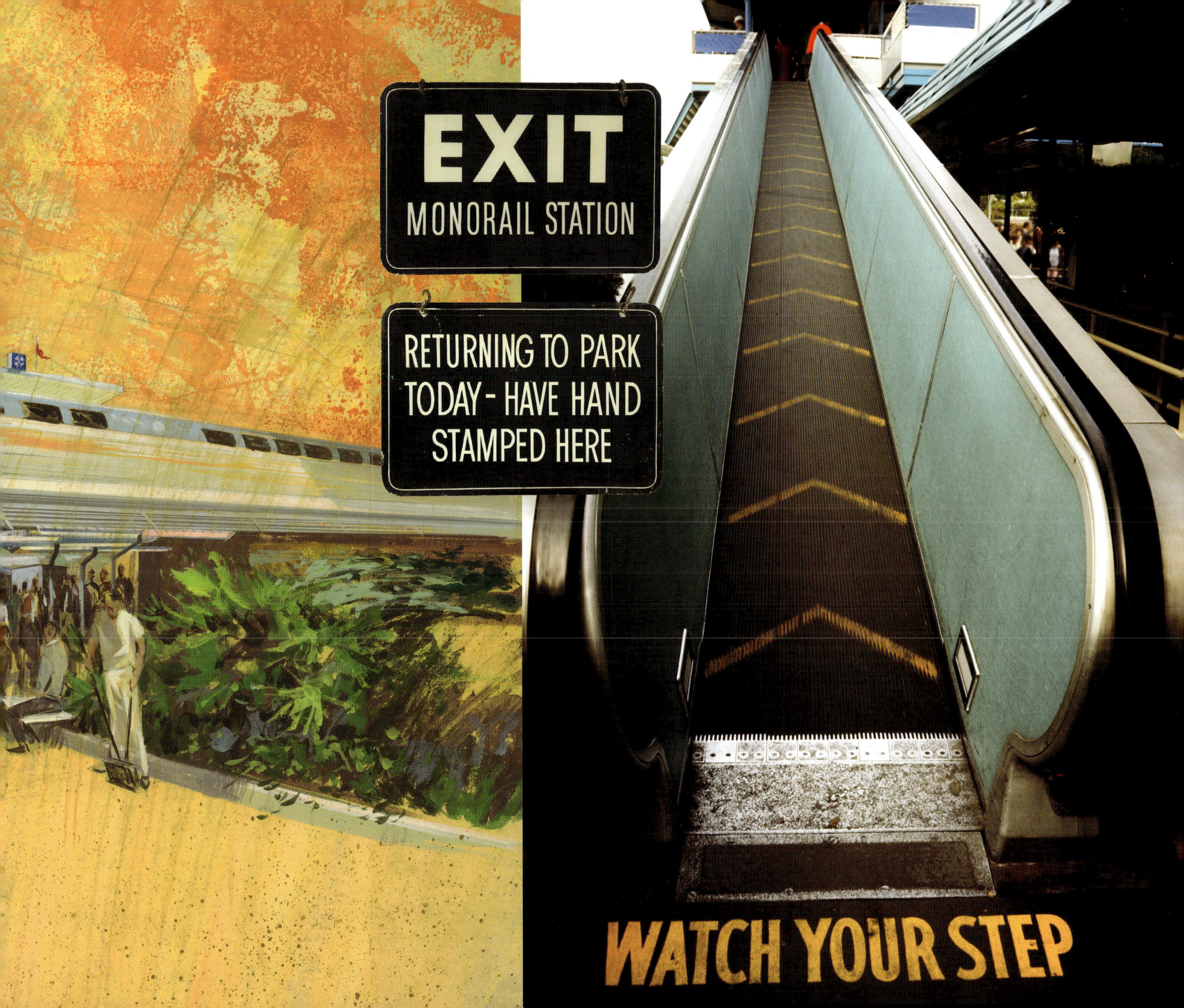
EXIT
MONORAIL STATION
RETURNING TO PARK
TODAY - HAVE HAND
STAMPED HERE
WATCH YOUR STEP

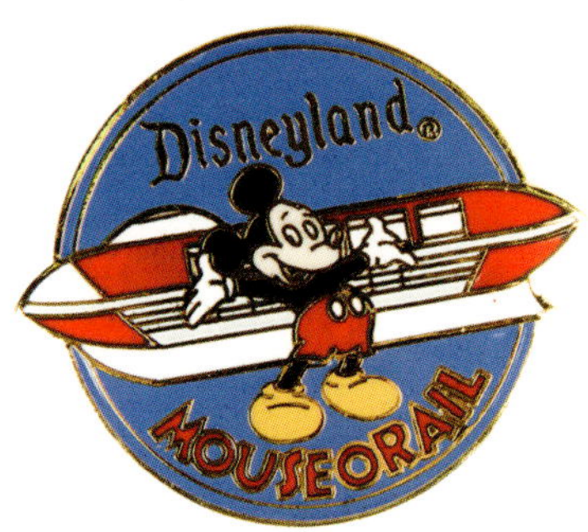

Monorail-mania
A Collectible Culture

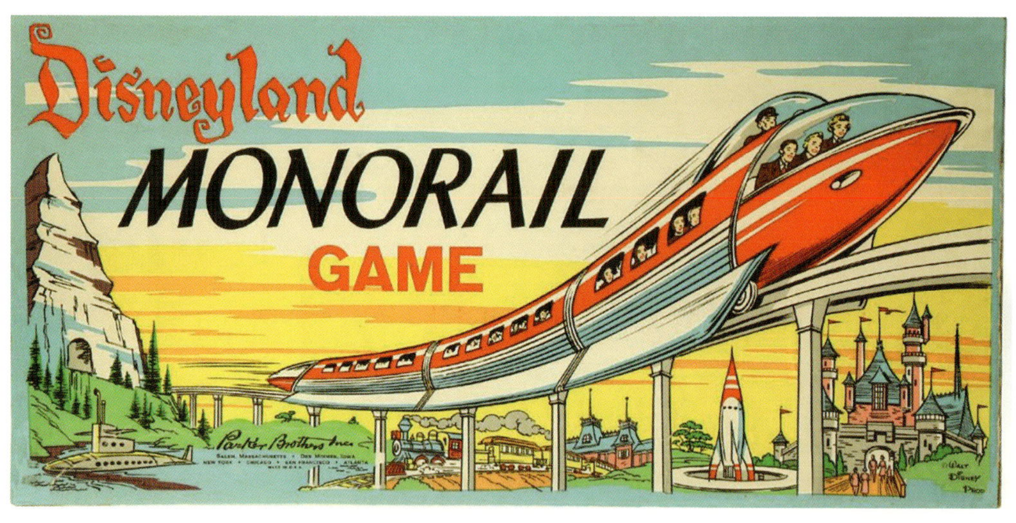

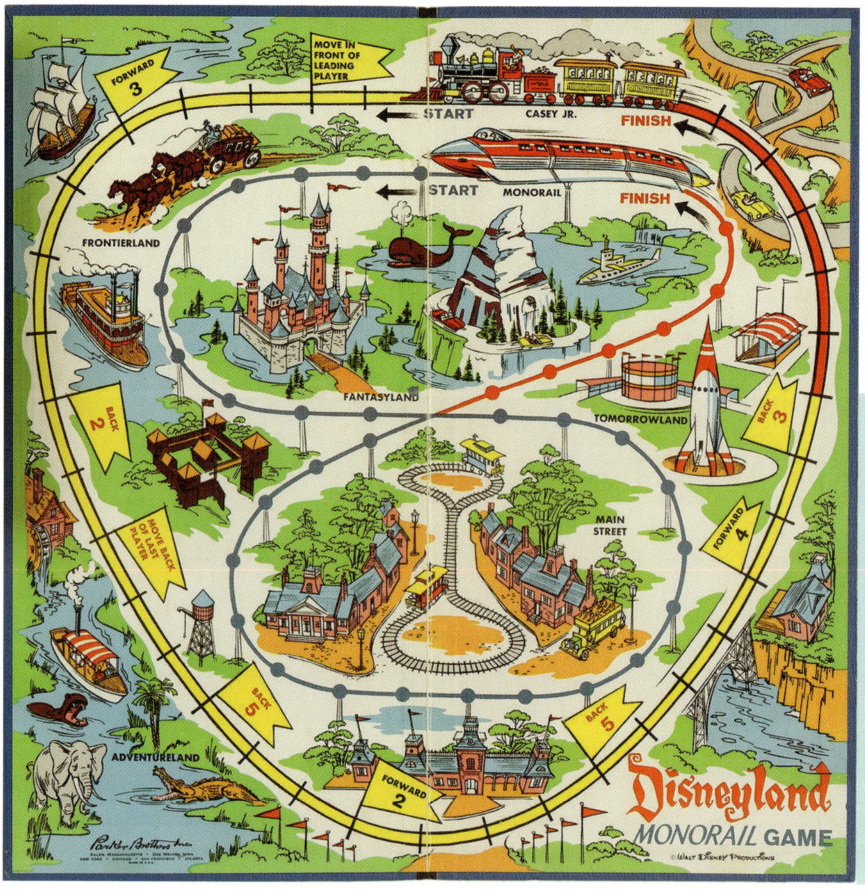

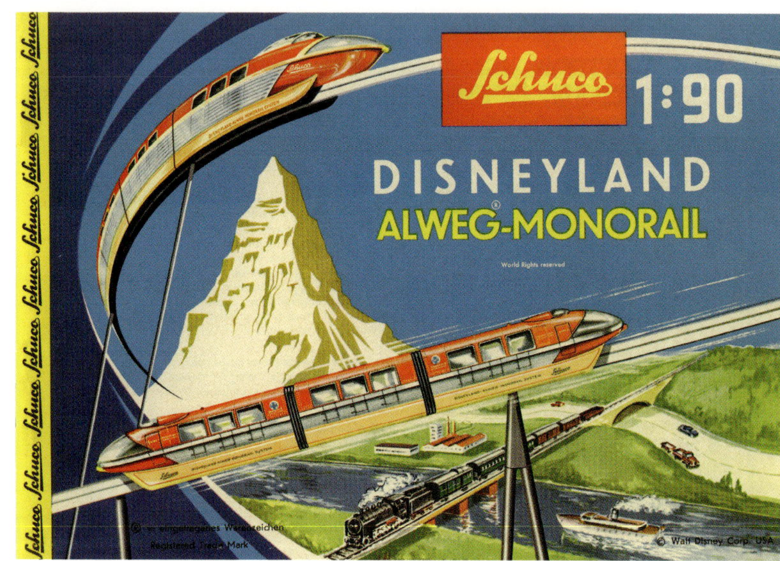

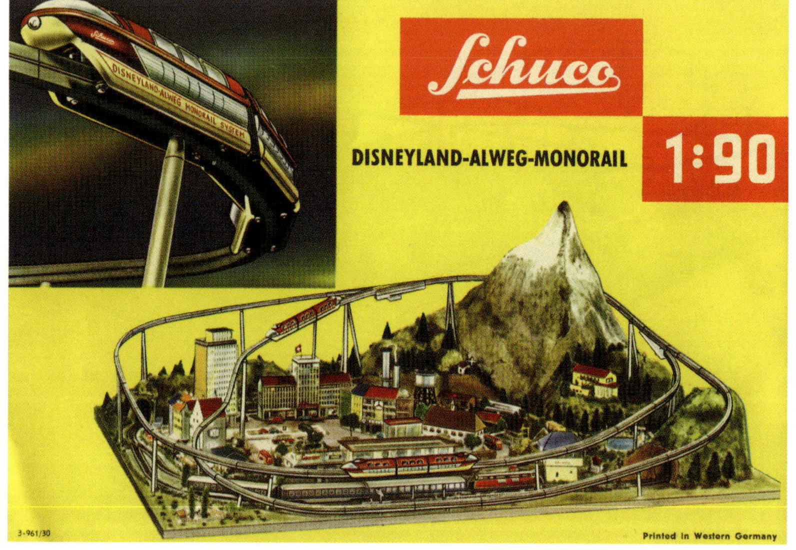

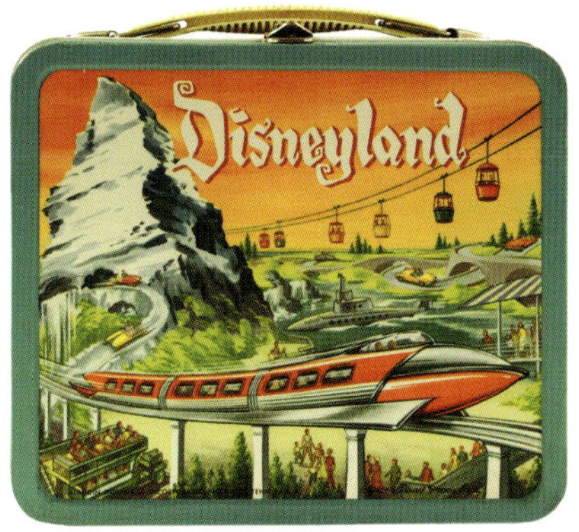

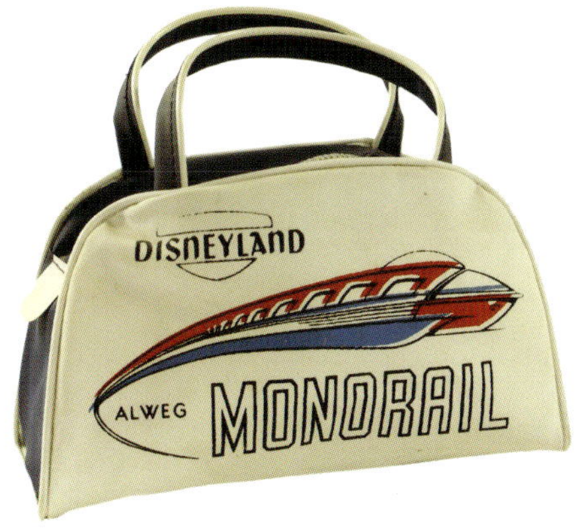

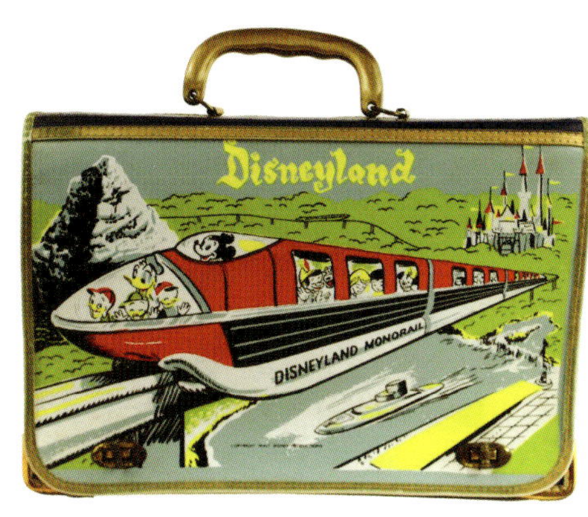

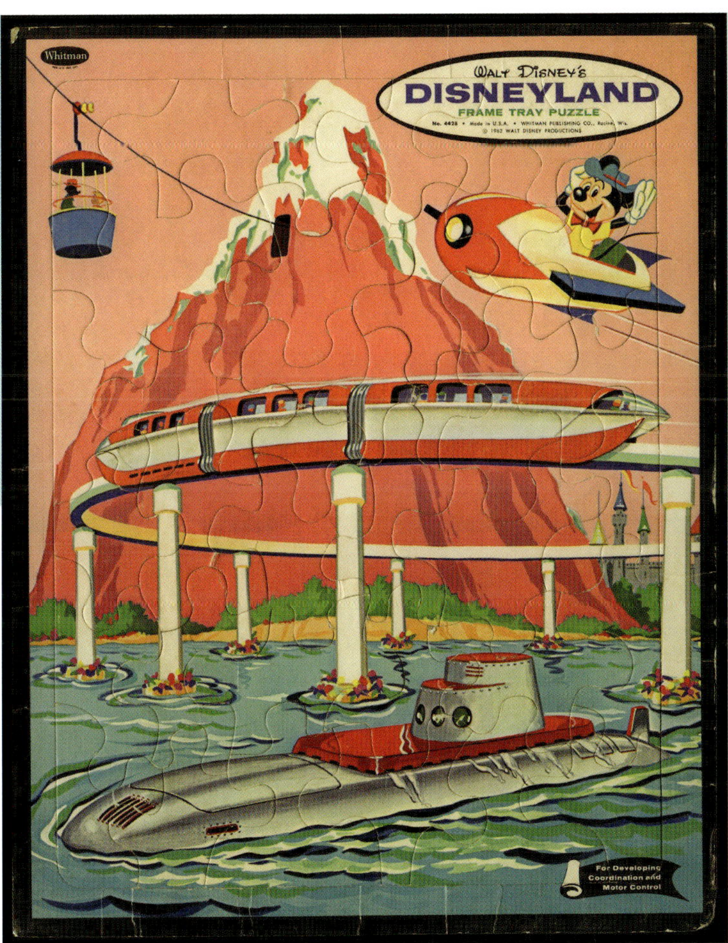

The Disneyland Monorail was not just a means of transportation or a tourist attraction; it was a potent symbol of a kind of cultural aspiration, of the science fiction future that was on its way to becoming a reality! At the same time it was as attractive and friendly as any other "Disney character"—even while it was ostensibly an attraction. As such, the Disneyland Monorail became a popular thematic, decorative, and storytelling component of a wide array of products and merchandise.

The Monorail also appeared in Disney publications and comic books, and magazines and paper ephemera, created by Disney itself, and by a variety of licensees and partners, and are sought-after collectibles today. They further established the ongoing cultural connection of "Disney" and "Monorail."

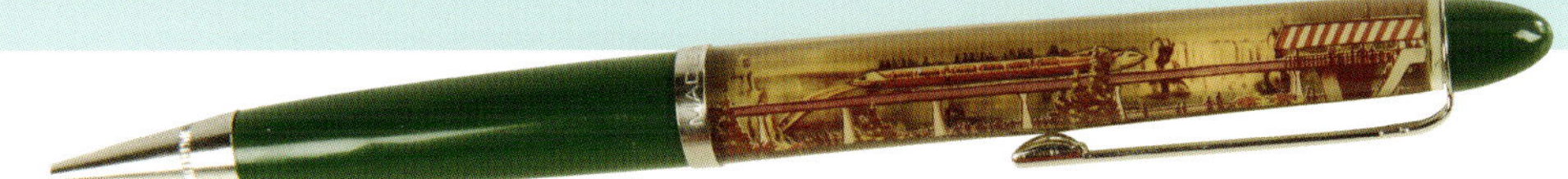

OPPOSITE (DOWN FROM TOP LEFT): *Disneyland Mouseorail* from the Disney Decade Pin collection, 1990; game box and board for a Disneyland Monorail Game, 1960; and front and back of the box for a Schuco 1:90 Disneyland-Alweg Monorail D/C model train, 1961.

ABOVE (CLOCKWISE FROM TOP LEFT): Disneyland Monorail lunch kit, Aladdin Industries 1960; souvenir camera tote bag, 1961; schoolbag, c. 1960; a "floaty" fountain pen; and Whitman frame tray jigsaw puzzle, 1960.

An Expanding System and Function: The Mark II

Although the Monorail was initially just a prototype and excursion attraction, Walt naturally had a bigger idea. So just two years after its maiden journey, the monorail beam was extended to a two-and-a-half-mile route and became an actual transportation link with a new station at the Disneyland Hotel.

The existing Mark I trains were expanded from three to four cars, and an additional train of that design, in gold, was built, creating the Mark II fleet.

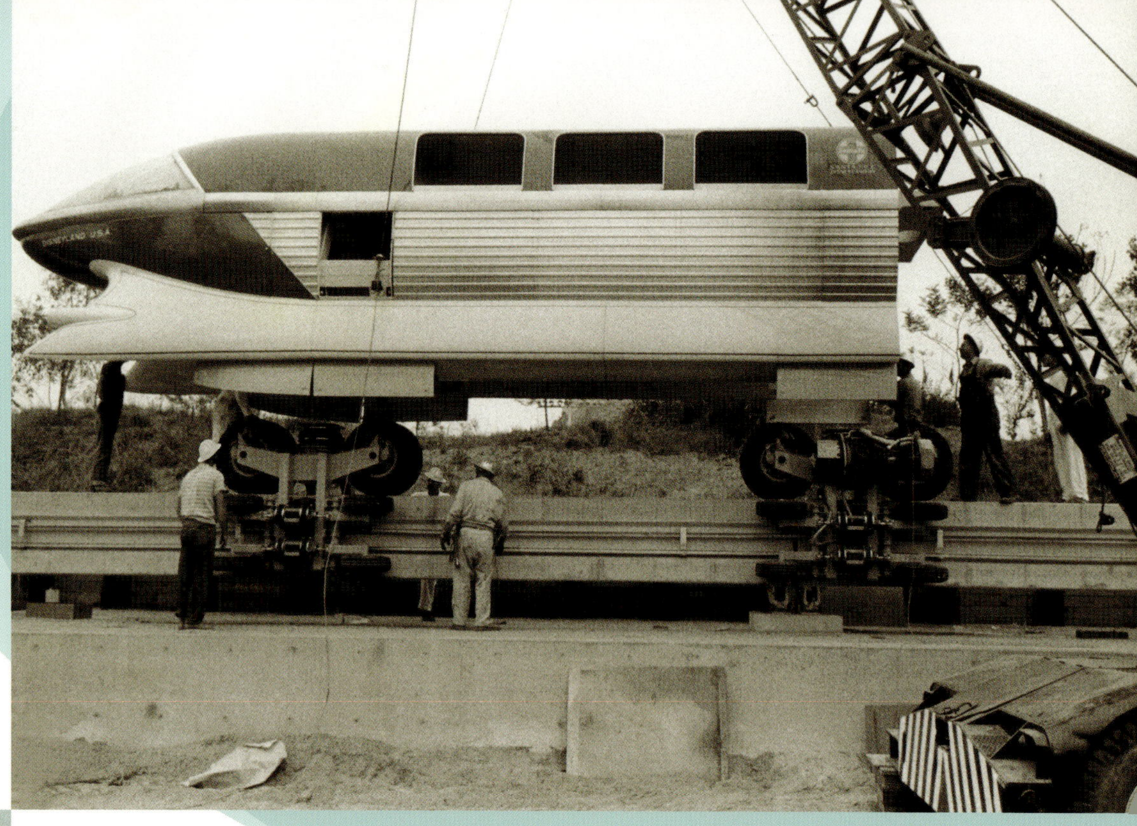

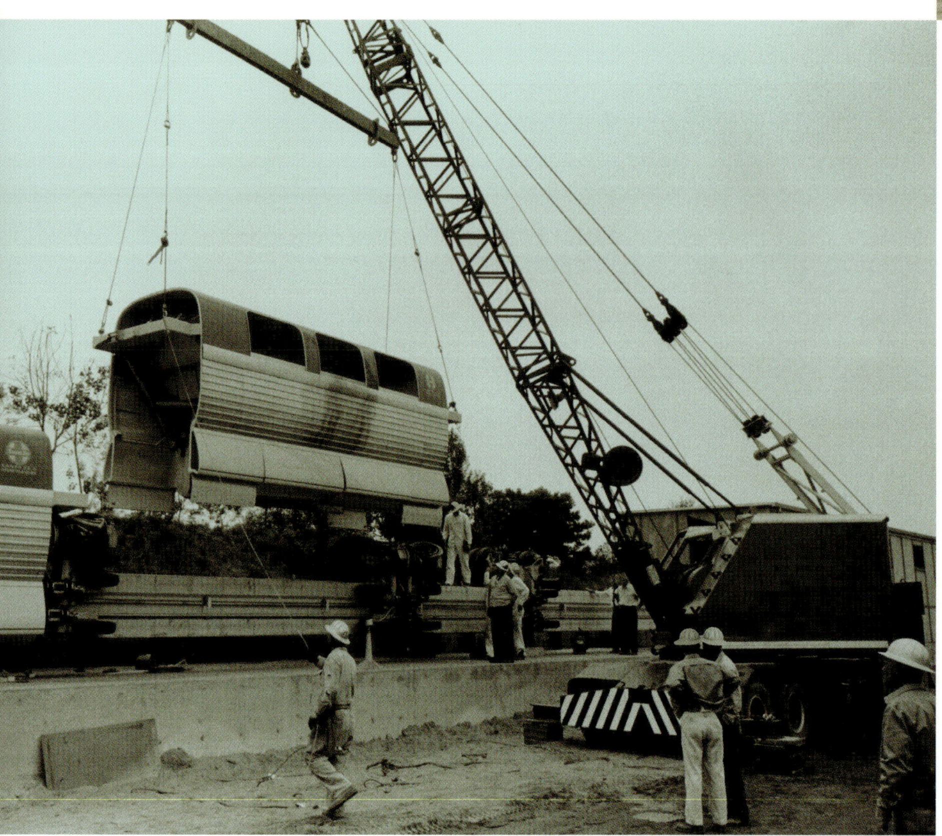

Now park Guests could embark on a monorail trip to the hotel to enjoy the amenities and experiences exclusive to that property (including adult beverages), and hotel Guests could board the Monorail at the new station, gaining special entry into the park in Tomorrowland.

Guests leaving the park, or Guests at the hotel who had park admission, could buy one-way tickets from the park to the hotel station, or head from the hotel to the entrance in Tomorrowland. Guests without park admission could buy round-trip tickets from the hotel. To keep them from entering the park without paying, they were seated in a separate passenger car that did not open at the Tomorrowland Monorail Station.

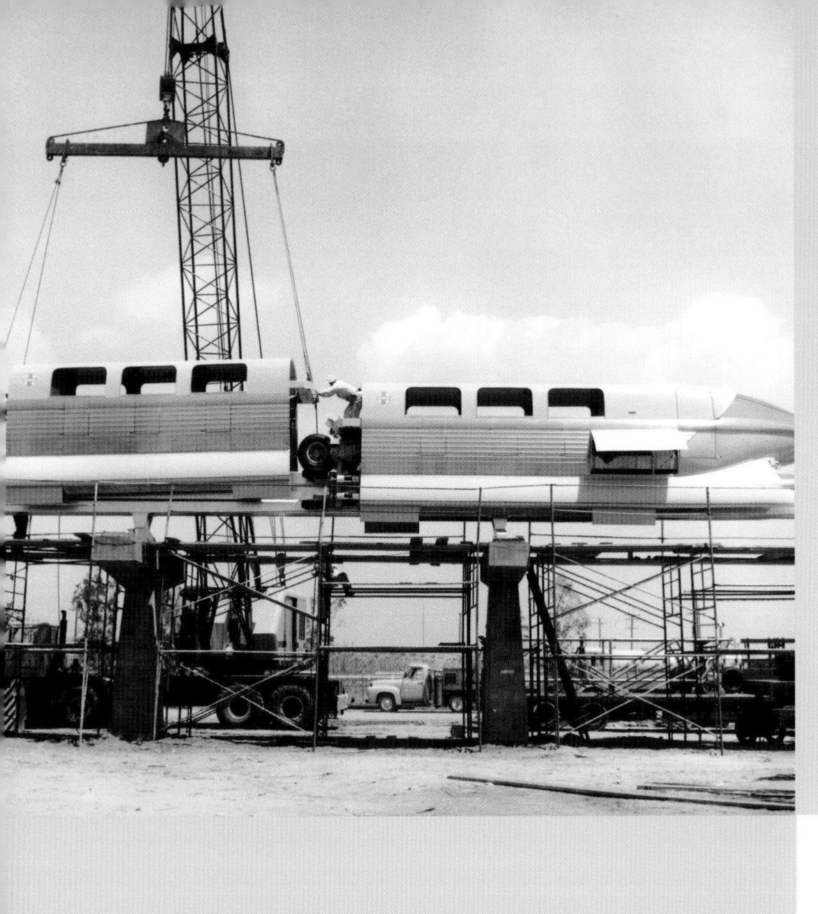

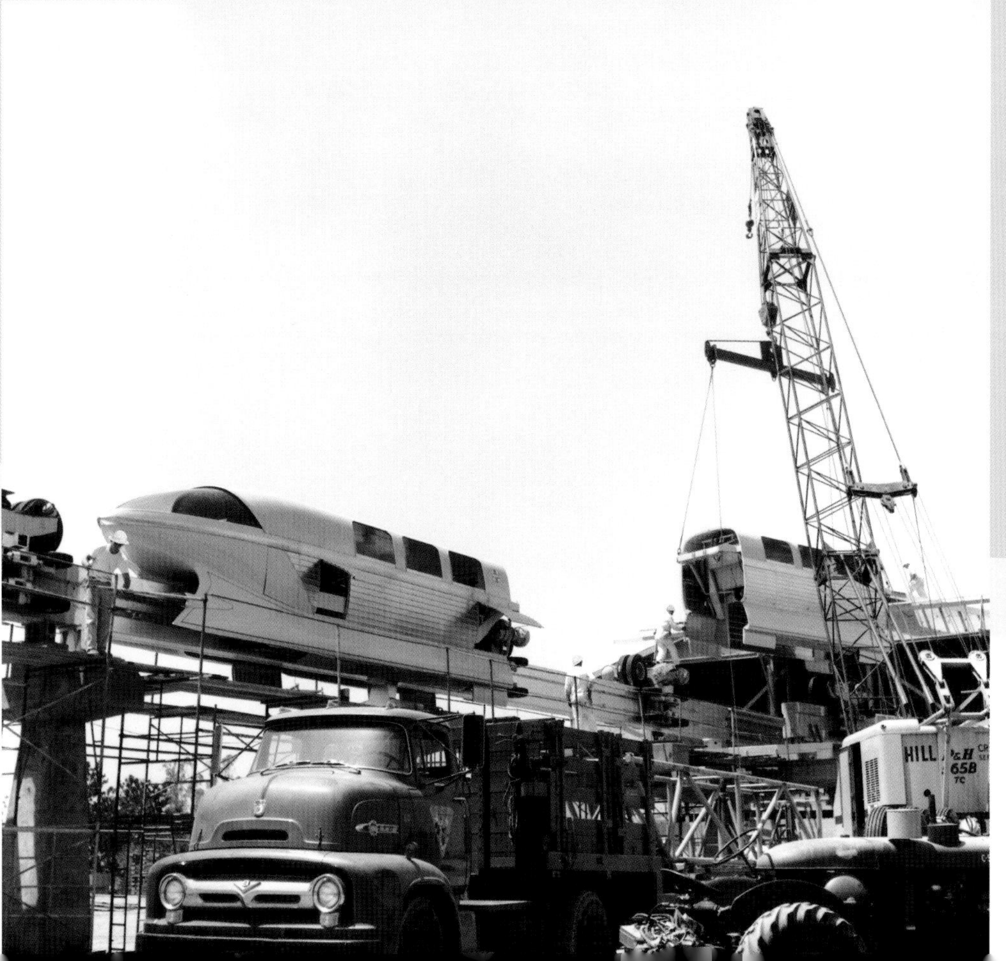

Luxurious Accommodations at the End of the Line

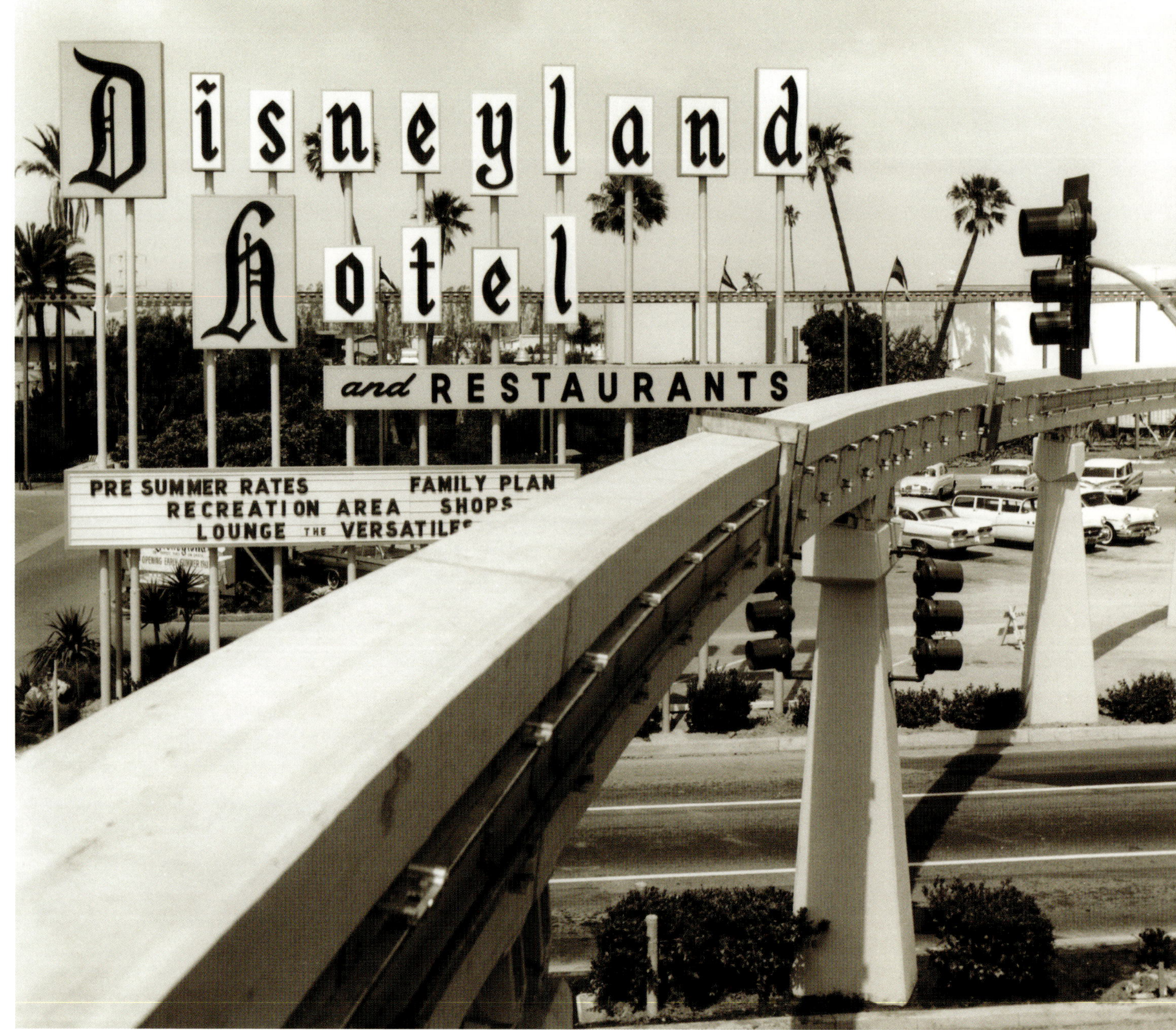

From Attraction to Transportation System

In 1961, the Monorail, which had been solely a park attraction since its 1959 opening, had its beam extended, turning the just under a mile draw into an impressive two-and-a-half-mile route that transported Guests to and from the Disneyland Hotel.

The placement of a hotel at his ambitious park had been a part of Walt's dream, but his finances were strained to the limit. So in 1954 Walt invited his friend, the entrepreneur, petroleum businessman, and television producer Jack Wrather, to develop a hotel (with attendant amenities) in what was then an orange grove across from the park. Ground was broken on March 18, 1955, a scant four months before Disneyland's opening day.

Designed by famed Los Angeles architects Pereira & Luckman, the original plans called for three hundred (later increased to 650) motel and hotel rooms, suites, and garden apartments. Due to several setbacks, including labor and material shortages, the still-unfinished Disneyland Hotel quietly opened—with seven available Guest rooms—on October 5, 1955.

Finally, in August of 1956, the Disneyland Hotel had an "official" grand opening, and included 204 Guest rooms and suites, an Olympic-size swimming pool, seventeen shops, and restaurants and cocktail lounges.

In 1960, Walt and Jack Wrather announced plans to extend the Disneyland-Alweg Monorail System to link the hotel to the park. The full line opened to the public on June 11, 1961.

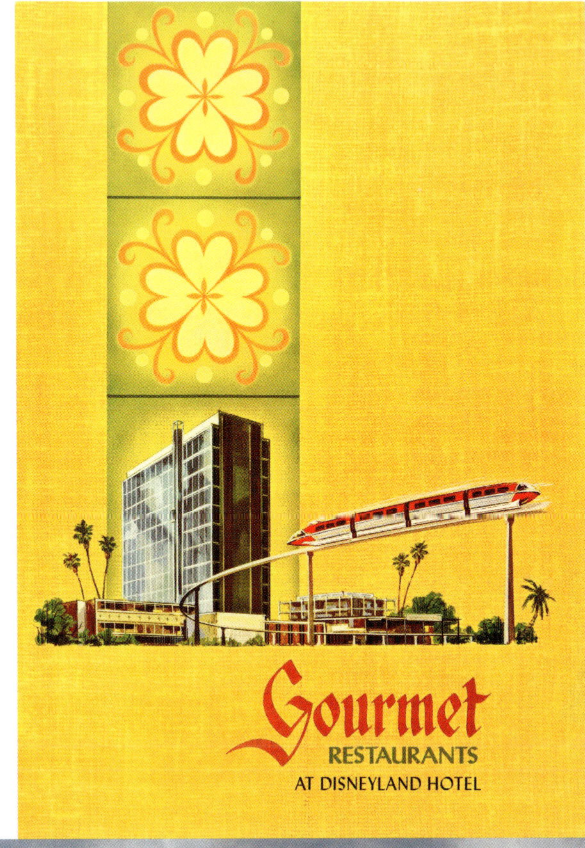

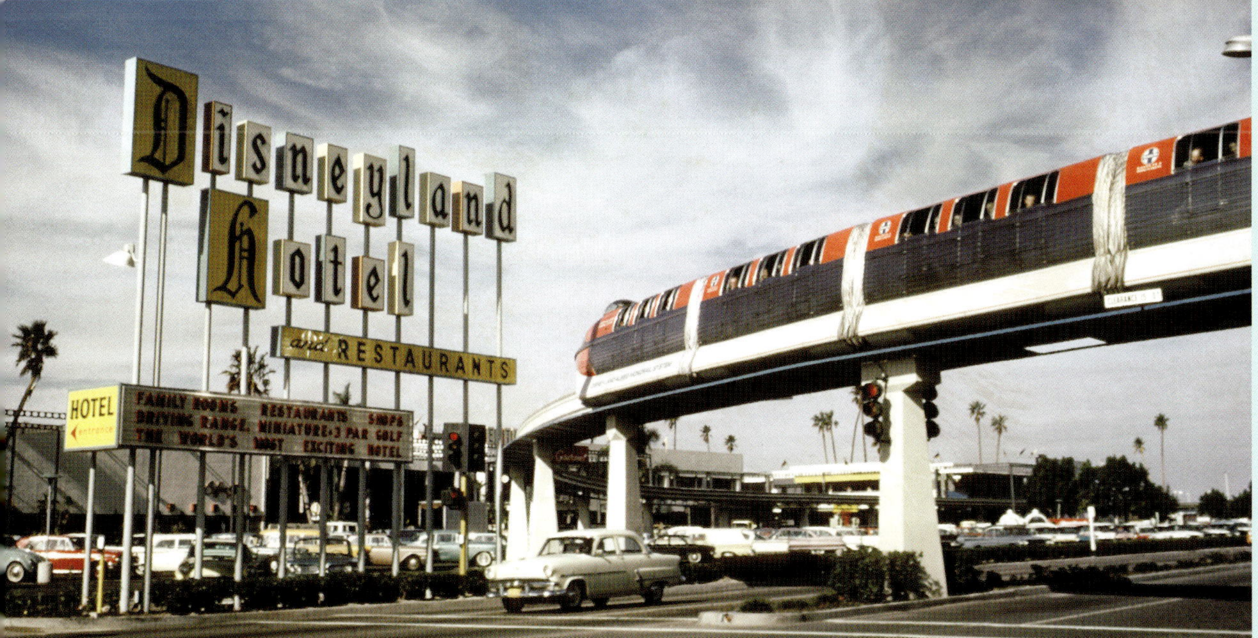

Monorails and Mad Men

The "Cocktail Culture" of the "Highway in the Sky"

". . . Americans enjoy ritual," journalist Jacki Lyden says, "particularly ritual that allows us to mix fantasy and pleasure."

As the Monorail itself symbolized an age of aspiration and modernism, so did its era comport with that of a kind of then-current sacrament of social sophistication embodied in the "imbibition destination" at the Disneyland Hotel: alcohol was forbidden at the park itself, but the "Highway in the Sky" led to a unique and long-gone quintessence of that era: the Monorail Bar.

The warm, intimate lounge offered a "streetcar'" themed environment with transportation-related decor—and a futuristic display of modern mixology. Looking at the few remaining relics of the Monorail Bar today, it is not only a recollection of the Disneyland Hotel's past, but of a postwar culture that aspired to leave its terrible past to memory. "They had won the war and displayed a sureness and strength which following generations have not been able to tap," Medium writer Ladylee observes. "But the drinks flowed and banter moved around the room in shared jokes and innuendo. It's hard to believe that world existed when I was a child; it all seems removed from today's realities and, to be honest, the realities of most people of that time."

After Walt, the Mark III

Although Walt Disney passed away in 1966, his creative heirs were infused with his powerful and restless ideas about progress: they kept his park moving forward, by observing and applying the continuing advances in technology that had been so important to him. In July 1969, the Disneyland Monorail fleet was completely replaced, and the four all-new 137-foot-long five-car Mark III trains began service. (Monorail Green joined Red, Blue, and Gold.)

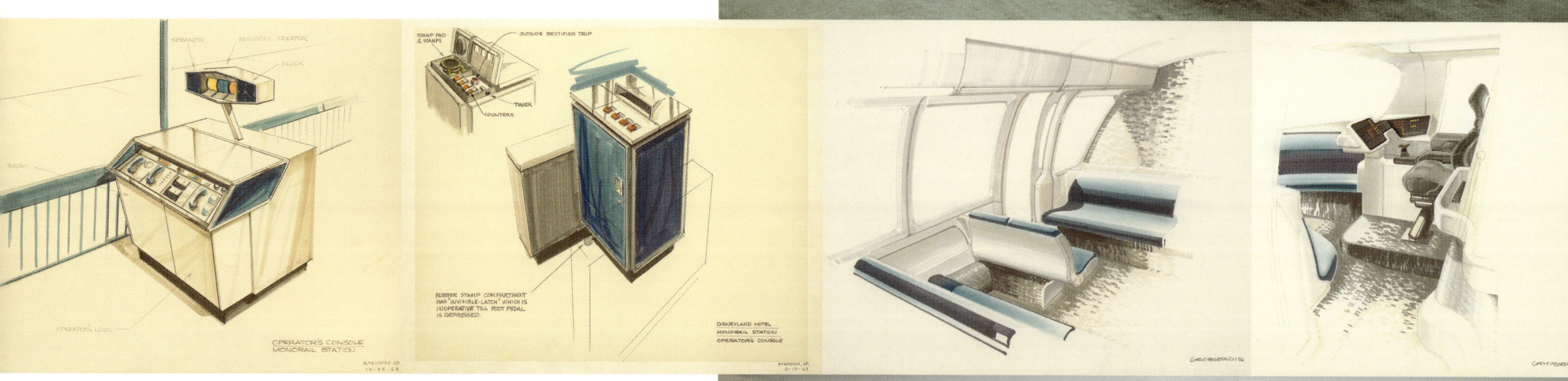

The Mark II Monorails were designed and assembled at MAPO, on the WED Enterprises campus in Glendale, California. In the wake of the 1964–1965 New York World's Fair, and using his personal profits from *Mary Poppins*, Walt founded MAPO as an engineering and manufacturing subsidiary. The "Mary Poppins" portmanteau was later reverse-engineered to the acronym to stand for "Manufacturing and Production Organization."

DIRECTLY ABOVE: Interior Monorail concept art; the two left pieces are dated 1969 and so were for the Mark III trains, while the right two are dated 1986 and were for Mark V.

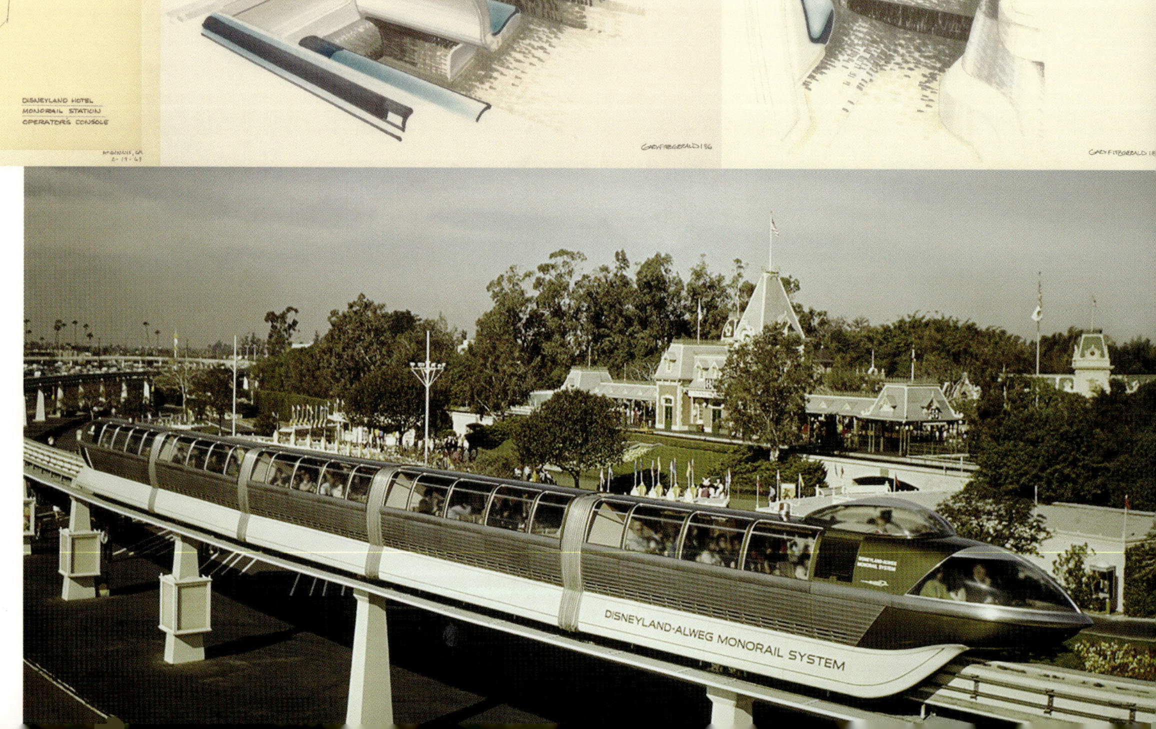

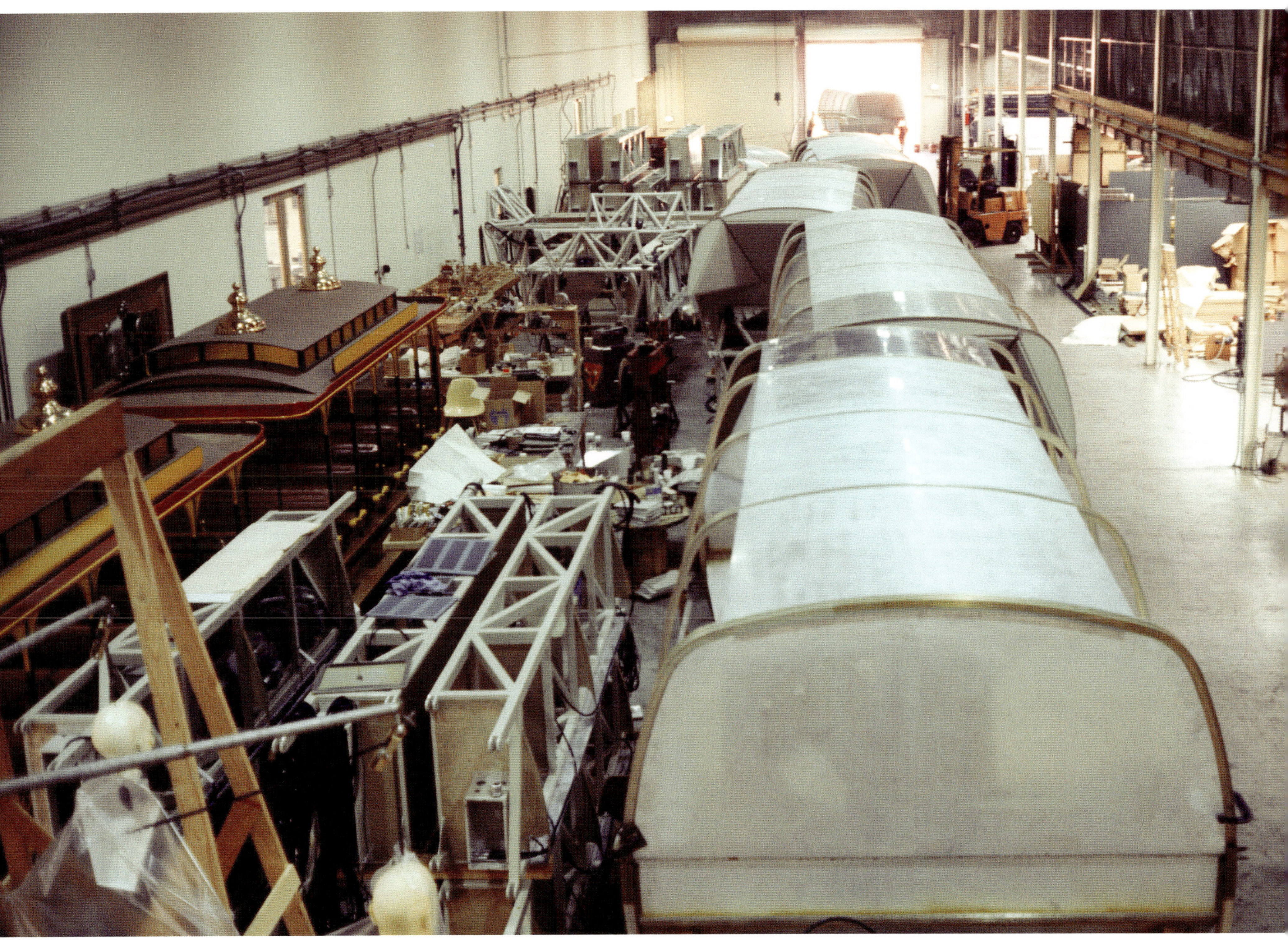

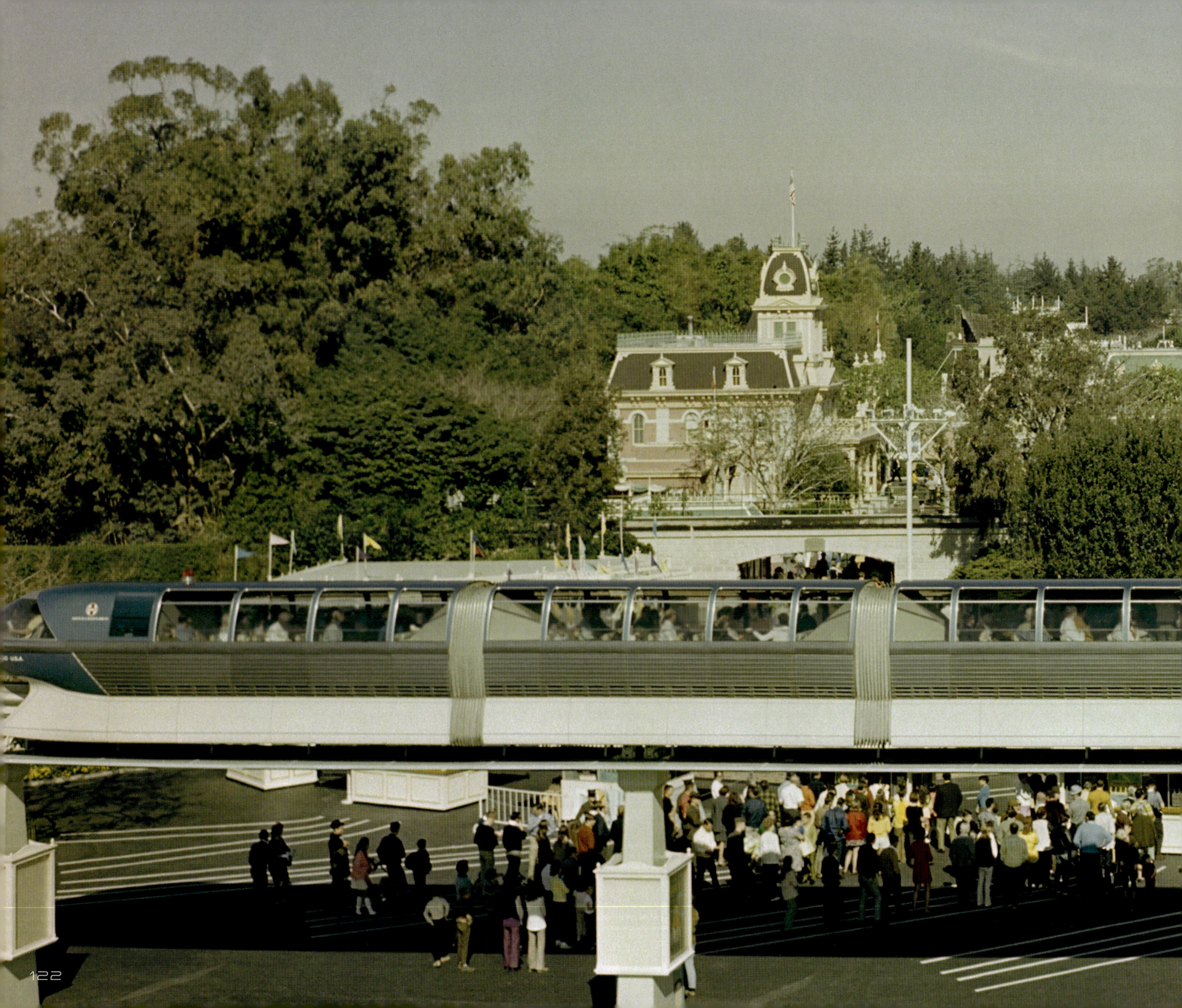

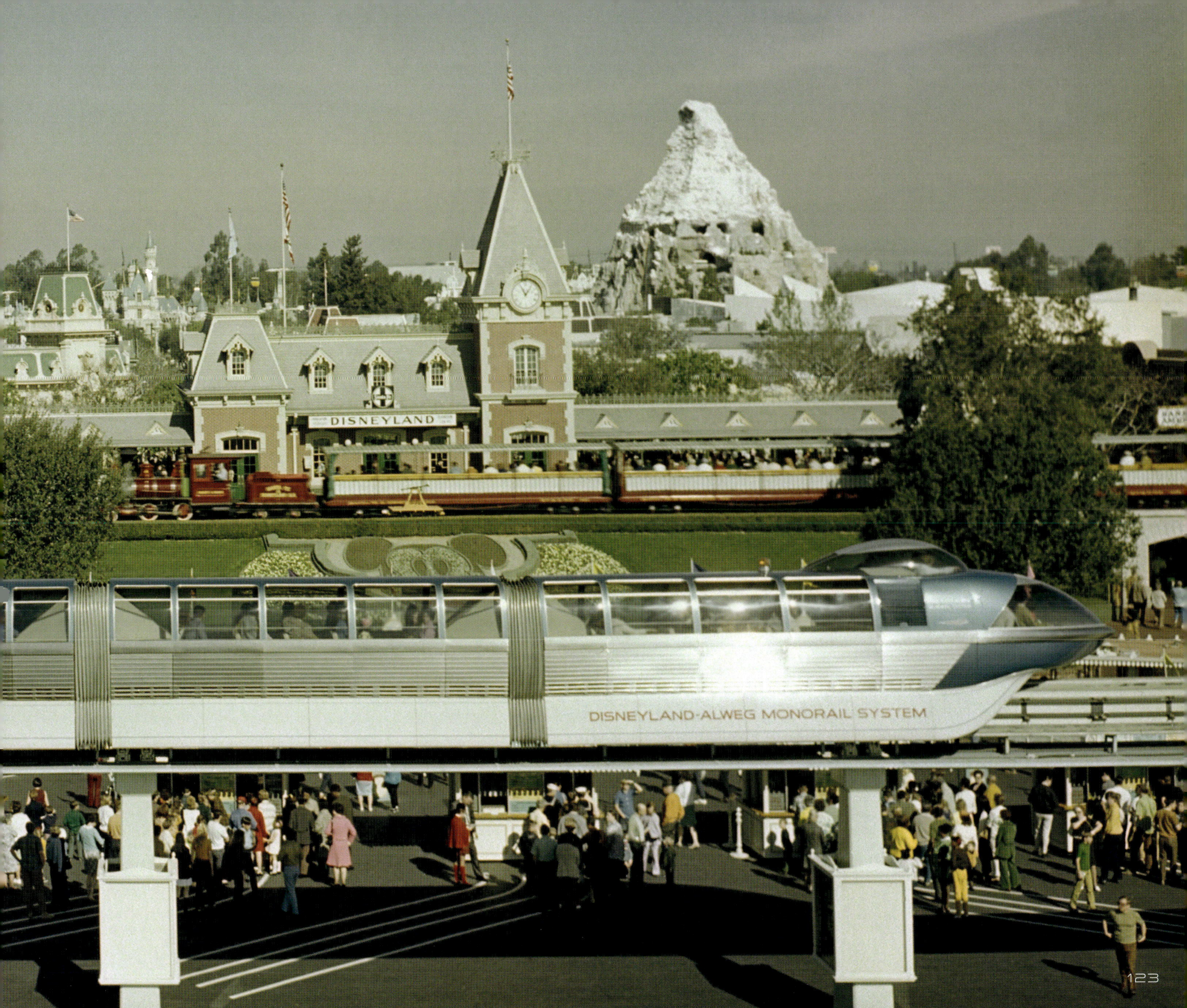
DISNEYLAND
DISNEYLAND-ALWEG MONORAIL SYSTEM

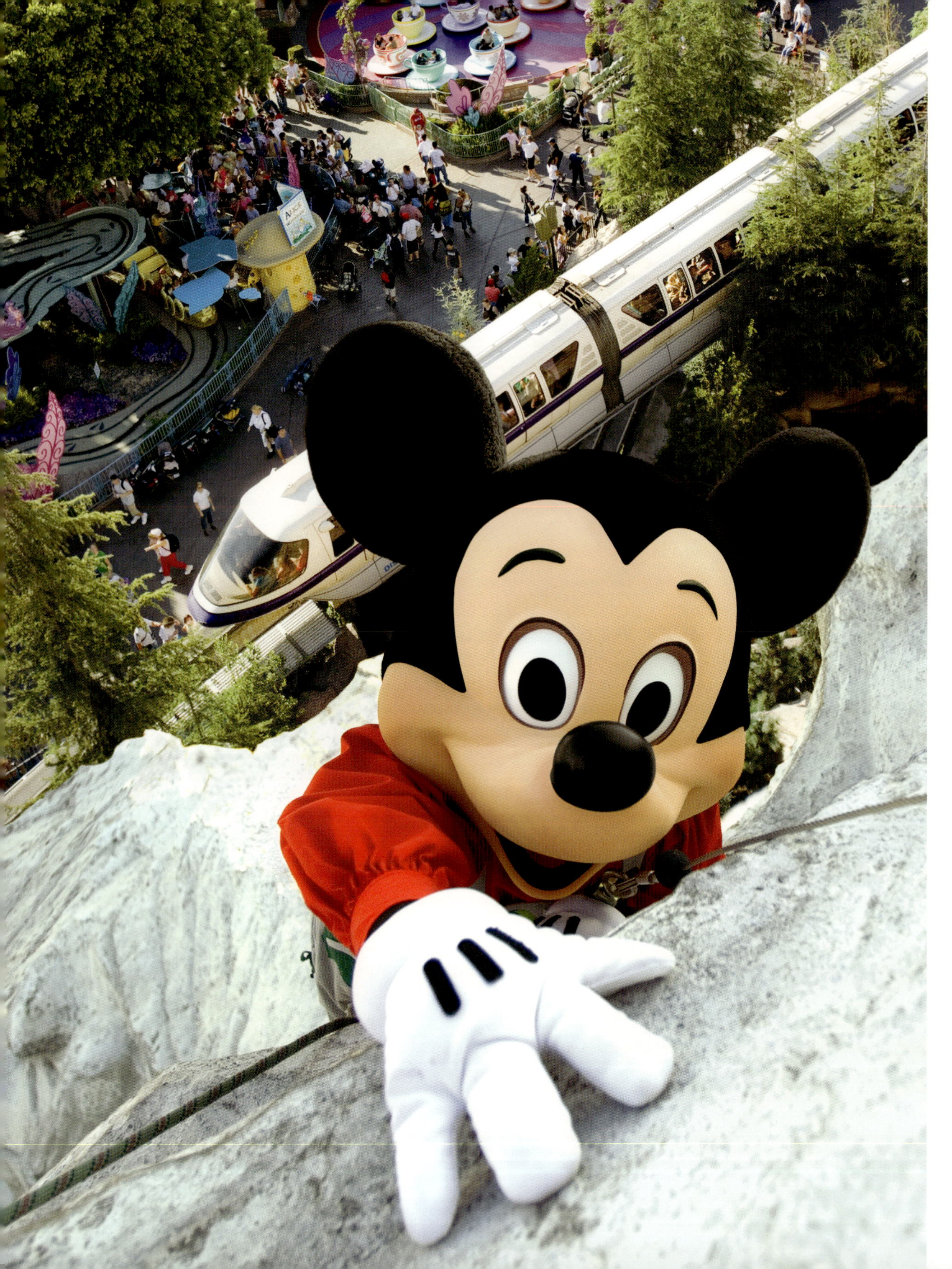

Into the 1980s: The Mark V

By the early 1980s, the Mark III trains were no longer operating with the desired efficiency, and all were showing the wear and tear of fifteen years of nearly nonstop service. Disneyland began phasing out the Mark III trains one by one in 1985, stripping the cars down to the superstructure. Ride & Show Engineering, Inc., of San Dimas, California, utilized body components from Messerschmitt-Bölkow-Blohm of Germany to rebuild the cars as the new Mark V fleet. (Mark IV was designated for the first Walt Disney World Monorail fleet, but more on that later.)

Mark III Green was rebuilt as Mark V Purple and debuted in the fall of 1986; Mark III Gold became Mark V Orange, and went into service in mid-1987. Mark III Blue was still blue, but a lighter shade, and began running in early 1988. Mark III Red became Mark V Red and returned to service in 1988. The bubble-top pilot car was redesigned, using a design similar to the Mark IV trains at Walt Disney World (see page 146).

The new trains seated twenty-four passengers in each of the five cars, plus seven passengers in the tail cab and five in the cockpit cab. The Mark V fleet remained in service for more than twenty years.

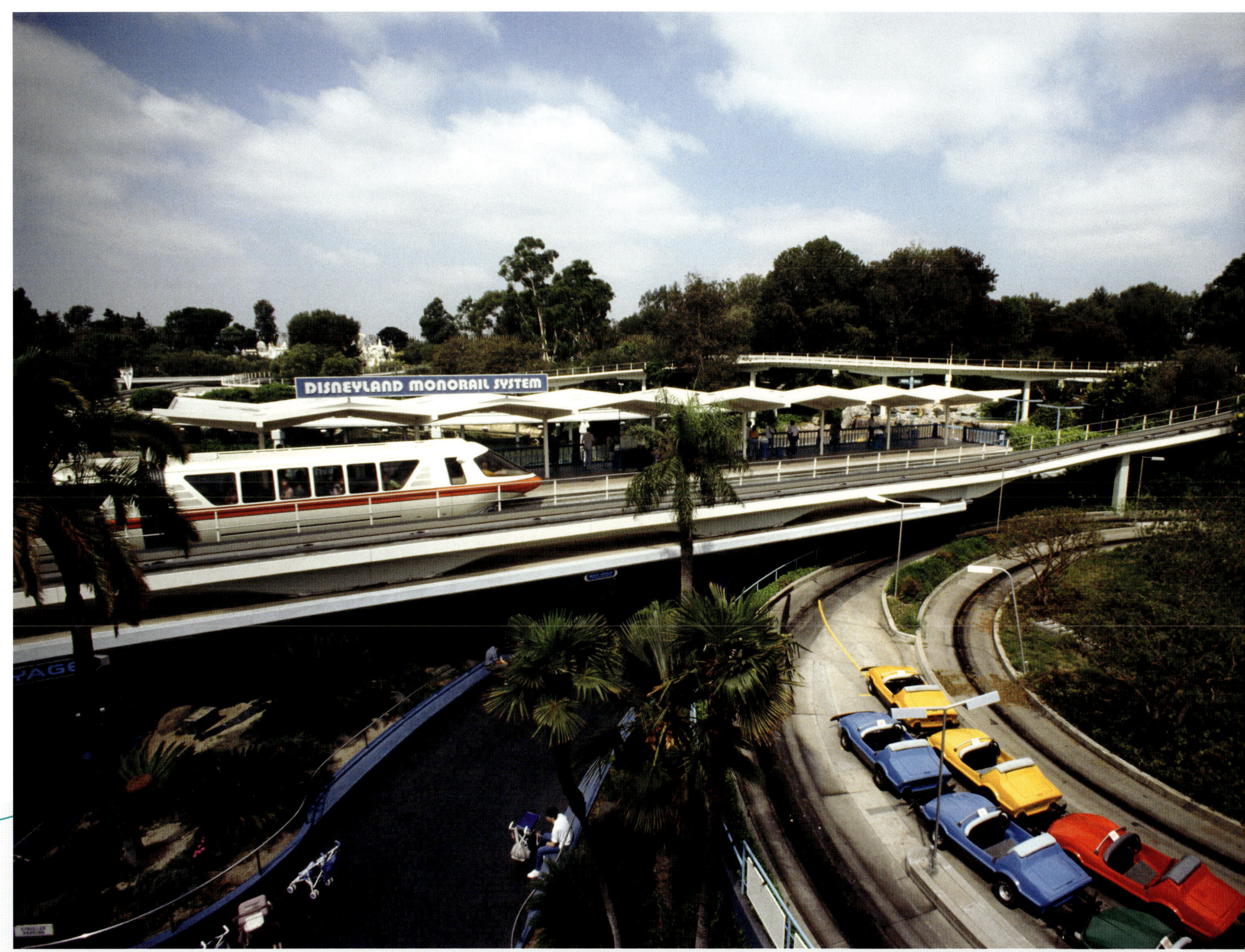
DISNEYLAND MONORAIL SYSTEM

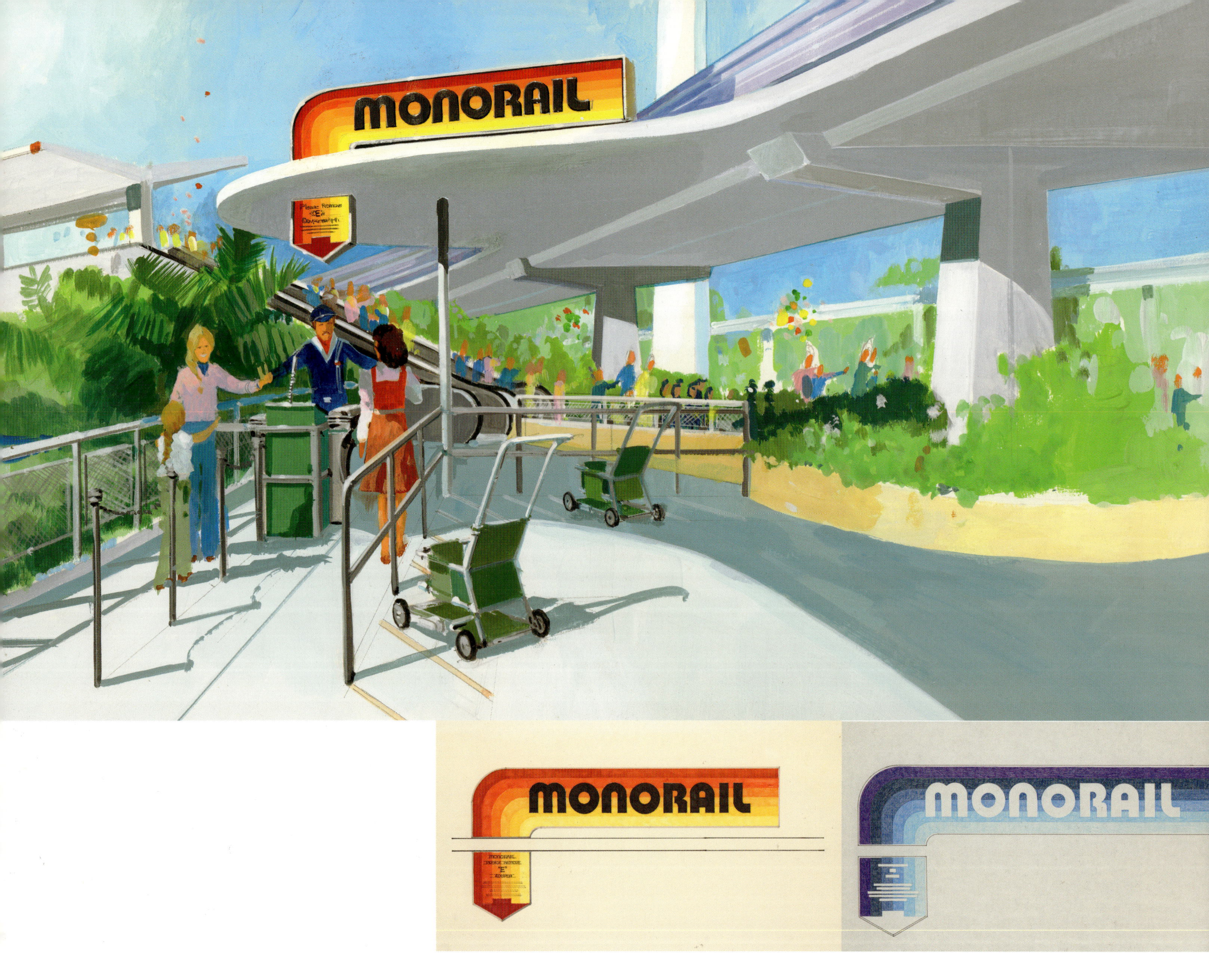
MONORAIL
MONORAIL
MONORAIL

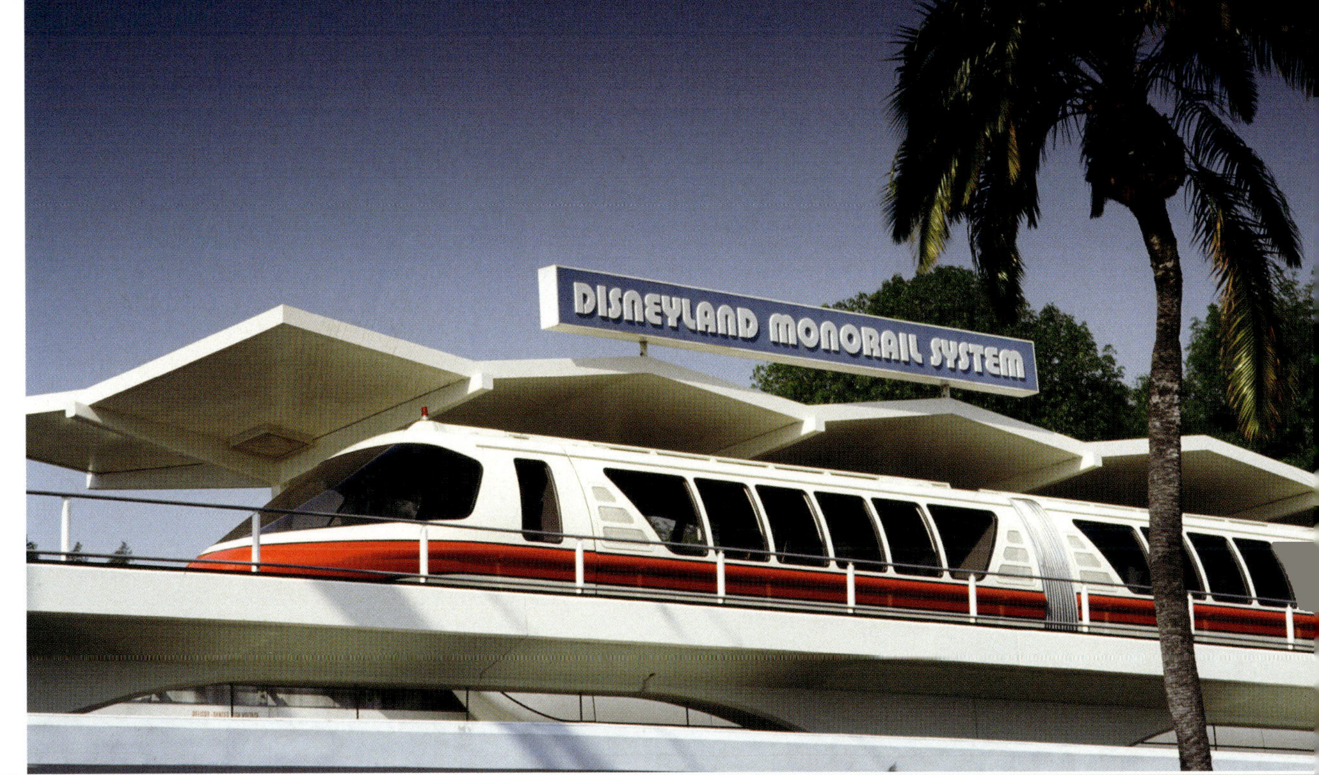

Graphics and signage are details that perhaps escape the notice of park Guests, but add to the overall theme and show quality. A late-1970s redesign and rebranding of the Monorail by Rudy Lord resulted first in a warm "sunset" of orange and gold; the same design was then restyled with a cool blue gradation to better harmonize with, rather than contrast with, the station and area color palette.

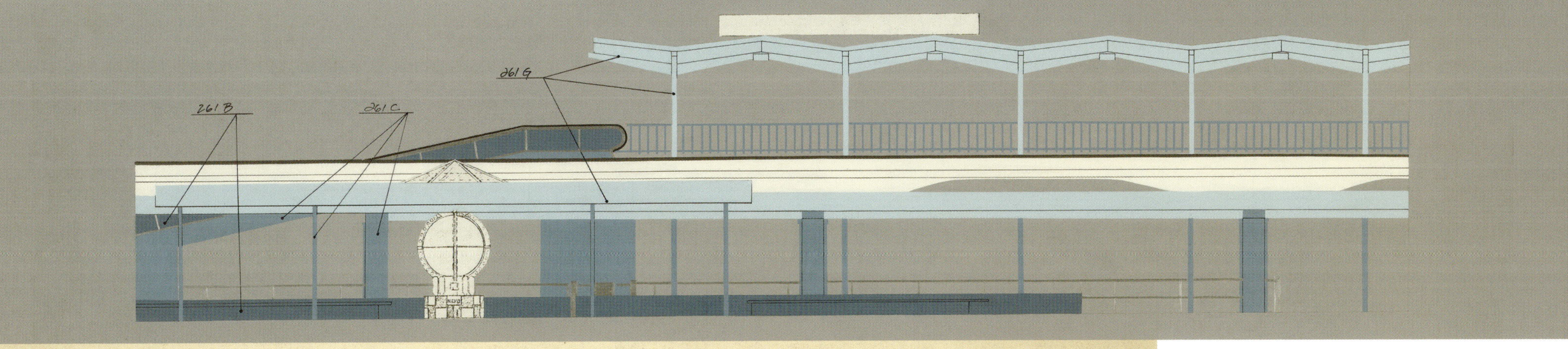

DISNEYLAND MONORAIL SYSTEM

ELEVATION OF MONORAIL MARQUEE SIGN

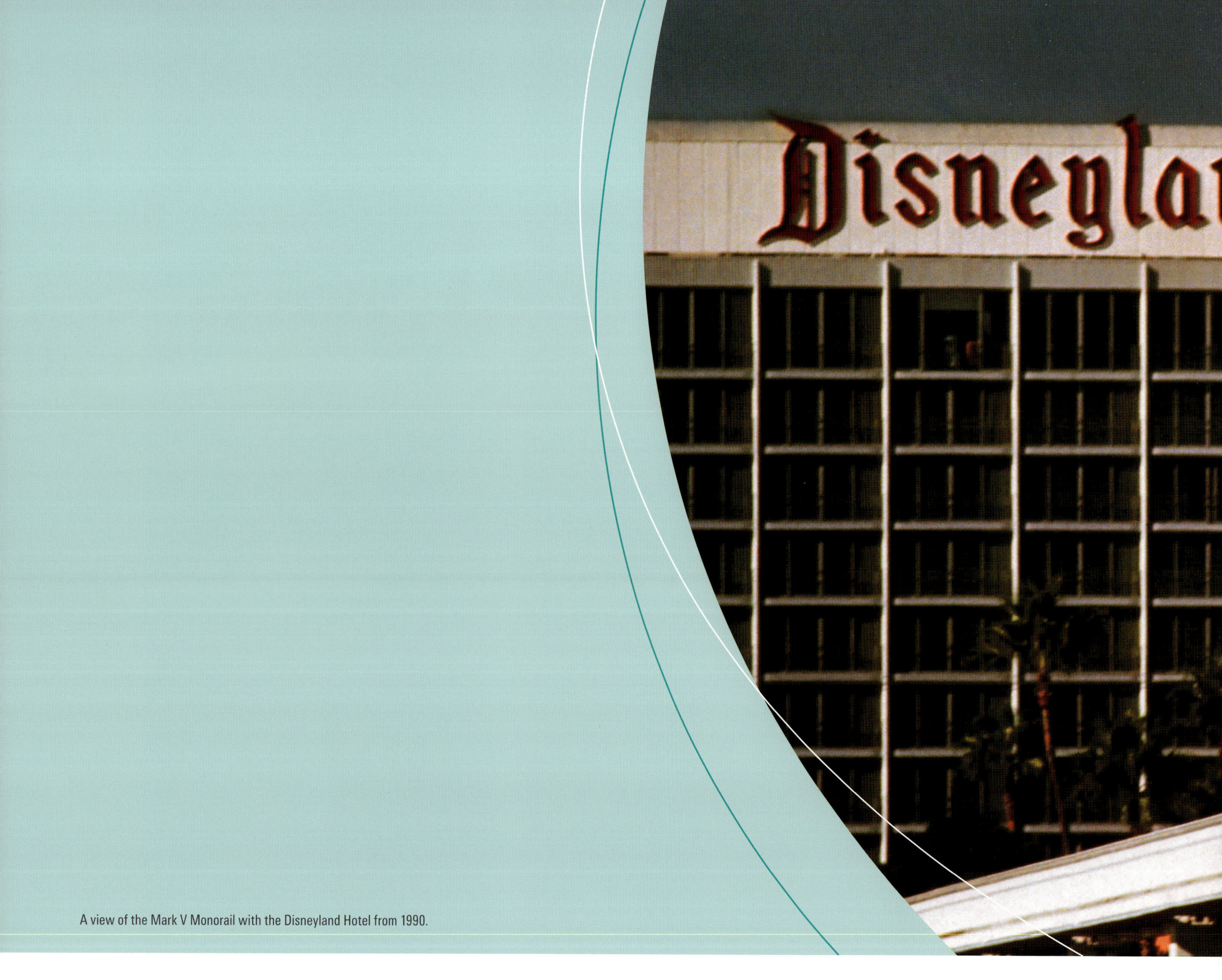

A view of the Mark V Monorail with the Disneyland Hotel from 1990.

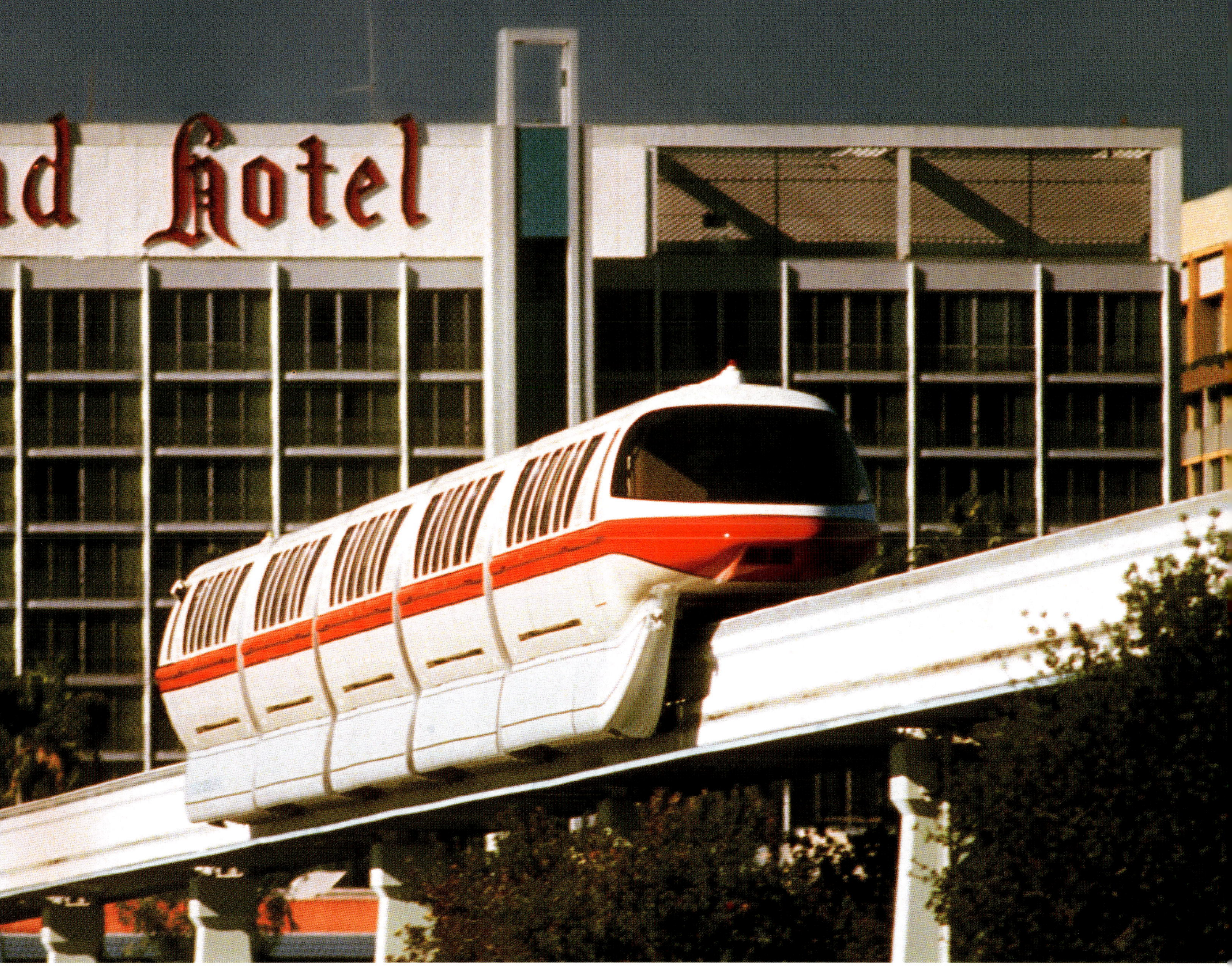
Hotel

How to Identify

MONORAILS OF DISNEYLAND AND WALT DISNEY WORLD

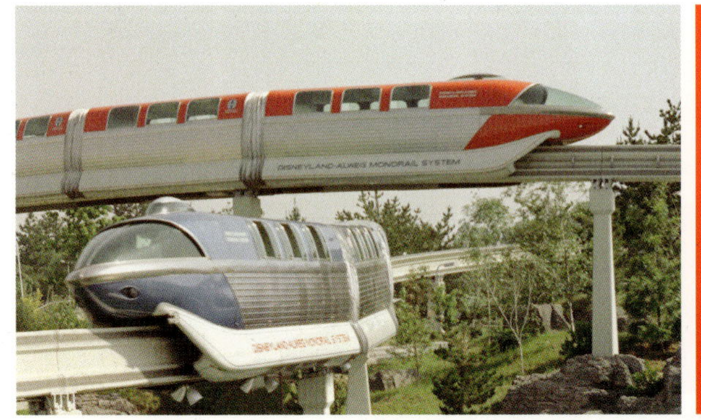

MARK I DISNEYLAND

JUNE 14, 1959 – 1961

COLORS: RED ◦ BLUE

LENGTH: 85 FEET

FEATURES: THREE CARS ◦ SMALL BUBBLE TOP ◦ ALWEG LOGO

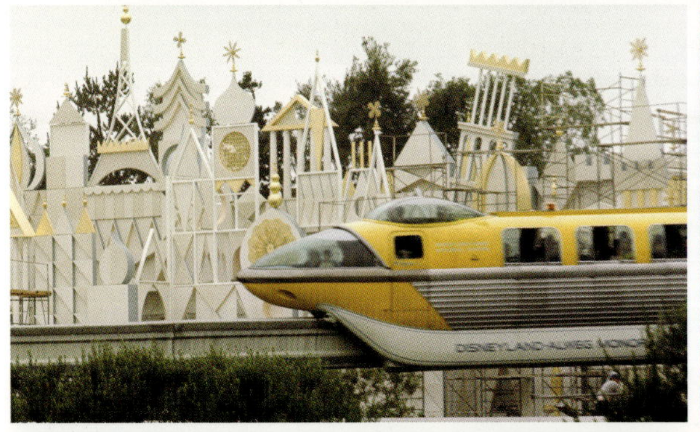

MARK II DISNEYLAND

JUNE 1961 – 1969

COLORS: RED ◦ BLUE ◦ GOLD

LENGTH: 112 FEET

FEATURES: FOUR CARS ◦ LARGE DOME ON TOP OF FRONT CAR ◦ ALWEG LOGO ◦ TRACK CONNECTED TO DISNEYLAND HOTEL

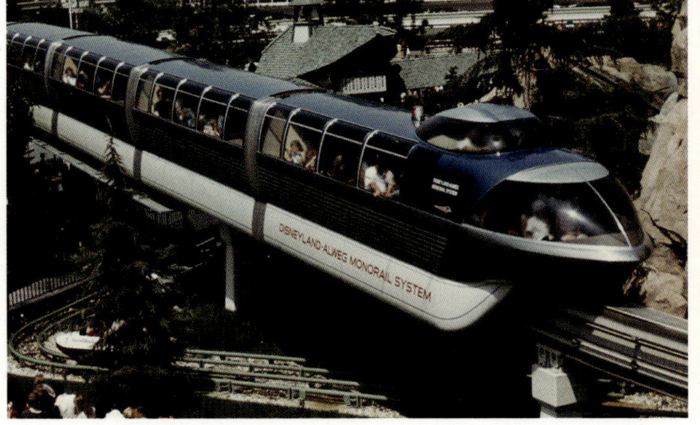

MARK III DISNEYLAND

JULY 1969 – 1987

COLORS: RED ◦ BLUE ◦ GOLD ◦ GREEN

LENGTH: 137 FEET

FEATURES: FIVE CARS ◦ LARGE DOME ON TOP OF FRONT CAR ◦ ALWEG LOGO ◦ LARGER WINDOWS

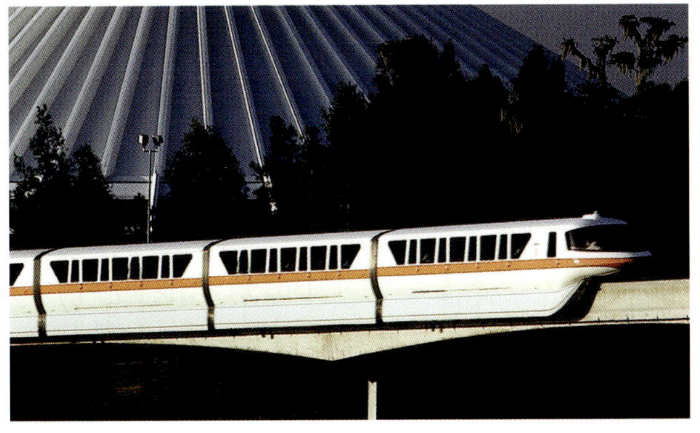

MARK IV WALT DISNEY WORLD

1971 – 1989

COLORS: RED ◦ BLUE ◦ GOLD ◦ ORANGE ◦ YELLOW ◦ GREEN ◦ SILVER ◦ BLACK ◦ PURPLE ◦ PINK ◦ LIME AND CORAL JOIN IN 1984

LENGTH: 171 FEET

FEATURES: FIVE CARS ◦ NINE WINDOWS ◦ SOME TRAINS BECOME SIX CARS AND 201 FEET LONG IN 1978

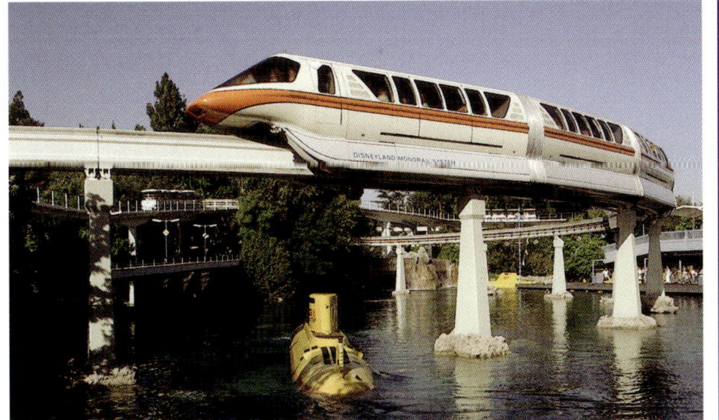

MARK V DISNEYLAND

1986 – 2008

COLORS: RED ◦ BLUE ◦ ORANGE ◦ PURPLE

LENGTH: 150 FEET

FEATURES: FIVE CARS ◦ RESEMBLES THE MARK IV AT WALT DISNEY WORLD

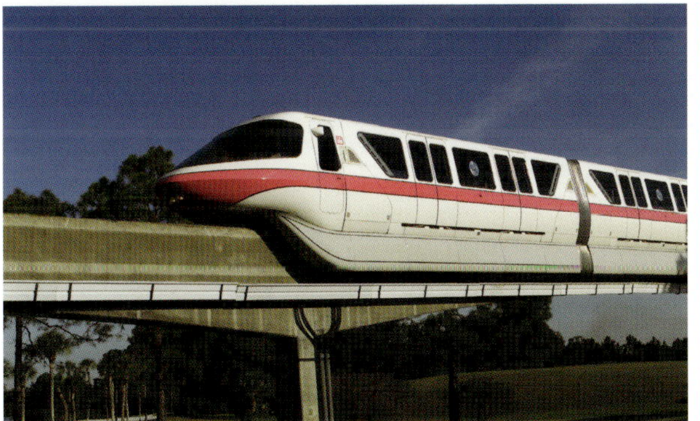

MARK VI WALT DISNEY WORLD

DECEMBER 1989 – PRESENT

COLORS: RED ◦ BLUE ◦ GOLD ◦ ORANGE ◦ YELLOW ◦ GREEN ◦ LIME ◦ CORAL ◦ SILVER ◦ BLACK ◦ PINK AND PURPLE RETIRE JULY 2009 ◦ PEACH AND TEAL JOIN IN 2011

LENGTH: 203.5 FEET

FEATURES: SIX CARS ◦ SEVEN WINDOWS ◦ WIDER DOORS

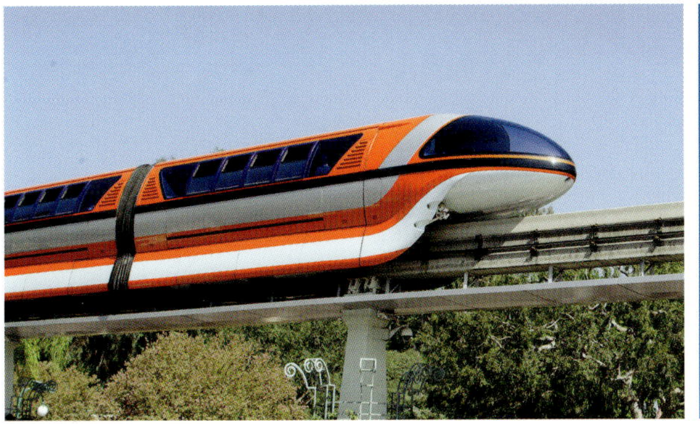

MARK VII DISNEYLAND

JULY 2008 – PRESENT

COLORS: RED ◦ BLUE ◦ ORANGE

LENGTH: 140 FEET

FEATURES: FIVE CARS ◦ SIMILAR TO THE MARK I

Landmark Status

In December of 1986, the Disneyland Monorail System was named a National Historic Mechanical Engineering Landmark by the American Society of Mechanical Engineers (ASME). The program, initiated in 1973, recognizes international and regional landmarks each representing a step forward in the evolution of mechanical engineering with its own influence on society. As of 2019, 273 landmarks were on the ASME list of honorees.

"The landmarks program illuminates our technological heritage and serves to encourage the preservation of the physical remains of historically important works," the ASME declaration said. "It provides an annotated roster for engineers, students, educators, historians and travelers and helps establish persistent reminders of where we have been, where we are, and where we are going along the divergent paths of discovery." A plaque was installed at the entry of the Tomorrowland Monorail Station. A slightly updated plaque (shown at right) replaced the original in 2004 when it was rededicated.

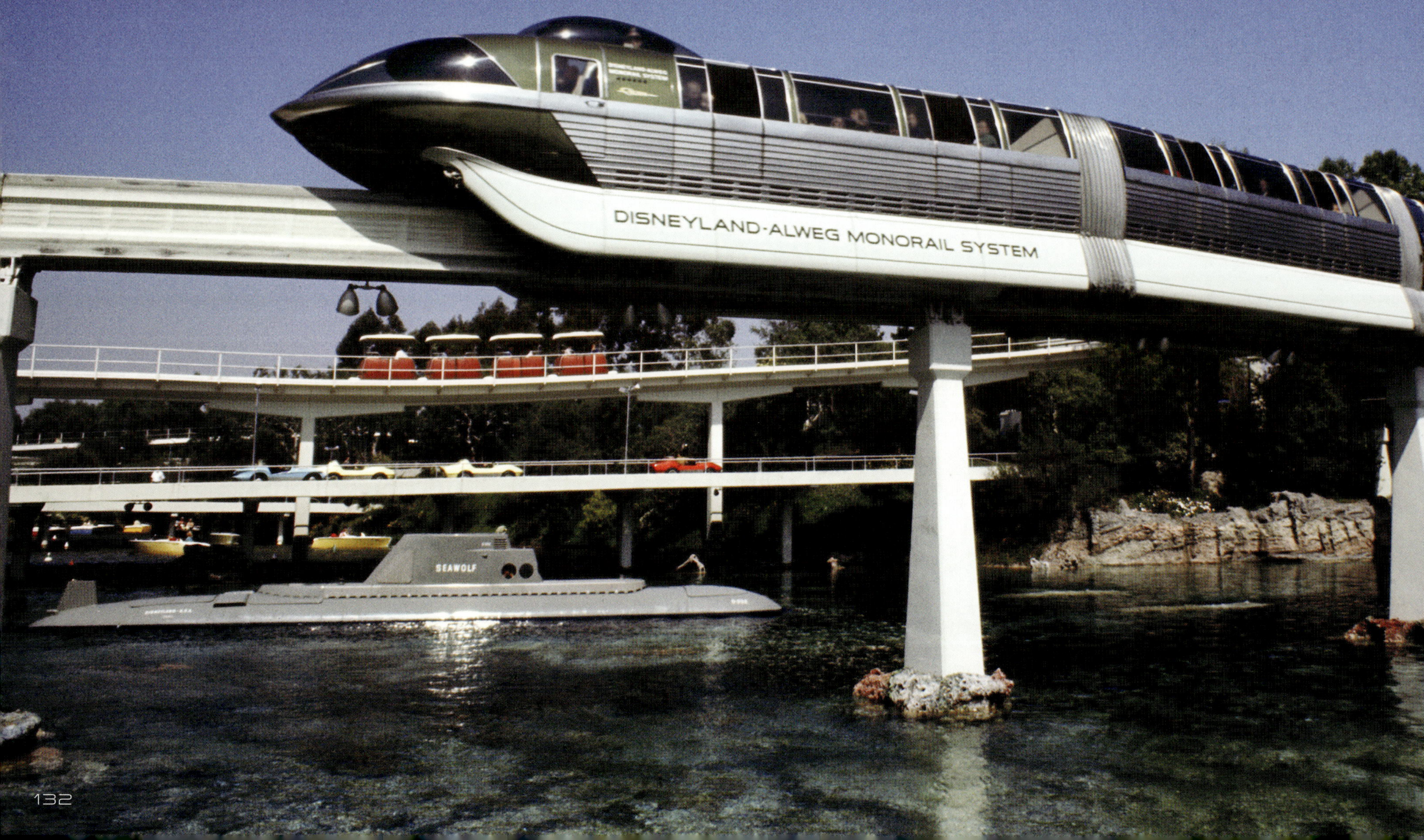

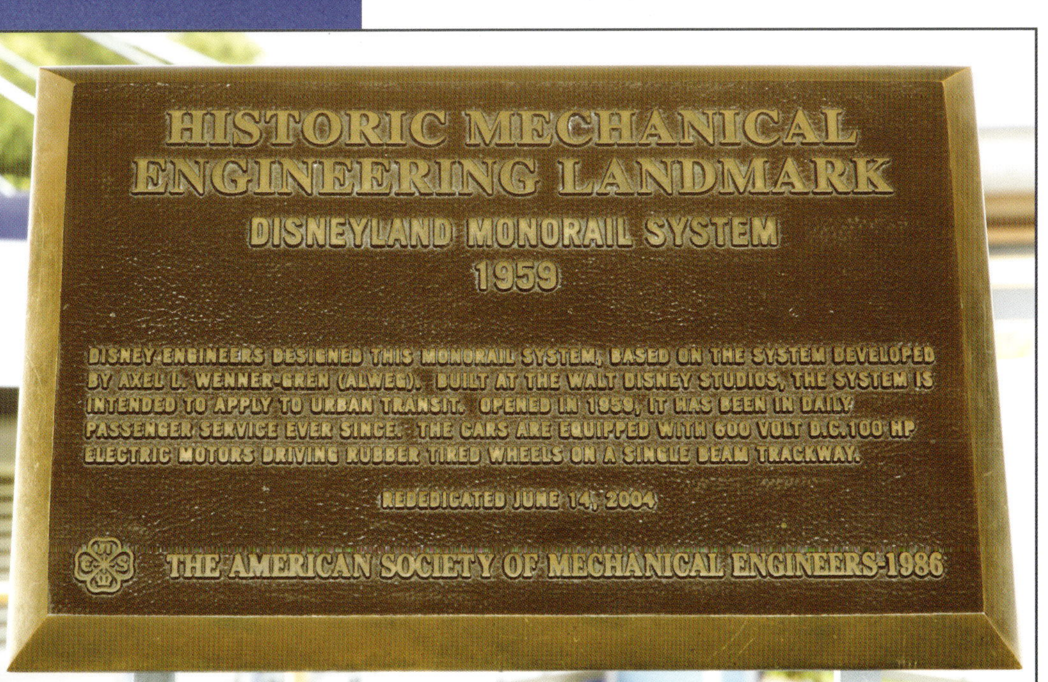

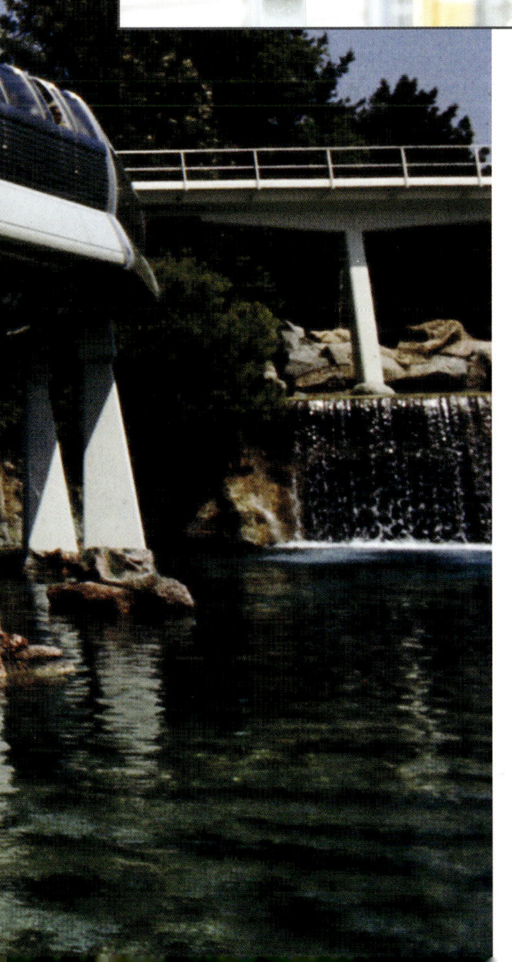

There's little doubt that Walt Disney would have taken special pride in such recognition.

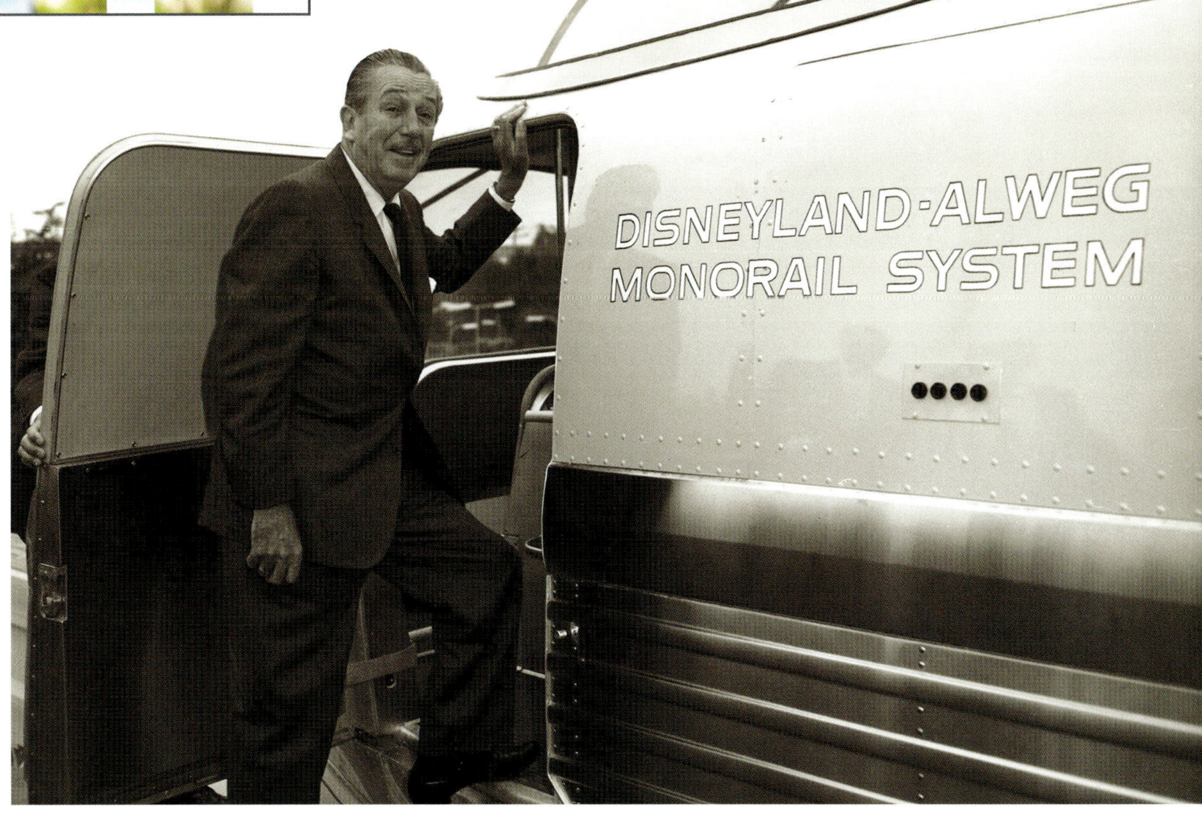

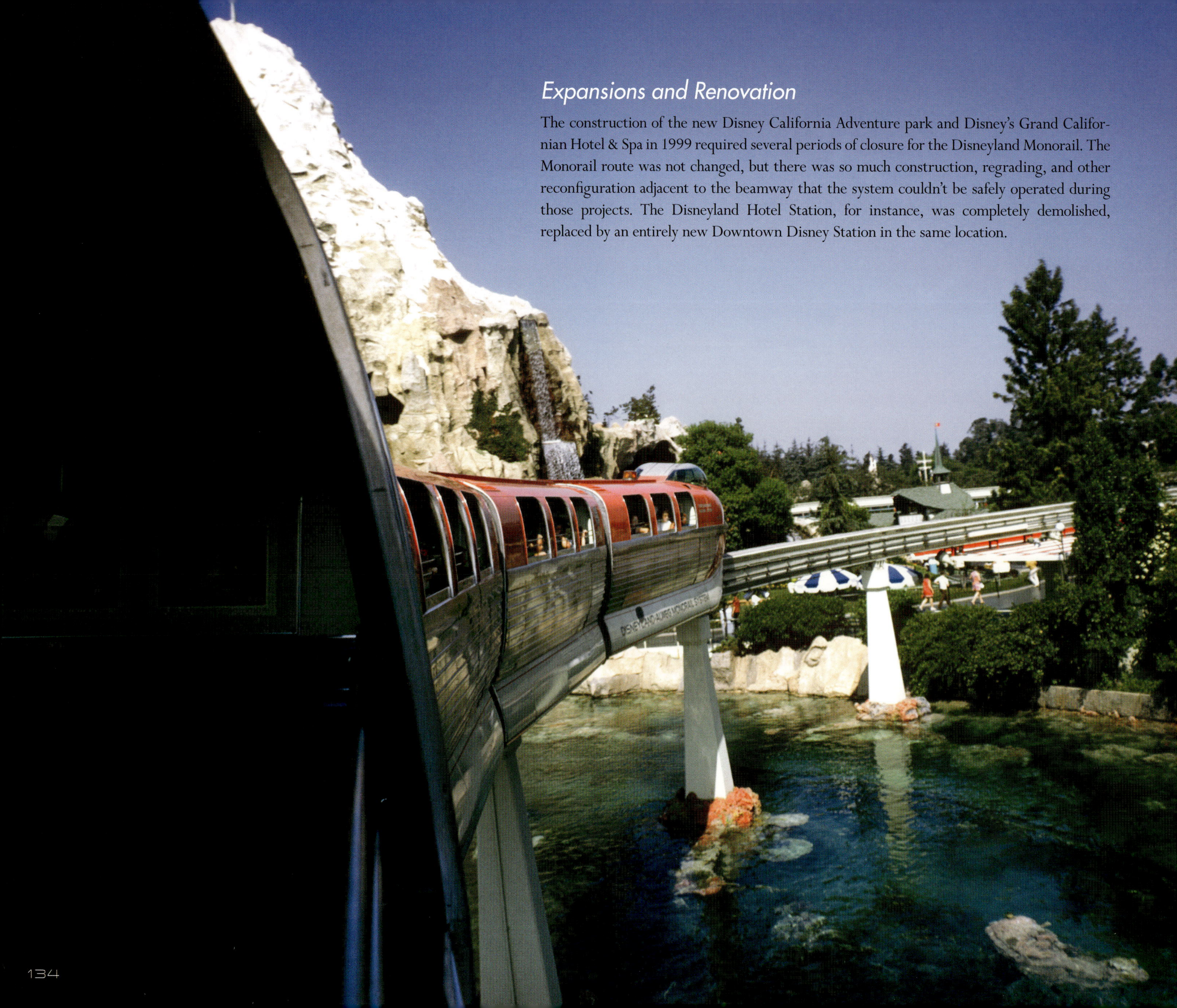

Expansions and Renovation

The construction of the new Disney California Adventure park and Disney's Grand Californian Hotel & Spa in 1999 required several periods of closure for the Disneyland Monorail. The Monorail route was not changed, but there was so much construction, regrading, and other reconfiguration adjacent to the beamway that the system couldn't be safely operated during those projects. The Disneyland Hotel Station, for instance, was completely demolished, replaced by an entirely new Downtown Disney Station in the same location.

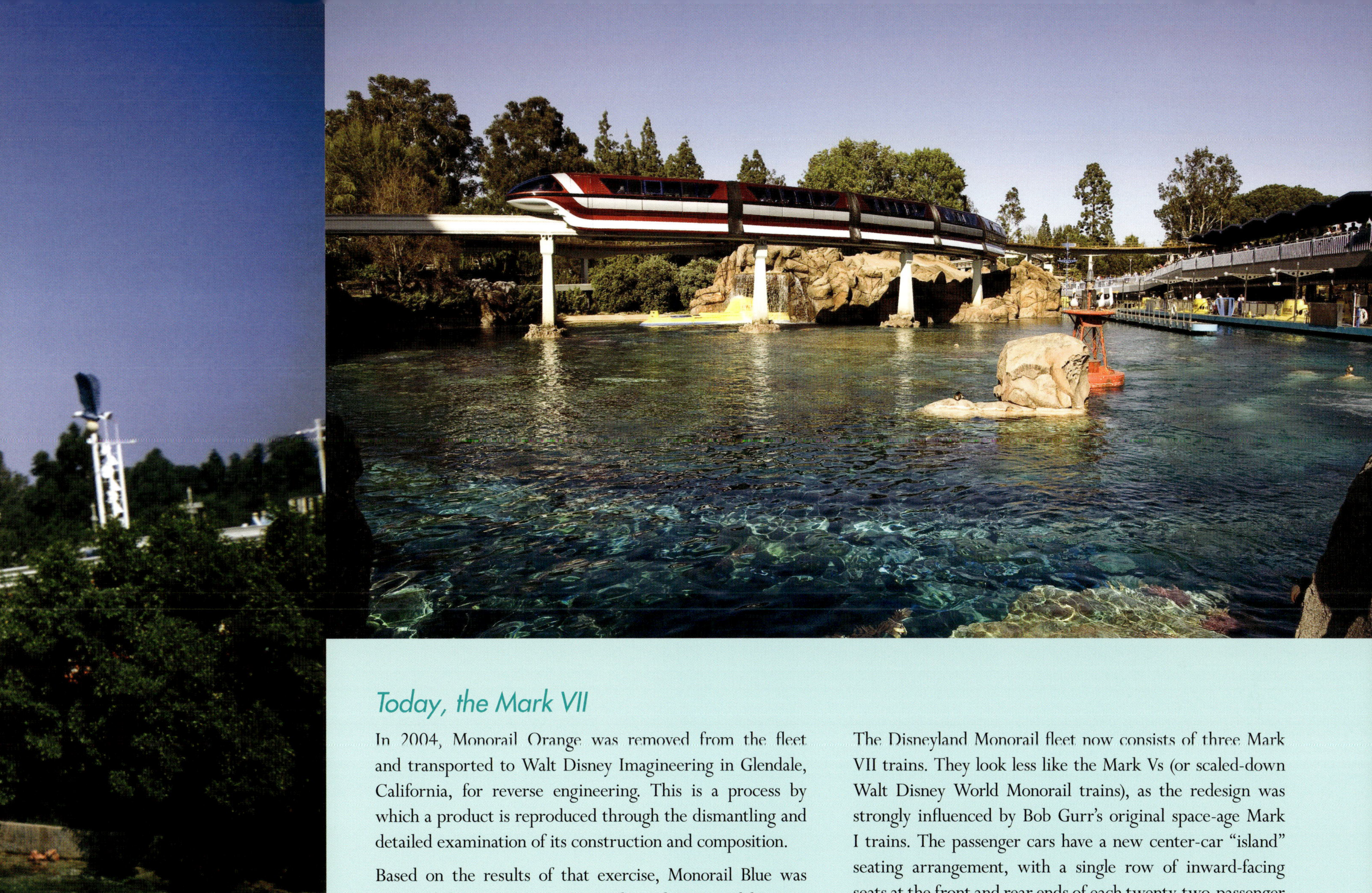

Today, the Mark VII

In 2004, Monorail Orange was removed from the fleet and transported to Walt Disney Imagineering in Glendale, California, for reverse engineering. This is a process by which a product is reproduced through the dismantling and detailed examination of its construction and composition.

Based on the results of that exercise, Monorail Blue was removed from service in September of 2006 and began a process of redesign and rebuilding by Walt Disney Imagineering and TPI Composites to transform it into a new Mark VII model. This process was continued, train by train, for the next three years. The new Monorail Red began service in July 2008, and Monorail Blue went back into service in September of that year. They were joined by Monorail Orange in April 2009.

The Disneyland Monorail fleet now consists of three Mark VII trains. They look less like the Mark Vs (or scaled-down Walt Disney World Monorail trains), as the redesign was strongly influenced by Bob Gurr's original space-age Mark I trains. The passenger cars have a new center-car "island" seating arrangement, with a single row of inward-facing seats at the front and rear ends of each twenty-two-passenger car. The tail cone has a capacity of seven passengers; the nose cone holds five and a pilot.

In the fall of 2006, the Tomorrowland Monorail Station was remodeled (due to Finding Nemo Submarine Voyage attraction construction), and the original speed ramp entries were removed, replaced with standard concrete ramps and concrete stairs on the west end of the station for exiting passengers.

Still an Inspiring "Highway in the Sky"

Today, the Monorail retains its well-deserved status as an "E Ticket" attraction. Passengers board at the Tomorrowland Monorail Station, after which the train crosses the Disneyland Railroad and follows Harbor Boulevard along the east side of the park. It enters Disney California Adventure, passing adjacent to Hollywood Land, then crossing the Hyperion Bridge at the park's entry. The Monorail then glides through an outdoor concourse at Disney's Grand Californian Hotel & Spa, then curves right to arrive at the Downtown Disney Station.

After loading and unloading passengers, the train departs through Downtown Disney, loops through the area, crosses the esplanade shared by the two parks, and then returns to Disneyland. Once inside, the Monorail again crosses the Disneyland Railroad, then glides into a series of graceful bends and gentle curves, giving an excursion tour of Tomorrowland. The beamway passes above Submarine Lagoon and Autopia, crossing the lagoon four times, circling the Matterhorn, and offering an aerial view of Fantasyland before returning to the Tomorrowland Monorail Station.

Still a popular and inspiring sight and an elegant ride, the Disneyland Monorail continues to represent what Imagineer John Hench declared: "Transportation as an attraction has become a design element characteristic of Disney theme parks."

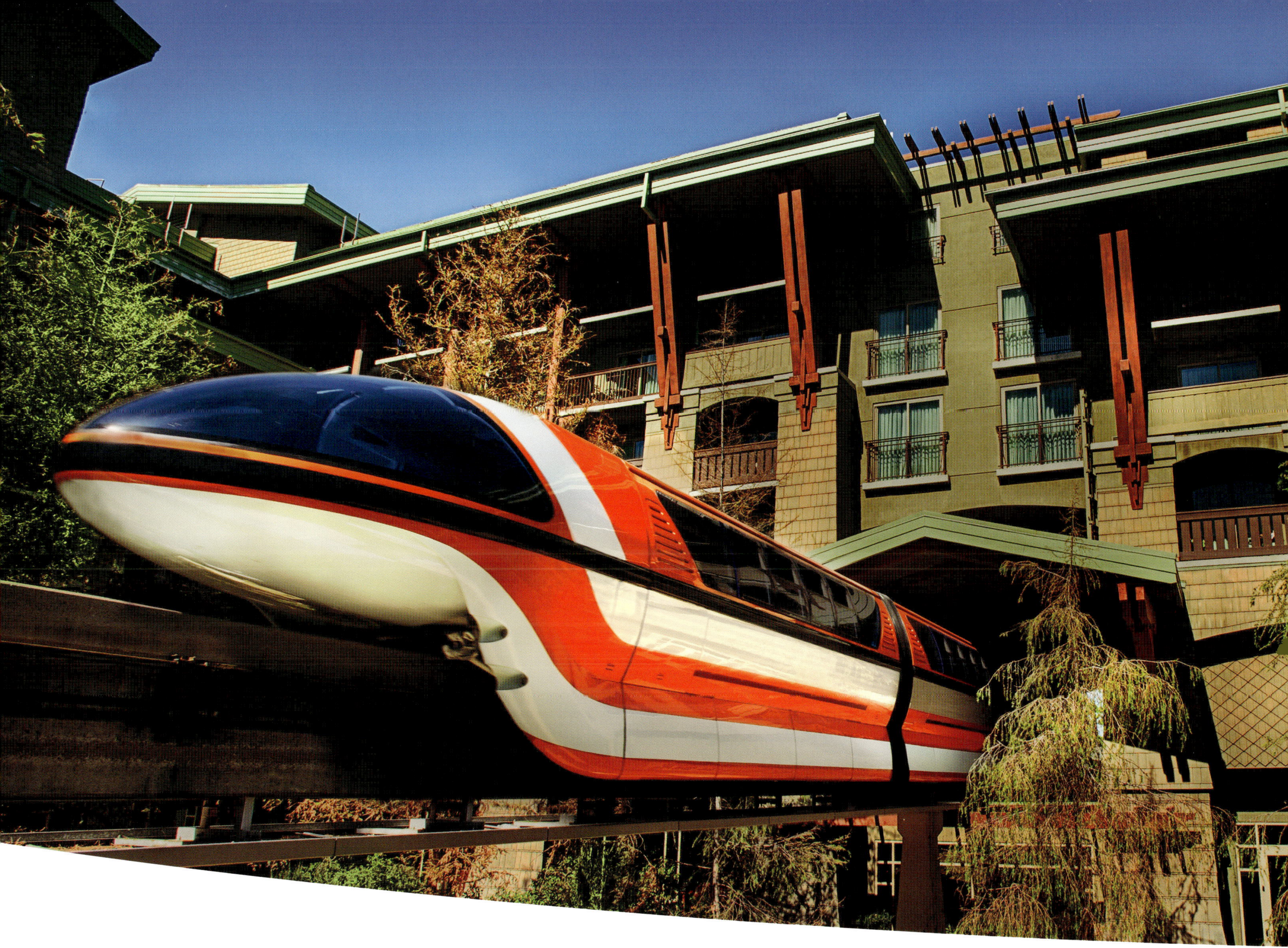

The Monorail glides through an interior courtyard of Disney's Grand Californian Hotel & Spa. Opened in 2001, the hotel (designed by architect Peter Dominick) was inspired by National Park Service lodges such as the Ahwahnee in Yosemite National Park and the Old Faithful Inn in Yellowstone. The existing Monorail beam was incorporated into the layout of the hotel during its design.

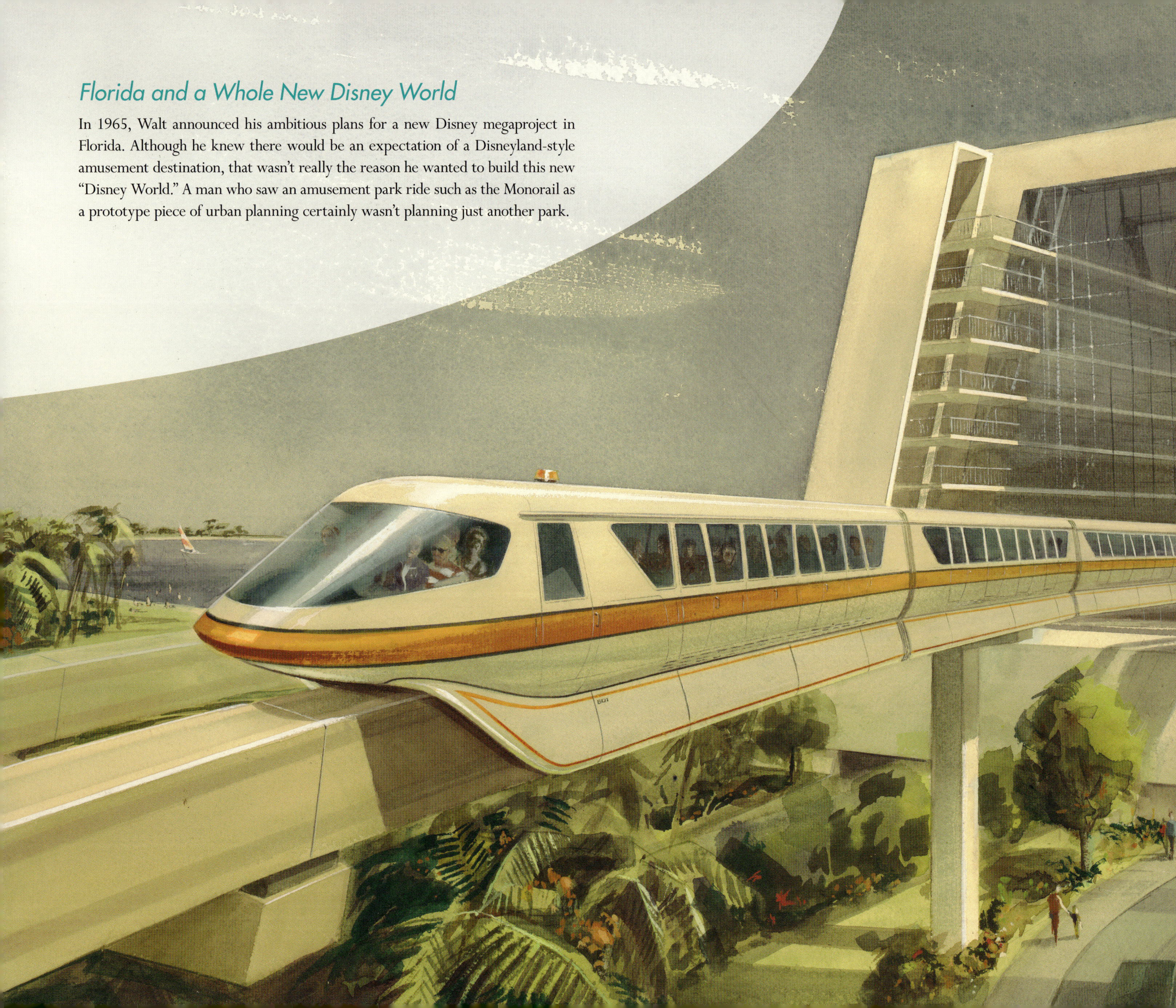

Florida and a Whole New Disney World

In 1965, Walt announced his ambitious plans for a new Disney megaproject in Florida. Although he knew there would be an expectation of a Disneyland-style amusement destination, that wasn't really the reason he wanted to build this new "Disney World." A man who saw an amusement park ride such as the Monorail as a prototype piece of urban planning certainly wasn't planning just another park.

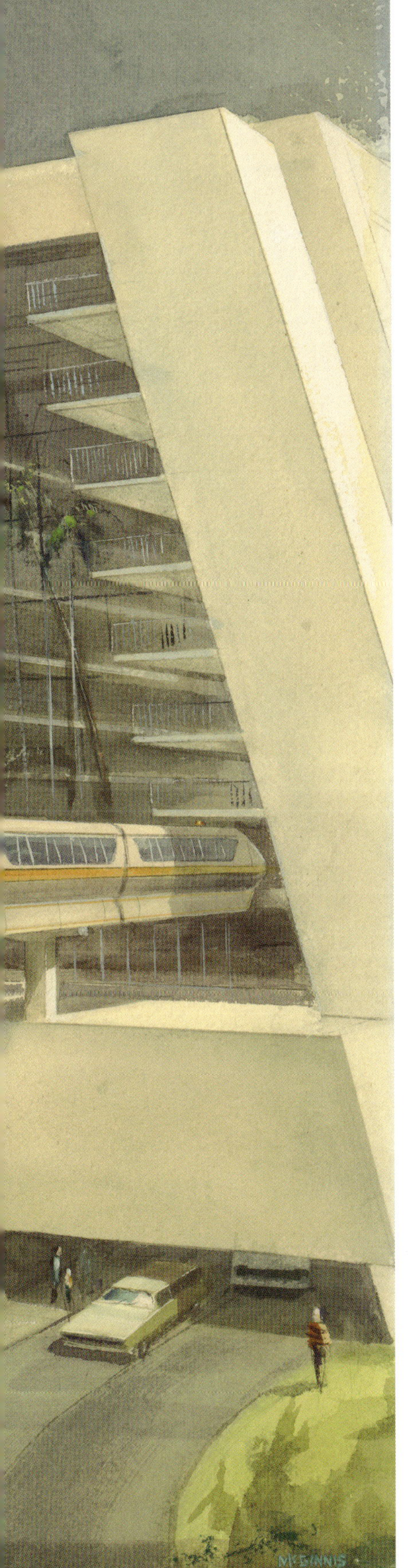

"With Walt Disney World, you know Walt didn't spend *any* time on the park," Marty Sklar said. "In fact, he said this in a press conference he had when he announced Walt Disney World in 1965, that people would expect certain attractions that had been at Disneyland and we were certainly going to bring them there. But his whole focus was on EPCOT, an experimental prototype community of tomorrow—he kind of used the words city and community interchangeably. But it really was on finding a way to bring new technology that would influence and inform people's lives in a way that they would understand and perhaps be introduced to."

John Hench recalled, "I think Walt wanted to have a place with more ideas than we could have possibly had in Disneyland. But he was—he really did believe that people would profit by an experience. And where they could—and the problems that he saw in city life and the way things were beginning to feel about the problems of communities at large, and Walt figured that he'd build a place where they could have an experience of some solutions for these things. He believed that the experience was the important thing. That people could read about ideas, or see photographs or pictures or images of ideas, but if they experienced it, if they went through this themselves, it would be much more compelling. It would really answer something. That they could go home then in their own communities and make changes."

Included with the expected theme park and resort amenities was a fully developed model city, which was the focus of Walt's vision. It included single-family and apartment residences, business and research parks, shopping, parks, and even a self-contained airport.

Of course, in order to link all the elements of the new Florida Project, innovative mass transit would be required.

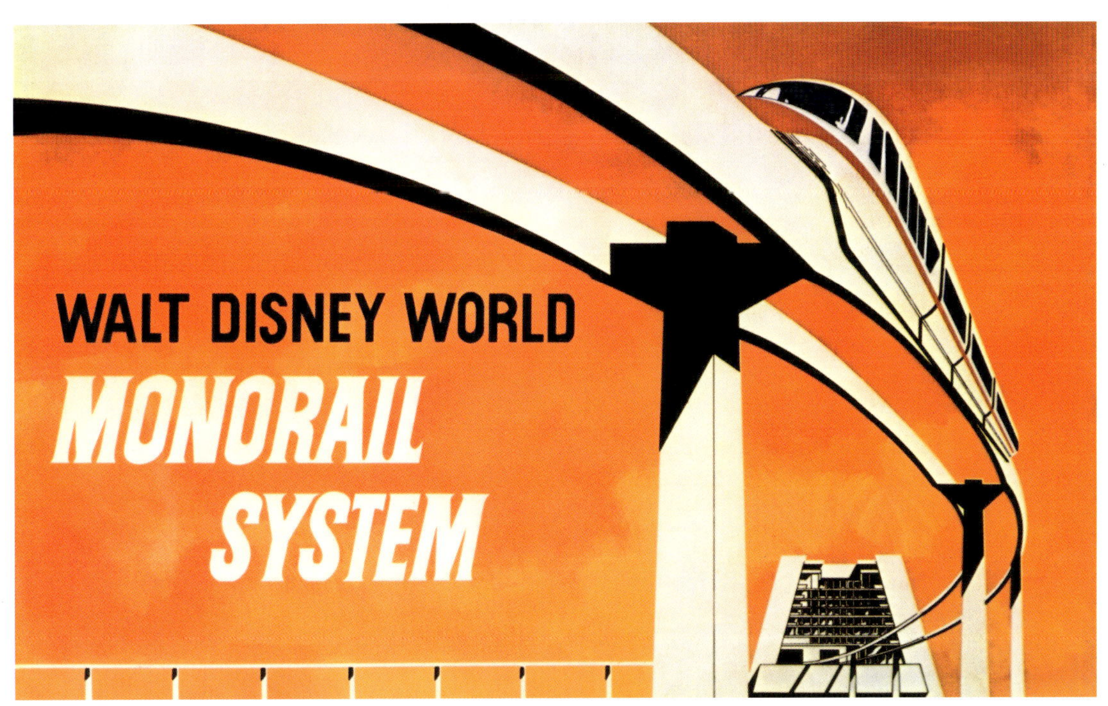

OPPOSITE: This acrylic and watercolor painting by George McGinnis is a masterpiece of design and staging; the color palette speaks of lightness and modernity; the perspective creates a palpable sense of motion and speed.

LEFT: Less successful is this tram card design by an uncredited artist; the eye focuses on shadows; the staging makes the train oddly boxy and seemingly motionless.

The "New Disneyland" Park

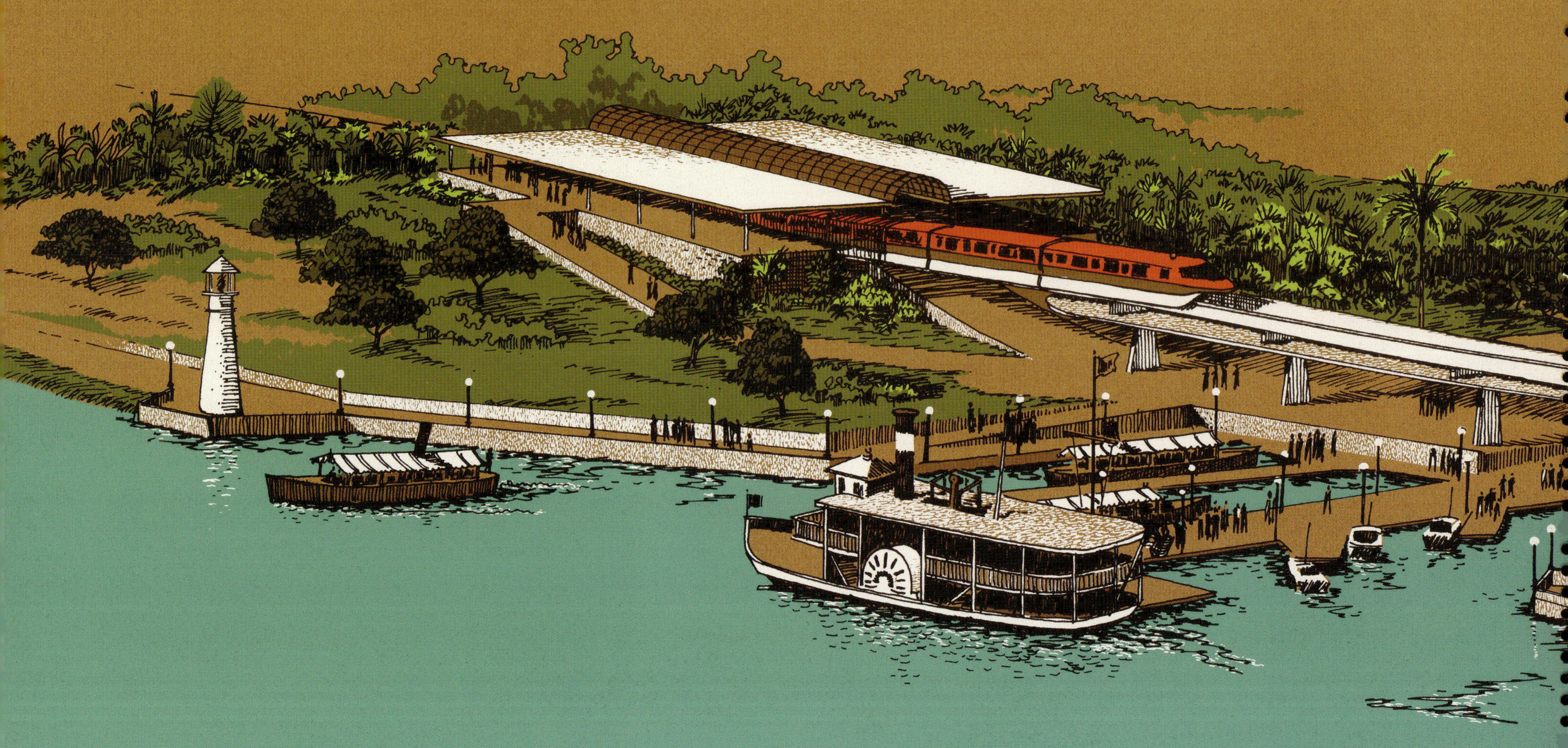

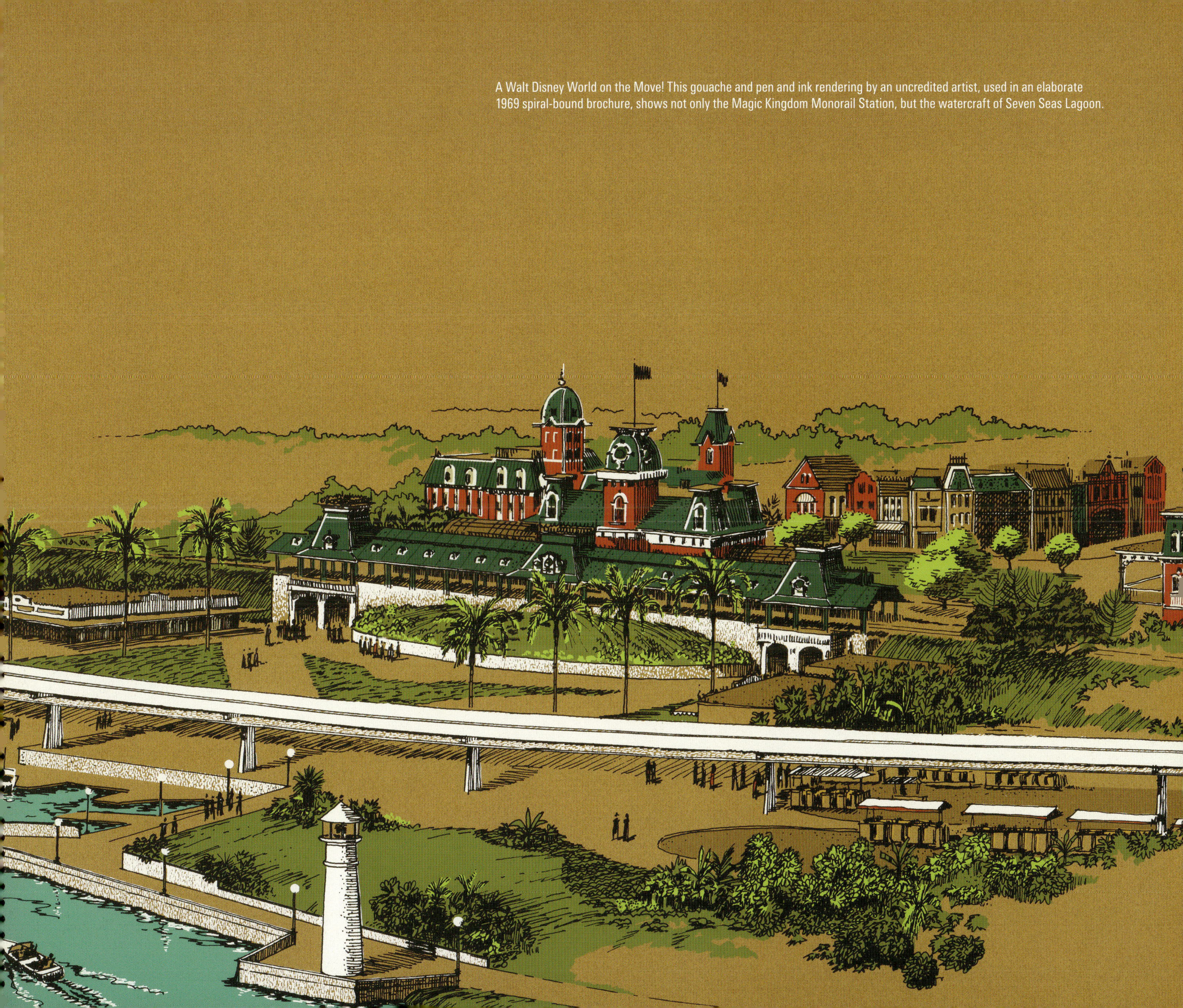

A Walt Disney World on the Move! This gouache and pen and ink rendering by an uncredited artist, used in an elaborate 1969 spiral-bound brochure, shows not only the Magic Kingdom Monorail Station, but the watercraft of Seven Seas Lagoon.

"They were going to be automatic trains that came on, based on demand," Disney Legend and past Imagineering president Carl Bongiorno recalled. "You'd go to a station, you'd push a button, and if there wasn't a train coming or if a lot of people pushed the buttons at various stations, new cars would come on the line because they knew that there were additional load requirements. And as demand decreased, then cars automatically went back into the barn. Now, that was the concept, and again, that had to be designed and engineered. Walt always said, 'I want a car there within three minutes.' He had some great ideas."

From the very first property plans, including one drafted by Walt himself, the Monorail was a key element of what would become the Walt Disney World Resort.

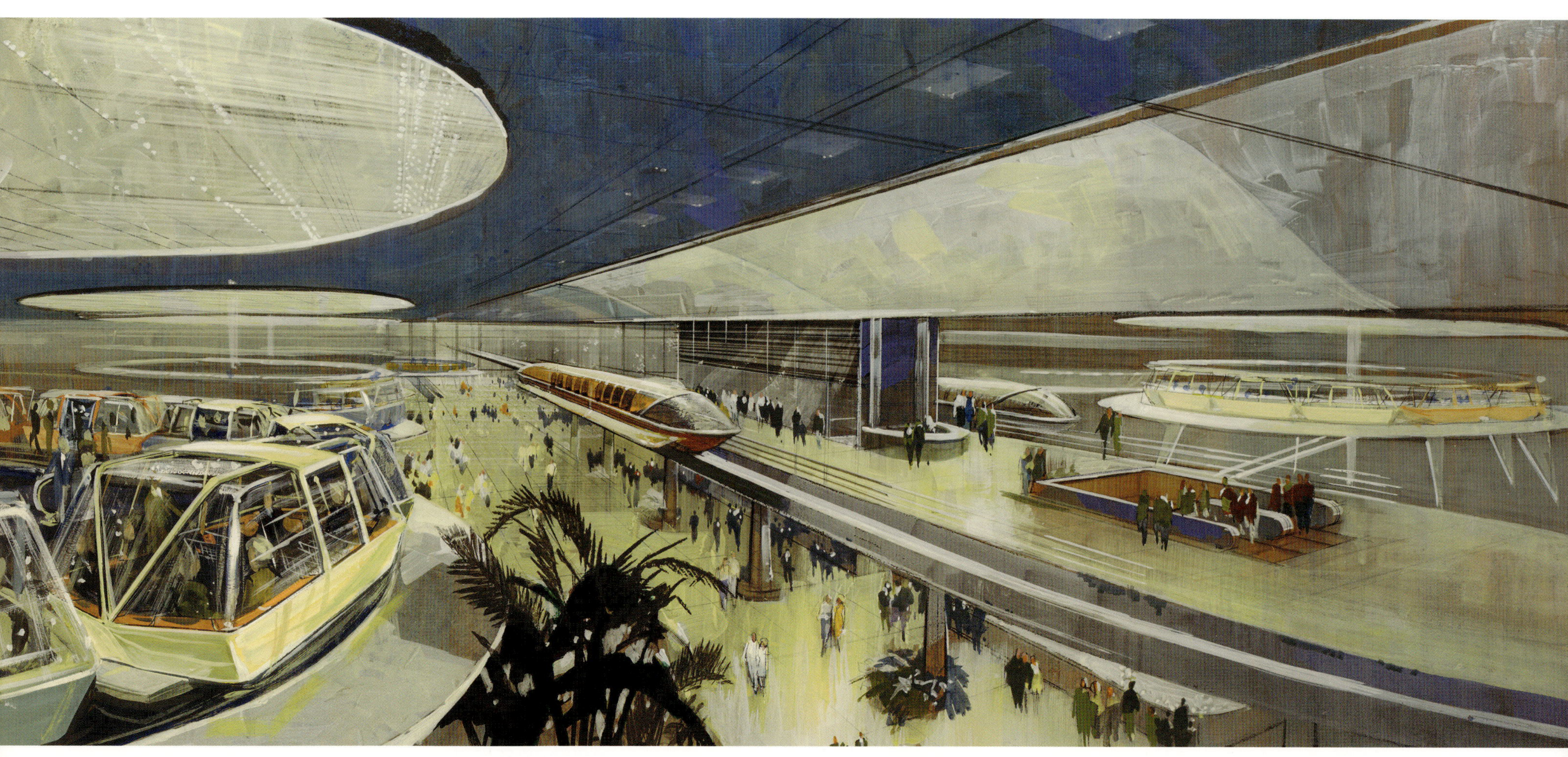

A 1966 acrylic painting by Herb Ryman of an idea for Walt Disney's original planned community concept. Here in the "Transportation Lobby" beneath the hotel tower in the EPCOT "Central City," separate but interconnecting transportation systems come together: the shorter-range WEDWay PeopleMover system, and the high-speed Monorail system for rapid transit over longer distances.

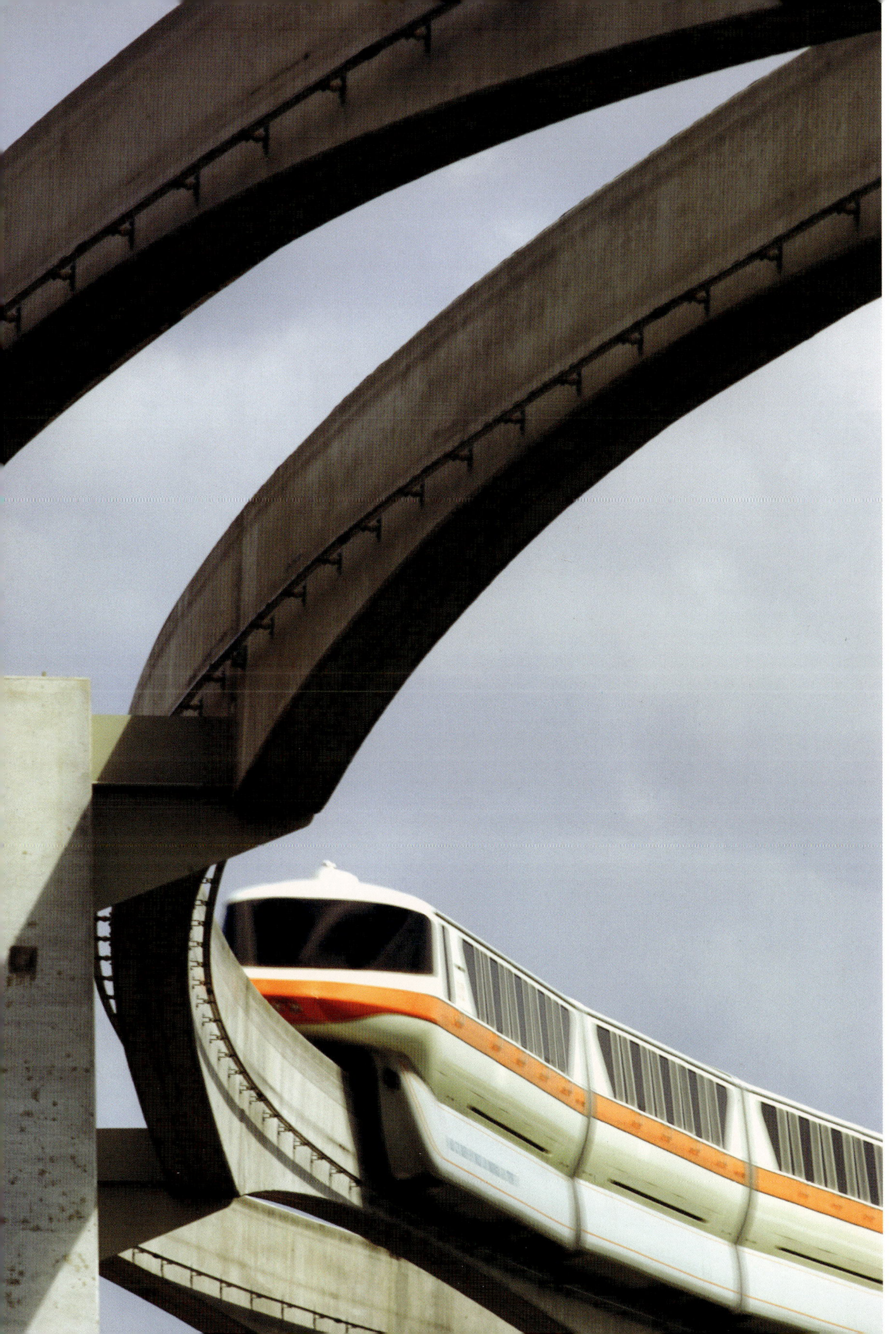

Florida After Walt

With Walt's passing in 1966, the plans for Florida changed. A vision without its driving visionary simply can't be sustained. Roy O. Disney postponed his own retirement in order to at least get Disney World—which he renamed Walt Disney World, so his brother's personal influence on the project would never be forgotten—into its initial construction, and to attempt a phased development plan in order to realize Walt's prophetic aspiration.

Although it never became the straightforward "model city" of Walt's design, Walt Disney World did indeed become an idea lab, as Walt wanted: "an experimental prototype community of tomorrow that will take its cue from the new ideas and new technologies that are now emerging from the creative centers of American industry. It will be a community of tomorrow that will never be completed, but will always be introducing and testing and demonstrating new materials and systems. And EPCOT will always be a showcase to the world for the ingenuity and imagination of American free enterprise. . . . It will never cease to be a living blueprint of the future."

Today, the Mark VI Monorail trains at Walt Disney World are a testament to Walt's faith in the technology and the ideas behind it. They incorporate more than fifty years of research and development in monorail expertise. The system, in operation since 1971, was expanded in 1982 with a four-mile extension to the (then) brand-new EPCOT Center, and updated in the late 1980s and early 1990s with new trains to create today's twelve-train fleet. The 14.7-mile Walt Disney World Monorail System of elevated beamways services seven stations between EPCOT, the Magic Kingdom, and three resort hotels, plus carries hundreds of thousands of Guests each day.

The double-beam track circles the Seven Seas Lagoon and initially featured four stations: the Transportation and Ticket Center, Disney's Polynesian Village Resort, the Magic Kingdom, and Disney's Contemporary Resort. The four-mile single-beam EPCOT line and its station were added during that park's construction, opening on October 1, 1982. The most recent addition was Disney's Grand Floridian Resort & Spa Station, along the original resort beamway, which was opened in 1988 along with the resort.

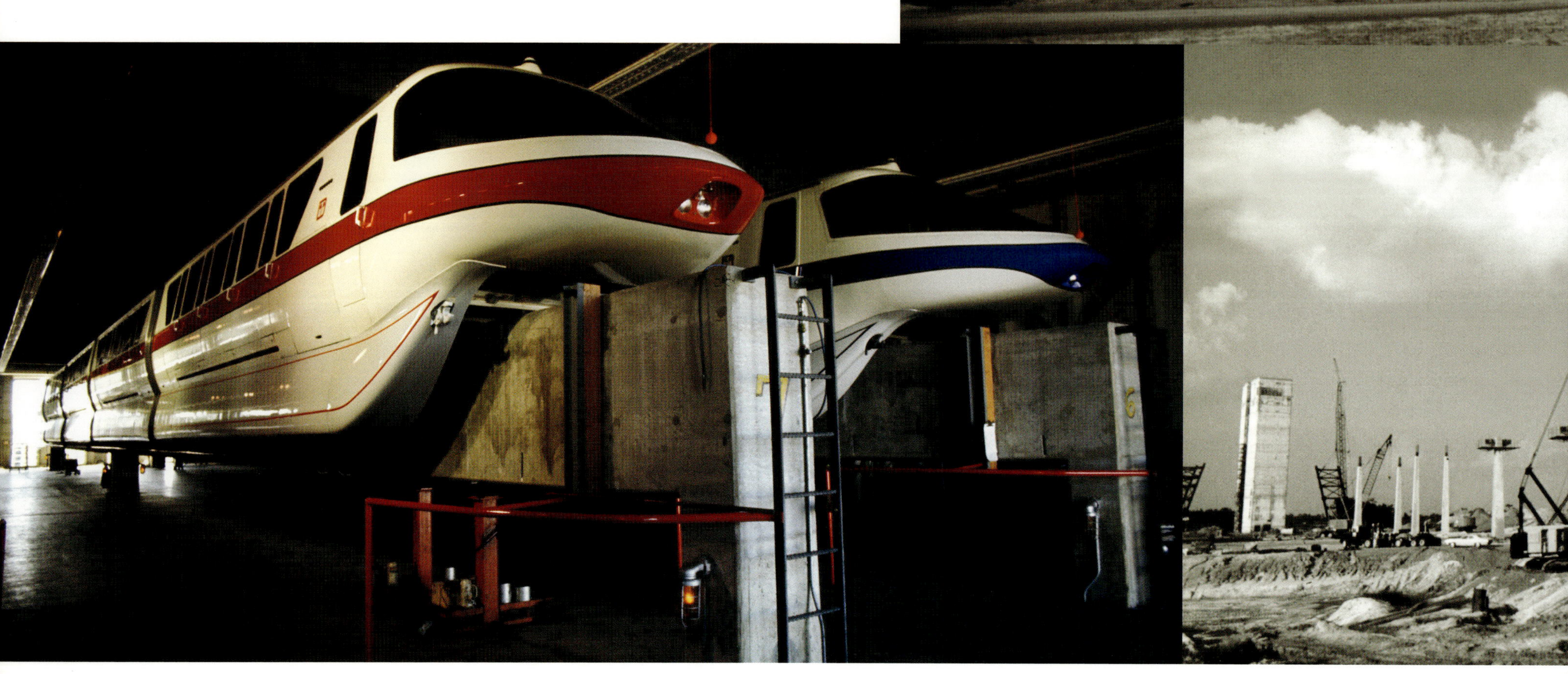

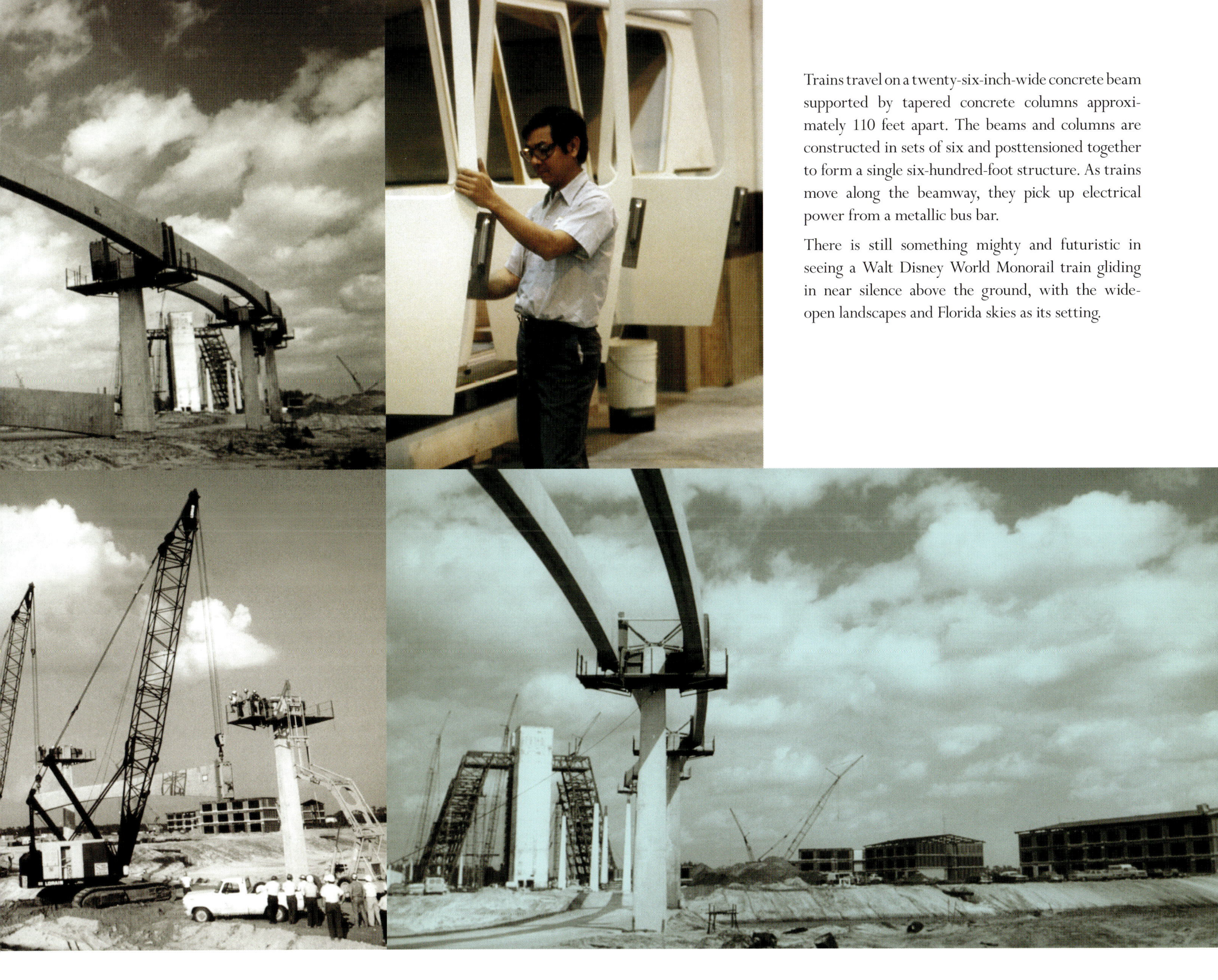

Trains travel on a twenty-six-inch-wide concrete beam supported by tapered concrete columns approximately 110 feet apart. The beams and columns are constructed in sets of six and posttensioned together to form a single six-hundred-foot structure. As trains move along the beamway, they pick up electrical power from a metallic bus bar.

There is still something mighty and futuristic in seeing a Walt Disney World Monorail train gliding in near silence above the ground, with the wide-open landscapes and Florida skies as its setting.

The WDW Original Mark IV

The original Mark IV Monorail debuted at the opening of Walt Disney World in October 1971. While the Monorail system, like the project itself, would not be as ambitious and expansive as Walt's original plans, the decision was made that the Monorail would be both an iconic element of the project and a primary mode of Guest transport. The Monorail in Florida would not be a demonstration or prototype. It was, as Walt had envisioned, a necessary operational component of the entire property.

Walt had bemoaned the rampant commercial development that took place around Disneyland once it had become a success; he disliked the lack of cohesion and the visual cacophony that encircled his beloved park. His Florida property would be big enough to prevent that, and so the primary initial parking facility for Walt Disney World was located nearly a mile away from the Magic Kingdom and resort hotels, across the two-hundred-acre Seven Seas Lagoon. There, Guests could leave their vehicles (and the visual intrusion they created) behind and board a monorail or watercraft to the primary on-property destinations.

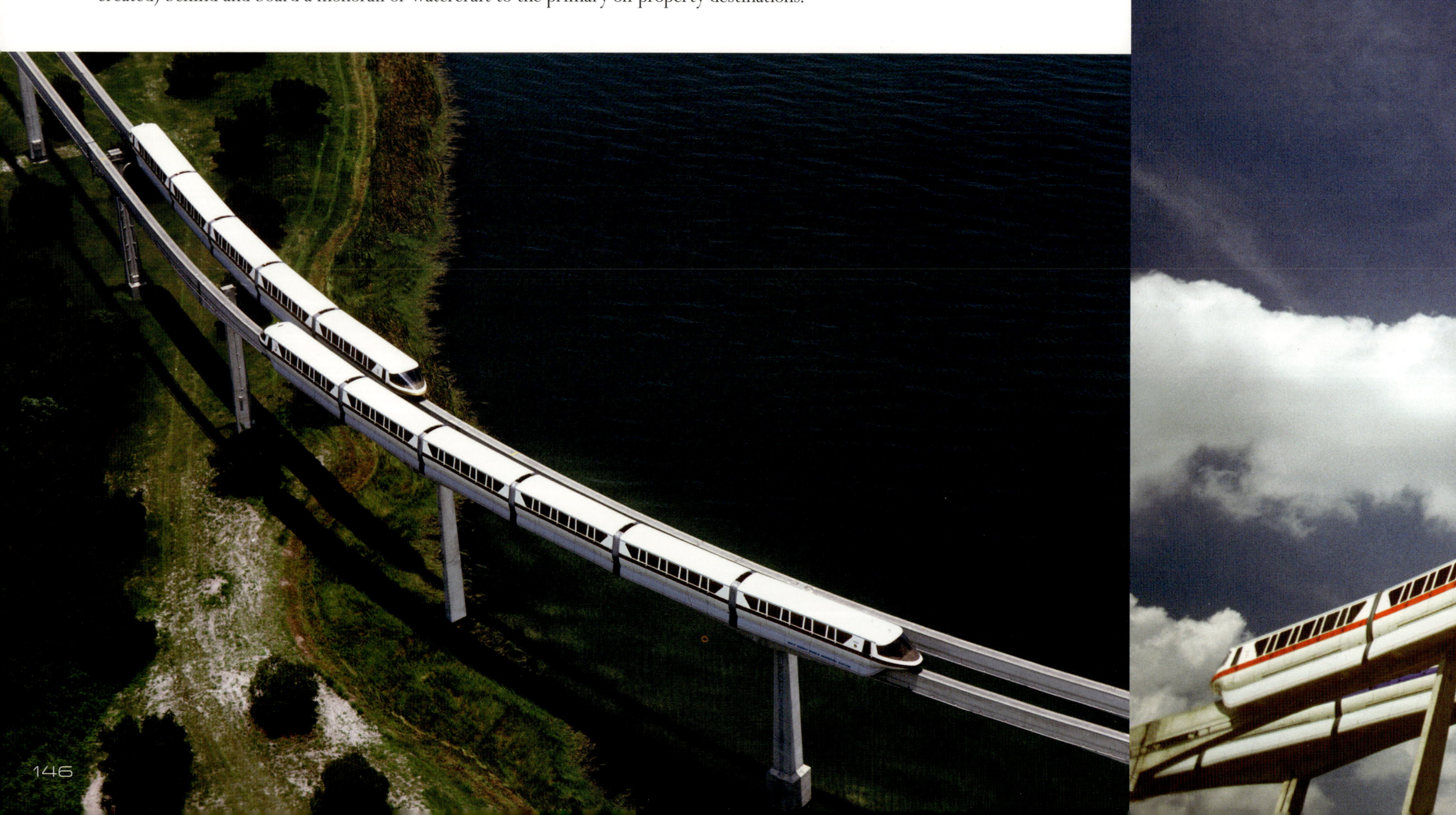

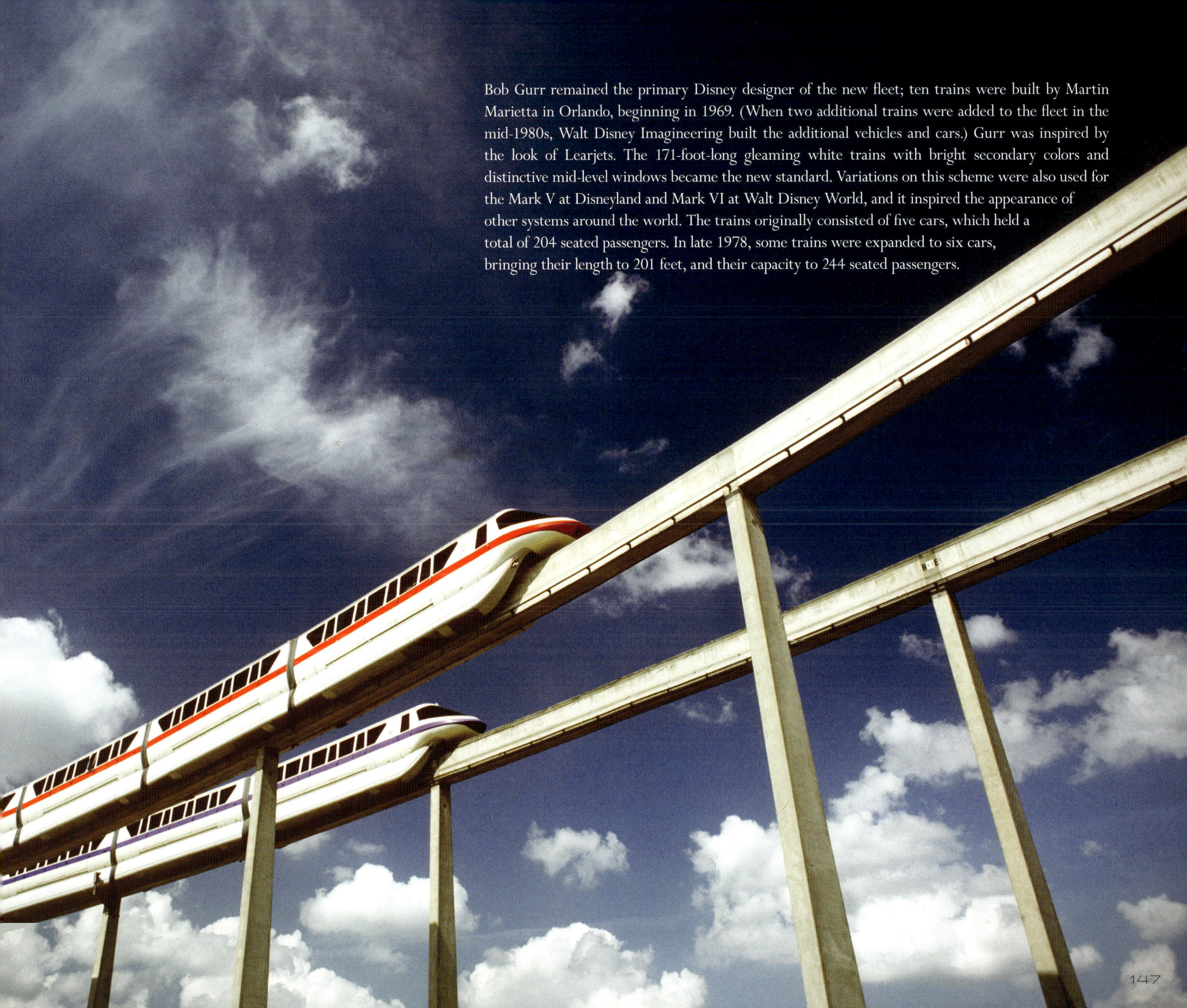

Bob Gurr remained the primary Disney designer of the new fleet; ten trains were built by Martin Marietta in Orlando, beginning in 1969. (When two additional trains were added to the fleet in the mid-1980s, Walt Disney Imagineering built the additional vehicles and cars.) Gurr was inspired by the look of Learjets. The 171-foot-long gleaming white trains with bright secondary colors and distinctive mid-level windows became the new standard. Variations on this scheme were also used for the Mark V at Disneyland and Mark VI at Walt Disney World, and it inspired the appearance of other systems around the world. The trains originally consisted of five cars, which held a total of 204 seated passengers. In late 1978, some trains were expanded to six cars, bringing their length to 201 feet, and their capacity to 244 seated passengers.

From the Mark IV to the Mark VI

By the waning days of the 1980s, the Mark IV had served for almost two decades of eighteen-hour-a-day operations. In that time, the trains had traveled nearly 67,500 miles annually—with a reliability rate of 99.9 percent!

But that admirable service was beginning to show in deterioration and increasing maintenance, and a new fleet was begun. Bombardier, a leading Canadian manufacturer of planes and trains, had been licensed by The Walt Disney Company to market the Monorail design. Walt Disney Imagineering and Bombardier manufactured twelve all-new Mark VI trains beginning in 1989.

The six-car trains are 203 feet and 6 inches long with a seated-passenger capacity of twenty per car, and an additional capacity of forty standing passengers. Each train can accommodate up to 364 riders. On a typical day, more than 150,000 Guests utilize Monorail transportation.

The Bombardier design featured upgraded air-conditioning, sliding door systems, new safety features, and a redesigned interior, onboard monitoring and communications, and control.

Each of the twelve Monorails is identified by a colored stripe: Red, Blue, Gold, Orange, Yellow, Green, Lime, Coral, Silver, and Black (Pink and Purple were retired in July 2009, and Peach and Teal joined in 2011).

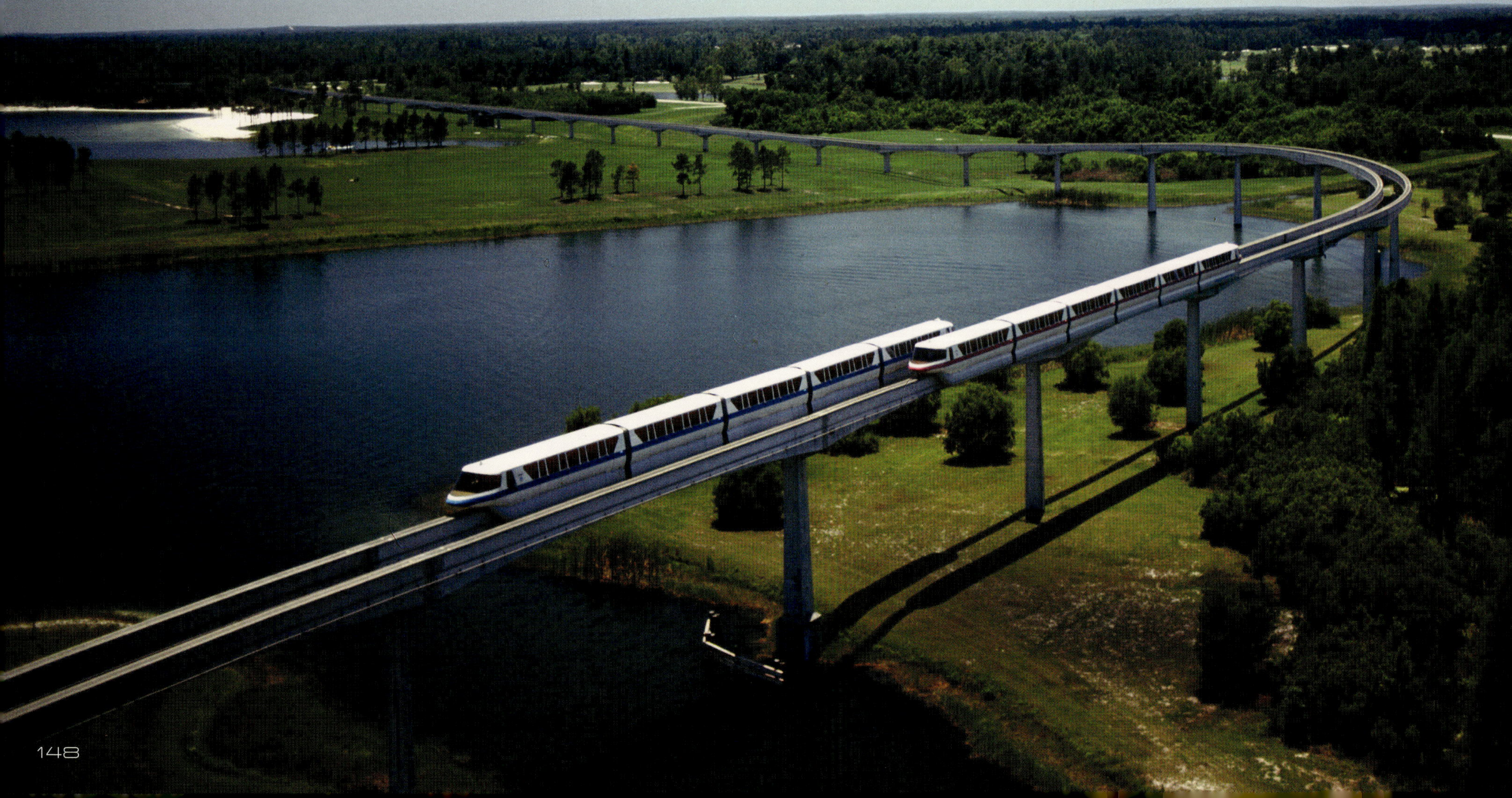

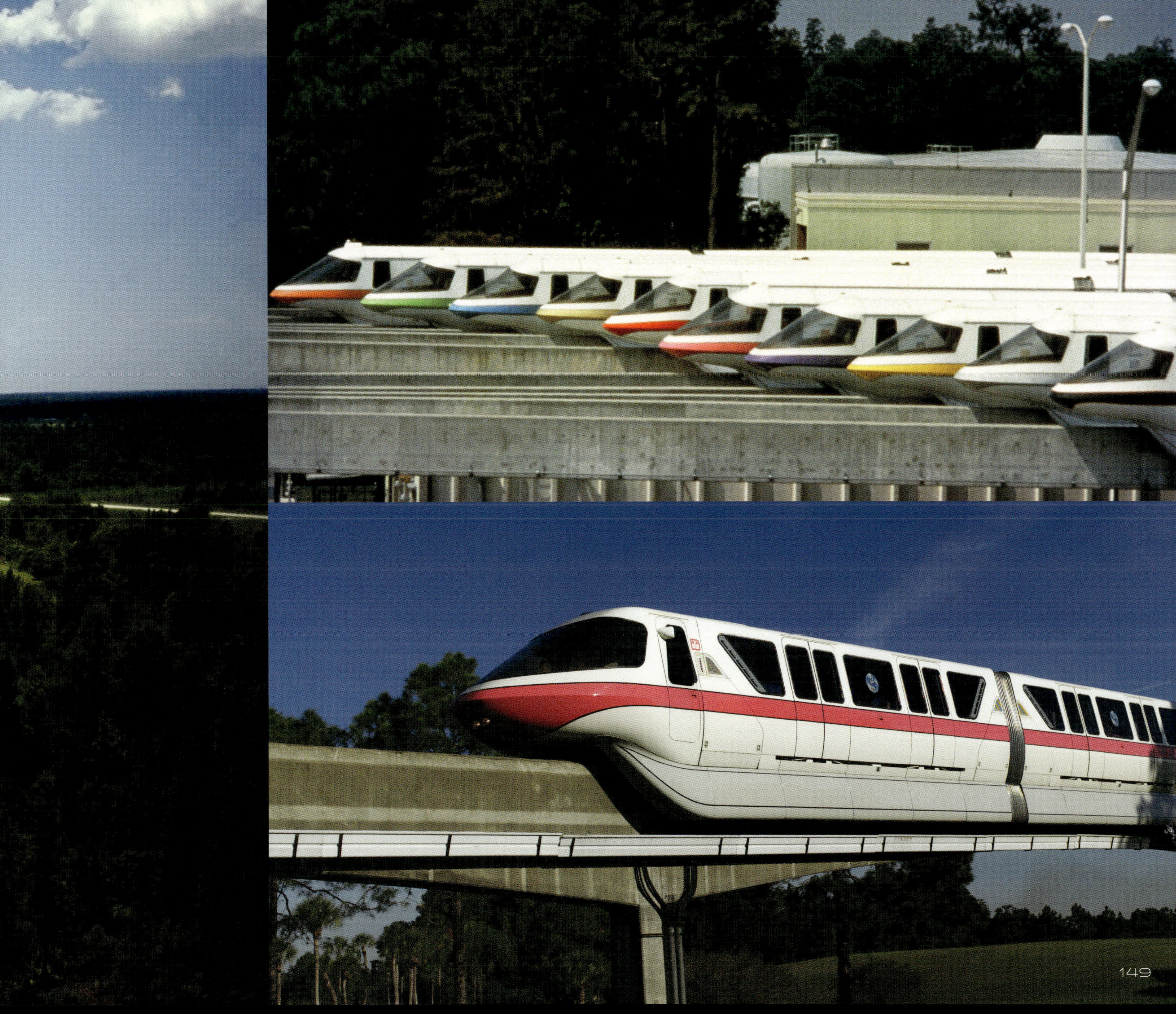

Speed with Safety

Maximum speed during normal operations on the Walt Disney World Monorail System is forty miles per hour, and there are speed zones throughout the system with limits ranging from fifteen to thirty-five miles per hour. These speed limits are strictly enforced by the train's computer and for the sake of complete safety cannot be overridden without the operator engaging a special "lockout." (Attempting to drive the train too quickly in a given speed zone will result in an "overspeed stop.")

A new automation of the Monorail system, initiated in 2014, improves safety and provides more efficient service by creating more frequent dispatch of the trains, faster switching times, and more accurate Monorail arrival information.

As of 2016, the system is one of the most heavily used monorail systems in the world, with more than 150,000 daily riders. It is surpassed only by the Tokyo Monorail, which has more than three hundred thousand daily riders, and the Chongqing Rail Transit monorail system in Chongqing, China, which has more than nine hundred thousand daily riders.

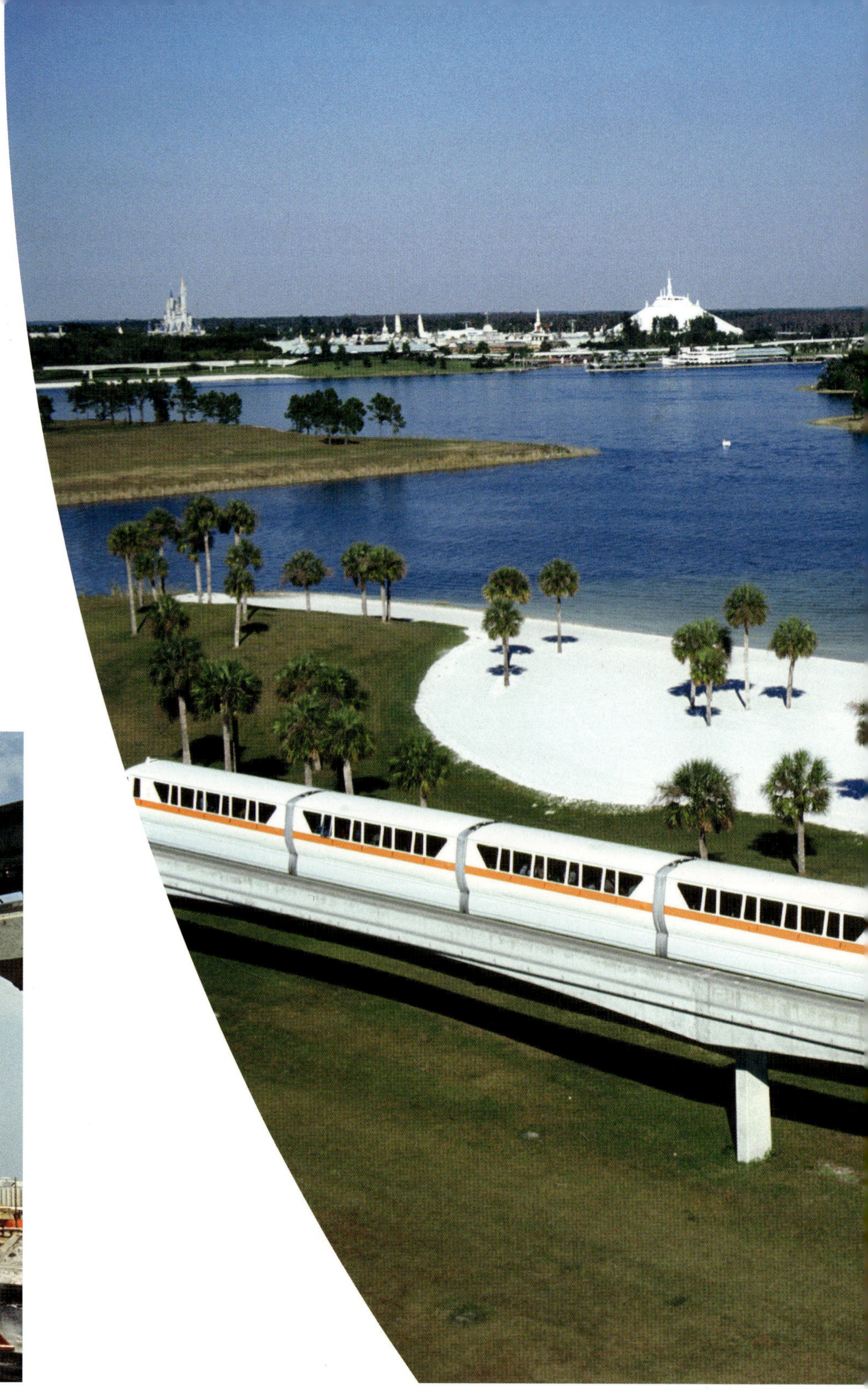

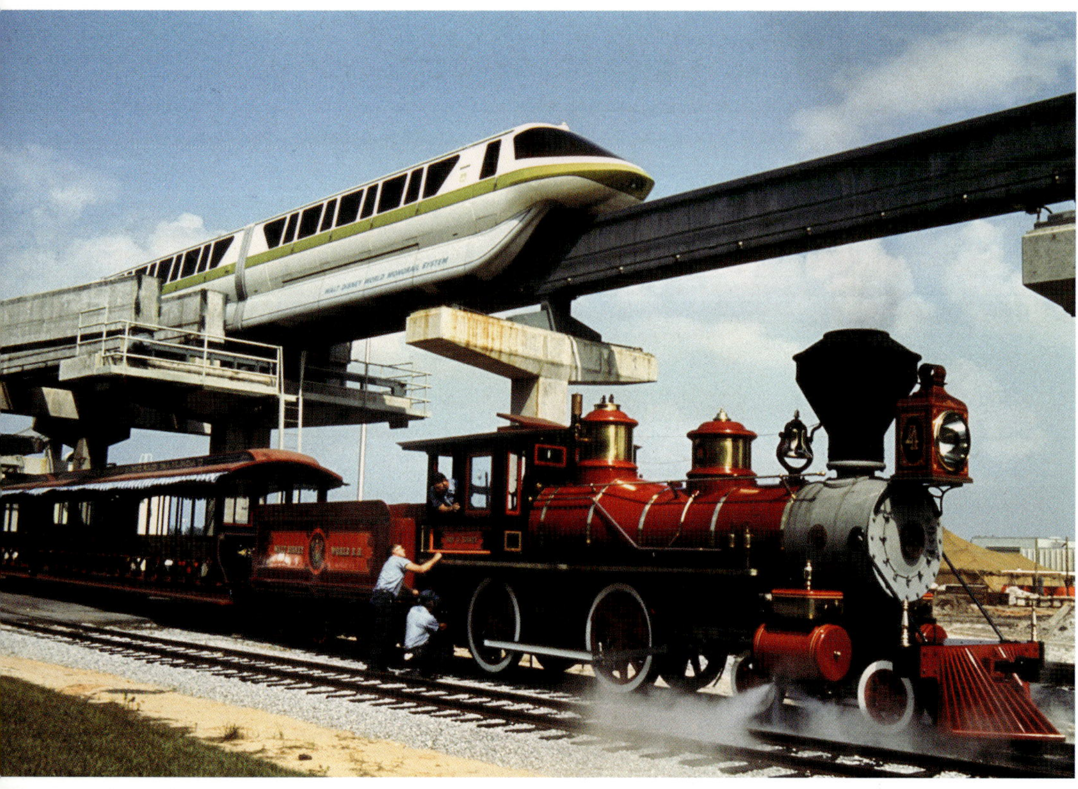

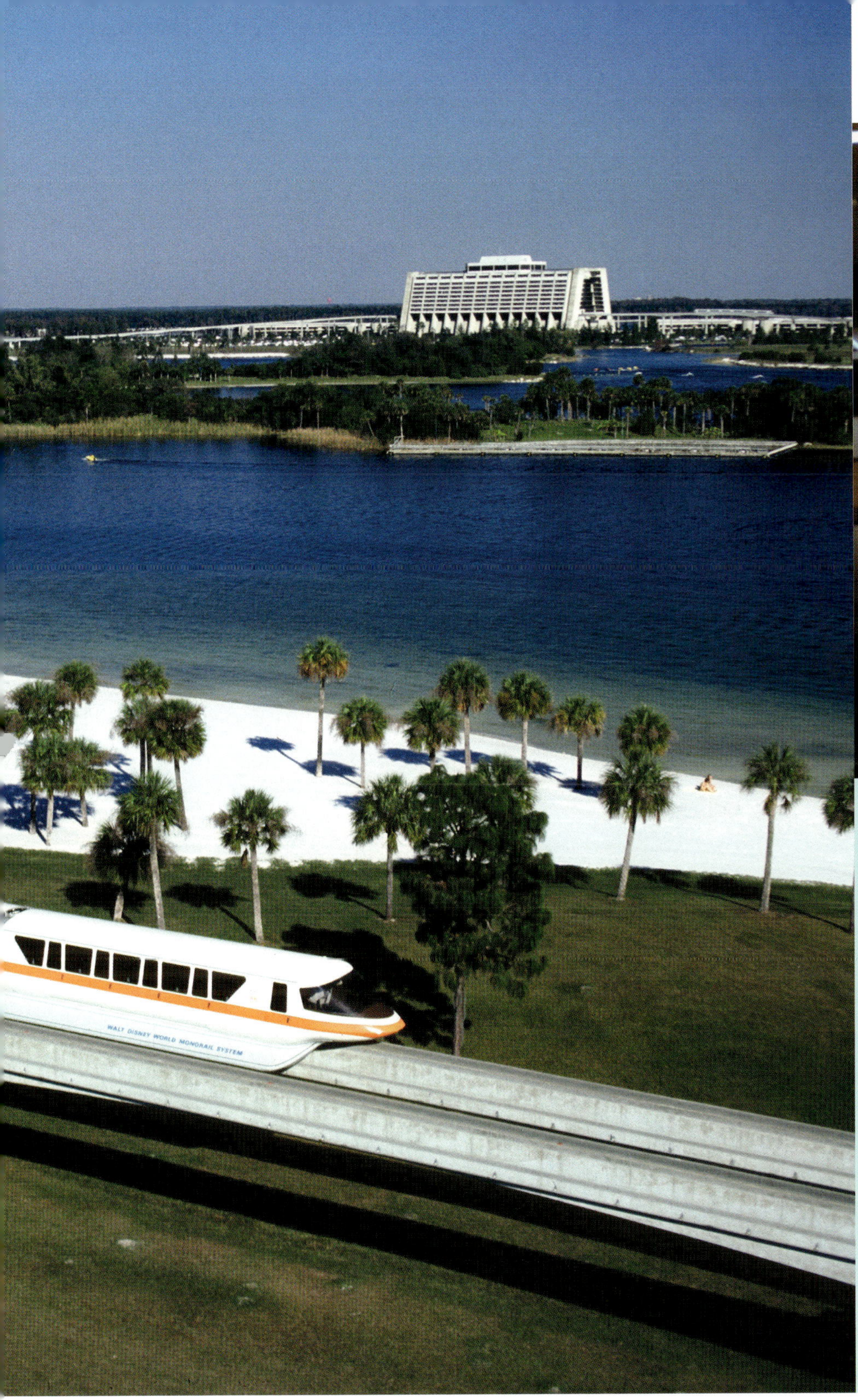

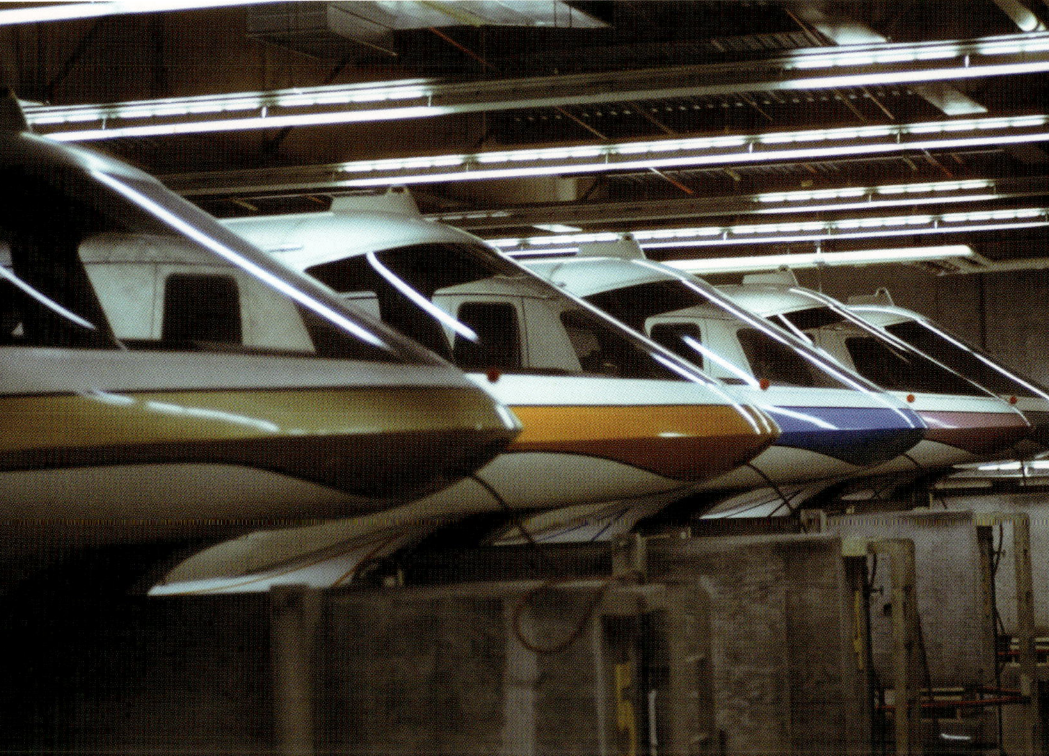

Walt's ideas for the monorail technology and his vision of how it could be applied to improve the daily life of the average citizen seemed strangely unattractive during the waning decades of the twentieth century.

"He wanted to try improving, going beyond the park experience, and he wanted to try improving the environment, the urban setting," research economist and Disney Legend Buzz Price reflected. "And he was full of ideas on what that place would be like. . . . Where you could try to improve the way people live—in the schools, the transportation, the intimacy of the life, the control of our frantic, automobile existence."

Although Walt did not live to see them realized—nor was his enthusiasm for them shared by civic and government leaders during his lifetime—his transportation ideas have endured for nearly sixty years. They continue to resonate, and are finally being consistently implemented and applied for daily use all around the world.

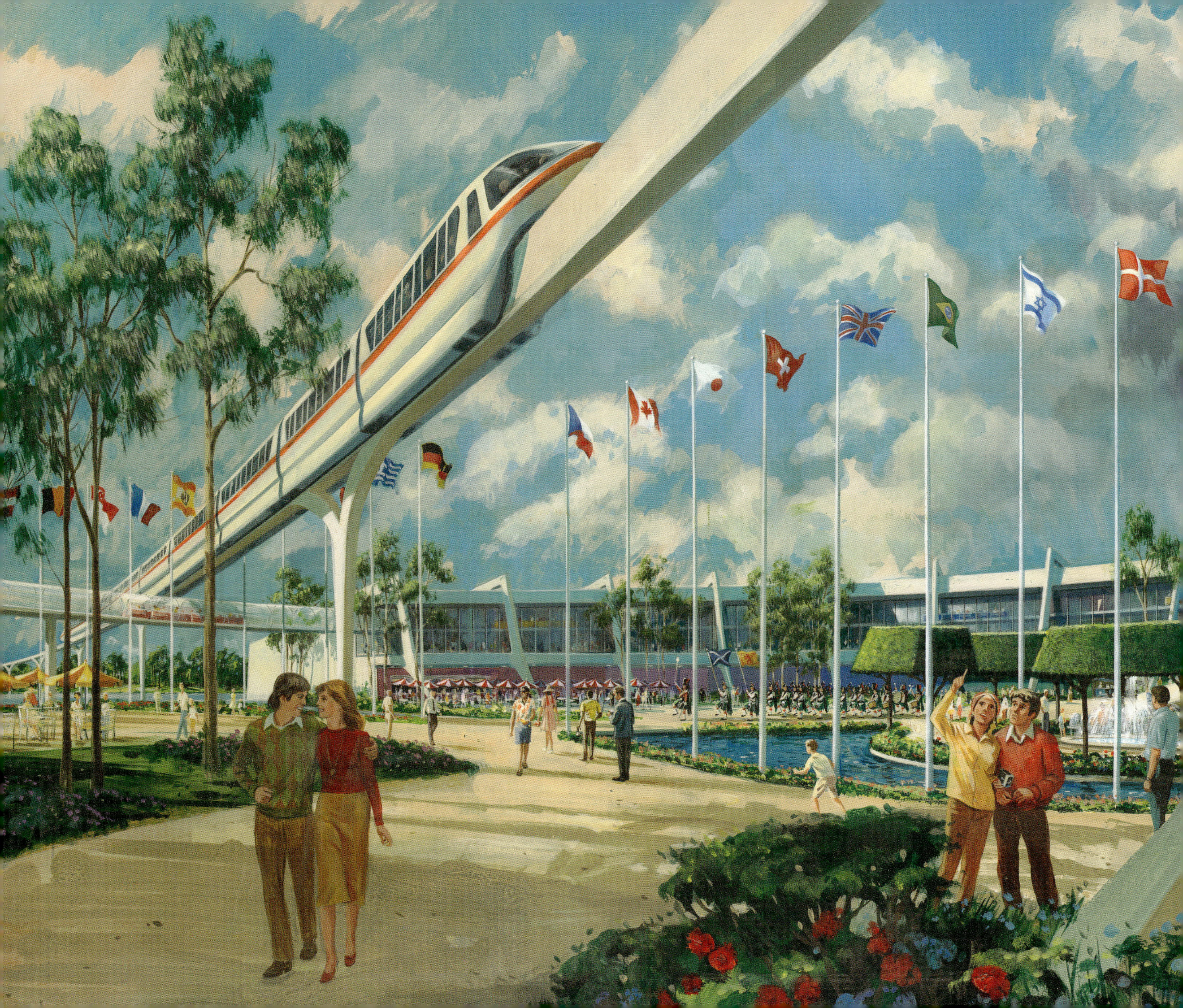

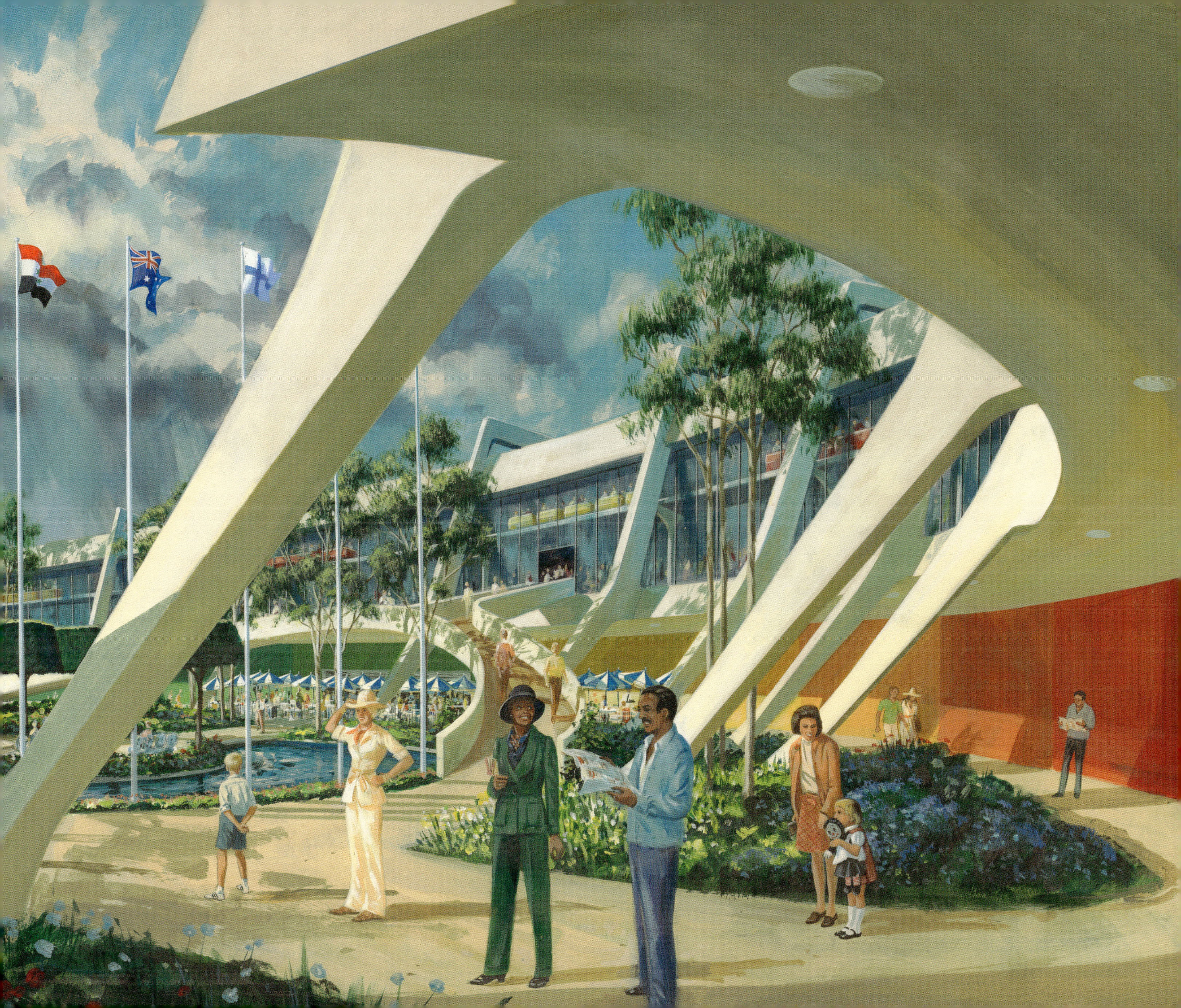

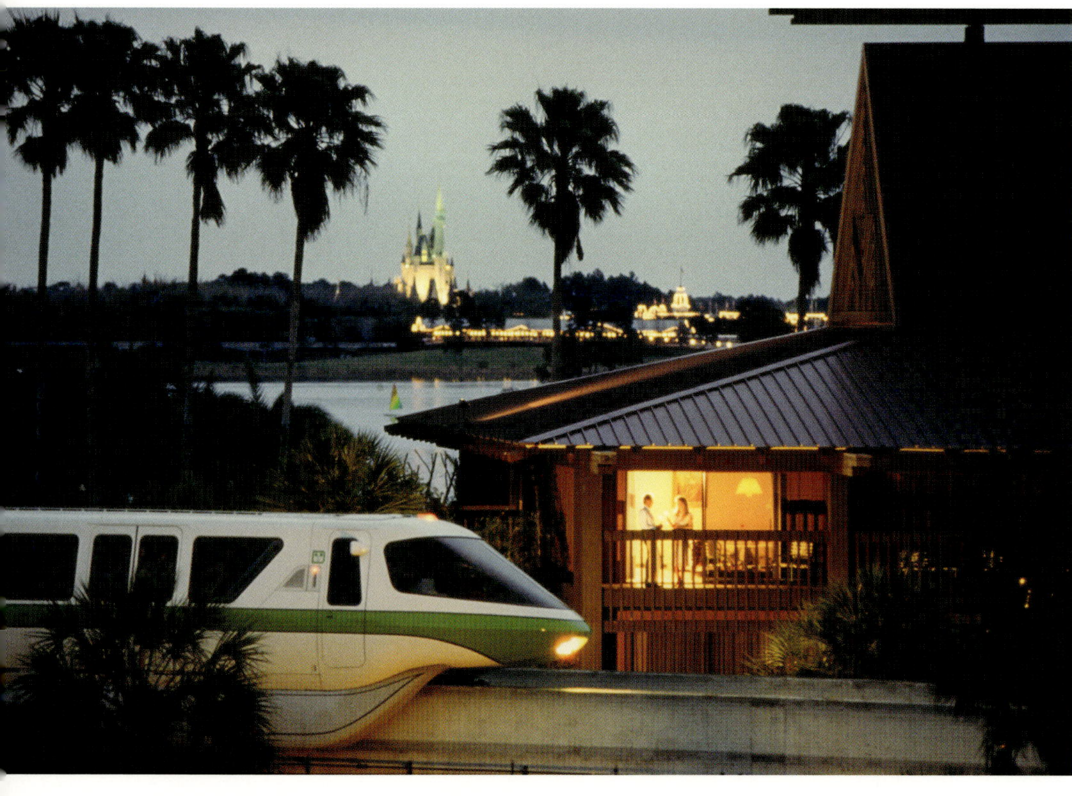

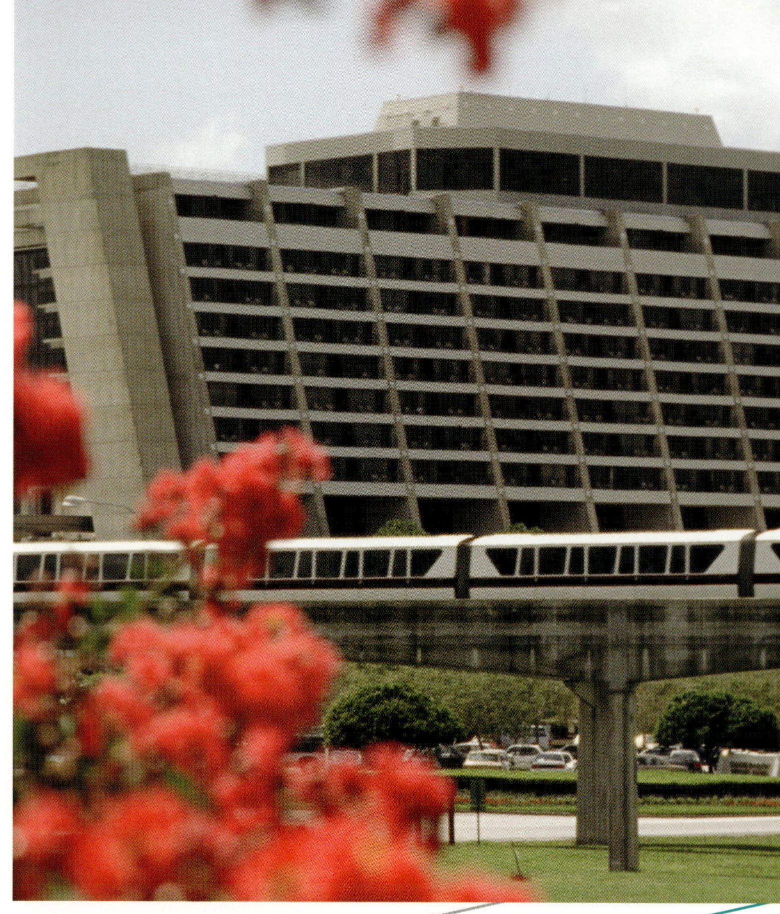

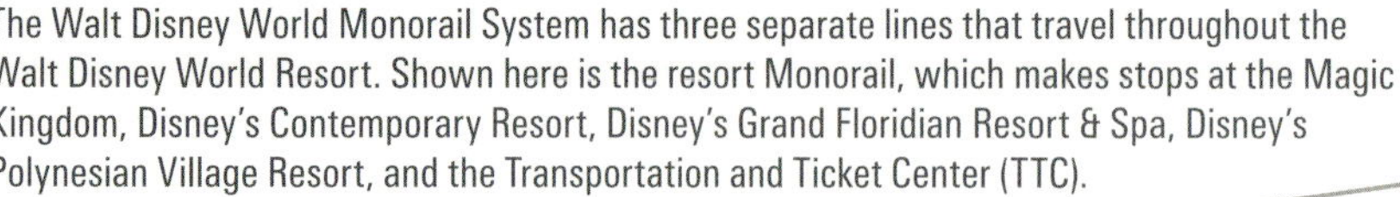

The Walt Disney World Monorail System has three separate lines that travel throughout the Walt Disney World Resort. Shown here is the resort Monorail, which makes stops at the Magic Kingdom, Disney's Contemporary Resort, Disney's Grand Floridian Resort & Spa, Disney's Polynesian Village Resort, and the Transportation and Ticket Center (TTC).

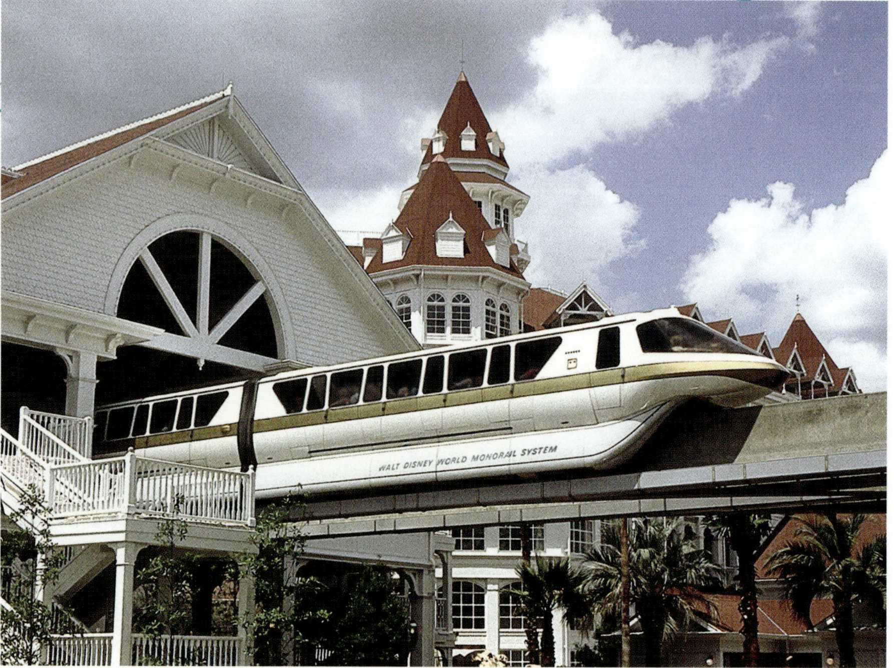

PREVIOUS SPREAD: A 1975 acrylic painting by Collin Campbell, this exterior concept for EPCOT Center (now EPCOT), might be mistaken for Communicore, but in fact is an early idea for World Showcase, where each country pavilion had equal street frontage, and the "show" was on the interior.

BELOW: At Disney's Contemporary Resort, the Monorail runs through a central cavernous space created by architect Welton Becket's innovative A-frame design. Early on nicknamed "The Grand Canyon," because of its imposing scale and size, what otherwise might have been simply a massive and impersonal public space was instead made warmer and more intimate by the creation of discrete areas within the Grand Canyon Concourse, and the inclusion of a warm-toned and fanciful nine-story ceramic tile mural designed and supervised by Disney Legend Mary Blair.

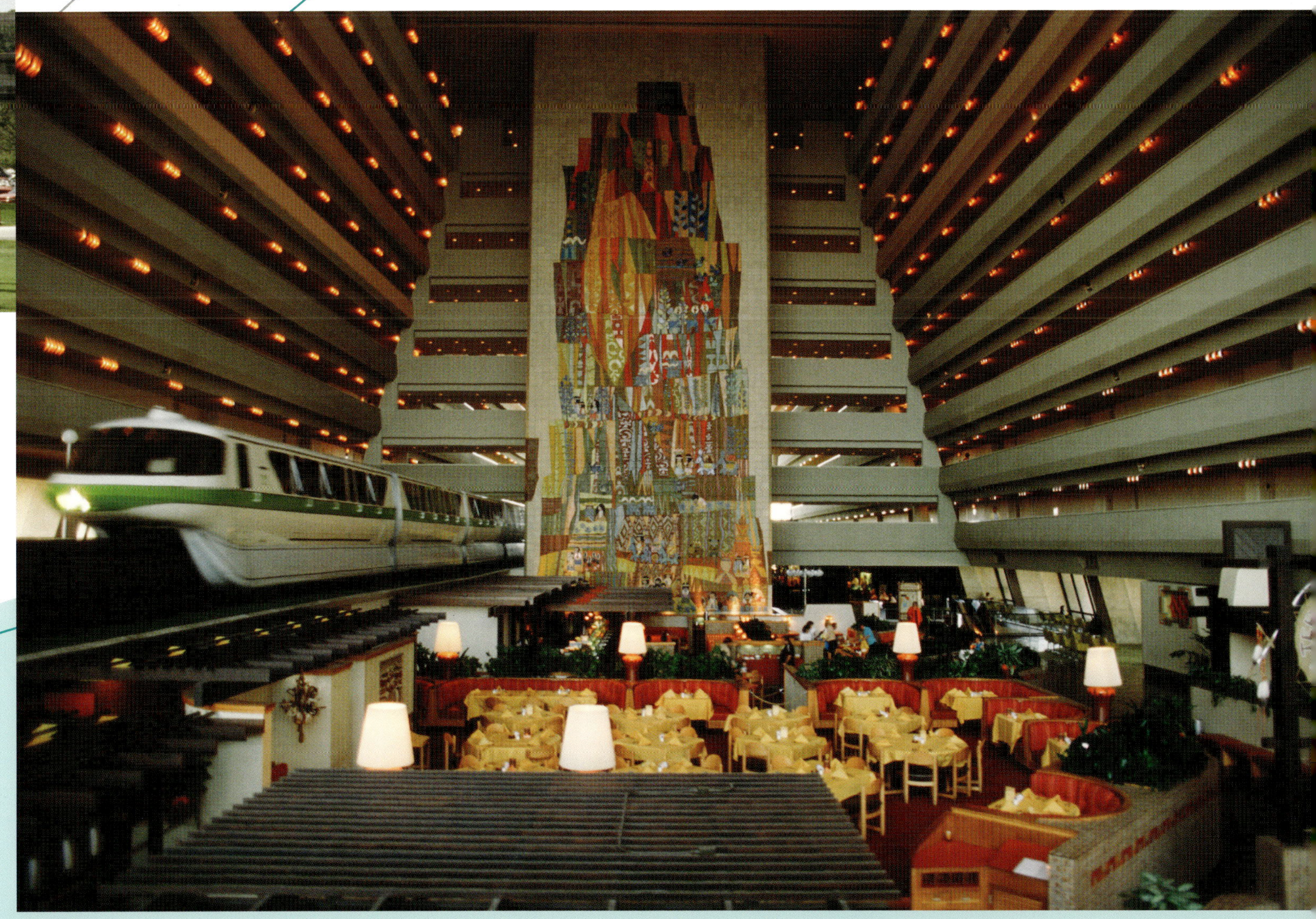

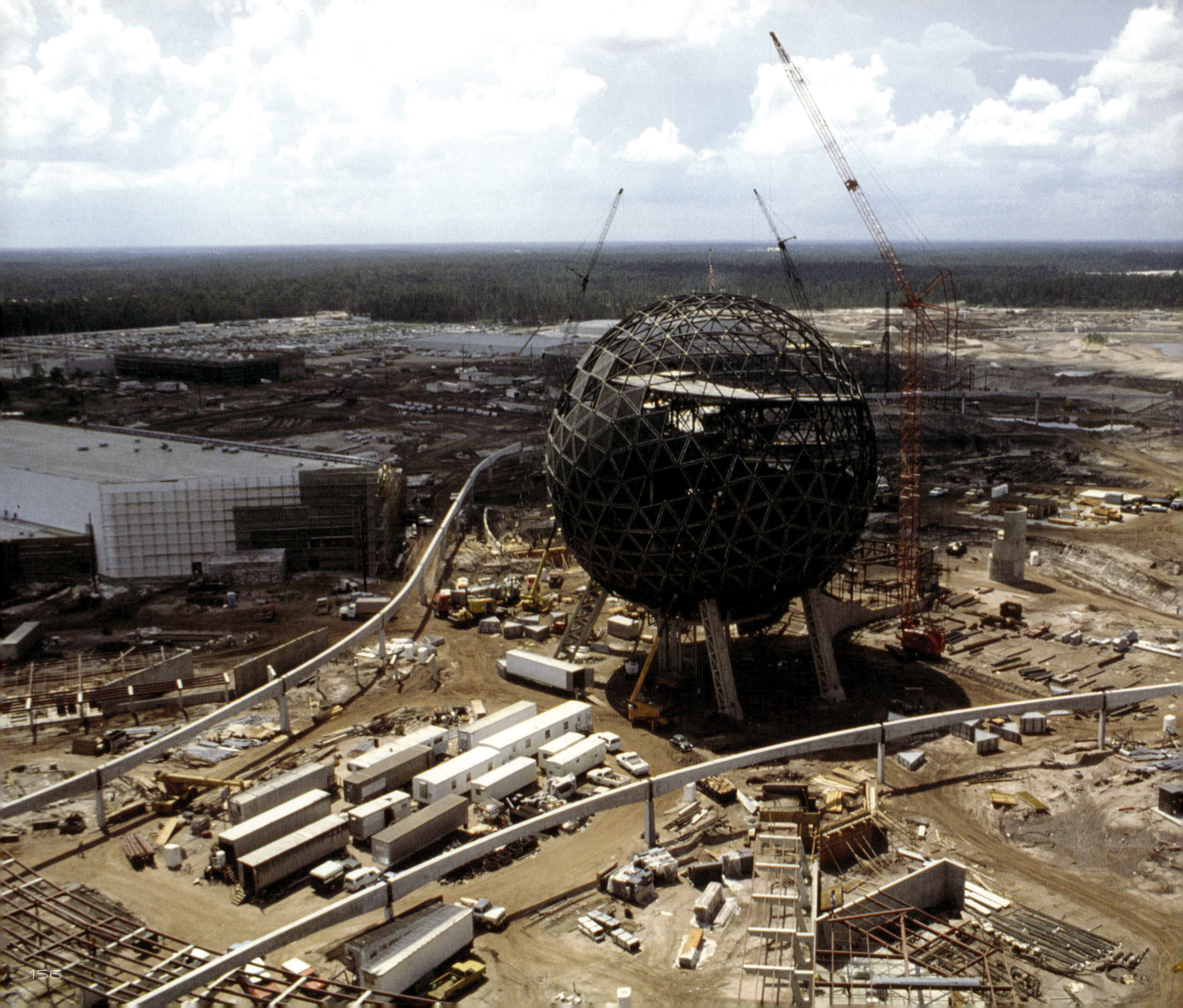

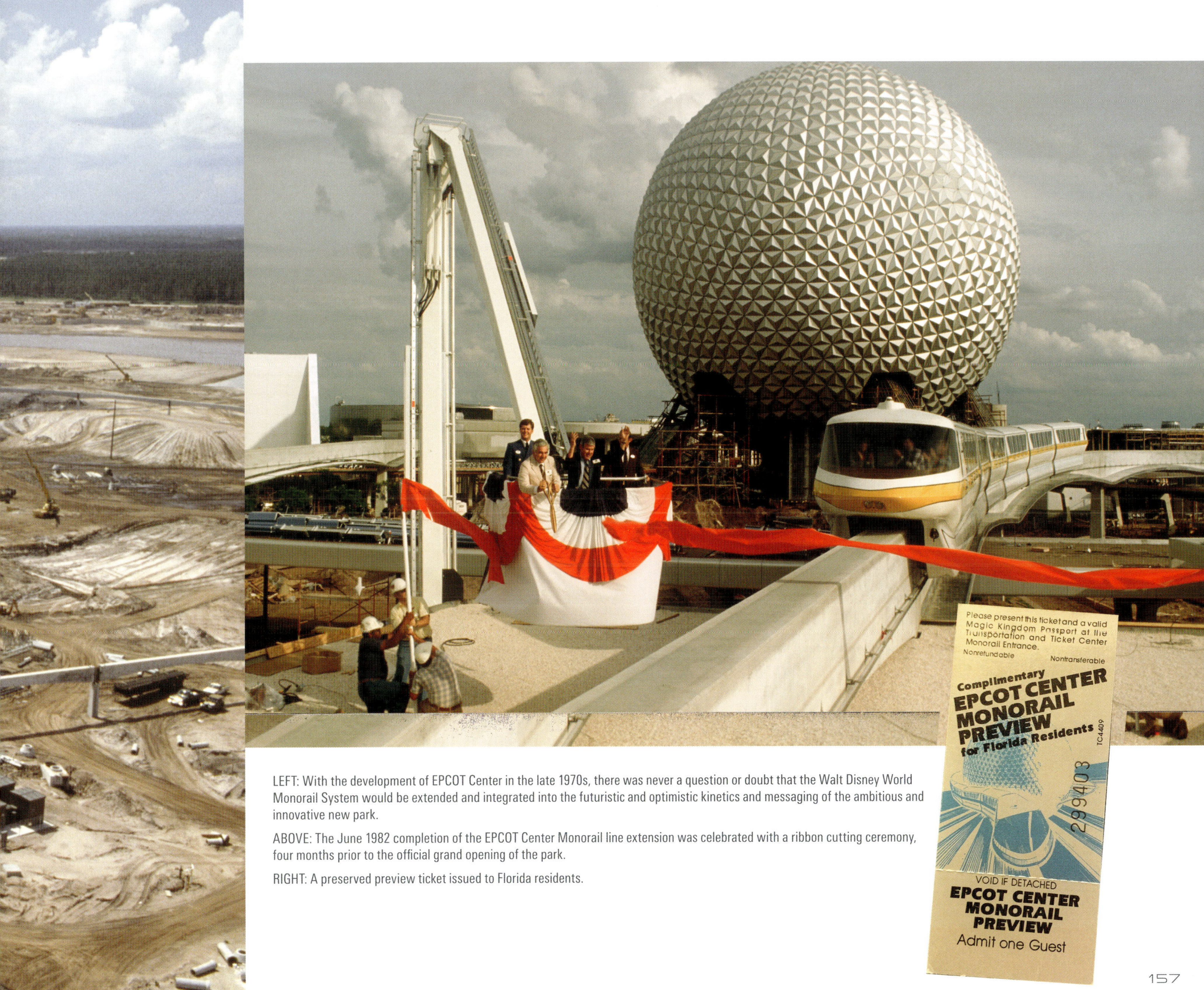

LEFT: With the development of EPCOT Center in the late 1970s, there was never a question or doubt that the Walt Disney World Monorail System would be extended and integrated into the futuristic and optimistic kinetics and messaging of the ambitious and innovative new park.

ABOVE: The June 1982 completion of the EPCOT Center Monorail line extension was celebrated with a ribbon cutting ceremony, four months prior to the official grand opening of the park.

RIGHT: A preserved preview ticket issued to Florida residents.

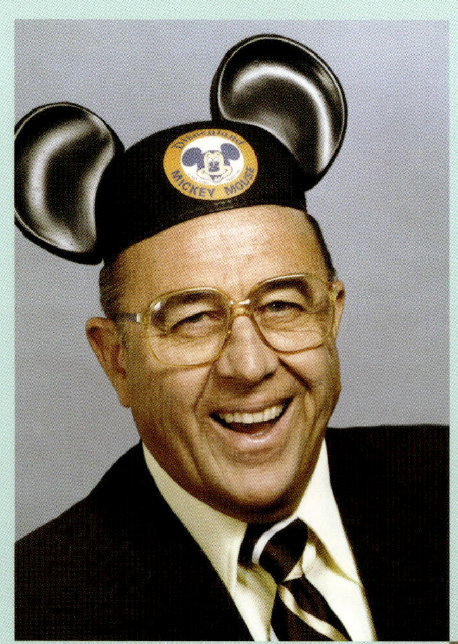

Jack Wagner, a Voice on the Move

"The Voice of Disneyland" Rides the Rail

"Please stand clear of the doors. Por favor manténgase alejado de las puertas."

For many, along with sleek futuristic vehicle styling and familiar Grover air horn blasts, a key "Monorail Memory" is the silky authority of the voice of Jack Wagner.

For more than two decades, Jack's cheerful, friendly tone vocally captured the Disney spirit, making announcements at the Disney Parks, in touring ice and arena shows, and doing voice-over for television programs, commercials, and audio-visual presentations.

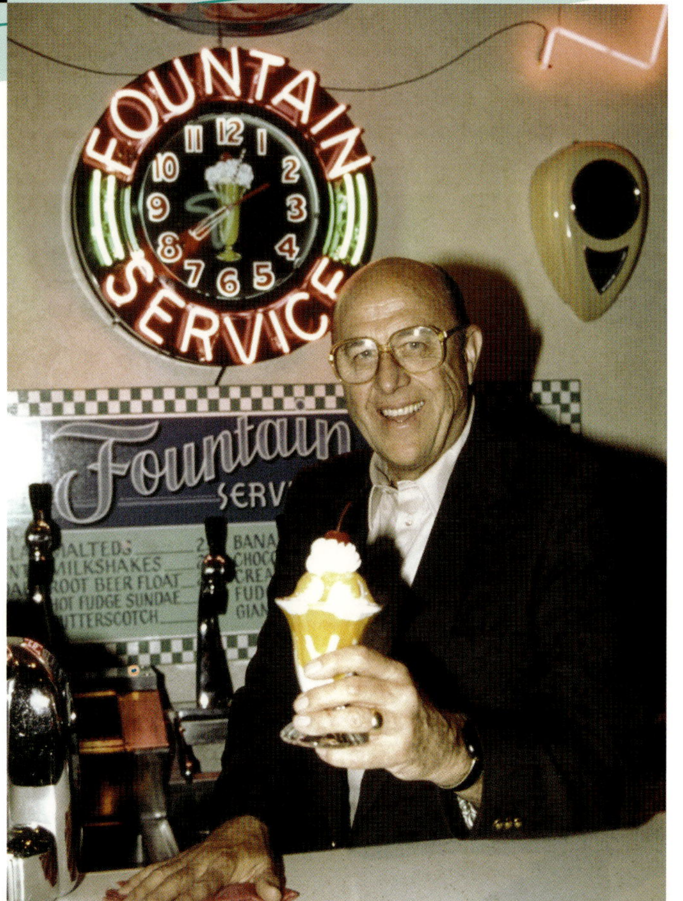

Born December 17, 1925, Jack's French-born parents were both musicians; his late older brother, Roger, was director of the world-famous Roger Wagner Chorale. Jack began his own performing career at age four, dubbing American-made movies into French for foreign release. As a teenager, he was an MGM contract player, and in the 1950s, he made appearances on the classic television program *The Adventures of Ozzie and Harriet*. He was also featured on *The Ann Sothern Show*, *Sea Hunt*, *Dragnet*, and other popular series of the decade. Los Angeles' top ranked radio personality, Jack also had an interview show, Hollywood on a Silver Platter, that was syndicated to more than 1,200 radio stations worldwide.

Jack's association with Disneyland began in 1955 when he was invited to attend opening day. In the ensuing years, he did guest announcing and narration for Christmas parades and other special programs, coming on board full-time as a production consultant in 1970, and shortly thereafter being named park announcer as well. "From there, it just kind of snowballed," he recalled.

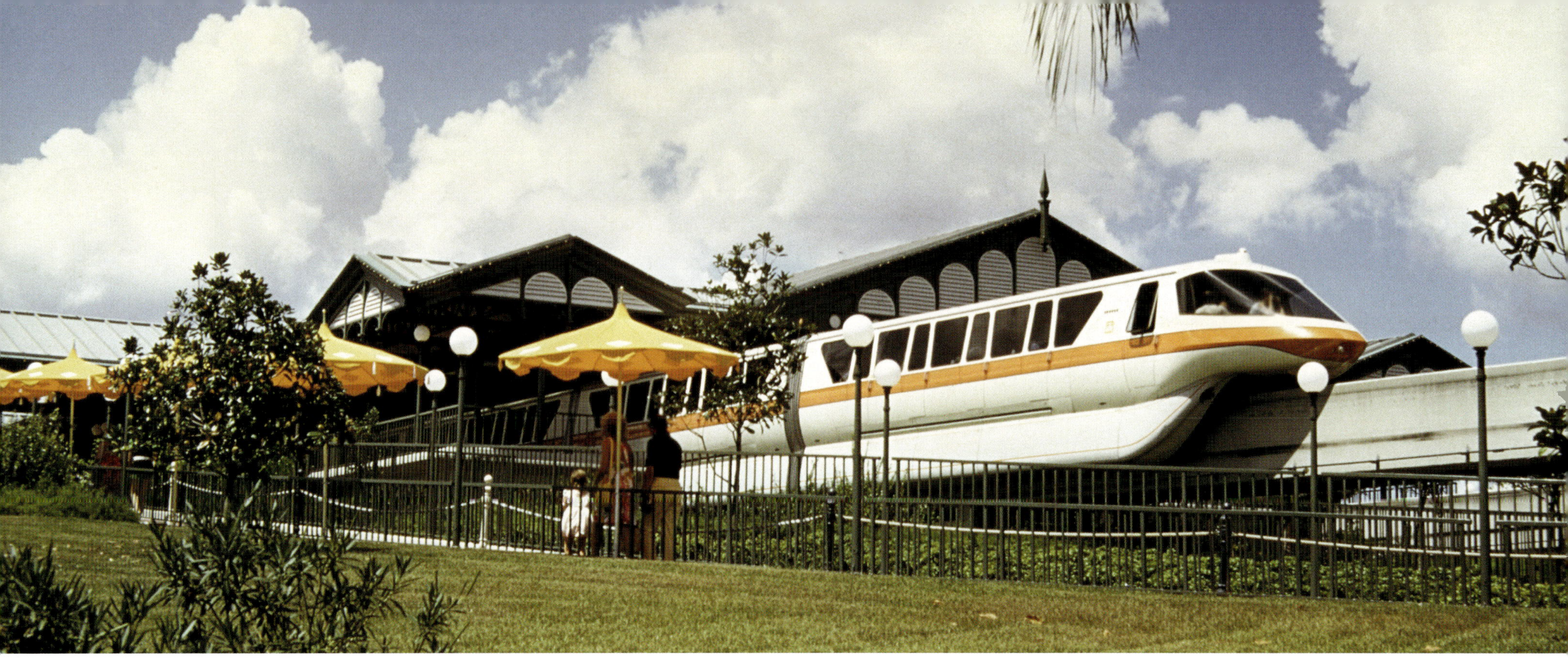

Because of the prevalence of his voice over the park, his nickname was "The Voice of Disneyland." It has been said that no other man's voice has been heard over so many loudspeakers by so many people. Jack also produced music and sound for many of the parades and live shows at both Disneyland and Walt Disney World, provided background music for the themed lands in those Parks and Tokyo Disneyland, and produced record albums featuring Park talent.

Jack's recording for Disney was done at his own studio, two miles from Disneyland, in rooms filled with sophisticated audio and video equipment and walls lined with memorabilia: Theme Park opening day tickets, a golden spike commemorating the Big Thunder Mountain Railroad opening, posters, badges, clocks, and plaques of appreciation for his years of service.

Perhaps his most enduring legacy is a famous line from a Matterhorn Bobsleds safety announcement: "Remain seated please; permanecer sentados por favor."

This famous quote was also heard in the Disneyland fireworks show Remember . . . Dreams Come True, and in the Pixar animated feature *Toy Story 2*. Barbie (voiced by Jodi Benson) offered the safety warning. The Disney animated series *Phineas and Ferb* (the episode titled "Rollercoaster: The Musical!") used the line; even Anaheim ska punk band No Doubt used Jack's safety spiel in the opening of their hit song "Tragic Kingdom" (from the album of the same name).

Although vocal cord surgery forced his retirement in 1991, Jack continued to make short announcements for Disneyland. Wagner's son Mike, a former disc jockey and radio programmer, is a Disney executive and also provided park announcements for Disneyland Paris.

Jack passed away on June 16, 1995, and was posthumously made a Disney Legend in 2005.

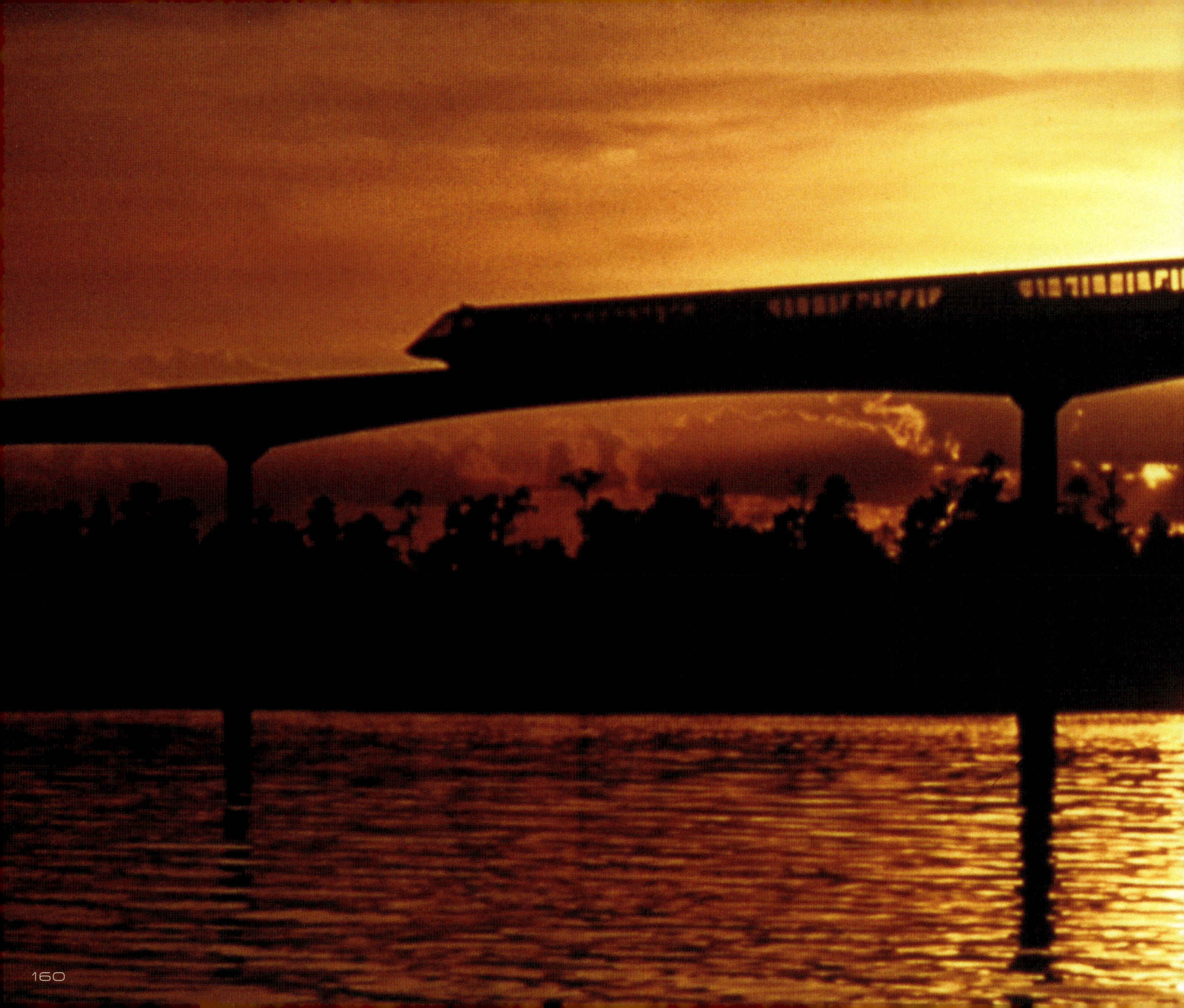

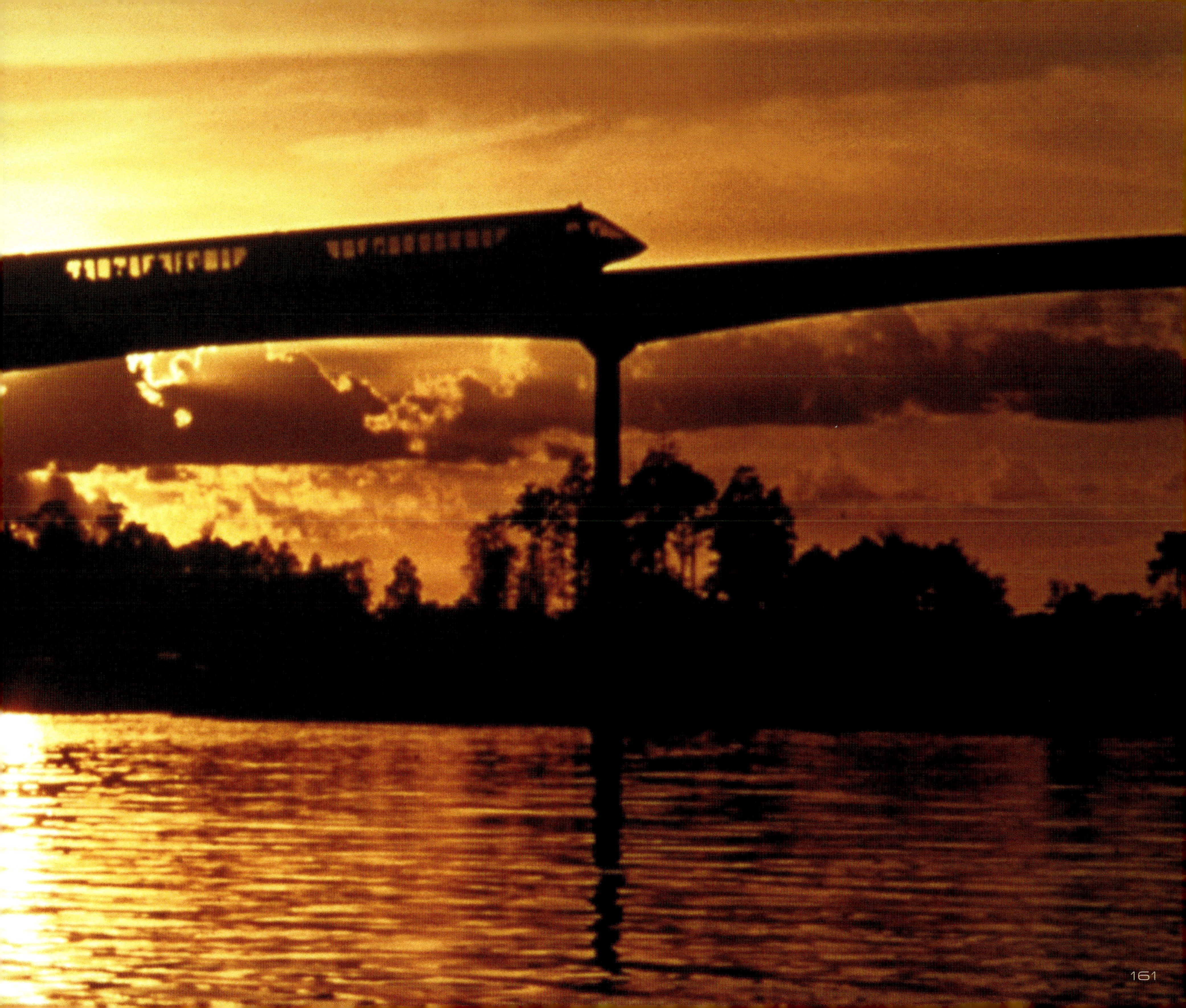

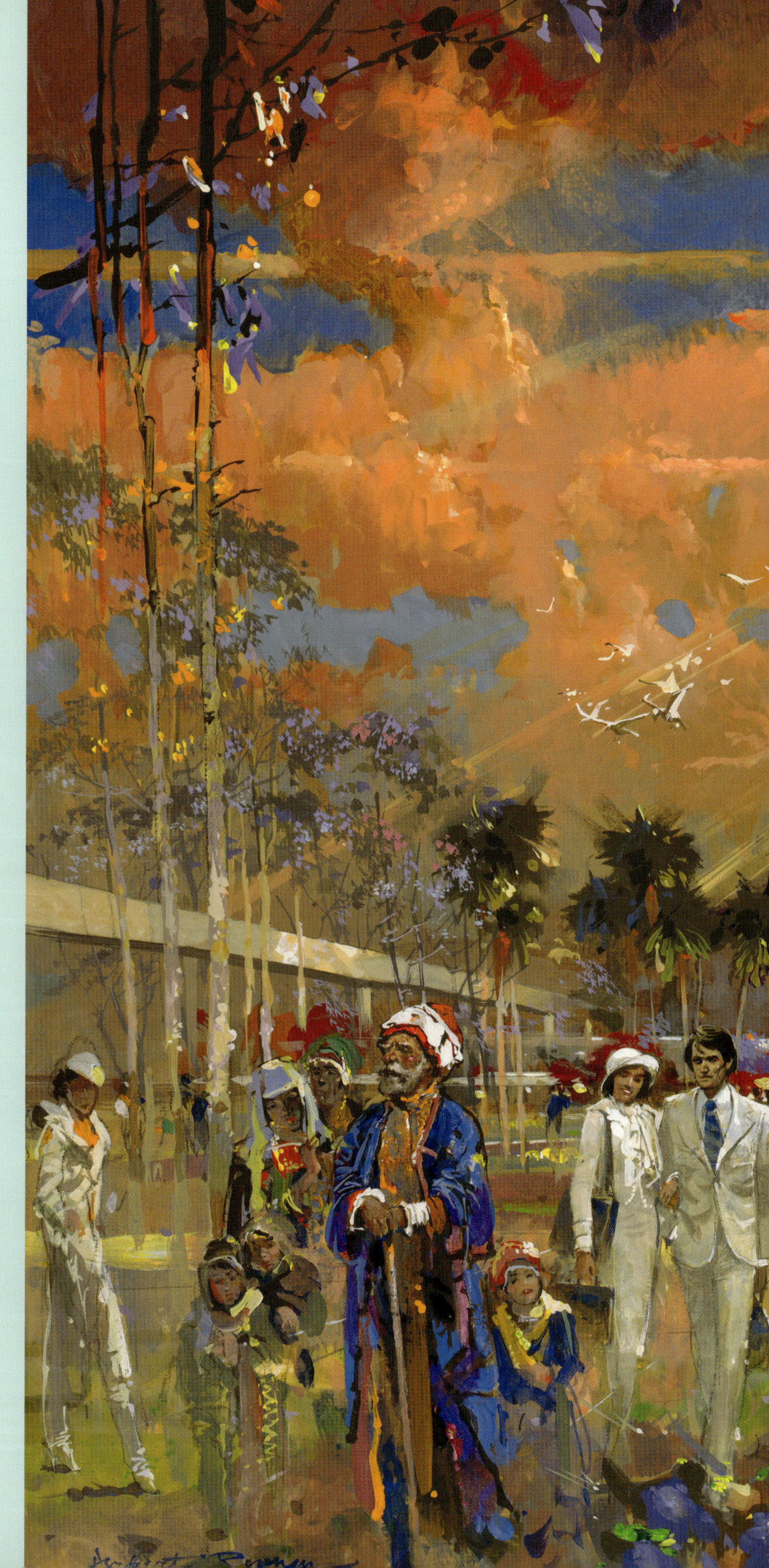

One of several Herb Ryman visualizations for EPCOT Center, this 1981 acrylic work was described in a contemporary publication as "the wedding of history, technology, and entertainment, presented in a unique setting under the Florida sun. The artist's rendering of the entrance to Epcot Center [sic] . . . says it all."

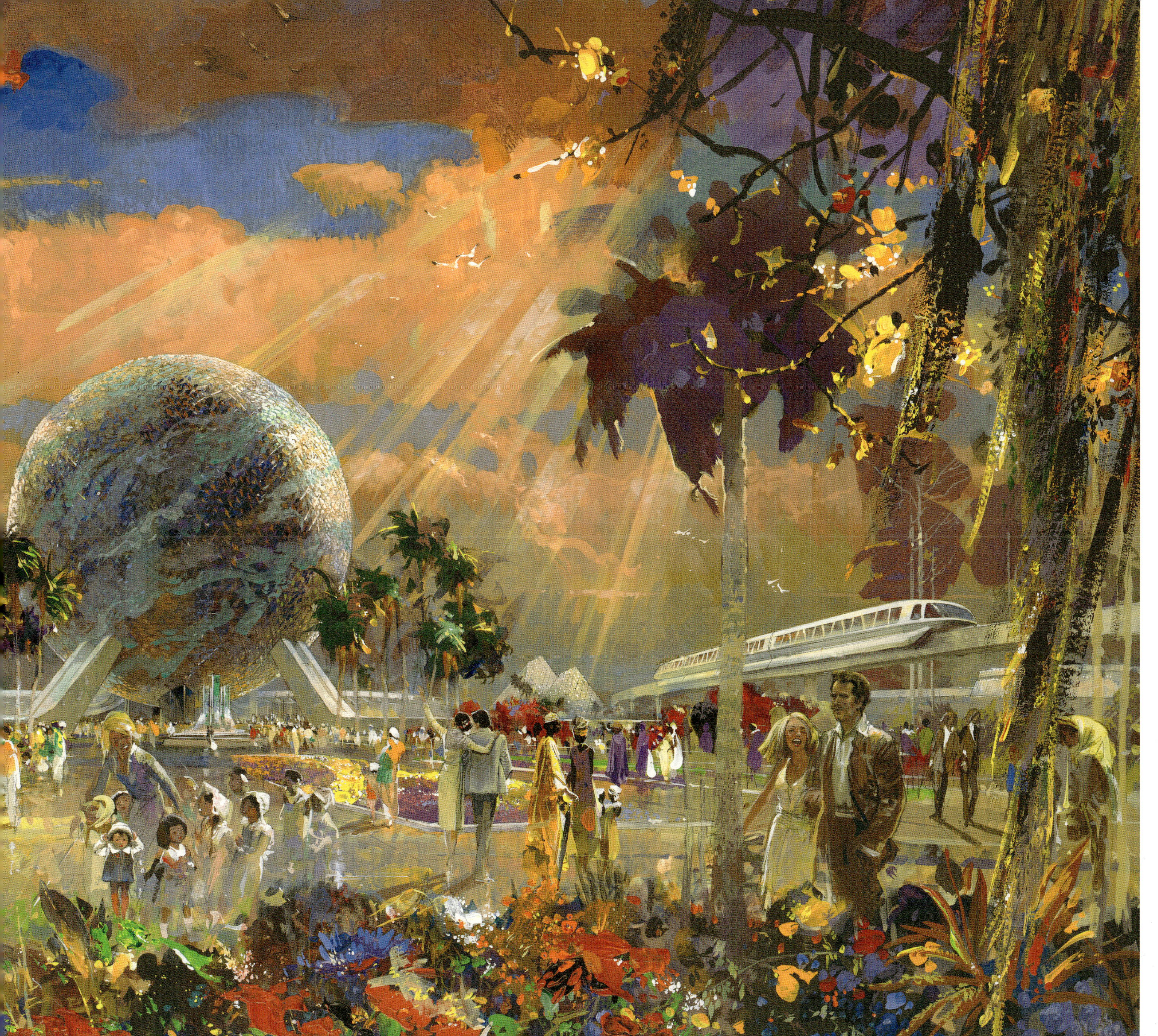

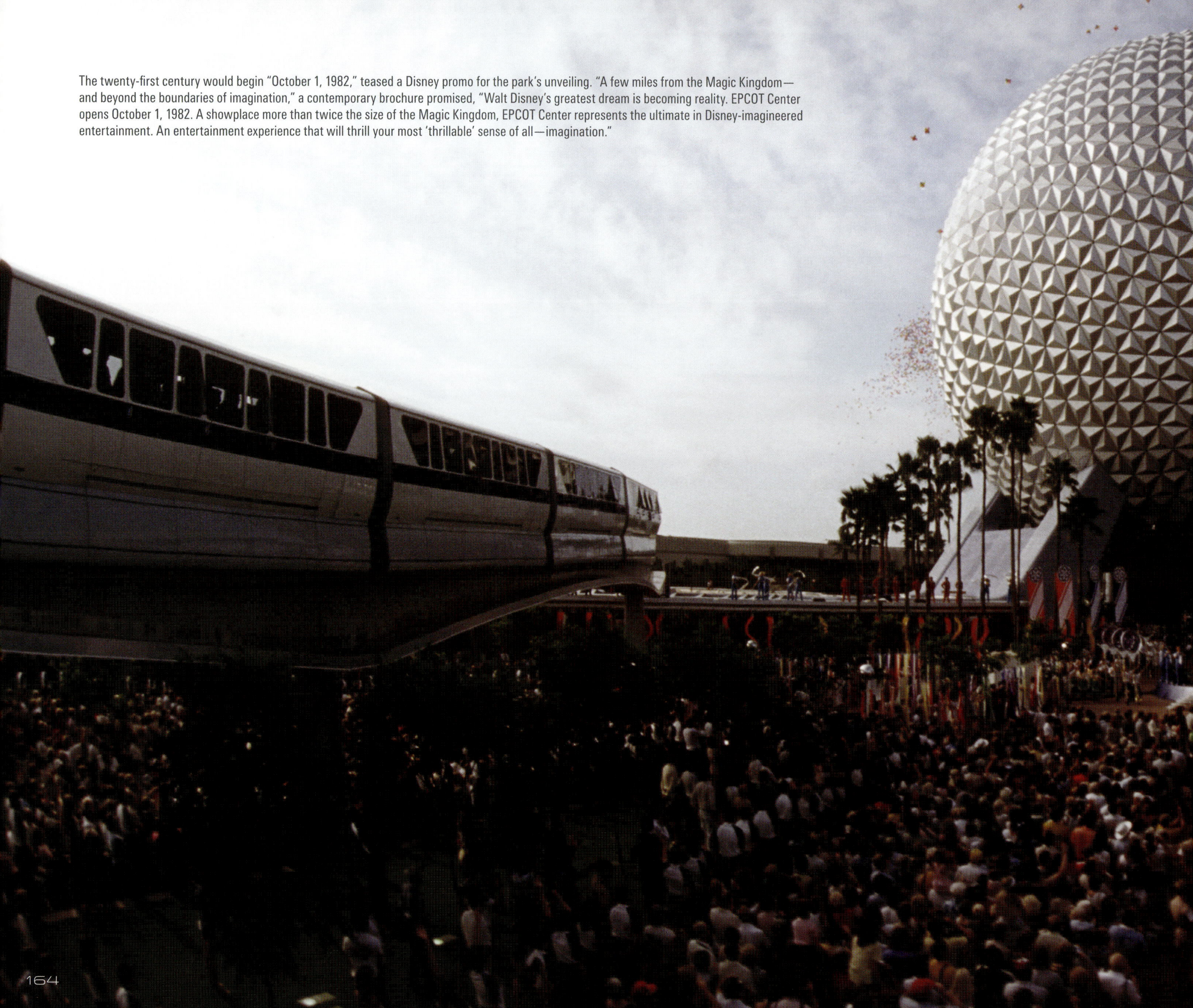

The twenty-first century would begin "October 1, 1982," teased a Disney promo for the park's unveiling. "A few miles from the Magic Kingdom—and beyond the boundaries of imagination," a contemporary brochure promised, "Walt Disney's greatest dream is becoming reality. EPCOT Center opens October 1, 1982. A showplace more than twice the size of the Magic Kingdom, EPCOT Center represents the ultimate in Disney-imagineered entertainment. An entertainment experience that will thrill your most 'thrillable' sense of all—imagination."

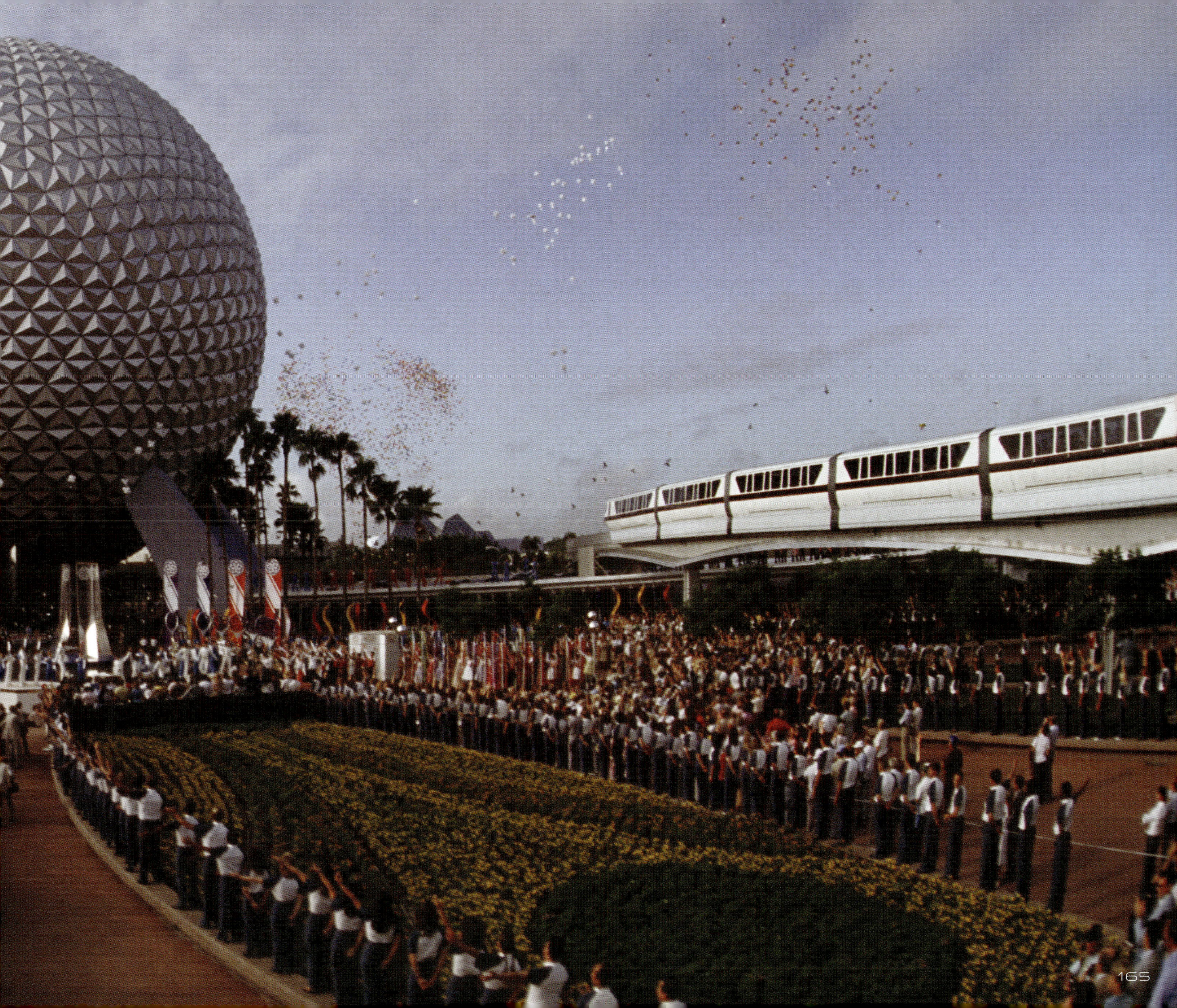

THREE-DAY WORLD ADVENTURE

Allows one

ADULT

the following for three days:

Unlimited admission to WALT DISNEY WORLD EPCOT Center and Magic Kingdom.

Unlimited use of transportation within the WALT DISNEY WORLD Vacation Kingdom.

Unlimited use of all EPCOT Center and Magic Kingdom attractions (except Shootin' Gallery, Discovery Island and River Country).

№ 003001

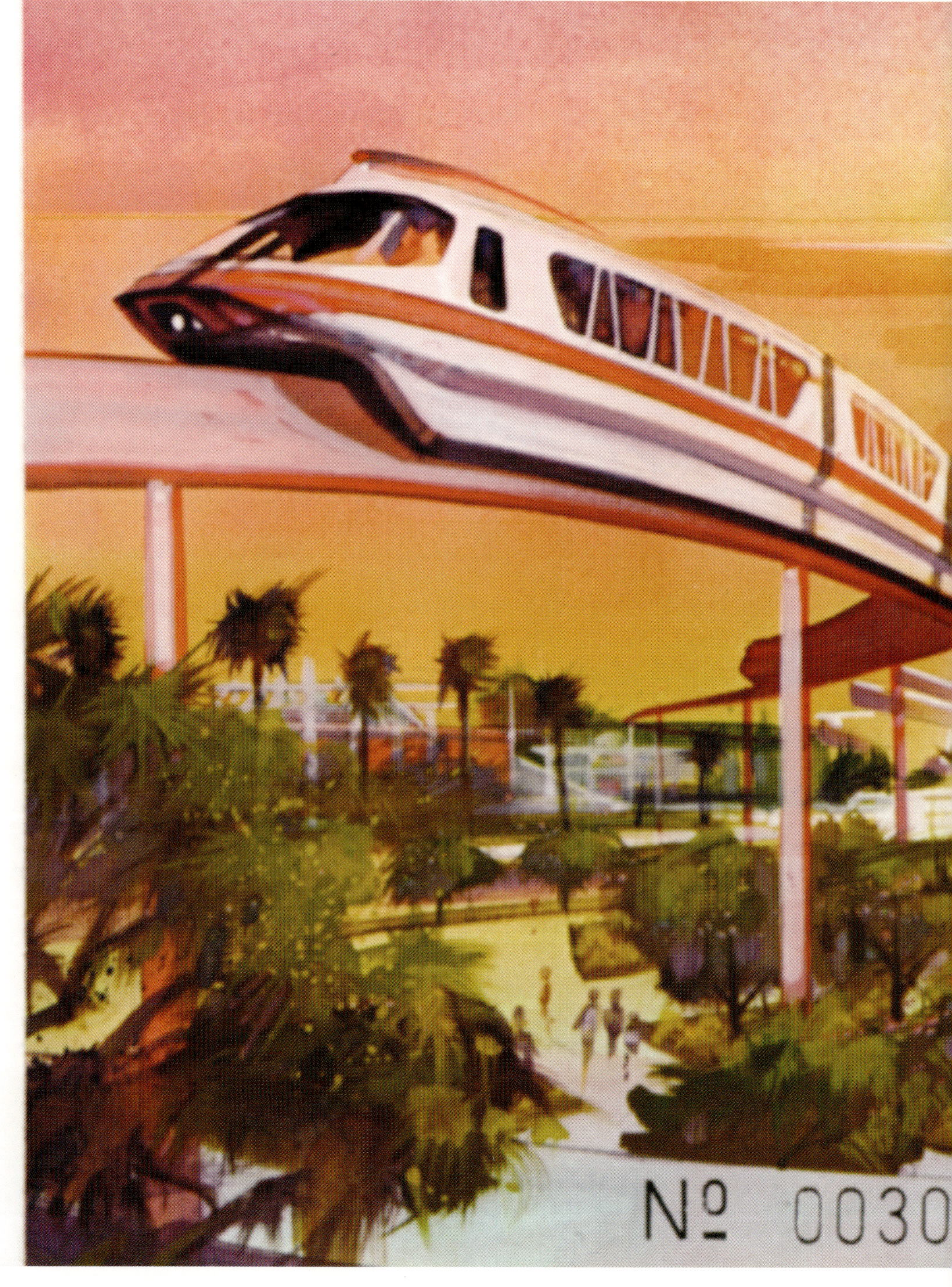

Even more than two decades after their debut, Disney Monorails still symbolized the future, progress, and technology for the betterment of mankind. This EPCOT Center Special Edition commemorative ticket was a "first series keepsake," and entitled the bearer to a three-day World Adventure, featuring "unlimited use of all EPCOT Center and Magic Kingdom attractions (except Shootin' Gallery, Discovery Island, and River Country)," as well as "unlimited use of transportation within the Walt Disney World Vacation Kingdom." (The example shown here is an unused and preserved ticket purchased at the EPCOT Center Preview Center on Main Street, U.S.A. in the Magic Kingdom.)

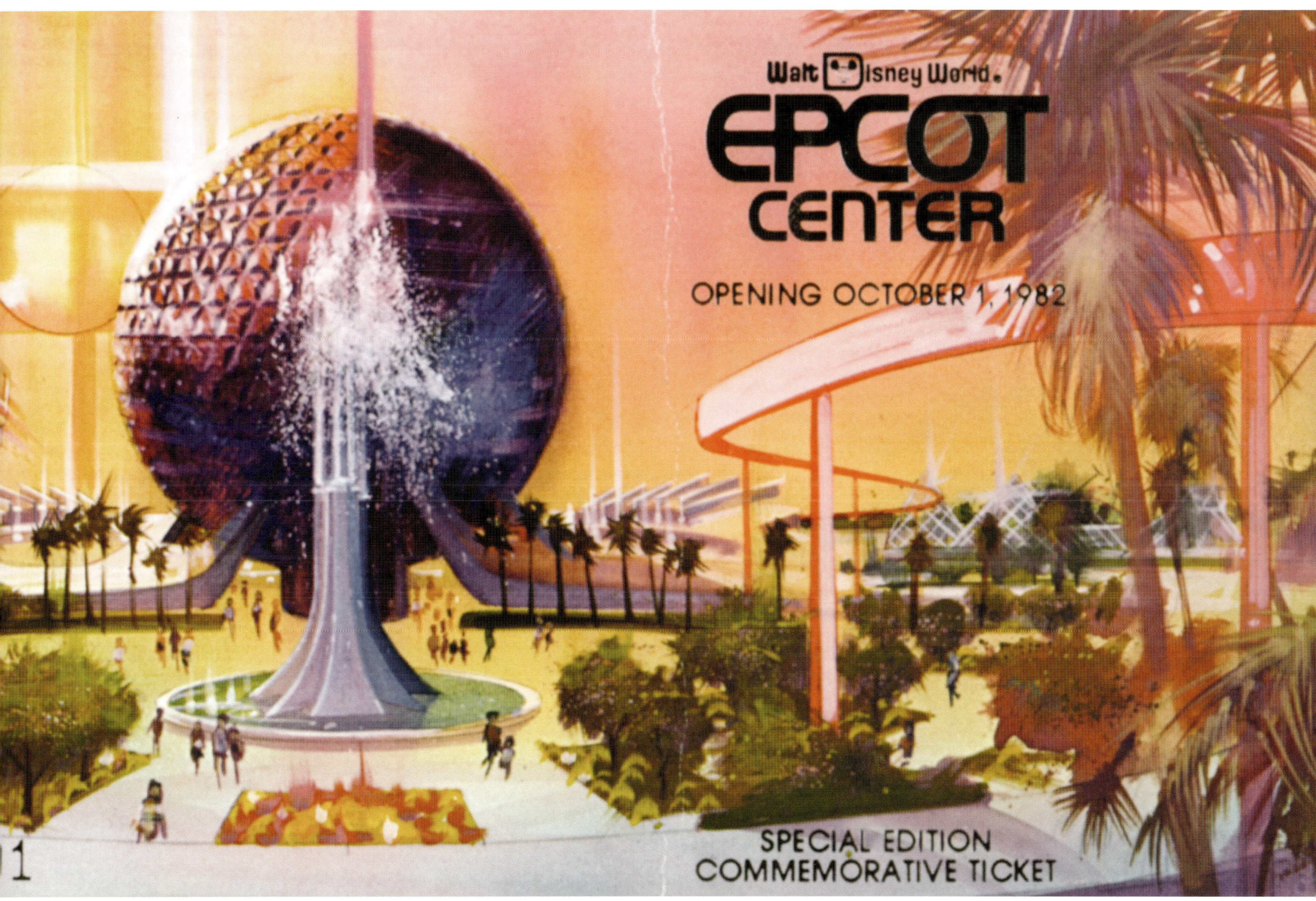
Walt Disney World.
EPCOT CENTER
OPENING OCTOBER 1, 1982
SPECIAL EDITION
COMMEMORATIVE TICKET
1

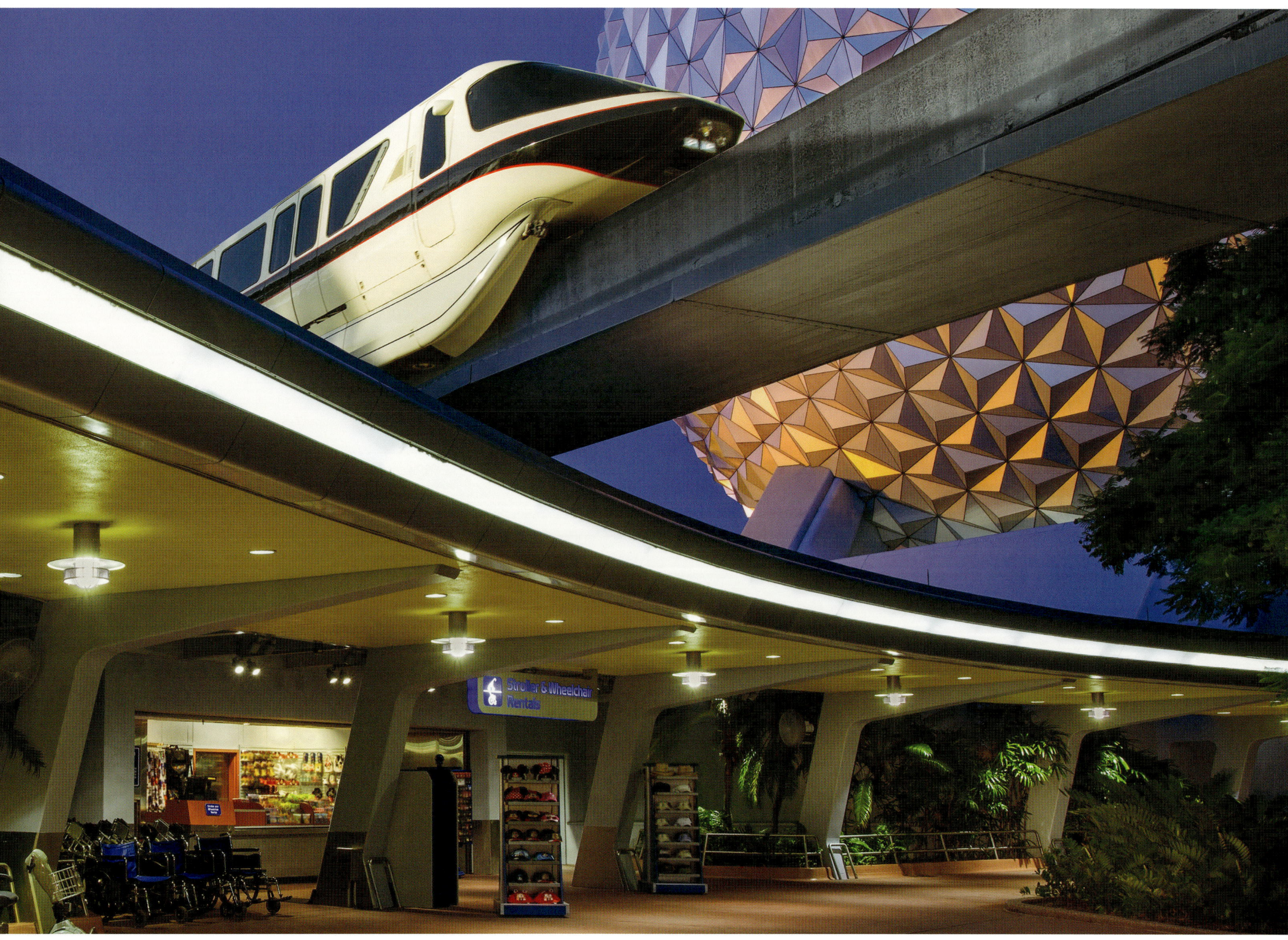
Stroller & Wheelchair
Rentals

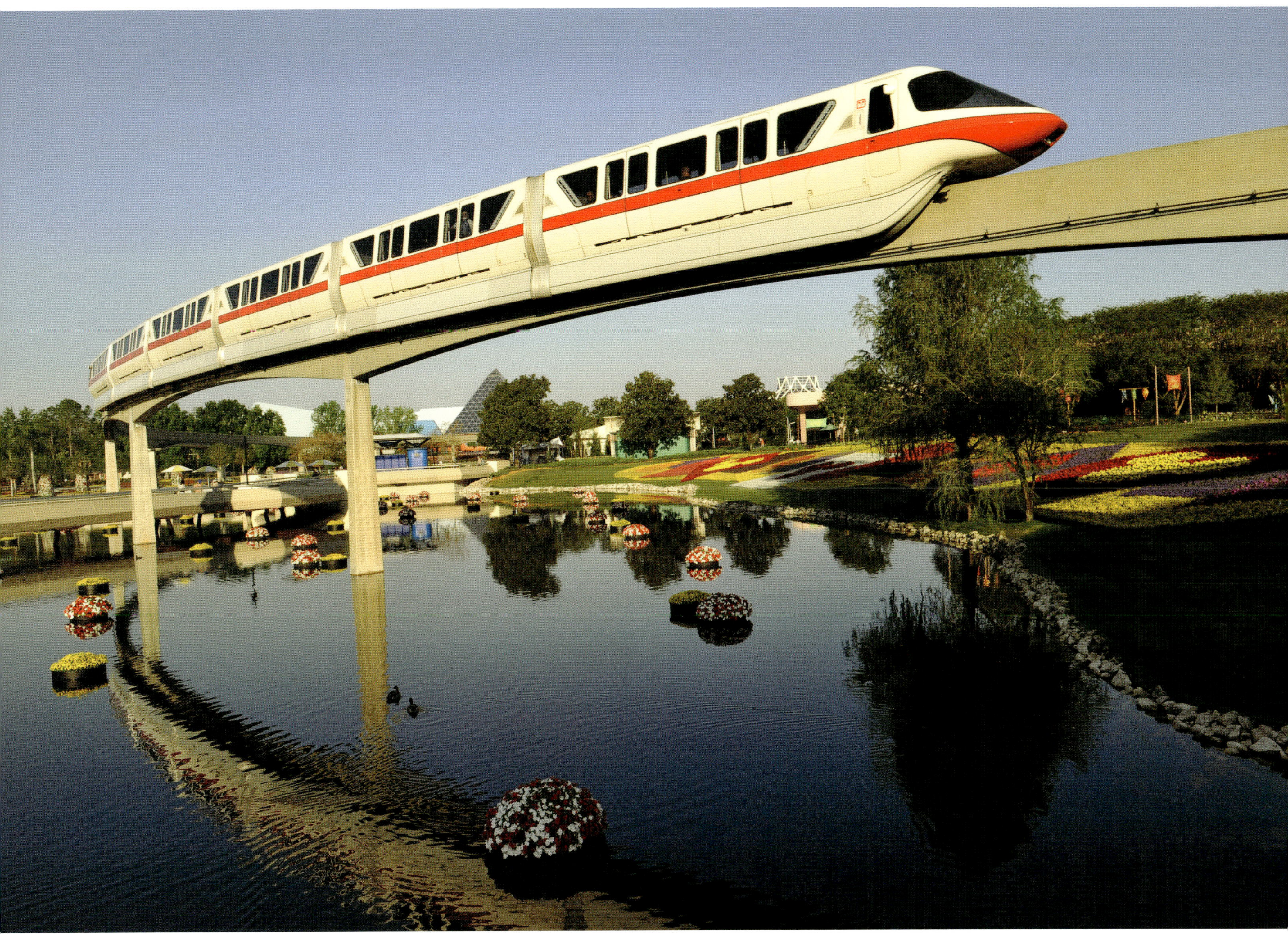

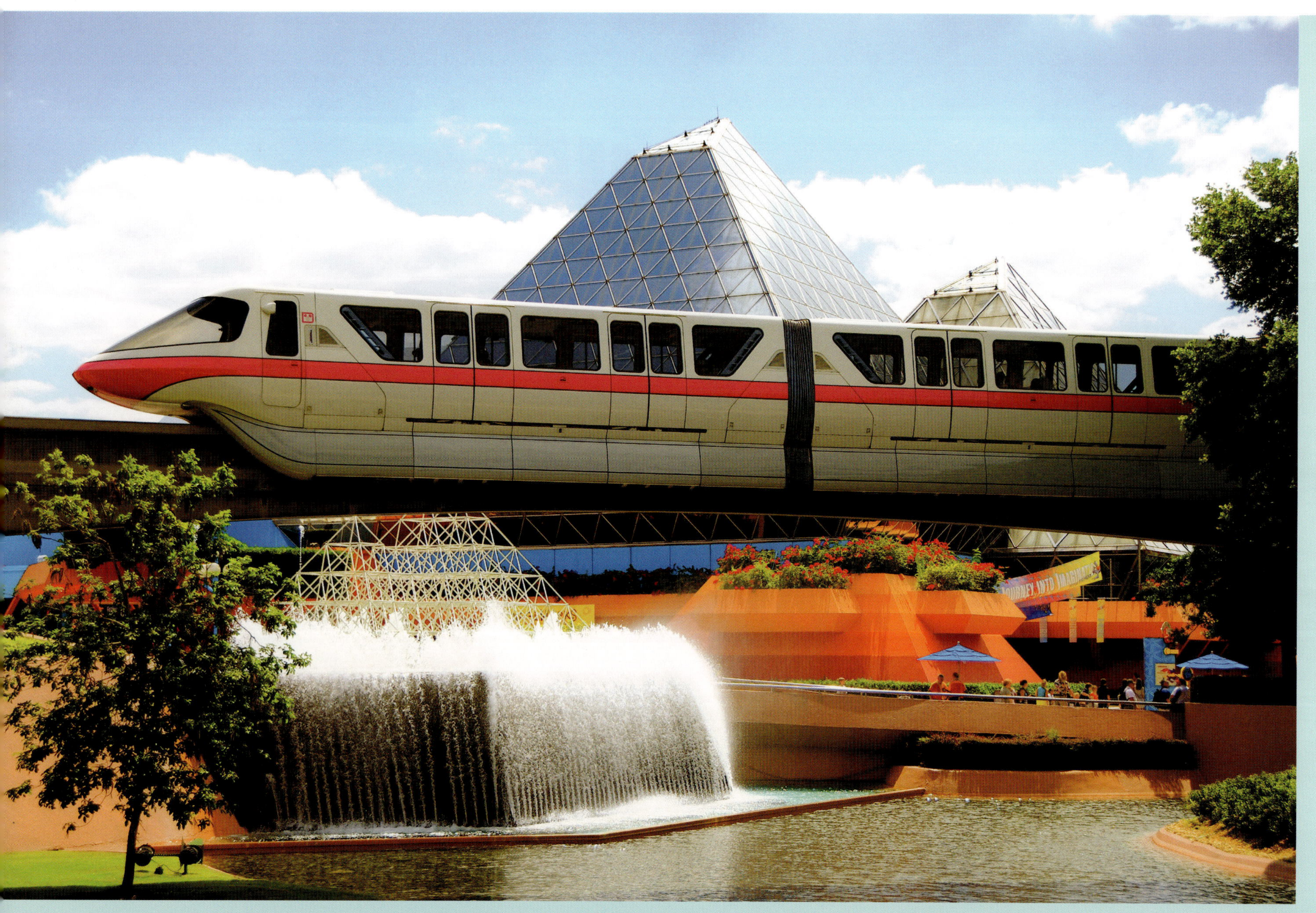

PREVIOUS SPREAD AND THESE PAGES: The sweeping grandeur of the EPCOT Monorail loop through Future World is still as thrilling to ride and to behold as it has always been. Keeping Spaceship Earth as the steady central icon, the elevated view from within the Monorail changes through the years as the park itself has evolved—and continues to evolve. The view even shifts seasonally, such as with enhanced flora during the EPCOT International Flower & Garden Festival (see page 169 for a view from 2011).

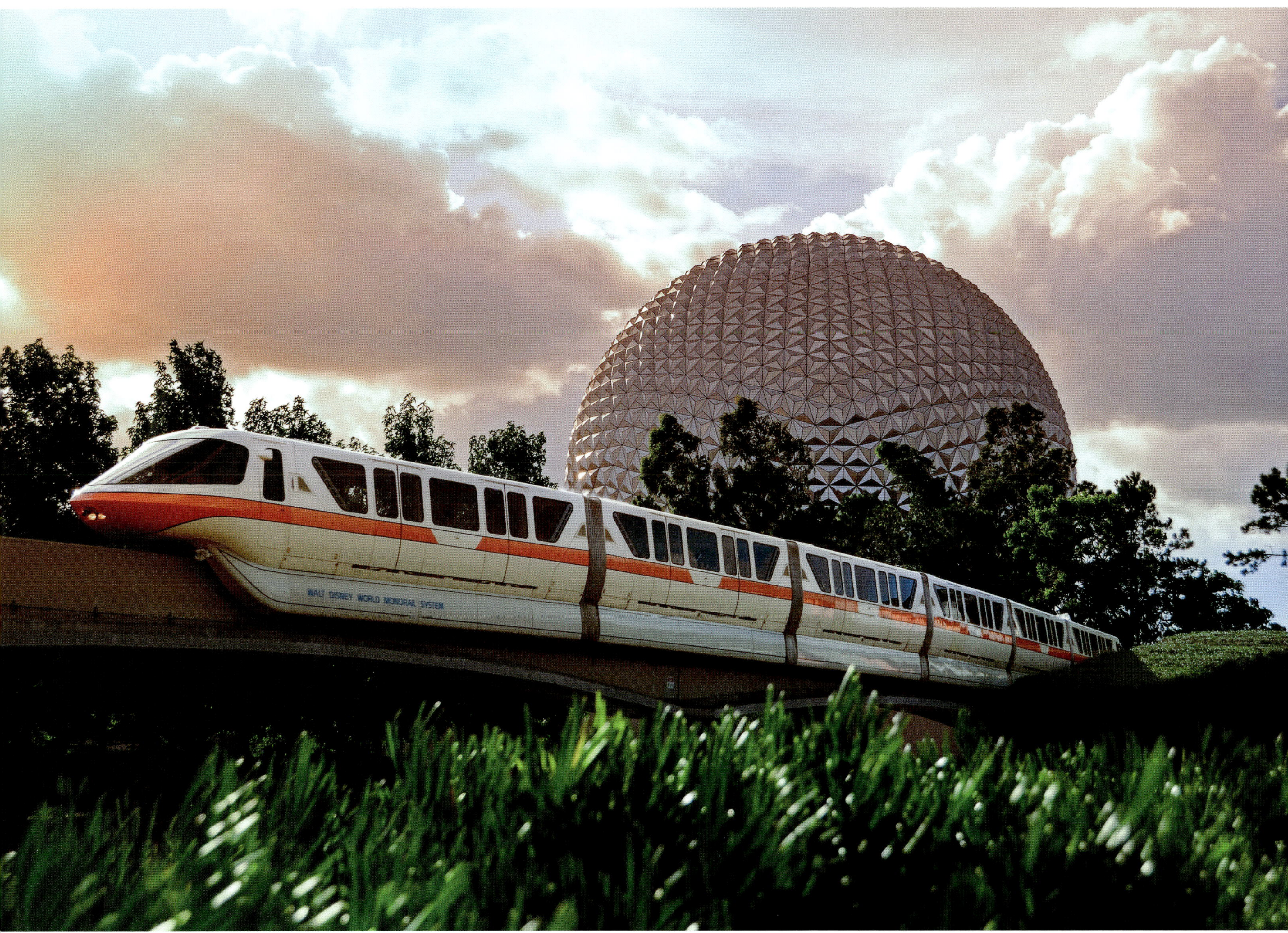
WALT DISNEY WORLD MONORAIL SYSTEM

Disneyland Turns 50

Celebrating an icon of innovation

For the celebration of Disneyland's fiftieth anniversary in 2005, a Disneyland Red Monorail Mark I (below) commemorative replica (right) was researched and designed by Jody Daily and Kevin Kidney. Kevin and Jody are the founders of the Kevin & Jody Show, a unique creative studio in Southern California. Their portfolio includes "limited edition and replica collectible merchandise, parades, and stage shows, toys, films, and other fun things."

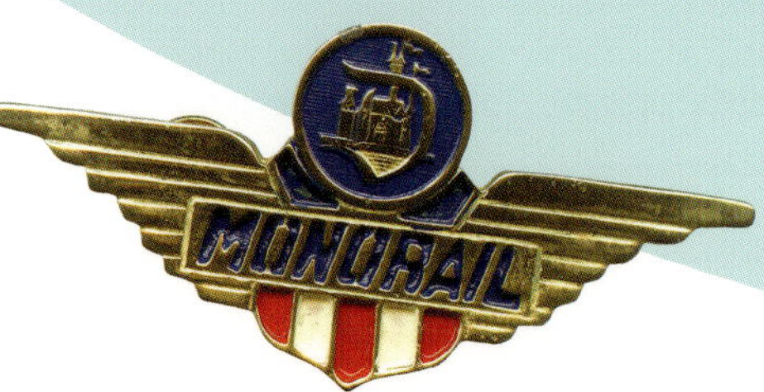

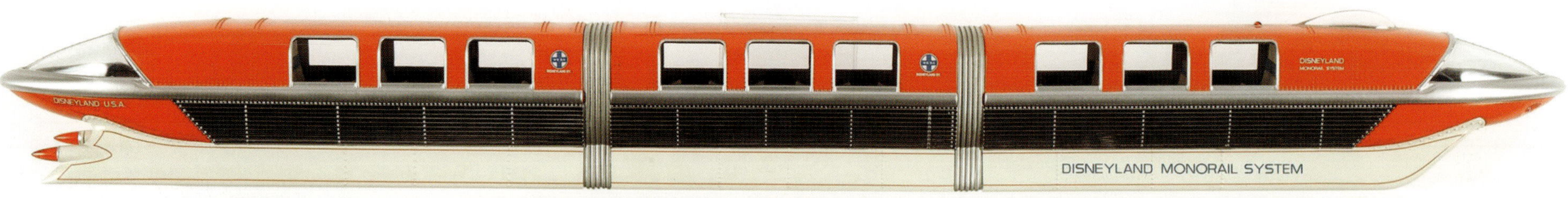

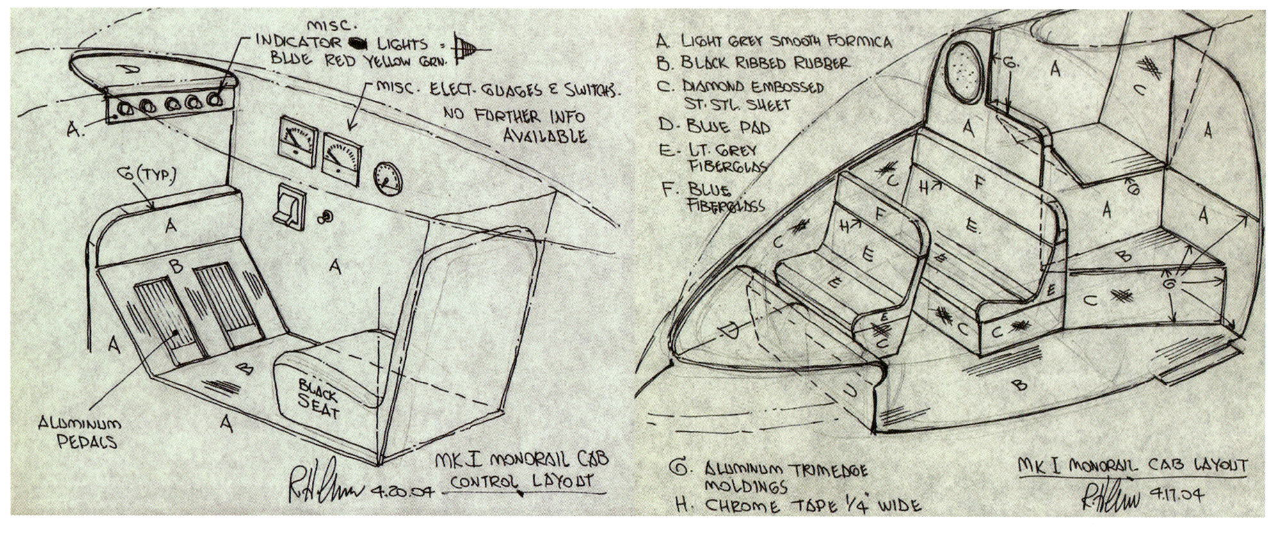

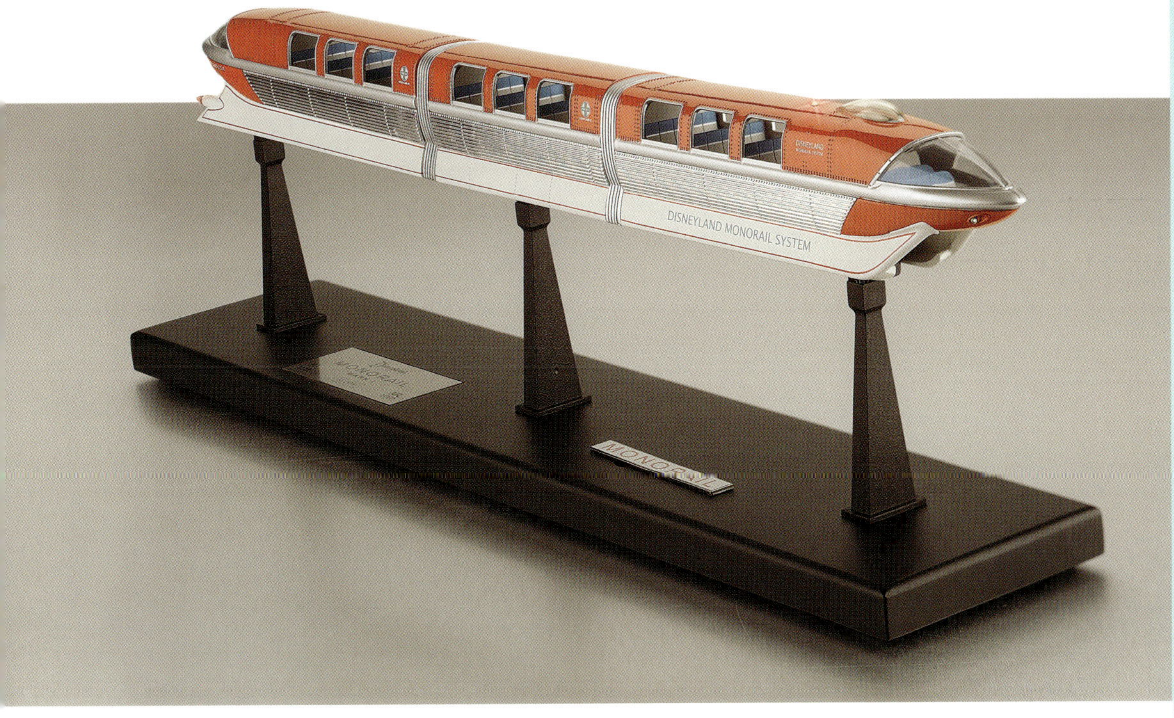

“We started working together in 1990 as designers in the Disneyland Entertainment Art Department,” Kevin says. “Since then we’ve created all kinds of things for Disney from illustrating books to designing toys and, of course, *theme park* entertainment. Everything we do starts with a ton of research.”

That research included collaborating with the original Monorail designer, Bob Gurr, who even provided Kevin and Jody with new cab interior detail drawings (see page 172).

As a result, this twenty-two-inch die-cast metal O scale model (manufactured by Master Replicas and released in spring 2005, in a limited edition of 1,959 units) contains authentic details such as foot pedals, working headlights, taillights, and a top beacon light.

The model came with a special pin (shown on page 174) based on the attraction’s original signage.

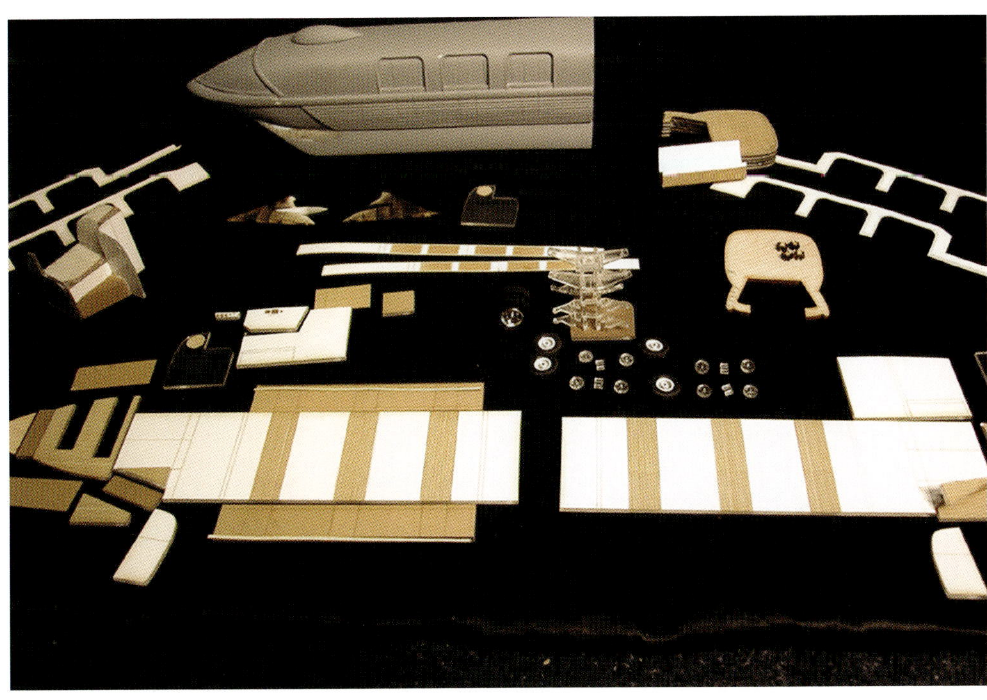

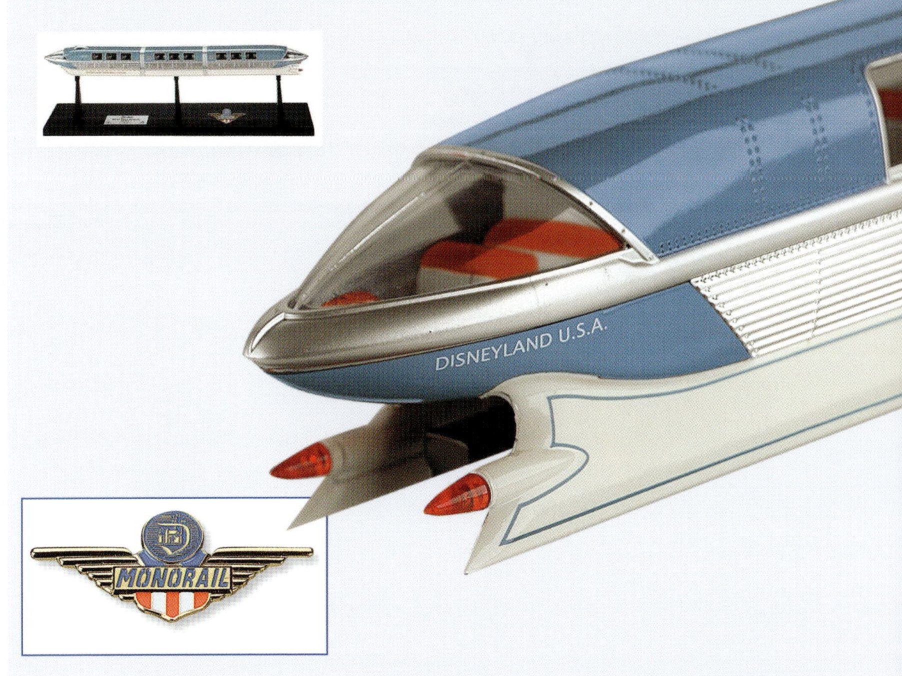

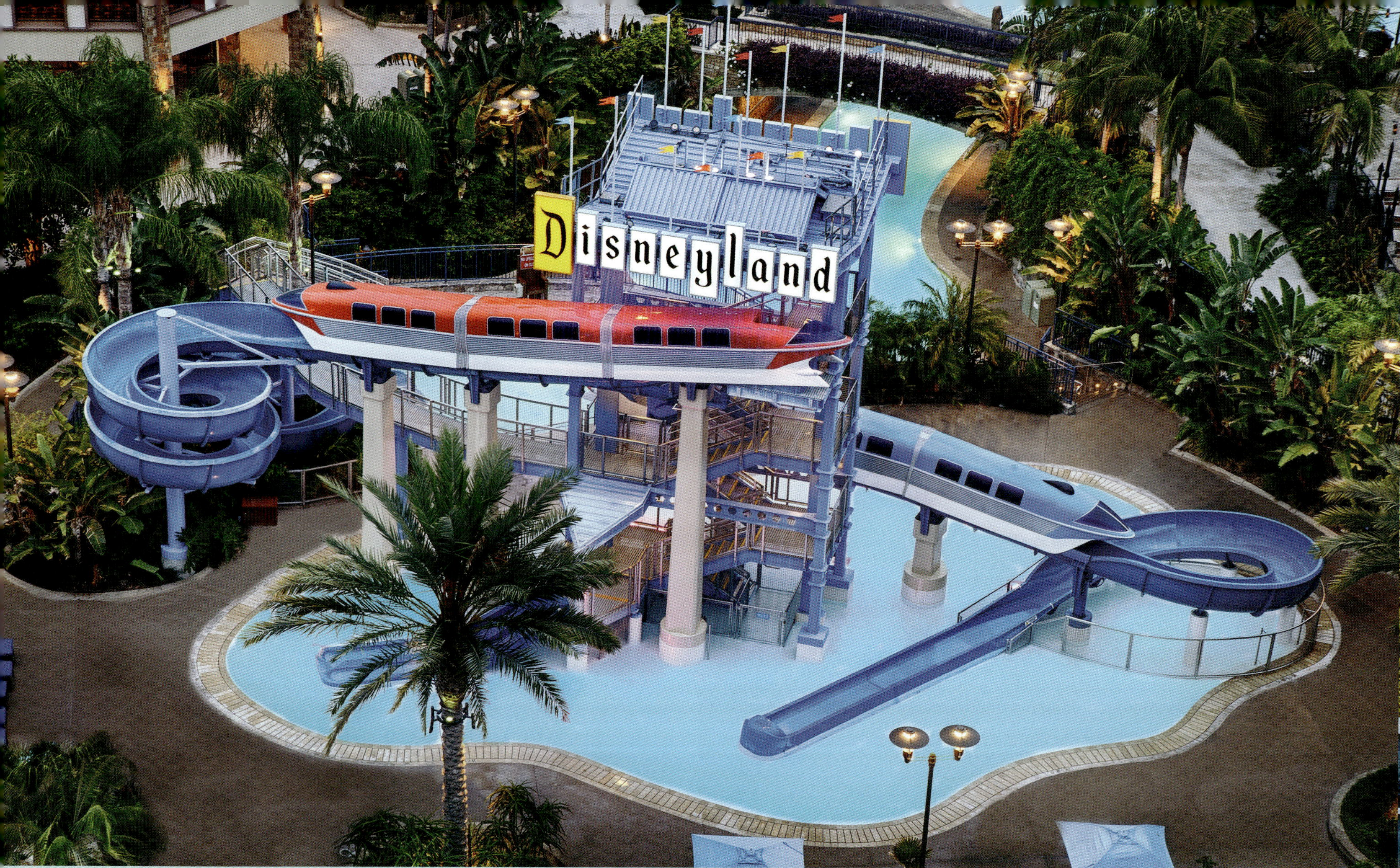

A 2011 renovation to the Disneyland Hotel pool area was designed with a nod to the iconic original Harbor Boulevard entrance marquee—with "Disneyland" spelled out in familiar box letters—atop a platform inspired by the original hotel Monorail Station, which supports a pair of waterslides. Each slide's entrance is a "Monorail car" that sliders glide through as they twist and turn their way to the water below. It's a remarkable cultural fusion, a simultaneous celebration of nostalgia, futurism, and Disney. (Note the 2014 photo above depicts the original Monorail Red and Blue color choices, while the 2017 photo on the opposite page shows the current Monorail Red and Gold color choices.)

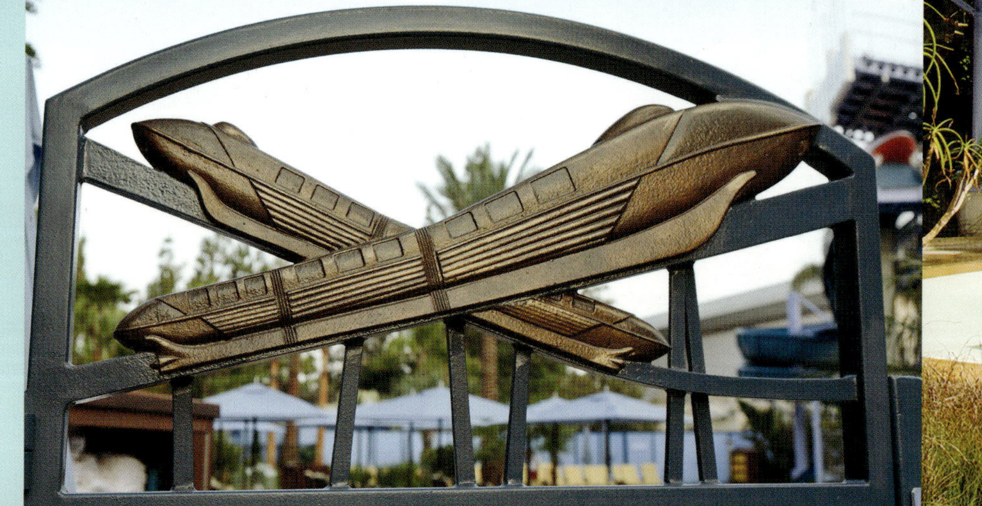

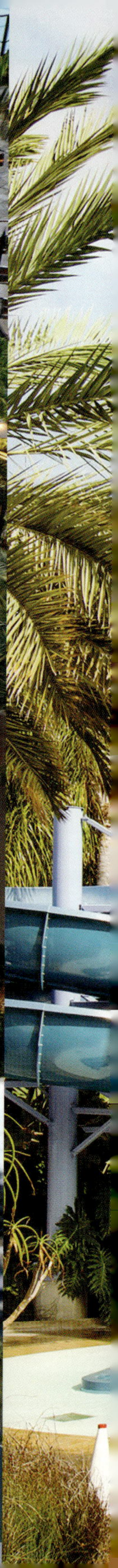

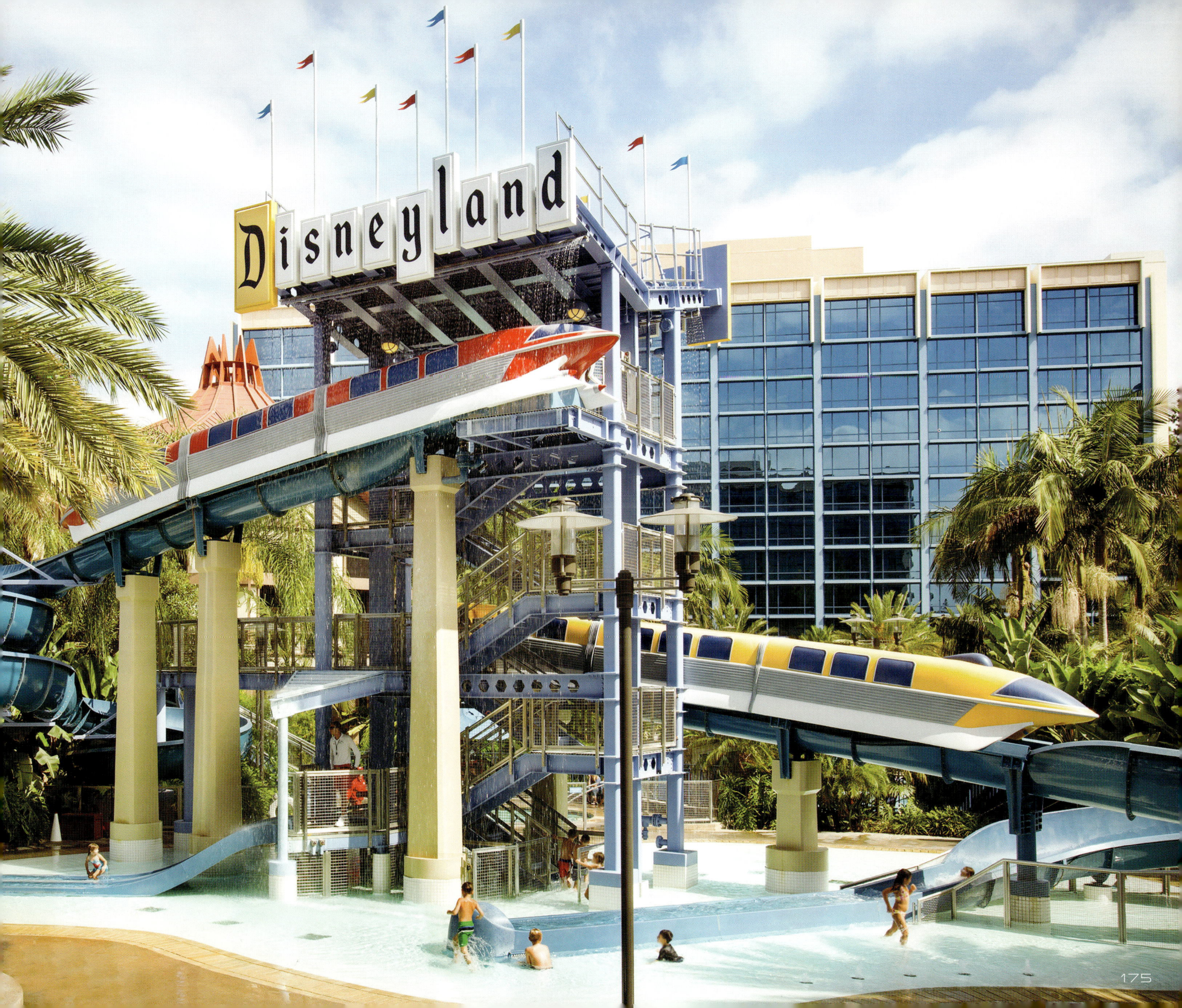
Disneyland

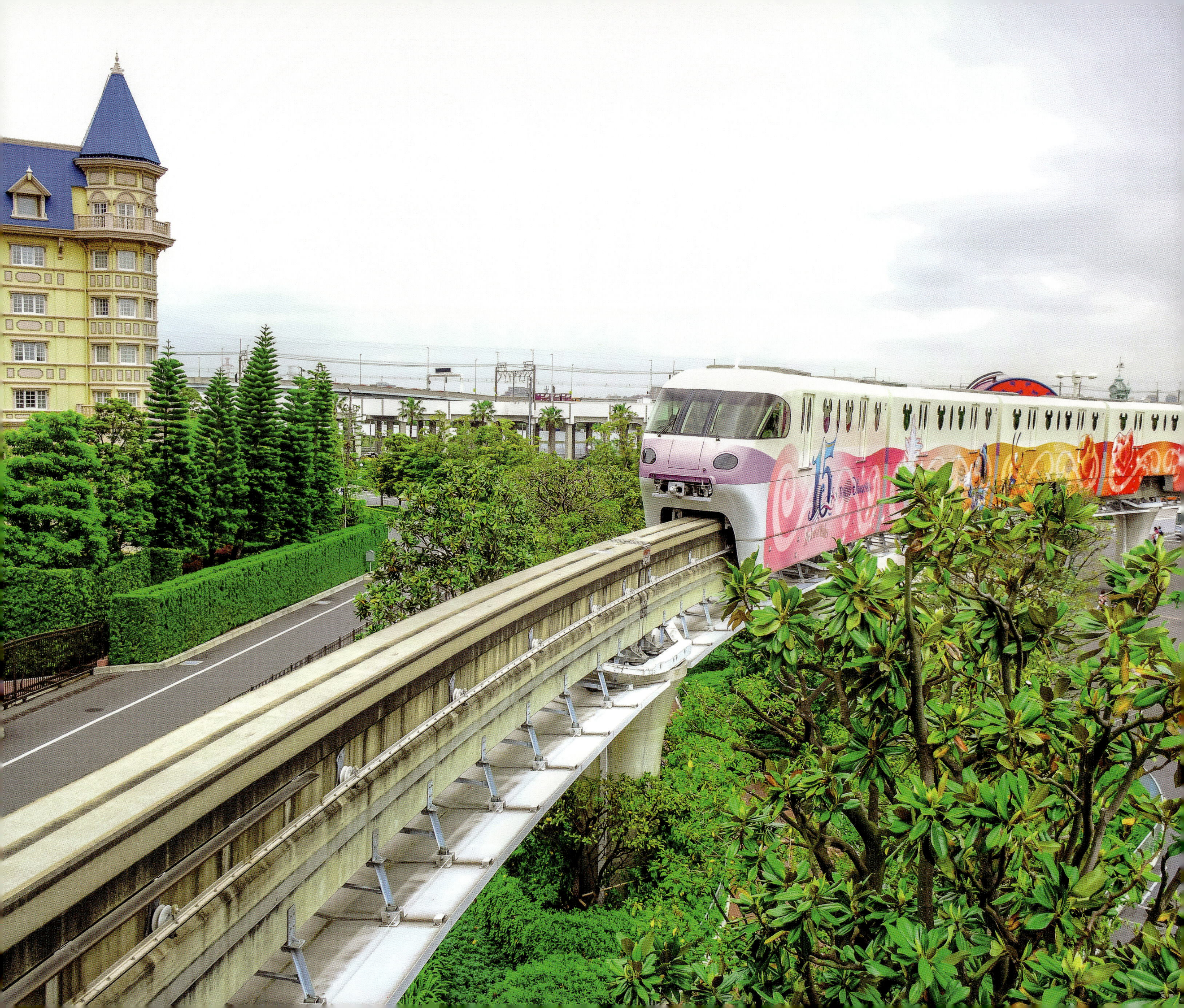
15

CHAPTER 7

A Rail Around the World

An Urban Visionary

Walt was convinced that the monorail system he had pioneered would be as much a part of his legacy as his work in film and television and on Disneyland. "He'd gone from cartoonist to feature motion picture producer to family entertainment activity," former Disney legal counsel Bob Foster recalled, "and now he was moving that next level into dealing with the ills of inner cities and was becoming a sociologist as he was doing it."

Little known is the fact that on May 4, 1959, Walt hosted a large group of representatives of the Los Angeles County Board of Supervisors at Disneyland in what was called an "Inspection of the Disneyland-Alweg Monorail System." In a morning briefing session at the Red Wagon Inn, Joe Fowler, Roger Broggie, Disneyland chief of engineering John Wise, and Alweg consulting engineer Colonel S. H. Bingham provided an overview of the project, including its background and development, application to daily use in the park, engineering and capacity specs and statistics, and economic data. This was followed by an inspection tour of the still-unfinished system, a comment-and-question period, and a luncheon service.

"You can't fight these things. I learned that a long time ago. I mean, it's progress. You can sit back and try to fight it, but it's stupid. I think, 'Go with it.'" —Walt Disney

The May 5, 1959, issue of the *Pasadena Independent* reported, "They pointed out that the cost per mile for a similar system in the county would be less than theirs because of research already completed by Disneyland. None of the officials, however, would hazard a guess as to the cost per mile for a county system."

Additional reporting and recollection of this passionate and proactive effort (including the aforementioned research study paid for by Walt) reveal an equally unenthusiastic response.

OPPOSITE: Tokyo Disneyland opened on April 15, 1983, in Urayasu, Japan, just outside of Tokyo. The Oriental Land Company had some land, reclaimed from Tokyo Bay, which had to be used for a recreational purpose and was an ideal size for a Disney park site. Walt Disney Imagineers assisted the Oriental Land Company to design the park and its surrounding resort area (see pages 180–181 and 188). By April 2014, Tokyo Disney Resort welcomed its six-hundred millionth Guest, and in 2016, it honored its fifteenth anniversary with a celebration called The Year of Wishes.

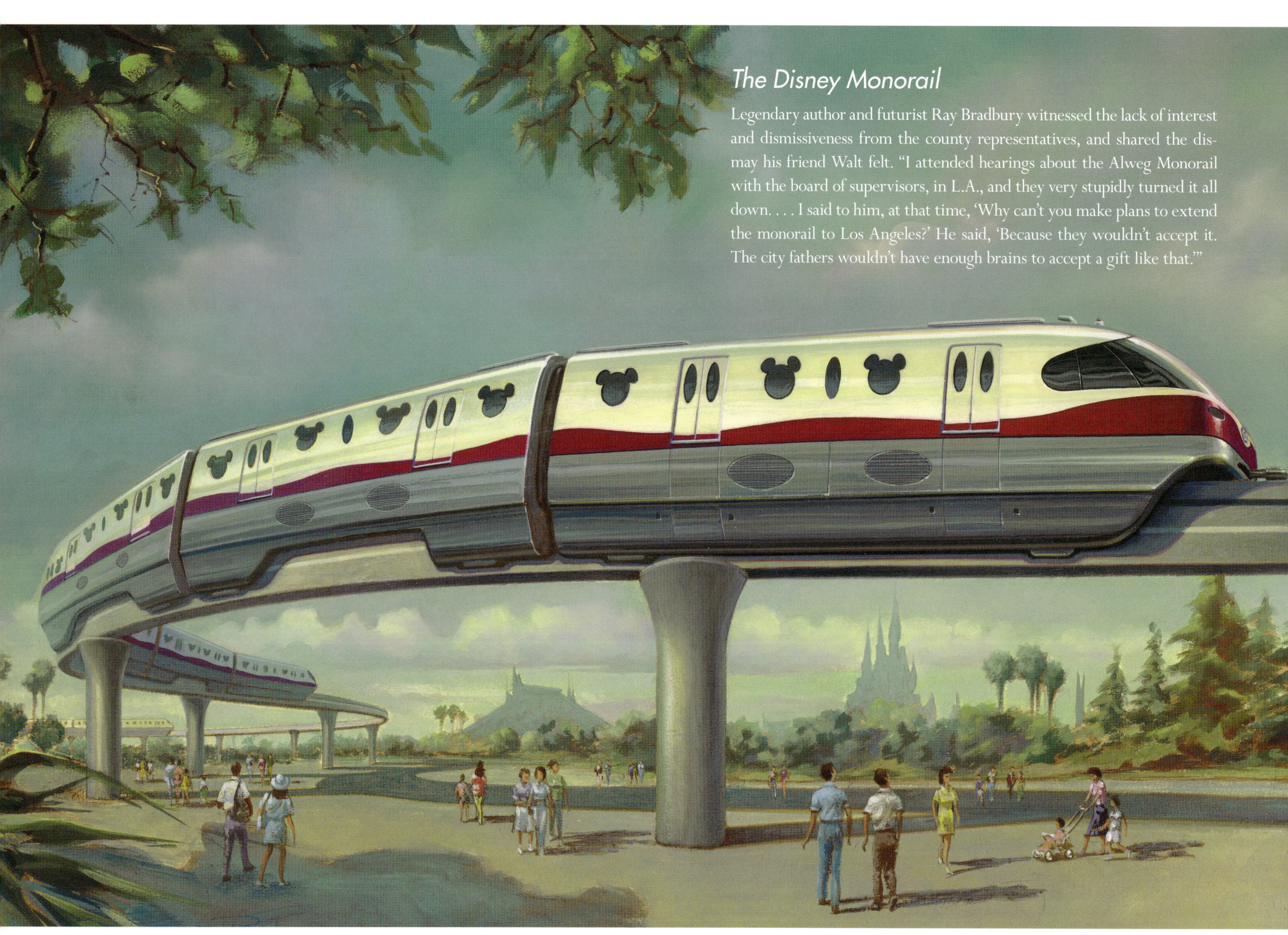

The Disney Monorail

Legendary author and futurist Ray Bradbury witnessed the lack of interest and dismissiveness from the county representatives, and shared the dismay his friend Walt felt. "I attended hearings about the Alweg Monorail with the board of supervisors, in L.A., and they very stupidly turned it all down. . . . I said to him, at that time, 'Why can't you make plans to extend the monorail to Los Angeles?' He said, 'Because they wouldn't accept it. The city fathers wouldn't have enough brains to accept a gift like that.'"

Instead of creating an immediate futurism in an actual urban setting, the lack of enthusiasm and civic vision displayed in Los Angeles and other urban areas (Alweg was reportedly preparing proposals for New Orleans; a locale in the province of British Columbia [in Canada]; and Brazil's São Paulo) led to the misconception of the monorail culturally as a "Disney thing," a fantasy creation. A connection of all monorails to Disney (at least in the United States) persists even today—although successful systems have actually been proving Walt's faith in such progress around the world for decades.

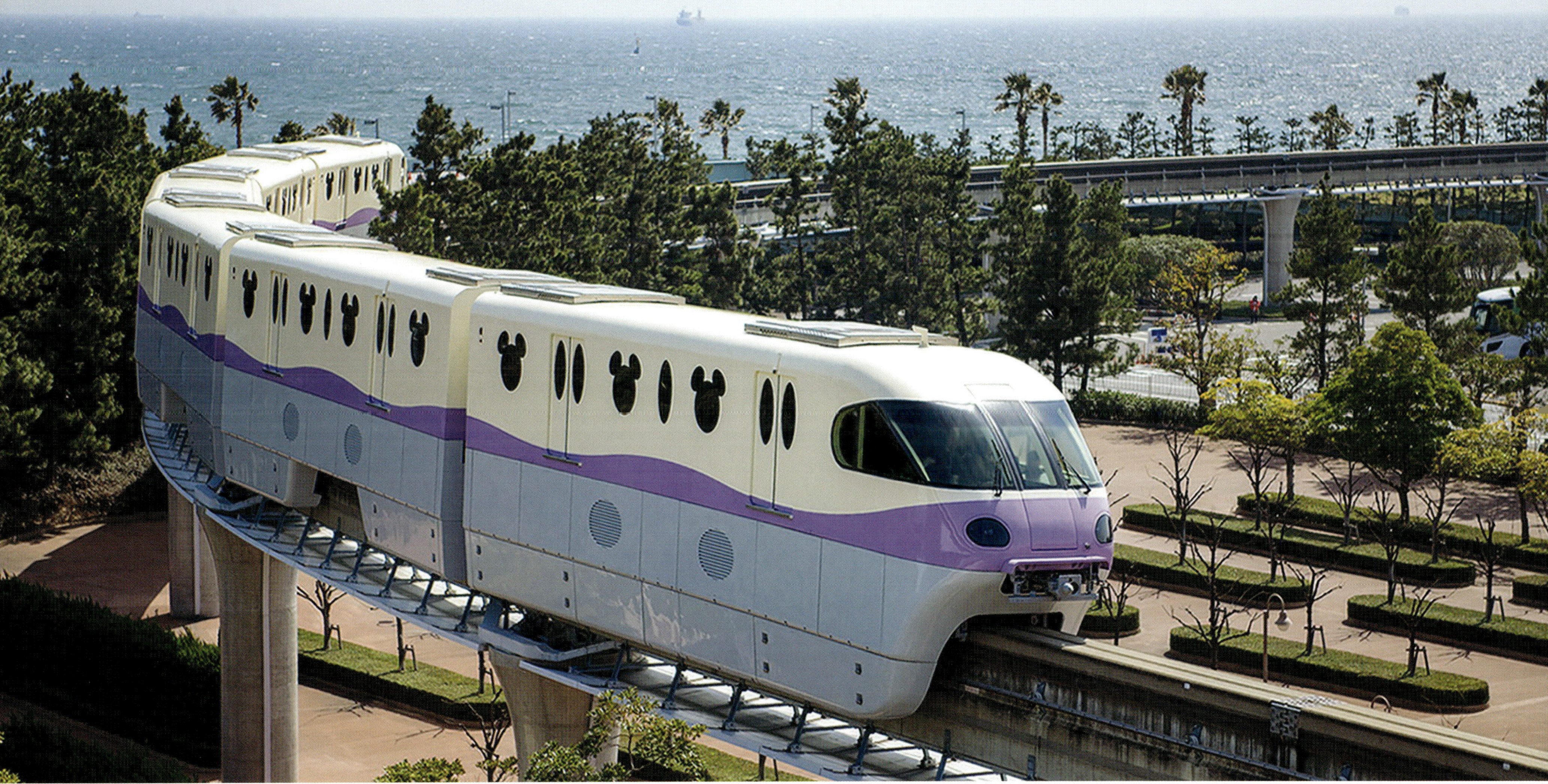

The Disney Resort Line trains on the loop line all travel in a counterclockwise direction. OPPOSITE: A concept rendering of the Disney Resort Line on the move by Erik van der Palen; gouache painting, 1998.

Disney Resort Line

Efficient Transportation and Elegant Showmanship

"With Disney it's never just about moving people from one place to another," past chairman of Disneyland International and Disney Legend Jim Cora says. "It's about moving people through their experience as efficiently as possible, while maintaining the proper atmosphere of theme and show.

"As we began the expansion at Tokyo Disney Resort in the late 1990s, the resort property just got too big to walk around," Cora recounts. "It became clear that we needed a more efficient and elegant means of getting Guests around what was now several discrete destinations."

So, as part of the opening of Tokyo DisneySea and its attendant expansion in 2001, the Disney Resort Line opened to passengers in July of 2001.

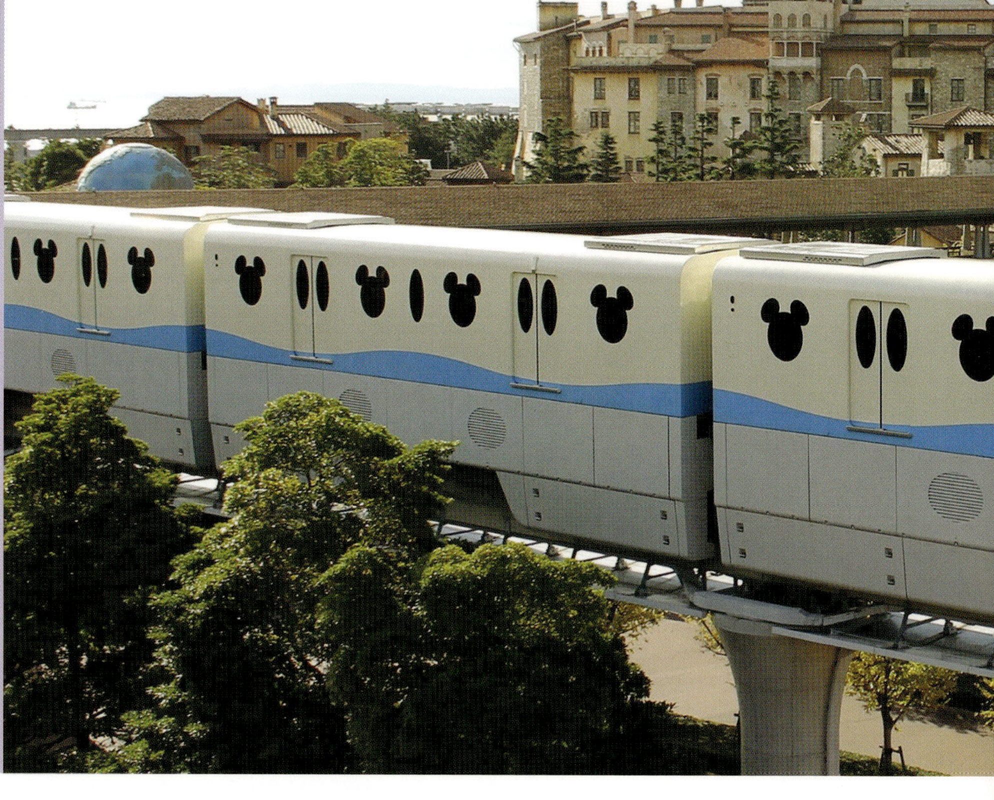

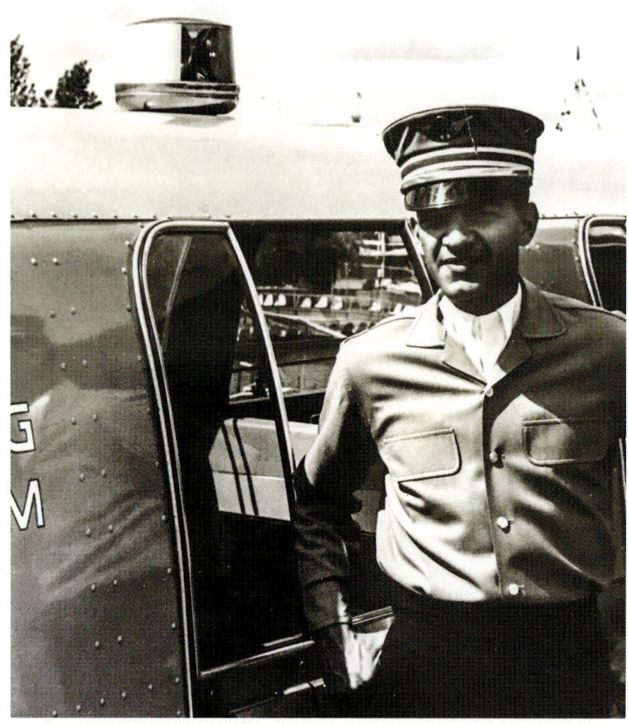

Jim Cora has a lifetime of authority on such things as the Monorail. Early in his Disney career, he was a supervisor on the Disneyland-Alweg Monorail at Disneyland in Anaheim.

The system (officially called Disney Resort Line) is an automated monorail loop line that moves Guests between four station destinations within the Tokyo Disney Resort property, and is operated by Maihama Resort Line Co., Ltd., a subsidiary of Oriental Land Company, Ltd. which owns and operates the resort.

Trains on the loop line all travel in a counterclockwise direction; a circuit of the entire route takes about thirteen minutes. All Disney Resort Line trains stop at every station on the circuit: they are the Resort Gateway Station (Disney Ambassador Hotel, Tokyo Disney Resort Welcome Center, and Ikspiari); Tokyo Disneyland Station (Tokyo Disneyland Park, Tokyo Disneyland Hotel, and Bon Voyage resort); Bayside Station (site of the Tokyo Disney Resort official hotels: Hilton Tokyo Bay, Hotel Okura Tokyo Bay, Sheraton Grande Tokyo Bay Hotel, Grand Nikko Tokyo Bay Maihama, Tokyo Bay Maihama Hotel, and Tokyo Bay Maihama Hotel First Resort); and finally at the Tokyo DisneySea Station (Tokyo DisneySea Park and Tokyo DisneySea Hotel MiraCosta).

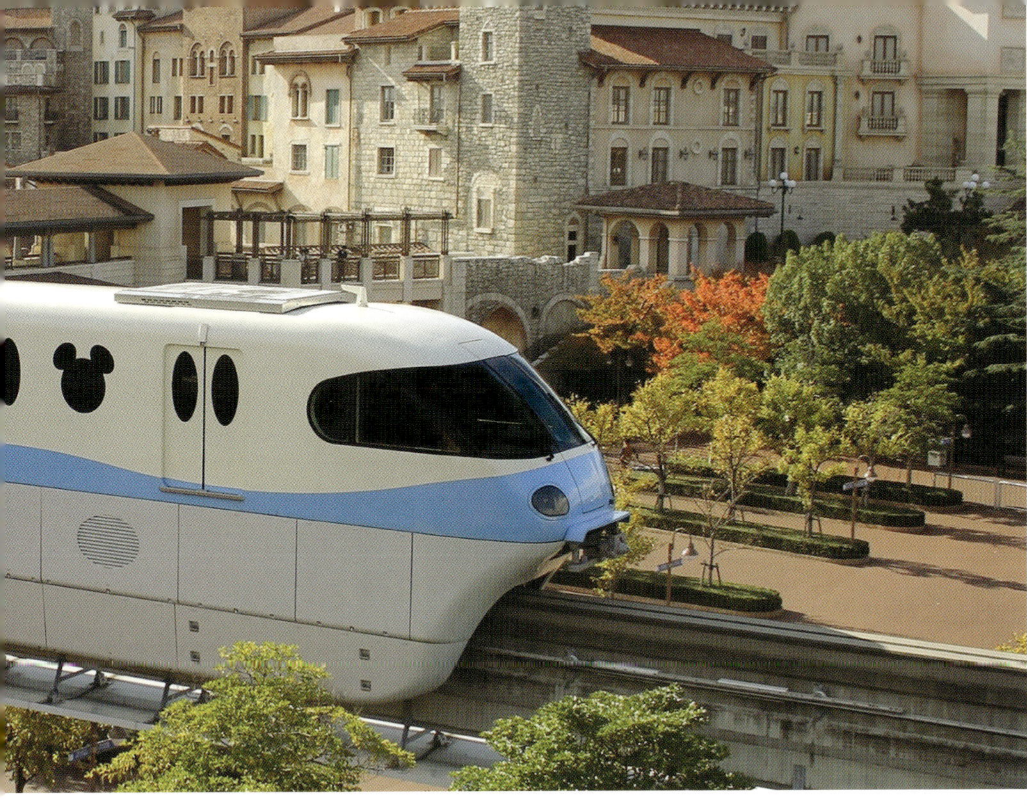

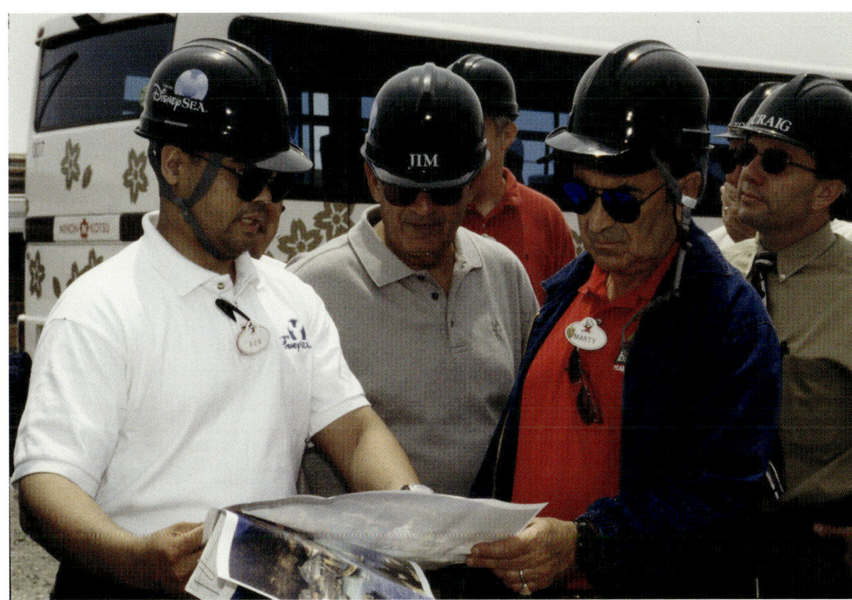

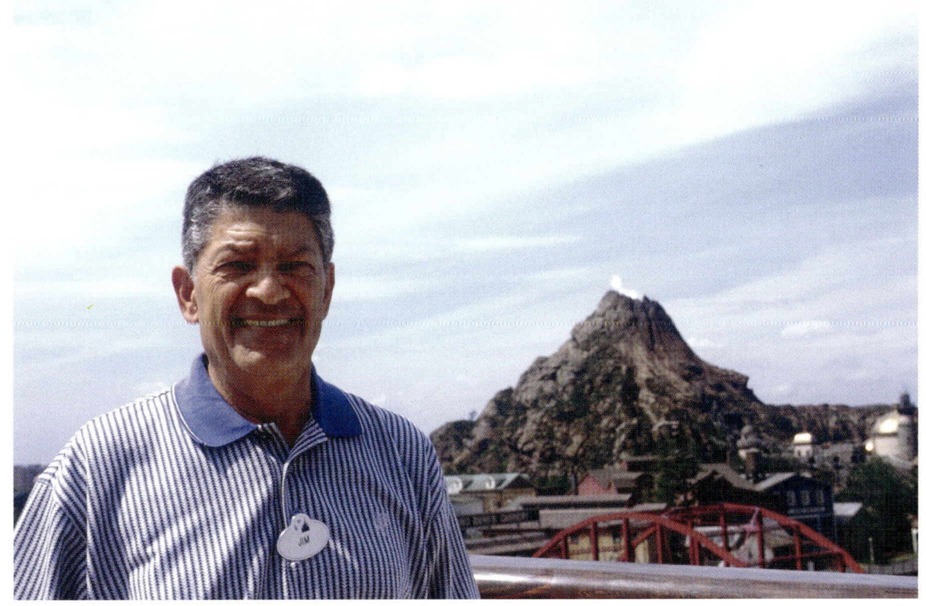

"Even though it never leaves the resort property," Jim says, "it still had to be permitted and approved as public transportation by all the proper government and authorities, which controls the Japanese Railway. It may seem like a simple 'ride,' but we had to go through a lengthy process, as you can imagine, to get a monorail at Tokyo Disney."

The line is operated using a fleet of five unclassified six-car "Resort Liner" monorail trains. Each train is finished in a different color. Up to four trains operate on the loop at one time, running with a minimum headway (the shortest time between vehicles in a transit system achievable without a reduction in the speed of vehicle) of approximately three-minute intervals.

"The Japanese saw the monorail both as a transportation system, but also as part of the overall show," Jim says. "They are pretty used to trains and practical transportation systems within Japan, so the idea of a monorail was not a big deal. Where we brought the Disney difference into the potentially mundane was in making the size of the windows larger, and making them in the shape of Mickey. Details are more luxurious, from wall coverings and upholstery colors. The cars themselves are wider and more spacious. Even the familiar Mickey silhouette is integrated as a passenger hang strap. These are not practical necessities—but what they have done is make a transportation system into an attraction."

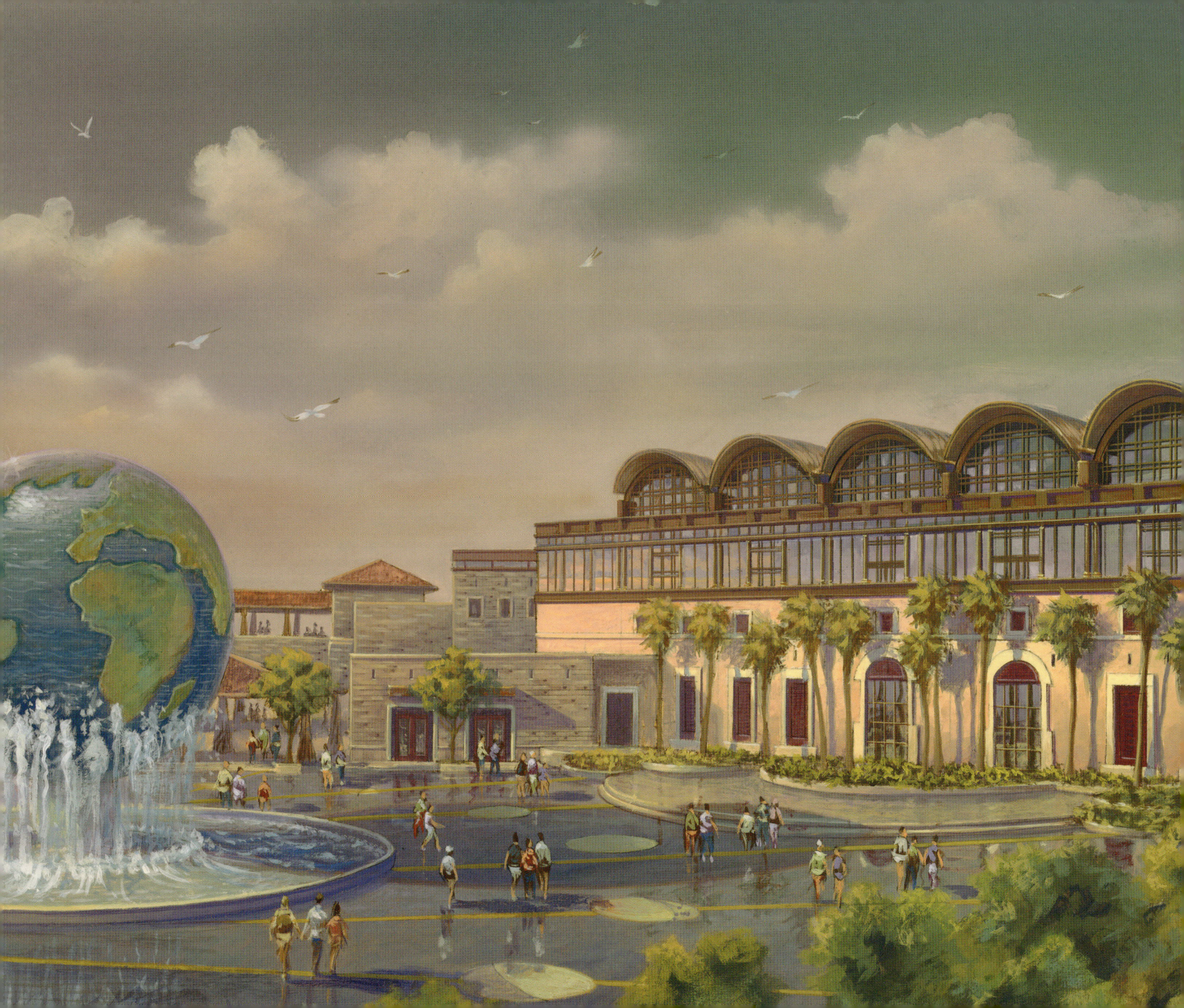

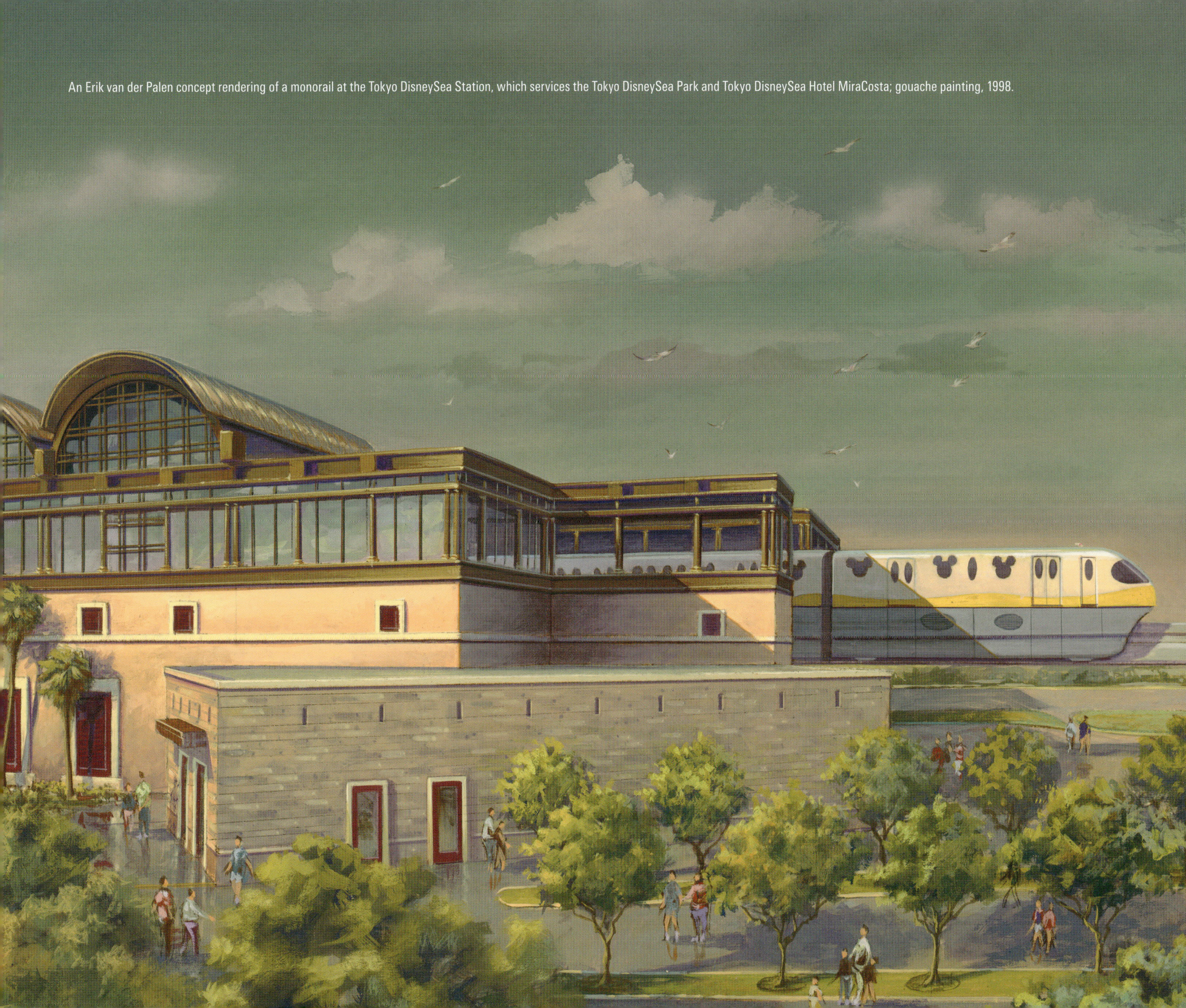

An Erik van der Palen concept rendering of a monorail at the Tokyo DisneySea Station, which services the Tokyo DisneySea Park and Tokyo DisneySea Hotel MiraCosta; gouache painting, 1998.

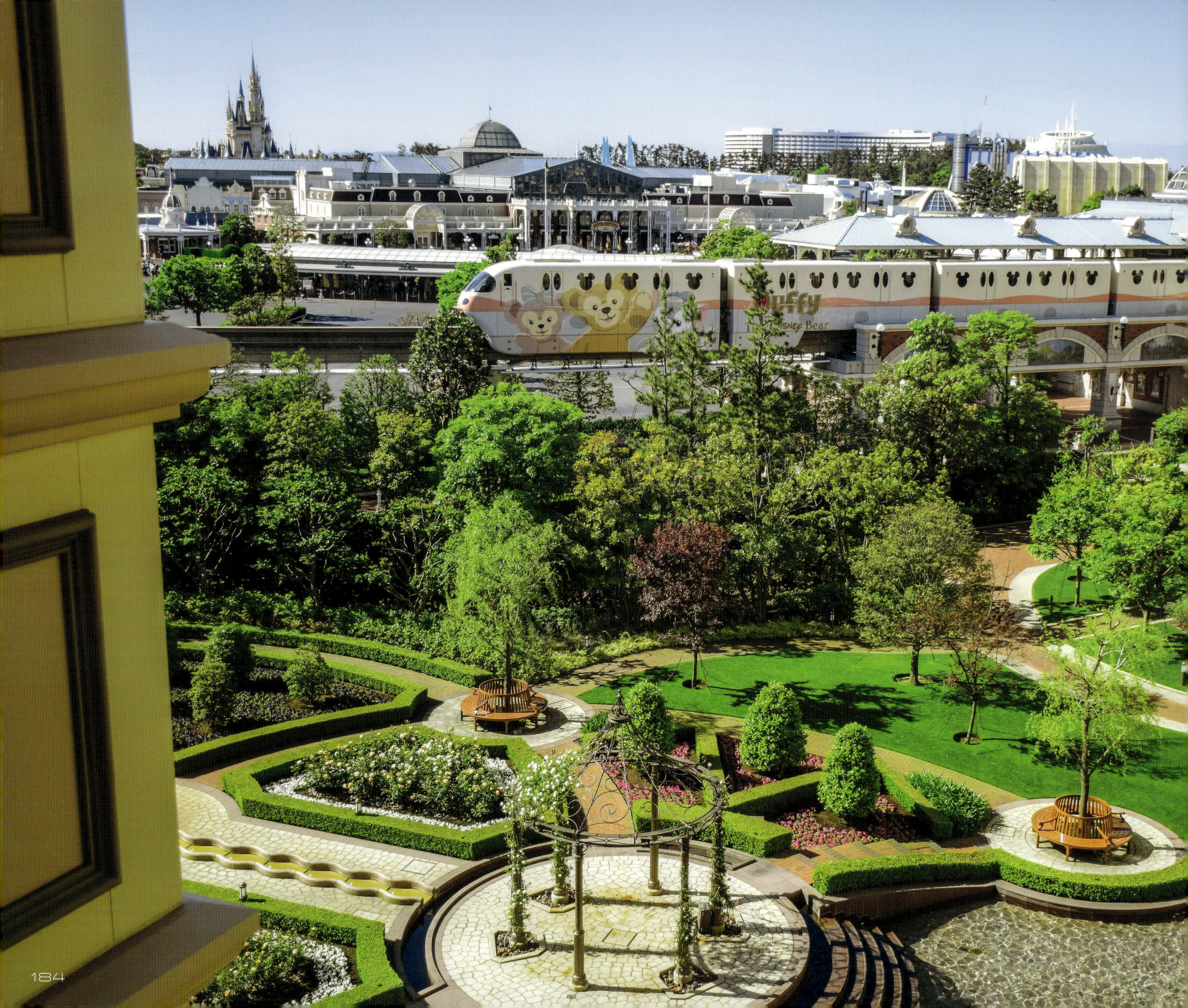

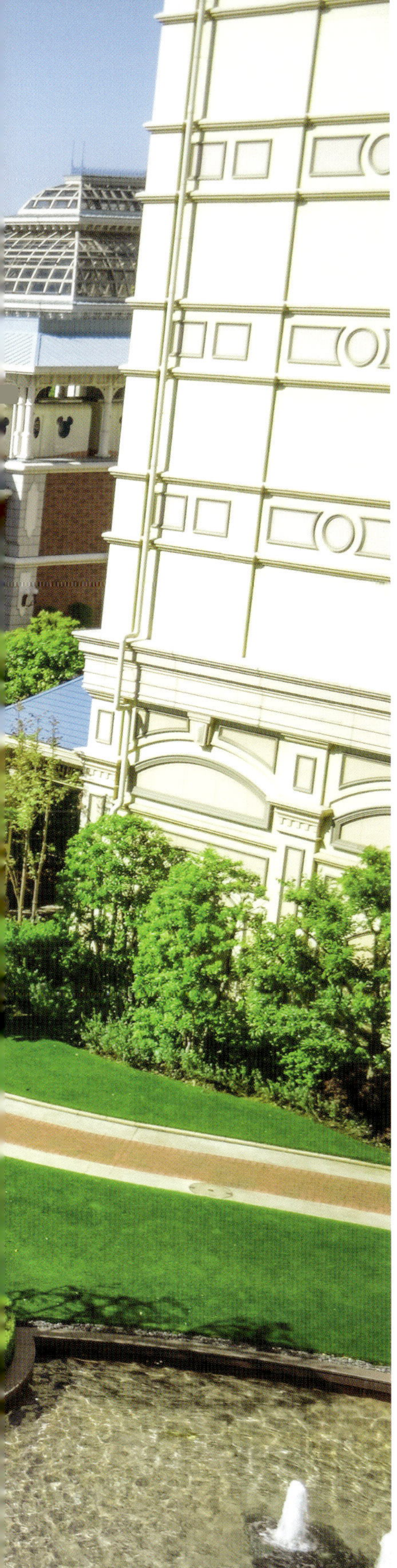

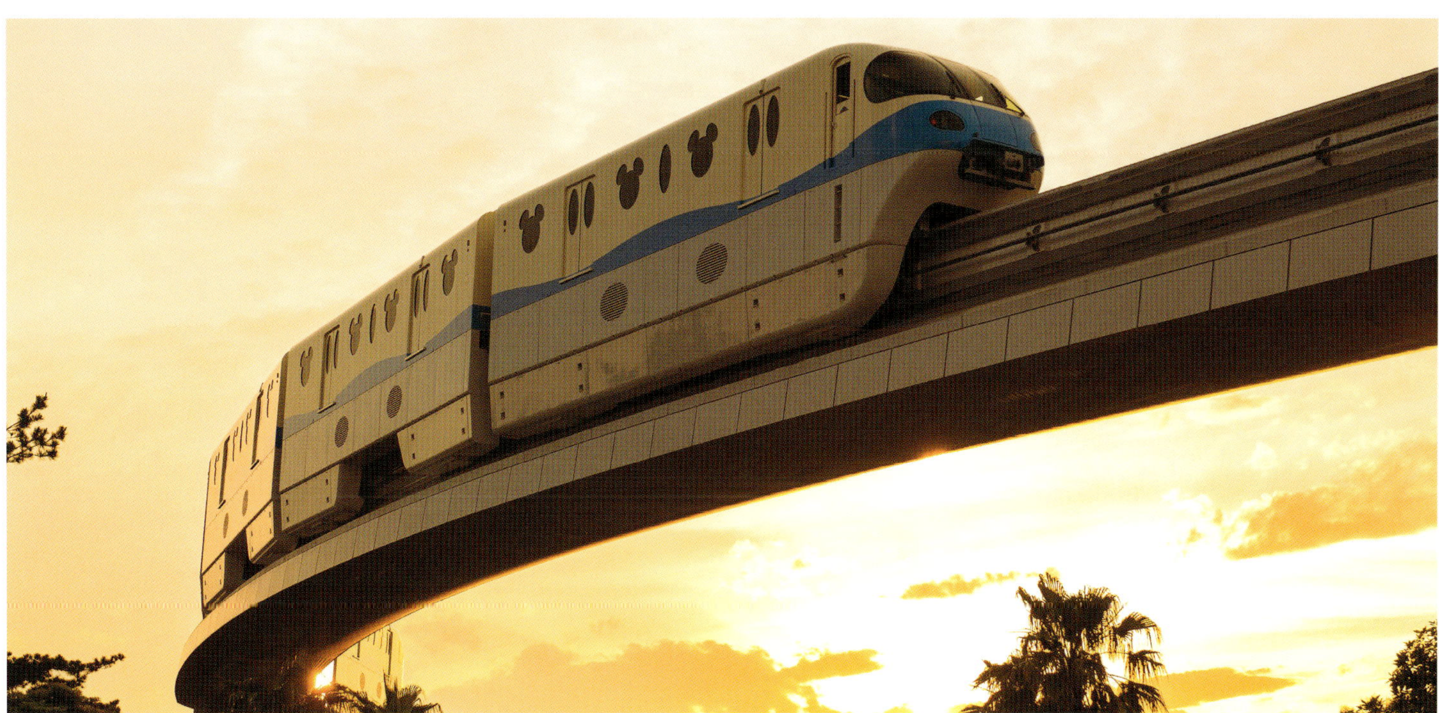

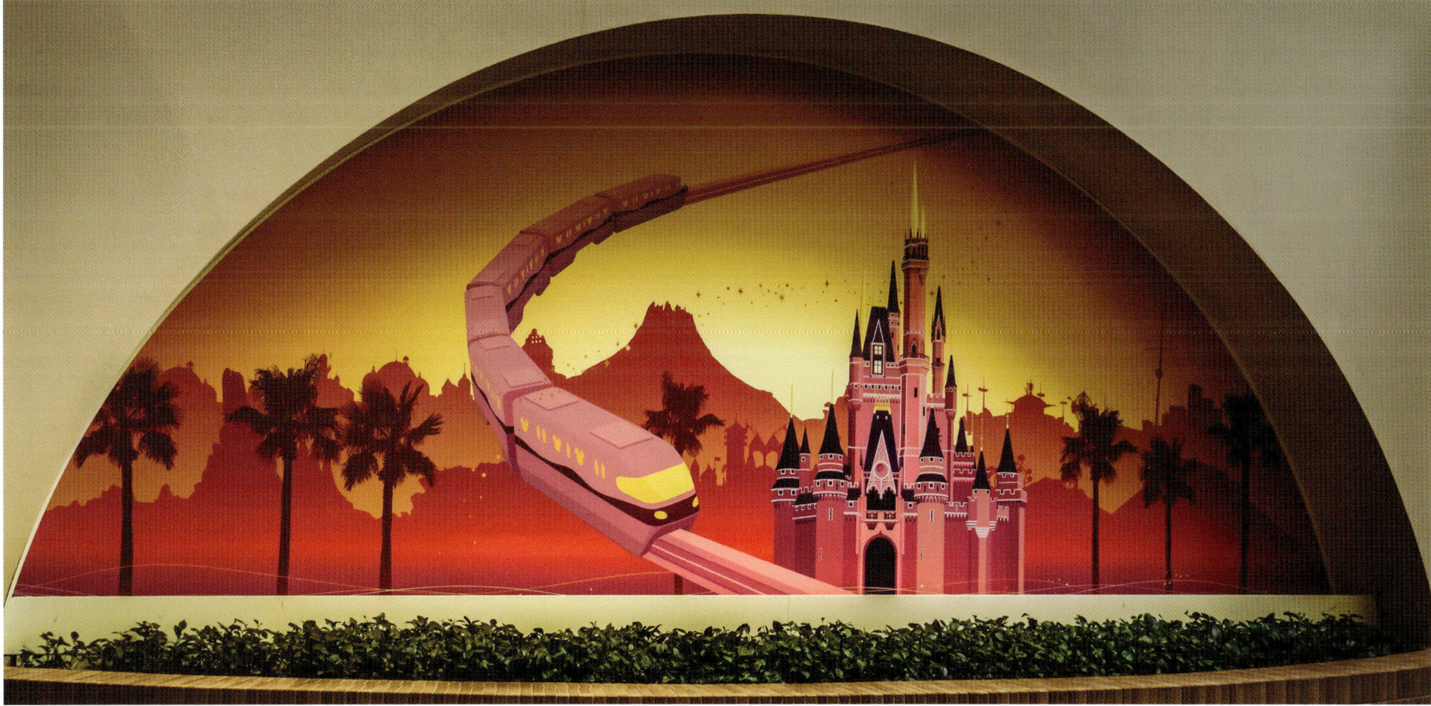

OPPOSITE: Also photographed in 2016 during the fifteenth anniversary celebration of Tokyo Disney Resort, this monorail features a wrap with the popular characters Duffy and ShellieMay. Imagineer Charlie Watanabe explains, "For those not familiar with Duffy, he is a teddy bear Minnie made for Mickey to keep him company during his long sea voyages. Duffy comes to life in Mickey's imagination and embodies *iyashi* (a heartwarming sense of comfort, healing, and being cared for) for many Japanese. The phenomenal success of Duffy has led to the creation of his many friends, such as a crafty bear friend named ShellieMay."

ABOVE: The Disney Resort Line against an orange sky and a vibrant mural at the Resort Gateway Station.

Global Monorails Today

Urban applications of monorail technology began to appear during Walt's lifetime and continue to be designed and built today. Although many of the monorails worldwide are used in theme parks, zoos, airports, and malls, and for other short-loop and amusement functions, there are many of the type Walt imagined: a kind of effectual, user-friendly, and even *fun* transportation that takes cars off the roadways, uses energy efficiently, reduces pollution, and provides affordable transit for everyone.

Tokyo, Japan

The Tokyo system has been consistently reliable and efficient since it was opened in time for the 1964 Summer Olympics in Tokyo. Today, its 11.06-mile route from Haneda Airport to Hamamatsuchō Station has eleven station stops and serves more than 120,000 passengers each day. As of 2013, the line has been used by more than one-and-a-half billion passengers and is one of few mass transit systems that operates at a profit.

Shōnan, Japan

The only kind of mass transit that is practical for the Shōnan corridor (which runs from the Ōfuna Rail Station in Kamakura, Kanagawa, to the coastal area of Enoshima, twenty miles southwest of Tokyo) is a monorail, due to space limitations and difficult topography. The 4.1-mile Shōnan route, based on the SAFEGE suspended monorail technology, opened in 1970. More than thirty thousand passengers a day embark at eight stations, which also serve as switches, since trains run on a single beam in both directions. "From purely an enthusiast's point of view, this monorail is one of the most fun to ride anywhere," monorail expert Kim Pedersen observed. "There is a sensation of a smooth flight through trees and above the traffic jams below. A couple of tunnels through hills add to the experience."

Kitakyushu, Japan

No new Alweg-type monorails had been built in Japan after the Tokyo-Haneda system until 1985 and the debut of the Kitakyushu City Monorail. This line, serving thirteen stations and nearly thirty-two thousand passengers a day, runs on a 5.4-mile route. This system is interesting in that long spans of track use steel guideways rather than concrete, and for its imaginative application of landscaping along the rail right-of-ways.

Osaka, Japan

Osaka is the second-largest metropolitan area in Japan, with a population of more than nineteen million. The Osaka Main Line runs on an elevated beamway between Osaka International Airport and Kadoma-shi Station, about seven miles to the southeast. Opened in 1990 and expanded since, the system serves more than one hundred thousand passengers per day through eight stations on a seventeen-mile route. The Osaka Main also links three Osaka University campuses. It was once in the Guinness Book of World Records as the longest monorail in the world, but this record has since been surpassed by the Chongqing monorail in China.

Chiba City, Japan

The Chiba City "Townliner" is distinctive in many ways. Incorporating lessons learned on the Shōnan monorail, it is the longest suspended monorail system in the world and the world's only dual-beam SAFEGE-type system. Current plans include extension to more than twenty-eight miles in length. The dual-track system was designed by the Mitsubishi Company and opened in 1988 to connect suburbs in Chiba Prefecture with the central downtown Chiba Rail Station. Currently its route serves eighteen stations on a ten-mile route, carrying more than forty thousand passengers daily.

Tama, Japan

The Tama Toshi Monorail Line in western Tokyo is a dual-track, Alweg-style "saddle-bag" system built by Hitachi. The ten-mile line carries more than 120,000 passengers daily through nineteen stations between the suburban cities of Higashiyamato and Tama via Tachikawa, Hino, and Hachiōji. The first section, from Kamikitadai to Tachikawa-Kita, opened in 1998, with an extension to Tama-Center Station in 2000. The Tama monorail build-out plan calls for nearly sixty miles of dual-beamed guideway.

Las Vegas, Nevada, USA

The Las Vegas Monorail is a nearly four-mile-long line located adjacent to the Las Vegas Strip, running between several large casinos. In 2013, total annual ridership was approximately 4.2 million passengers through seven station stops. The system began with Walt Disney World Monorail Coral and Lime trains, which were sold between 1991 and 1994 to the Las Vegas project, refurbished, and used when the initial two-station run commenced in 1995. In 2004, the Disney trains (by then renamed for MGM Grand and Bally's, the resorts that were the original two stations on the circuit) were replaced by fully automated Bombardier MVI four-car trains. Although beset by technical, electrical, and engineering problems over the years, the monorail continues to be a popular and efficient transport mode along the famous thoroughfare.

Shenzhen, China

The Happy Line monorail is a straddle-beam "light monorail" designed by Intamin Worldwide of Wollerau, Switzerland. The two-and-a-half-mile closed-loop system, opened in 1998, runs through four stations at major tourist attractions in downtown Shenzhen.

Tokyo Disney Resort, Japan

With the great success of Tokyo Disneyland, park owner Oriental Land Company expanded with an additional theme park, Tokyo DisneySea. Opened in 2001, the Disney Resort Line is approximately a three-mile, single-track closed-loop monorail system that loops the entire resort site with four station stops: Resort Gateway Station, Tokyo Disneyland Station, Bayside Station, and Tokyo DisneySea Station.

The Disney Resort Line trains are also *driverless*. The individual liners are operated from a central control station, and a single Disney Cast Member rides in each end of the train to ensure the safety of Guests during boarding and transport. (Also see pages 176–185.)

Naha City, Okinawa, Japan

The eight-mile-long Naha dual-beam monorail line opened in 2003 and connects thirteen stations with the airport. Starting at the airport, the line runs northeast through the city center and has an average ridership of thirty-five thousand passengers per day. In 2011, a two-and-a-half-mile, four-station extension was approved, from Shuri Station at the northeastern end of the line to Tedako Uranishi, with completion scheduled for March 2019. Each of the trains has two cars with sixty-five seats, and standing space for a hundred more passengers. The Okinawa Urban Monorail was the first rail system on the island of Okinawa since World War II.

Kuala Lumpur, Malaysia

Opened 2003, the KL Monorail is a five-mile system with eleven stations that serves approximately forty-five thousand passengers each day. Built by Monorail Malaysia, also known as MTrans (a monorail supplier with a background in bus manufacturing), the vehicles closely resemble the Alweg monorails in Seattle. In 2007, MTrans was acquired by Scomi Rail.

Chongqing, China

Serving the main business and public districts of Chongqing, China, the country's first Alweg-style monorail system officially opened on June 18, 2005. The system was also China's first heavy monorail line, built using Hitachi monorail technology.

Line 2 runs through three administrative districts in the central city (Yuzhong, Jiulongpo, and Dadukou), and covers 18.6 miles with service to twenty-five stations. It begins as a subway under downtown Jiefangbei, then runs west along the southern bank of the Jialing River on an elevated line, and then turns south into the city's southwestern inner suburbs, looping back east to terminate at Yudong in Ba'nan. It was subsequently expanded in 2006 from the Chongqing Zoo to Xinshancun, and, on December 30, 2014, to Yudong.

Line 3 (and the branch Airport Line) runs from north to south, linking the districts separated by Chongqing's two main rivers, the Yangtze (Chang Jiang) and Jialing. The first phase of the line from Lianglukou to Yuanyang (eighteen stations, 10.9 miles) opened in 2011, with a northern extension from Yuanyang to Chongqing Jianbei International Airport and a southern extension from Ertang to Yudong starting up in 2012.

At 34.5 miles, plus 6.20 miles for the Jurenba branch line that opened in 2016, Line 3 is the longest single monorail in the world by track length. At sixty-one miles in length, the system's two monorail lines form the world's largest monorail network. The system is also the world's busiest monorail system, with ninety-four million riders on Line 2 and 250 million on Line 3 when figures were last tabulated in 2015.

Moscow, Russia

The Moscow Monorail, located in the North-Eastern Administrative Okrug of the city, opened in 2005 and comprises a three-mile route with six stations. It runs from the Timiryazevskaya Metro Station to Sergei Eisenstein Street, and has a daily ridership of sixteen thousand. The system is based on Intamin technology, with modifications by the Moscow Institute of Thermal Technology. (For instance, due to harsh winter conditions, heating equipment has been installed in the guideway.)

Palm Jumeirah, United Arab Emirates

The Palm Jumeirah Monorail, opened in 2009, is a line on the man-made Palm Jumeirah island in Dubai, United Arab Emirates—and it's the first monorail in the Middle East. There are only two stations, Gateway Towers and Atlantis Resort, on the 3.3 mile beamway. Two unused stations on the route can be opened for future development. The line connects the Palm Jumeirah to the mainland, with a planned further extension to the Red Line of the Dubai Metro. The trains are driverless, like those of the Disney Resort Line, with attendants for loading and emergency situations.

Xi'an, China

Xi'an (population eight million) is the capital of Shaanxi Province, located in the center of the Guanzhong Plain in northwest China. Though one of the oldest cities in China, it now has a straddle-beam monorail line with a six-mile beamway that circles Qujiang New District, including Nanhu Park and residential districts in the vicinity. Three trains, designed and built by Intamin, can each carry forty-eight passengers and stops at eleven stations. Although the system was completed in 2012, it did not get approved until 2015!

Daegu, South Korea

Daegu is the fourth-largest city in South Korea. A fifteen-mile, thirty-station monorail line opened in 2015, connecting the southeastern and northwestern sections of the city, from Buk-gu's Chilgok Kyungpook National University Medical Center Station to Suseong-gu's Yongji Station. The monorail is Korea's first straddle-style monorail system, and has been especially praised for its aesthetics, including three spectacular bridges and generous attention to environmental integration and landscape design.

São Paulo, Brazil

The city of São Paulo is creating a major monorail network with a proposed sixty-two miles of monorail alignment—which would make it the largest and highest-capacity monorail system in the world. Three lines are completed or in development so far. The first section, Line 15 (formerly Line 2), opened as a two-mile segment with two stations in 2014. When completed, it will traverse sixteen miles of beamway with eighteen stations. The second monorail, Line 17, will be fifteen miles with eighteen stations; and Line 18 will run ten miles with thirteen stations. All the monorail lines will be integrated into the city's expansive rail system.

Mumbai, India

Mumbai Monorail, opened in 2014 in the city of Mumbai, Maharashtra, is the first monorail in India since the Kundala Valley Railway and Patiala State Monorail Trainways were closed in the 1920s. A first-phase 5.5-mile line with seven stations was supplemented by a second phase in 2017, increasing the line to 12.5 miles with eighteen stations.

191

Closing the Loop

Whatever his disappointments, Walt Disney kept moving forward, and no matter the obstacles or trials, kept making progress. He did everything he could to put forward-thinking, pioneering, and progressive urban planning into the real world—but without *direct* success. But he did not wallow in disappointment.

Ray Bradbury recalled, "He said, 'Look, I've given my services free to the board of supervisors and the city council of Los Angeles in connection with the L.A. Zoo.' They were rebuilding the zoo. He had some ideas on how it should be constructed. They didn't listen to a thing he said—and I was astounded to know that they would let him into a room and *not* listen to him. So he said he'd had his fill of politics at that point. And from then on, he would go his own direction, and try to do things with EPCOT and with Disneyland—and not worry about the politicians."

"Walt was an eternal optimist, and he really believed that things could be *better*," Marty Sklar said.

Bradbury disagreed—in nuance. "Walt was not an optimist, but an optimal behaviorist. Which means that every day of your life if you *behave* well, you begin to feel well. . . . You get your work done every day, at the end of a week, a month, a year, you turn around and say, 'Hey, look what I did,' so you feel good—that's real optimism. . . . He could look back at the end of each year and see his behavior, and it made him want to go on. A lot of people are pessimists because they've never done anything."

Sixty years on, one of Walt Disney's most enduring achievements is the Disney Monorail. A symbol of the man, his organization, his visionary scholarship, his showmanship—and his eternal belief that "there's a great big beautiful tomorrow, just a dream away."

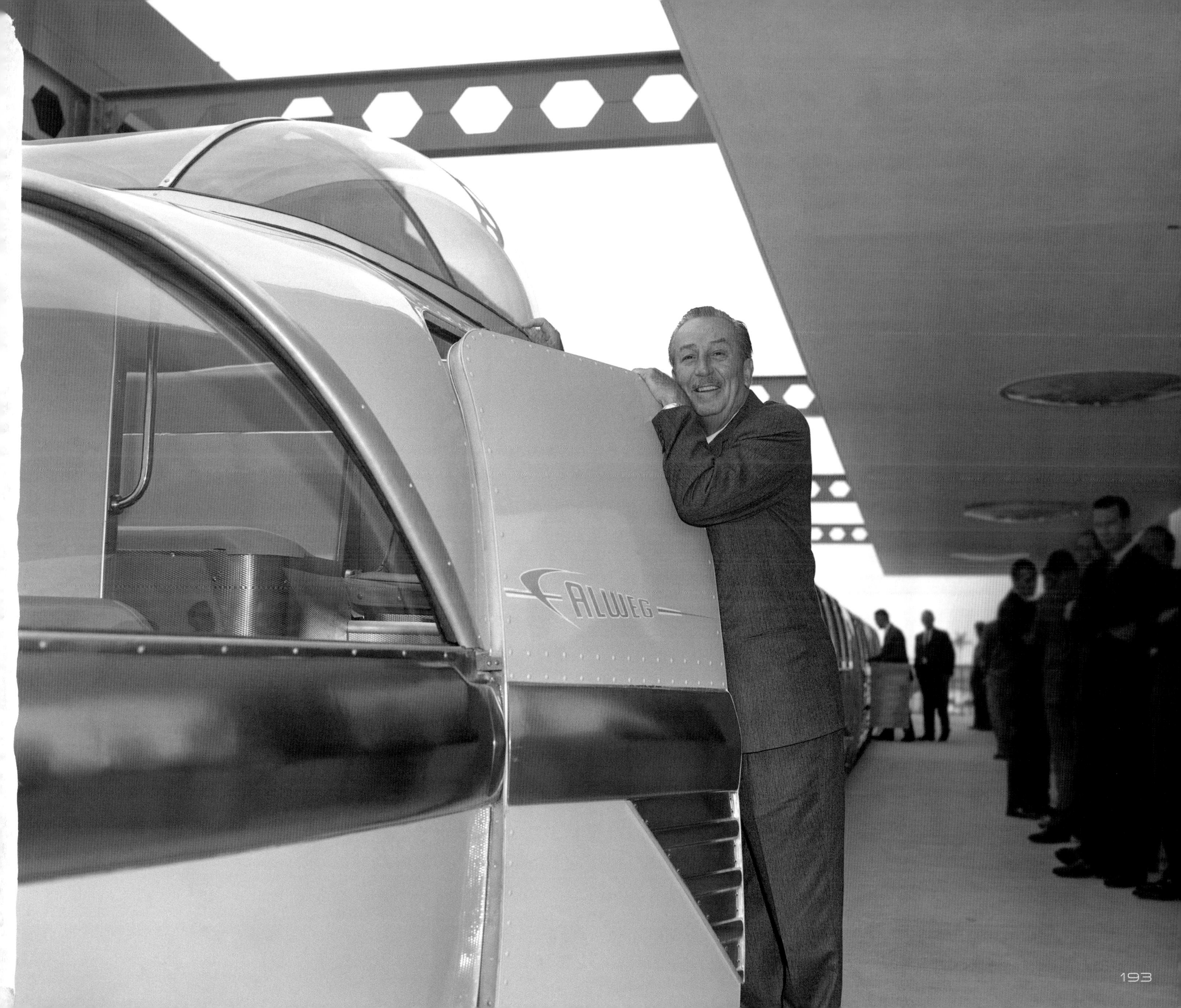
ALWEG

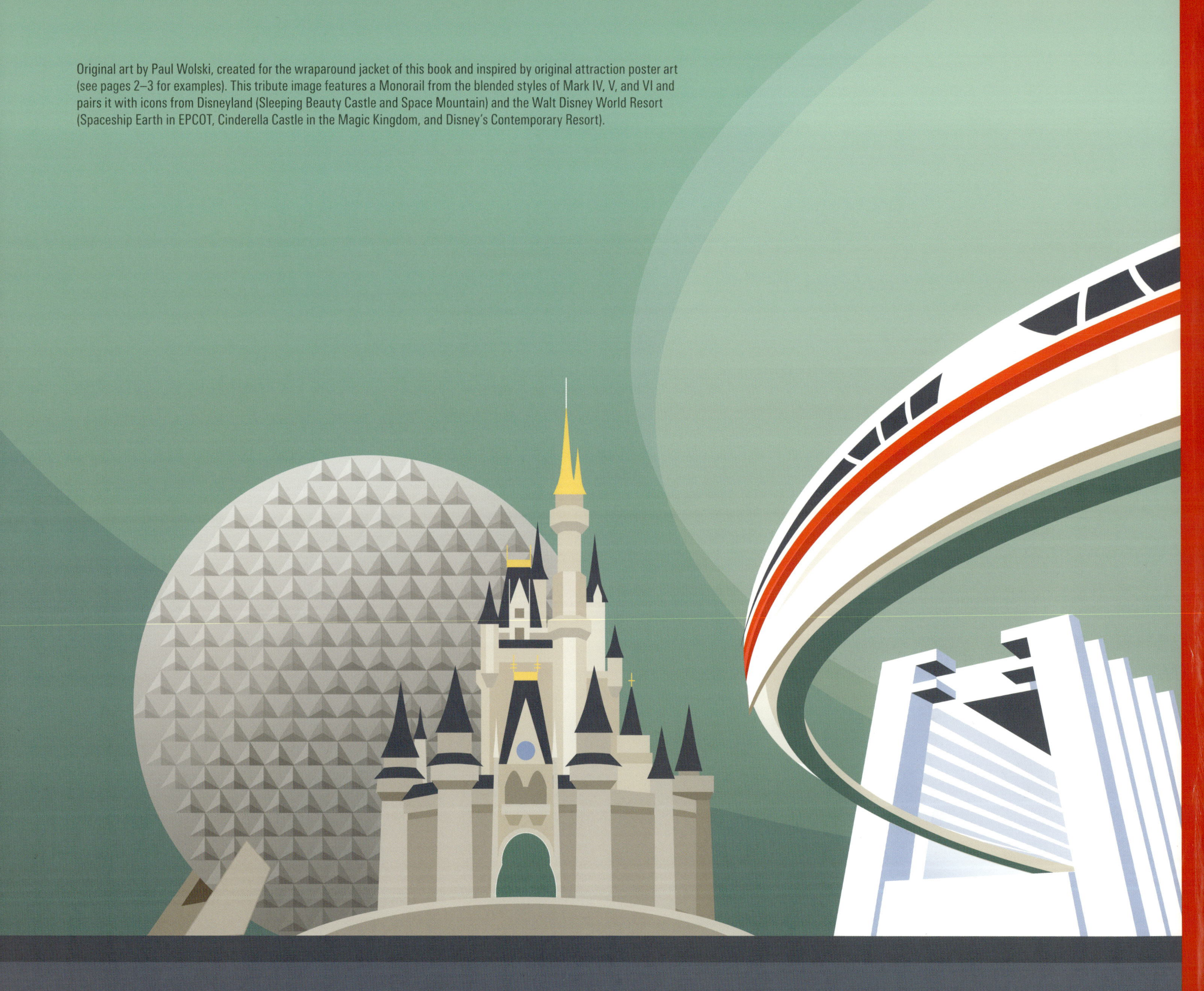

Original art by Paul Wolski, created for the wraparound jacket of this book and inspired by original attraction poster art (see pages 2–3 for examples). This tribute image features a Monorail from the blended styles of Mark IV, V, and VI and pairs it with icons from Disneyland (Sleeping Beauty Castle and Space Mountain) and the Walt Disney World Resort (Spaceship Earth in EPCOT, Cinderella Castle in the Magic Kingdom, and Disney's Contemporary Resort).

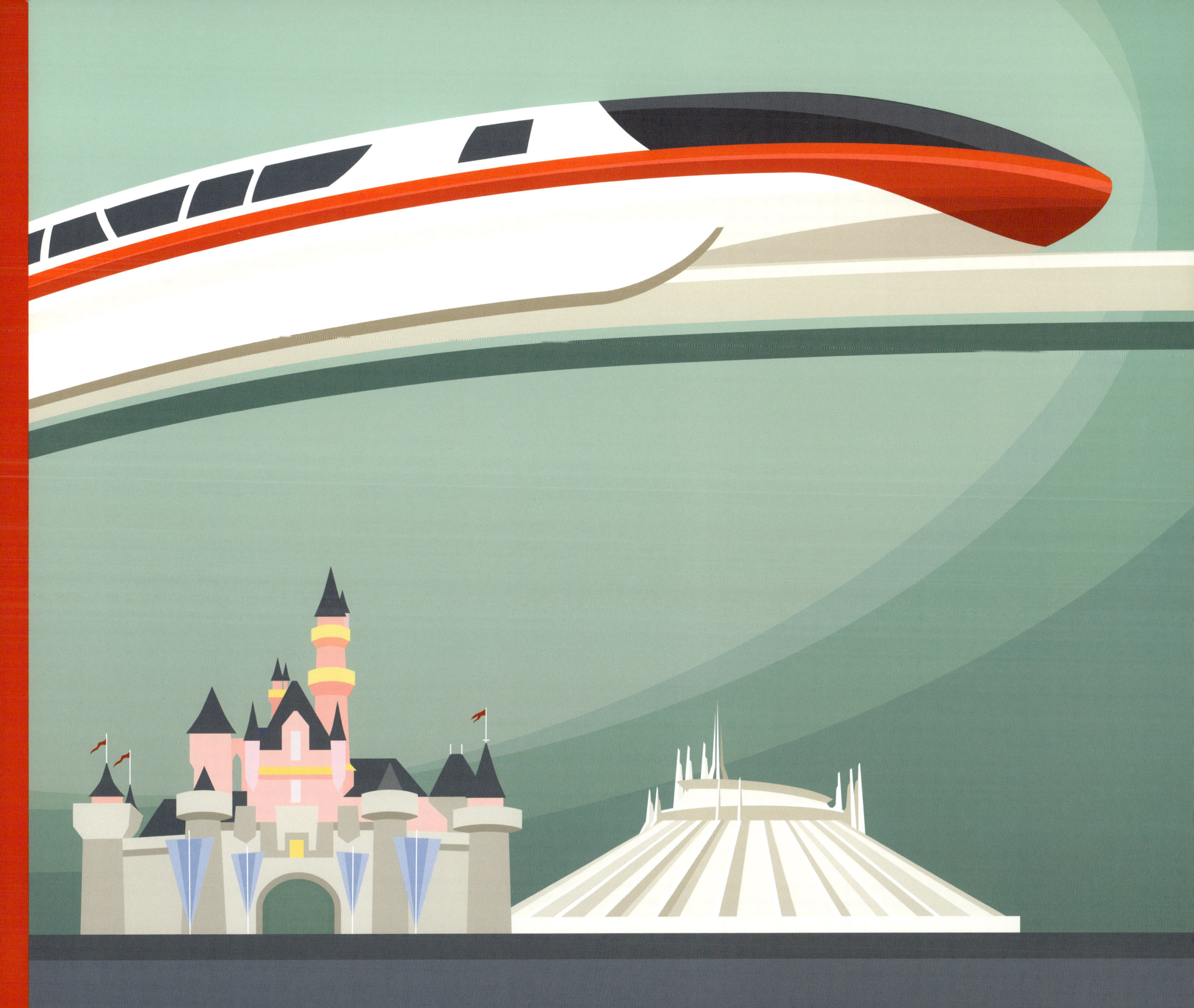

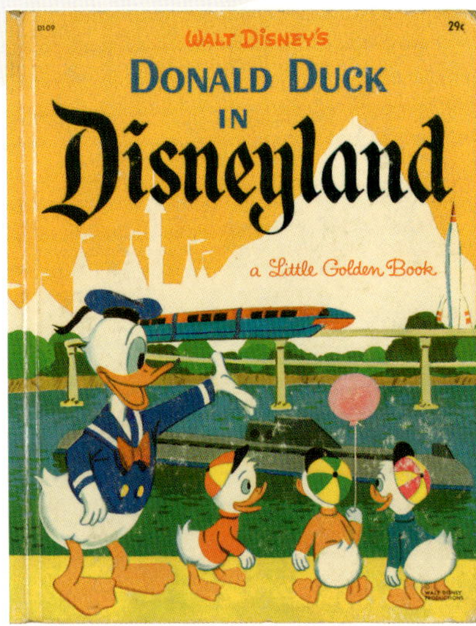
WALT DISNEY'S
DONALD DUCK
IN
Disneyland
a Little Golden Book

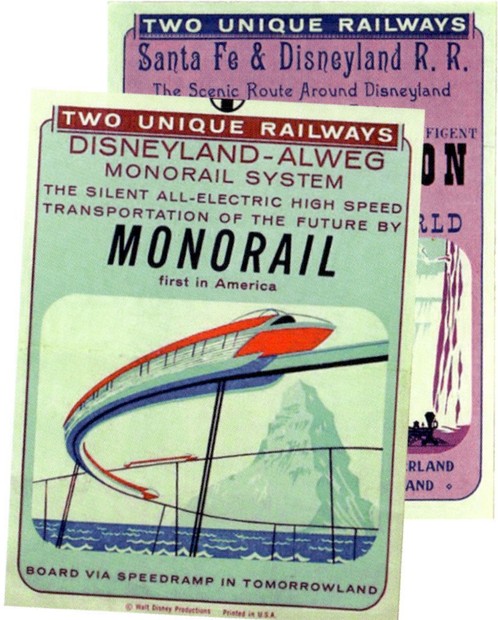
TWO UNIQUE RAILWAYS
Santa Fe & Disneyland R. R.
The Scenic Route Around Disneyland
TWO UNIQUE RAILWAYS
DISNEYLAND-ALWEG
MONORAIL SYSTEM
THE SILENT ALL-ELECTRIC HIGH SPEED TRANSPORTATION OF THE FUTURE BY
MONORAIL
first in America
BOARD VIA SPEEDRAMP IN TOMORROWLAND

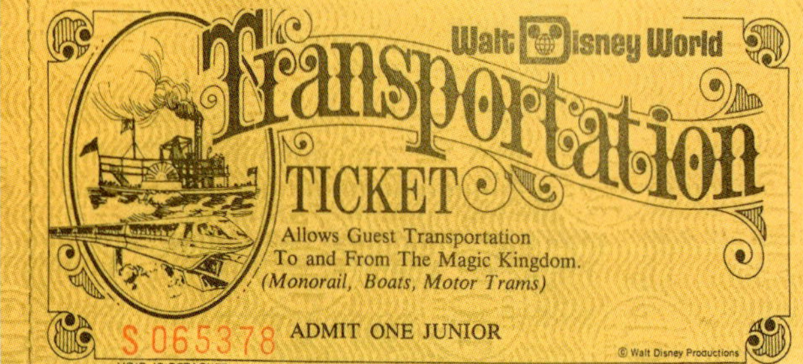
Walt Disney World
Transportation
TICKET
Allows Guest Transportation
To and From The Magic Kingdom.
(Monorail, Boats, Motor Trams)
S 065378
ADMIT ONE JUNIOR
© Walt Disney Productions

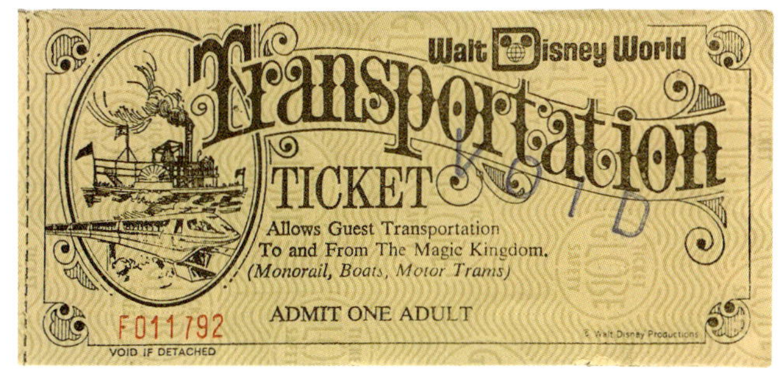
Walt Disney World
Transportation
TICKET
VOID
Allows Guest Transportation
To and From The Magic Kingdom.
(Monorail, Boats, Motor Trams)
F011792
ADMIT ONE ADULT
VOID IF DETACHED

Courtesy Michael Carroll / Disney Editions on page 135.

Courtesy Jim and Mimi Cora on page 180 (black-and-white photo).

Courtesy Jody Daily and Kevin Kidney on pages 14, 34, 79, 113 (EXIT sign photo), 114 (board game photos), 115 (lunch kit, school bag, travel bag, and puzzle photos), 119 (menu scan), 172 and 173 (all photos except for pin), and 197 (*Two Unique Railways* scans).

Courtesy Bob Gurr on page 68 (top photo).

Courtesy Stacey Hartley on page 204 (Paul Hartley photo).

Courtesy Resource Cafe on pages 124 (2005 photo by Jay Silverman), 128–129 (1990 photo), 137 (2014 photo produced by Justin Seeley), 154–155 (1990 Contemporary photo), 155 (1983 Grand Canyon Concourse photo), 156 (1981 construction photo), 157 (1982 ceremony photo), 164–165 (1982 photo), 168 (2013 photo), 169 (2011 photo), 170 and 171 (2011 photos by Andrea Barnett), 174 (2014 pool photo produced by Justin Seeley), and 175 (2017 pool photo by Nina Choi with creative by Dathan Shore).

Courtesy Stephen Russo on pages 68 and 69 (bottom photos).

Courtesy Stacy Shoff on page 201.

Courtesy Parinya Suwanitch / Alamy Stock Photo on pages 176 and 184.

Courtesy Derek Teo / Alamy Stock Photo on page 185.

Courtesy the Walt Disney Archives on pages 5, 21 (multiplane camera on display), 25 (book cover scan), 86 (program cover scan), 114 (pin and 1:90 model photos), 115 (pen photo), 173 (pin photo), 202 (pin photo), and 204 (book cover scan).

Courtesy the Walt Disney Archives Photo Library on pages 8, 10 and 11 (all photos), 15, 18 (all photos), 19 (all photos), 20 (all photos), 21 (multiplane camera in use, Walt with GARCO, and House of the Future Walt the TWA Rocket to the Moon photos), 22, 23, 24 (top and bottom photos), 27, 35, 57 (all photos) 83, 84, 88 (photo), 93 (color photo), 95, 99 (top photo), 122–123, 130 (Mark I photo), 133 (Walt photo), 158 (all images), and 193.

Courtesy the Walt Disney Imagineering Art Collection on pages 1, 2 (all art), 3, 6–7, 12–13, 16, 17, 20 (art), 26 (all art), 44, 46–47, 48–49, 50–51, 52, 53, 54–55, 56, 58–59, 60, 61, 62–63, 64 (all art), 65 (all art), 66, 66–67, 71, 72, 73, 76–77, 80–81, 86 (graphic detail), 88–89 (art), 90–91, 91, 92, 98–99 (art), 108 (art), 110–111, 112–113 (art), 120 (art), 126 and 127 (all art), 138–139, 139, 140–141, 142, 152–153, 162–163, 178, 182–183, 204 (poster art), 205 (all poster art), and 206–207, and 208.

Courtesy Walt Disney Imagineering Florida Research Library on pages 157 (preview ticket scan), 198, 199, and 203.

Courtesy the Walt Disney Imagineering Photography Collection on pages 21 (Clock of the World photo), 24 (book cover scan), 69 (right photo and logo design scan), 70, 74 (all photos), 75 (all photos), 82, 87 (newspaper supplement scan), 93 (all black-and white photos), 94, 96, 97 (all photos), 98 (photo), 99 (bottom photo), 100 and 101 (handbook scans), 102 (all photos), 103, 104, 105, 106 (all photos), 107, 108 (photo), 109, 113 (ramp photo), 116 and 117 (all photos), 118, 119 (photo), 120 (all photos), 121, 125, 127 (photo), 130 (Mark II and Mark III photos), 131 (all photos), 132, 133 (plaque photo), 134, 143, 144 and 145 (all photos), 146, 147, 148, 149 (all photos), 150 and 151 (all photos), 154 (Polynesian Village Resort and Grand Floridian Resort & Spa photos), 159, 160–161, 174 (gate detail photo), 181 (Jim Cora photos), and 196 (book cover scan).

Courtesy Paul Wolski on the jacket and pages 194–195.

Courtesy The Landrum Family Collection on pages 166–167.

Public Domain images on pages 28 (*Scientific American*, Publisher. 10 July 1886: World History Archive / Alamy Stock Photo.), 30 (top: *International Exhibition, Phila., Pa.: Elevated railway monorail on Centennial Grounds.* Photograph. Retrieved from the Library of Congress, www.loc.gov/item/ 2005676108/.), 30 (bottom: Alpha Stock / Alamy Stock Photo.), 31 (left: UtCon Collection / Alamy Stock Photo.), 31 (right, top: World History Archive / Alamy Stock Photo.), 31 (right, bottom: *Scientific American*, Publisher. 19 February 1887: Penta Springs LLP / Alamy Stock Photo.), 32 (left: *Scientific American*, Publisher. 10 July 1886. *Illustration of the interior of the passenger cab of the experimental Meigs monorail train.* Photograph. Retrieved from Wikimedia Commons, https://commons.wikimedia.org/wiki/File:Meigs_train_internal_viwe.jpg.), 32 (right: History and Art Collection / Alamy Stock Photo.), 33 (left: *Lexikon der gesamten Technik (Dictionary of Technology) by Otto Lueger.* Photograph. Retrieved from Wikimedia Commons, https://commons.wikimedia.org/wiki/File:L-Schwebebahn.png.), 33 (right: History collection 2016 / Alamy Stock Photo.), 36 (top: Sueddeutsche Zeitung Photo / Alamy Stock Photo.), 36 (bottom: Bain News Service, Publisher. *Louis Brennan and his gyroscope R.R. New York.* [No Date Recorded on Caption Card] Photograph. Retrieved from the Library of Congress, www.loc.gov/item/2014682972/.), 37 (top: History and Art Collection / Alamy Stock Photo.), 37 (bottom: The History Collection / Alamy Stock Photo.), 38 (top: *Wm. H. Boyes' monorail.* Photograph. Retrieved from the Library of Congress, www.loc.gov/item/2005680730/.), 38 (bottom: The History Collection / Alamy Stock Photo.), 39 (Dipper Historic / Alamy Stock Photo.), and 40 (Classic Image / Alamy Stock Photo.).

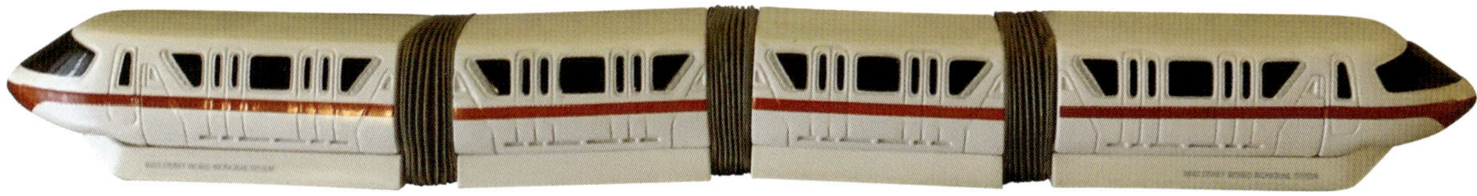

This book's authors and producers would like to thank

Alicia Chinatomby, Alison Giordano, Andrew Sansone, Annie Skogsbergh, Becky Cline, Bob Gurr, Chelsea Fallon, Charles Leatherberry, Courtney Rowley, Craig D. Barton, Cristina Diaz, Danny Saeva, David Jefferson, David Stern, Debra Kohls, Diana Brost, Denise Brown, Don Saban, Ed Ovalle, Elinor De La Torre, Elke Villa, Eric Boyd, Eva Lee, Evelyn Frederick, Fanny Sheffield, Gaby Biasi, Glendon Lee, the Imagineering Research Center (IRC) team, Jaime Gutierrez, Jason Grandt, Jeffrey Epstein, Jennifer Black, Jennifer Chan, Jess Allen, Jessie Ward, Jim and Mimi Cora, Jody Daily, Juleen Woods, Kelly Kipp, Ken Shue, Ken Stigen, Kevin Kern, Kevin Kidney, Kevin Lively, Kori Neal, Lia Murphy, Lynn Waggoner, Lyssa Hurvitz, Mary Ann Zissimos, Matt Moryc, Megan Granger, Meredith Lisbin, Michael Carroll, Michael Freeman, Michael Jusko, Mike Buckhoff, Monique Diman, Nancy Hickman, Nicole Carroll, Pat Van Note, Rachel Rivera, Roxolana Krywonos, Rudy Zamora, Scott Piehl, Seale Ballenger, Stacey Hartley, Stacy Shoff, Stephen Russo, Terry Downes, Tim Retzlaff, Vicki Korlishin, the Walt Disney Imagineering Photo Studio team, Warren Meislin, Winnie Ho, and Zan Schneider.

SELECTED BIBLIOGRAPHY

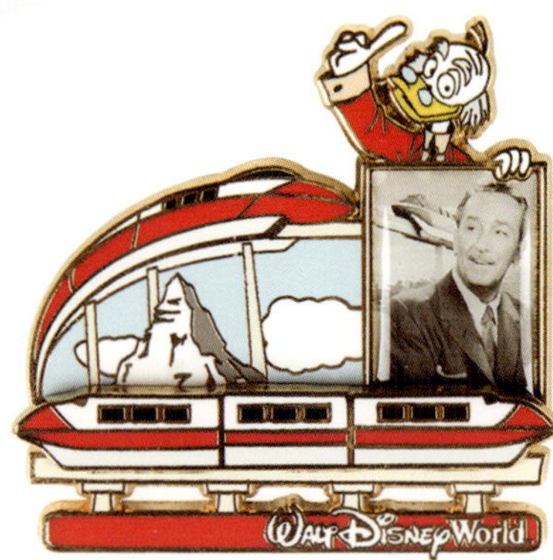

American Monorail Project. "Monorails: Historic Visions of the Future." *The American Monorail Project*. Date undocumented. Retrieved from http://www.theamericanmonorailproject.com/our-mission/monorails-historic-visions-of-the-future. Online.

Ballard, Donald W. "Design & History of the Disneyland Hotel California: 1955–1965." *Designing Disney*. Date undocumented. Retrieved from https://www.designingdisney.com/parks/disneyland-resort/design-history-disneyland-hotel-california-1955–1965. Online.

Beard, Richard R. *Walt Disney's EPCOT Center: Creating the New World of Tomorrow*. New York: Harry N. Abrams, Inc. 1982. Print.

Boothe Green, Amy. "Walt Disney Archives/ Disney Legends/ Bob Gurr." *D23.com*. Date undocumented. Retrieved from https://d23.com/walt-disney-legend/bob-gurr/. Online.

Disneyland, Inc. *Your Role in the Disneyland Show*. Anaheim, California: Disneyland. 1957. Print.

Freedogshampoo (YouTube Playlist). "1959 Monorail Dedication" (video, excerpt from *Kodak Presents Disneyland '59*). Posted 4 April 2007. Retrieved from youtube.com/watch?v=b5e129tiEcM/1959 Monorail Dedication. Online.

Gordon, Bruce, and Jeff Kurtti. *Art of Disneyland, The*. New York: Disney Editions. 2006. Print.

___________. *Walt Disney World: Then, Now, and Forever*. New York: Disney Editions. 2008. Print.

___________. *Art of Walt Disney World, The*. New York: Disney Editions. 2009. Print.

Gordon, Bruce, and David Mumford. *The Nickel Tour: A Postcard Journey Through Half a Century of the Happiest Place on Earth, Second Edition*. Santa Clarita, California: Camphor Tree Publishers. 2000. Print.

Gurr, Bob. *Design: Just for Fun: Collector's Edition*. Los Angeles: APP-Gurr Design. 2012. Print.

Hahn, Don. *Yesterday's Tomorrow: Disney's Magical Mid-Century*. Los Angeles • New York: Disney Editions. 2017. Print.

Handke, Danny, and Vanessa Hunt. *Poster Art of the Disney Parks*. Los Angeles • New York: Disney Editions. 2012. Print.

Harker, Michelle. "Celebrating the Art of . . . Kevin Kidney and Jody Daily!" *Disney Parks Blog*. 6 July 2010. Retrieved from https://disneyparks.disney.go.com/blog/2010/07/celebrating-the-art-of-kevin-kidney-and-jody-daily. Online.

Hench, John, with Peggy Van Pelt. *Designing Disney: Imagineering and the Art of the Show*. New York: Disney Editions. 2003. Print.

Imagineers, The. *Walt Disney Imagineering: A Behind the Dreams Look at Making the Magic Real*. New York: Disney Editions. 1996. Print.

___________. *Walt Disney Imagineering: A Behind the Dreams Look at Making More Magic Real*. New York: Disney Editions. 2010. Print.

Kurtti, Jeff. *Walt Disney's Imagineering Legends and the Genesis of the Disney Theme Park*. New York: Disney Editions. 2008. Print.

___________. *Disneyland Through the Decades: A Photographic Celebration*. 2010. New York: Disney Editions. 2010. Print.

___________. *Travels with Walt Disney: A Photographic Voyage Around the World*. Los Angeles • New York: Disney Editions. 2018. Print.

Ladylee (pseudonym). "Cocktail Culture in the '50s." *Medium, The MW Pub*. 27 March 27 2019. Retrieved from https://medium.com/ninja-writers/cocktail-culture-in-the-50s-94784950e138. Online.

Lyden, Jackie. "A Spirited Celebration of America's 'Cocktail Culture.'" *NPR Weekend Edition*. 11 June 2011. Retrieved from https://www.npr.org/2011/06/12/137106364/a-spirited-celebration-of-americas-cocktail-culture. Online.

Magical Hotel (pseudonym). "1967–1969 Disneyland Hotel Brochure." *The Original Disneyland Hotel*. 29 April 2010. Retrieved from http://magicalhotel.blogspot.com/2010/04. Online.

Mahne, Keith Michael. "Your Highway in the Sky: The Disney Monorail System." *DisneyAvenue*. 1 May 2015. Retrieved from https://disneyavenue.wordpress.com/2015/05/01/your-highway-in-the-sky-the-disney-monorail-system. Online.

Mumpower, David. "You Probably Don't Know This About Disney's Monorail . . ." *Theme Park Tourist*. 14 July 2015. Retrieved from https://www.themeparktourist.com/features/20150711/30416/walt-disney-and-rise-monorail. Online.

Neary, Kevin, and Susan Neary and Vanessa Hunt. *Maps of the Disney Parks*. Los Angeles • New York: Disney Editions. 2016. Print.

Pedersen, Kim A. *Monorails: Trains of the Future—Now Arriving*. The Monorail Society LLC. 2015. Print.

Polsson, Ken. "1952–1955." *Chronology of Disneyland Theme Park*. 30 January 2019. Retrieved from http://www.islandnet.com/~kpolsson/disland. Online.

Ryman, Herb. *A Brush with Disney: An Artist's Journey Told Through the Work and Words of Herbert Dickens Ryman*. Santa Clarita, California: Camphor Tree Publishers. 2000. Print.

Savvas, George. "A Look Back at June 14, 1959: Grand Opening of the Disneyland-Alweg Monorail System, Matterhorn Bobsleds and Submarine Voyage at Disneyland Park." *Disney Parks Blog*. 13 June 2014. Retrieved from https://disneyparks.disney.go.com/blog/2014/06/a-look-back-at-june-14-1959-grand-opening-of-the-disneyland-alweg-monorail-system-matterhorn-bobsleds-and-submarine-voyage-at-disneyland-park. Online.

Smith, Dave. *Disney A to Z: The Official Encyclopedia, Fifth Edition*. Los Angeles • New York: Disney Editions. 2016. Print.

University of Disneyland. *The Walt Disney Traditions at Disneyland*. Burbank, California: Walt Disney Productions. 1967. Print.

Weiss, Werner. "Disneyland-Alweg Monorail System Presented by Santa Fe Railroad." *Yesterland*, 27 July 2018. Retrieved from https://www.yesterland.com/monorail.html. Online.

Wikipedia. "Disneyland Monorail System." Wikipedia.org. 24 November 2019. Retrieved from https://en.wikipedia.org/wiki/Disneyland_Monorail_System. Online

___________. (Dynamic List). "List of Monorail Systems." Wikipedia.org. 5 December 2019. Retrieved from https://en.wikipedia.org/wiki/List_of_monorail_systems. Online.

___________. "Walt Disney World Monorail System." Wikipedia.org. 10 December 2019. Retrieved from https://en.wikipedia.org/wiki/Walt_Disney_World_Monorail_System. Online.

Wisdom Society for the Advancement of Knowledge, Learning, and Research in Education. *Wisdom: The Magazine of Knowledge for Lifetime Learning and Education*, Volume 32. Los Angeles. December 1959. Print.

Information and quotations were also sourced from numerous issues of The E Ticket, Vacationland, *and* Disney News *magazines. Various other sources and unpublished archival interview transcripts were also accessed for quotations and information within the text.*

PAUL HARTLEY

A Design Tribute to a Mid-Century Master

"There is a spirit to the subject matter of this book," says co-author Jeff Kurtti, "and it cried out for a design vernacular commensurate with its content. A mid-century concept of modernism, efficiency, speed, and optimism, but with an attendant sense of elegance, sophistication, style, and . . . well, fun."

"We found our visual muse in the print media work of Paul Hartley," co-author and visual curator Vanessa Hunt says. "Although his name is not as familiar as some of his contemporaries at Disney, his art style was influential and remains timeless. He represents a vernacular in Disney design that continues to be relevant."

In creating the design of this book, the authors looked extensively at Hartley's portfolio of work. "The Walt Disney Imagineering Art Collection houses scores of Hartley's works for Disneyland, Walt Disney World, and the 1964–1965 New York World's Fair," Hunt says. "Posters, signage, tram cards, and print collateral graphics were his forte."

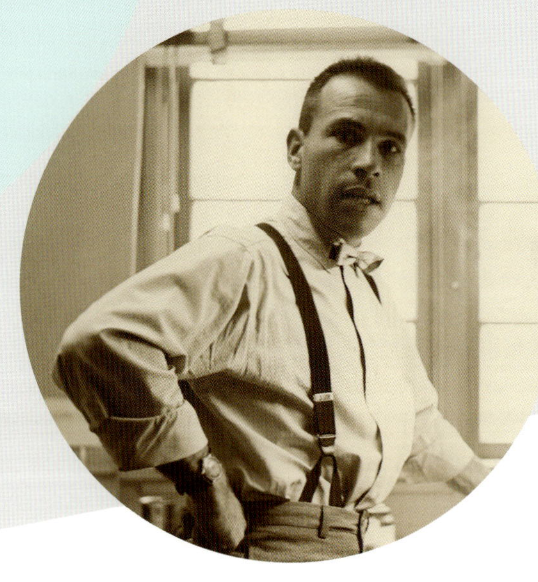

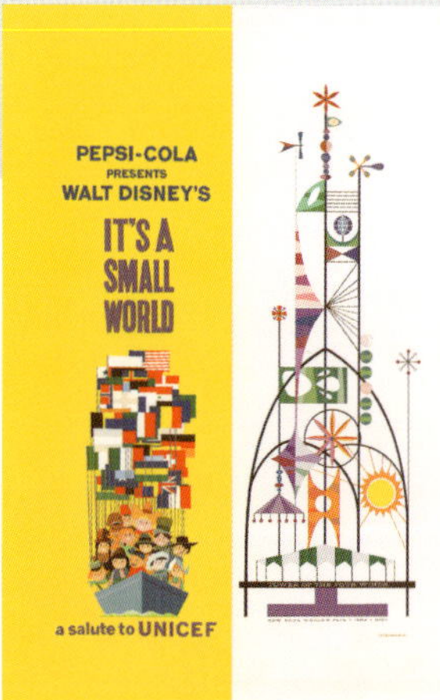

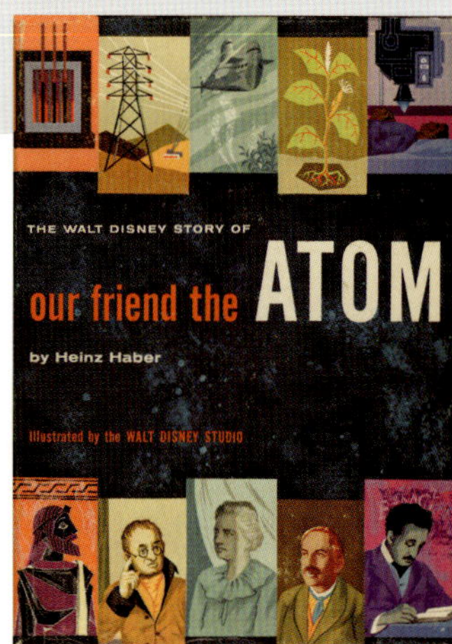

"Paul's prolific but largely-forgotten work in magazine and book design was the key resource for me," says co-author and designer Paul Wolski. "I looked through issues of *Mickey Mouse Club Magazine* and its successor *Walt Disney's Magazine*, published from 1955 to 1959. In addition, Paul's unforgettable designs for the books *The Art of Animation* and *Our Friend the Atom* were invaluable inspiration—and for me as an artist, something of an education.

"Our friends and colleagues Kevin Kidney and Jody Daily also maintain a significant selection of Paul's art layout boards from that era—their generous access to that art was invaluable.

"Paul not only did innovative things with bold style and layout, his design choices were efficient—for storytelling, evoking mood, and combining disparate art styles and media into cohesive visual statements," Wolski continues. "He uses typography as an illustrative element and balances white space and negative space like a master."

Like great artists through time, Paul influences succeeding generations. And like his colleagues at Disney, the body of work he left behind not only defines an epoch in Disney history, it continues to make a statement about the ongoing culture of Disney.

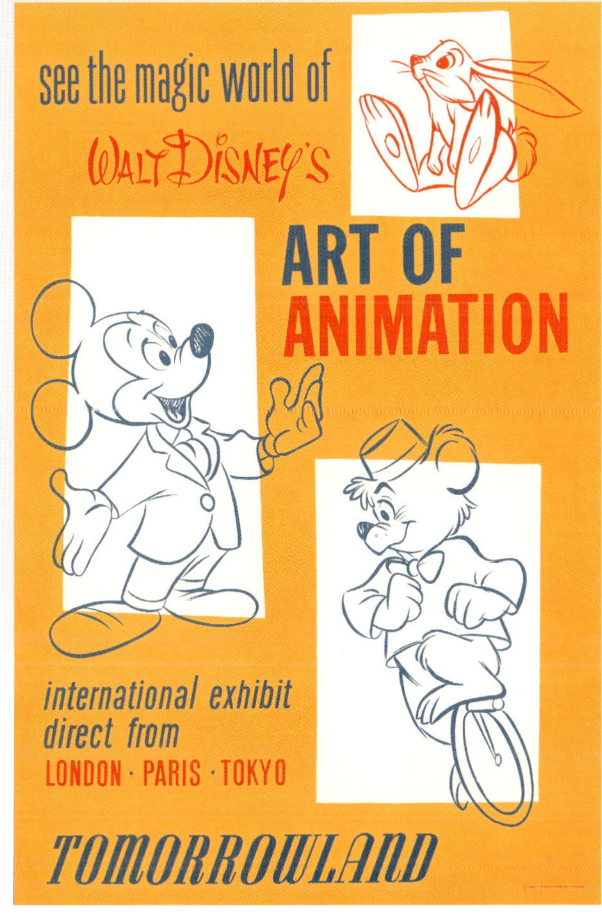

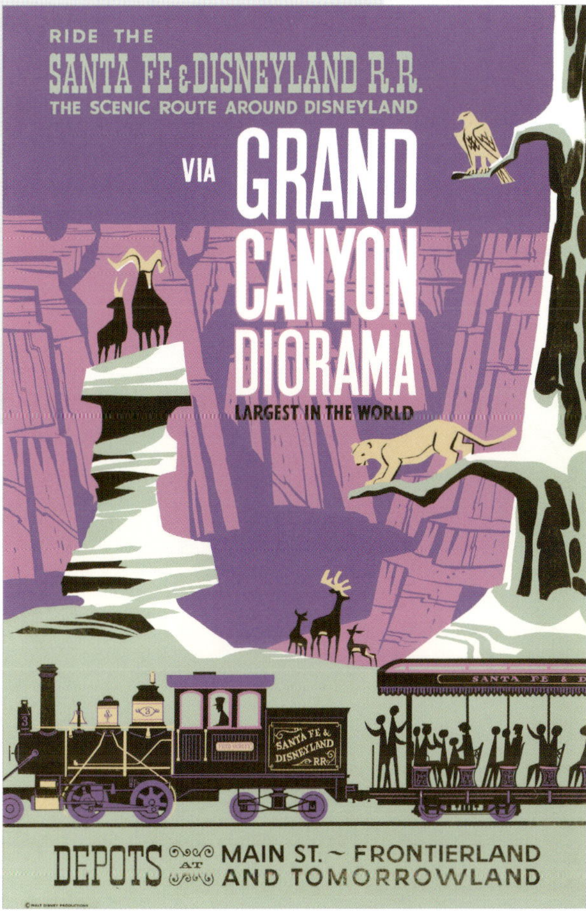

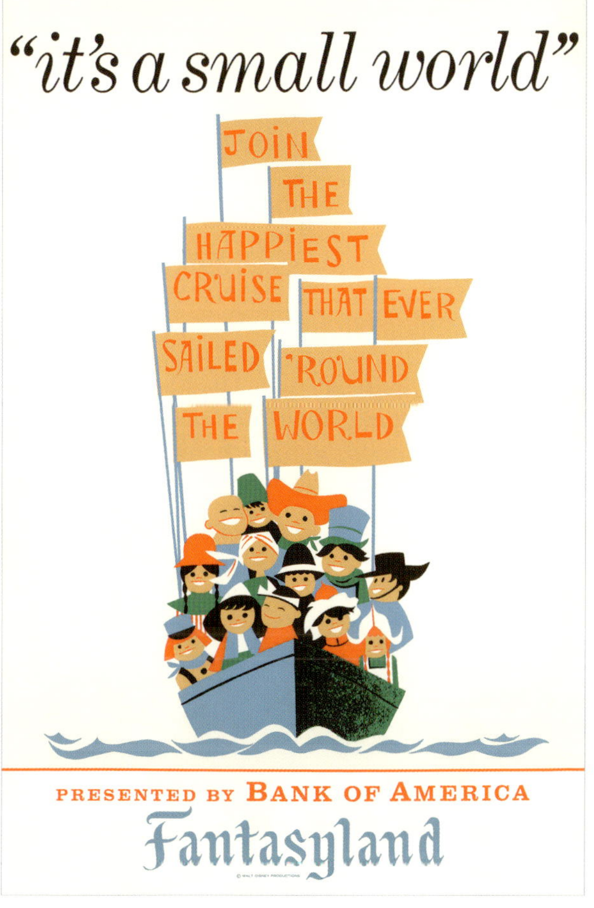

Paul Hartley

Paul Richard Hartley was born in Cheney, Kansas, on July 8, 1923. Always interested in art, Paul came in contact with "Sailor Gene," a tattoo artist, during the Depression and took over his stall in the lobby of the Rosslyn Hotel in Los Angeles at age fifteen.

After Pearl Harbor, Paul served in the Army for two years, stationed on Saipan. When he returned to California, he attended Art Center, Chouinard, and Otis Art schools on the GI Bill. He married Doris Callahan in 1949, and had a daughter, Stacey, in 1955.

After art school, he moved to New York, and worked for *Look* and *Esquire* magazines. He was hired by the Graphics Department at The Walt Disney Studios in 1955; one of his first assignments was art directing *Mickey Mouse Club Magazine*. He was also art director of two legendary books, *The Art of Animation* by Bob Thomas, and *Our Friend the Atom*, written by renowned German physicist and science writer Dr. Heinz Haber.

During a layoff at the studio in 1961, Paul moved to Palma de Mallorca, Spain, where he and Collin Campbell worked on illustrations for a Cathedral Films project on Moses. This period was one of the highlights of the artist's life. After returning, Paul spent most of his time painting. He was intelligent, multitalented, and a voracious reader—and self-educated, as he never finished high school; he was also blessed with a fine and biting sense of humor.

Paul returned to Imagineering from 1961 to 1964, and was working there from May 1968 until he took his own life on April 13, 1973.

"He was a true artist," colleague John Roberdeau Drury recalls. "Always drawing something on whatever scrap of paper might be handy—just a master with the pen and ink—or whatever drawing tool he had at hand. . . . I was fortunate to have known and worked with him . . . and I miss him still."

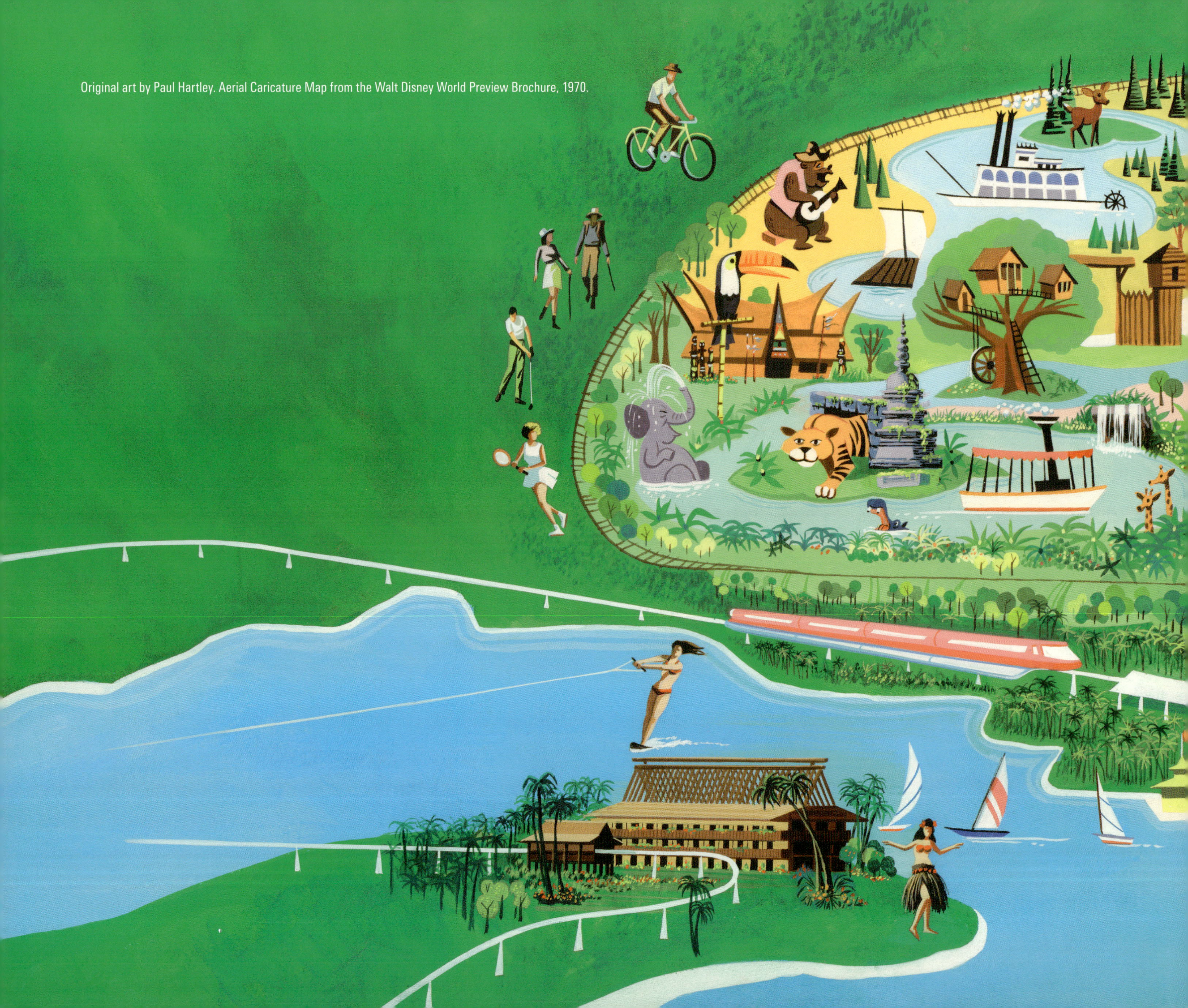

Original art by Paul Hartley. Aerial Caricature Map from the Walt Disney World Preview Brochure, 1970.

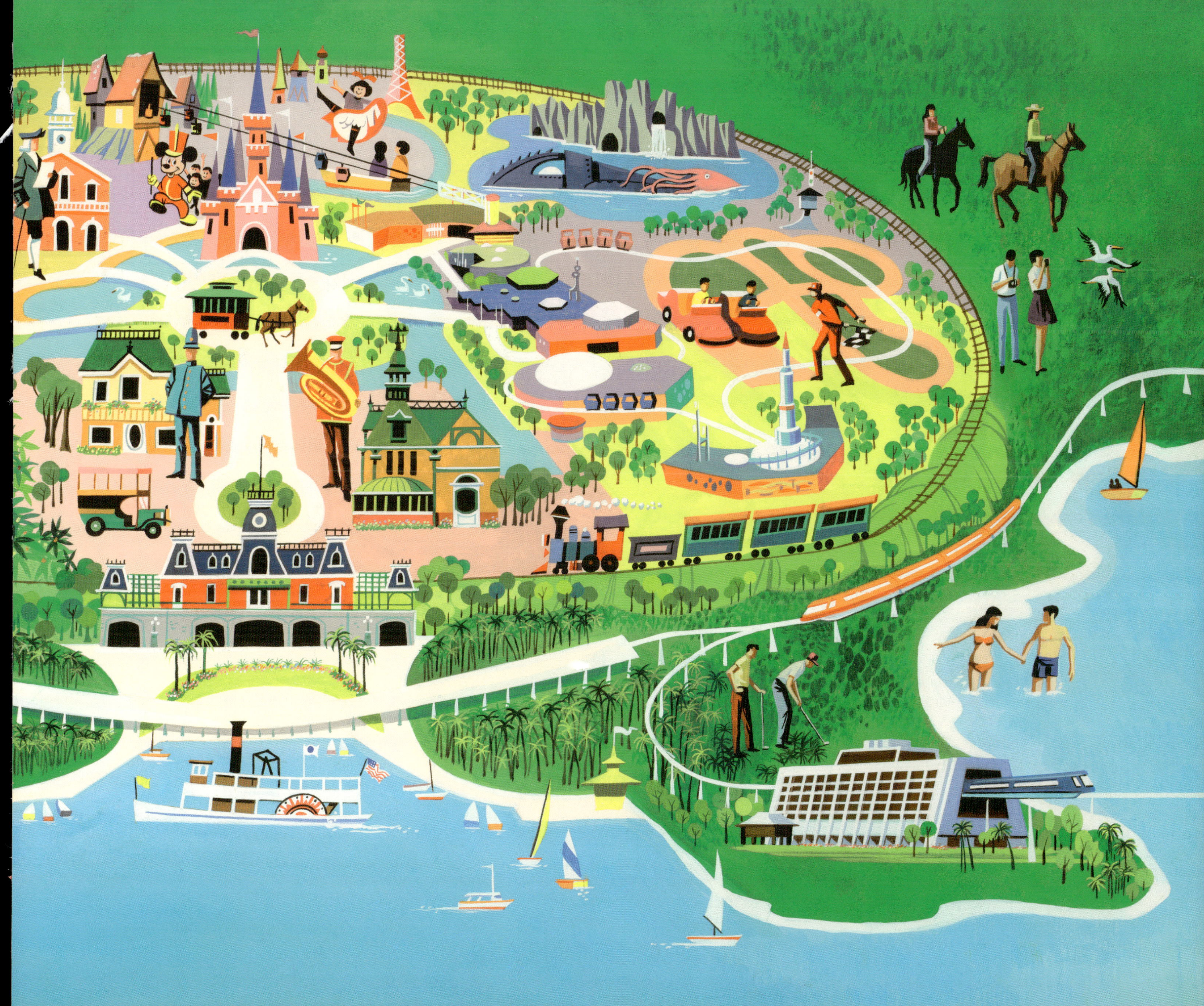

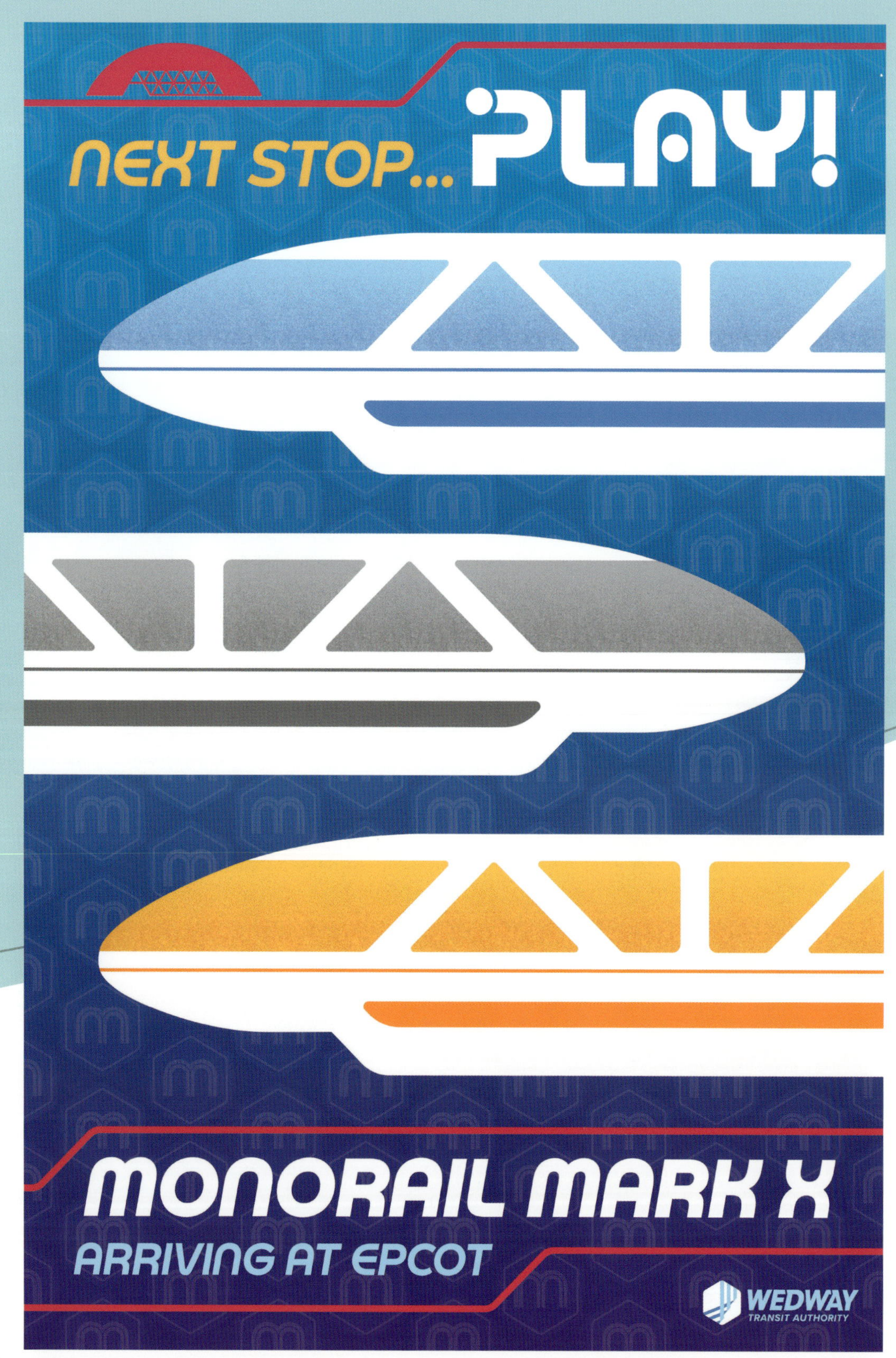

Calling all pilots! A new way to play arrives at the PLAY! pavilion at EPCOT.